A STUDY OF THE PROFESSIONAL CRITICISM OF BROADCASTING IN THE UNITED STATES 1920-1955

This is a volume in the
Arno Press collection

DISSERTATIONS IN BROADCASTING

Advisory Editor
Christopher H. Sterling

See last pages of this volume
for a complete list of titles.

A STUDY OF THE PROFESSIONAL CRITICISM OF BROADCASTING IN THE UNITED STATES 1920-1955

Ralph Lewis Smith

ARNO PRESS
A New York Times Company
New York • 1979

Editorial Supervision: Andrea Hicks

First publication 1979 by Arno Press Inc.

Reproduced from a copy in the University of Wisconsin Library

DISSERTATIONS IN BROADCASTING
ISBN for complete set: 0-405-11754-X
See last pages of this volume for titles.

Manufactured in the United States of America

Library of Congress Cataloging in Publication Data

Smith, Ralph Lewis, 1921-
A study of the professional criticism of broadcasting in the United States, 1920-1955.

(Dissertations in broadcasting)
Originally presented as the author's thesis, University of Wisconsin, 1959.
Bibliography: p.
1. Radio criticism. 2. Television criticism. 3. Broadcasting--United States. I. Title. II. Series.
PN1990.9.C73S6 1979 791.44'7 78-21739
ISBN 0-405-11775-2

A STUDY OF THE PROFESSIONAL CRITICISM OF BROADCASTING

IN THE UNITED STATES 1920-1955

BY

RALPH LEWIS SMITH

A thesis submitted in partial fulfillment of the requirements for the degree of

DOCTOR OF PHILOSOPHY
(Speech)

at the

UNIVERSITY OF WISCONSIN

1959

PREFACE

Audience broadcasting, sound and sight, is a major phenomenon of our age. Its impact has been felt upon almost every facet of society, upon government, business, education and the arts, upon family life and social custom; and we are just beginning to comprehend some of these changes and the strength of the new force which effected them. Broadcasting's social impact has been particularly strong in the United States, where scarcely an individual is without easy access to a radio or television set and where entertainment, diversion, and information have fast become necessities rather than luxuries.

To say that certain factors about these new mass media are just becoming clear, is not to imply that broadcasting elicited little comment until recently. Announced by reporters as a dazzling scientific achievement, trumpeted by press agents and ad men as a circus and super-market combined, enthusiastically accepted by the people, and damned by the intellectuals, American broadcasting has functioned from the very first in an atmosphere of high excitement. What it has lacked has been a steadier contemplation of its activities, a more widespread anticipation and recognition of its import, a more careful direction of its force.

This study sets forth the experiences and opinions of a small group of writers, who, over the years, have supplied a portion of that lack. It is an historical-descriptive account of a new fraternity of professional critics. References to the traditional elements of artistic criticism are only partly valid here. Though many of the functions of the literary or art or theater critic are similar to the functions of the broadcast critic, the material with which he so often deals, the operational structure under which it is composed, and the conditions under which it is perceived are different from the units of art scrutinized by critics of the older media.

Radio and television were inventions nurtured by scientists. In this country they have largely been utilized by businessmen for the sale of goods and the transmission of popular entertainment programs. They are also avenues for the dissemination of news and other information. And last, but by no means least, they are facilities licensed by the federal government to operate in the public interest. These are factors with sociological and cultural implications far out on the fringes of criticism's classic provinces. Consequently, the professional radio and television critic has had to build his critical structure, always conscious of older forms, but continually seeking new designs to accommodate a new discipline. And these chapters are the record of that process during audience broadcasting's first thirty-five years.

Previous scholarly attention to this new branch of criticism seems to have been slight. Perusal of the standard bibliographies dealing with radio and television, and of the standard thesis indexes, revealed only two masters' studies in this area, both of which were completed in 1955. One concerns the influence critics who write for newspapers and periodicals, or who deliver reviews over the air, have on their audiences.[1] Since film, literary, and drama criticism receive major emphasis, only a small portion of the material was helpful to the present study. The second thesis is an examination of the criticism of Gilbert Seldes.[2] Its narrow concentration gave it only partial relevance to a more comprehensive study of broadcast criticism. In addition, its author did not have the benefit of Mr. Seldes' latest statement about broadcasting, The Public Arts.[3] Thus, the present work, comprising a detailed investigation into factors influencing the practice of professional criticism, into the procedures and aims of the critics, and into their opinions about the major phases of broadcasting, attempts to fill a gap in the written history of radio and television.

The study has further significance in that it focuses attention on an area of endeavor which government spokesmen, educational leaders, and media executives, themselves, have emphasized as important to the future development of broadcasting. Charles Siepmann,[4] Lewellyn White,[5] and Edward R. Murrow,[6] to mention but a few, have complained about the lack of sustained, perceptive commentary to help guide the production and the reception of art and communication forms which have a well-nigh total population audience. A starting point for the solution to such a lack lies in an analysis of what has happened to date in the area of concern. This study attempts to provide that starting point.

In addition, by comparing major critical opinions with respect to broadcasting's artistic and informational achievements as well as shortcomings, and with respect to its persistent problem of commercial-cultural conflict, the study permits the presentation of viewpoints which acquire added strength because thoughtful minds are seen to have reached similar conclusions. Such a juxtaposition of opinions brings fresh emphasis to strengths and weaknesses in the philosophy and techniques of programing, in the unique structure of American broadcasting, and in our society as the result of these media.

And finally, the ideas herein presented testify to the valuable contribution of professional critics toward the improvement of broadcasting, and they point up the need for action on suggestions the critics have offered for strengthening their own profession.

Having briefly projected the purpose and content of this study, the obvious question arises as to how its leading figures were selected, or in other words, how the term professional broadcast critic was defined. The factors of remuneration, regularity, and type of journal qualify the definition of professional as far as this study is concerned. The persons included were hired by a newspaper or periodical of general circulation to write regular pieces for the purpose of keeping their readers informed about occurrences in the field of broadcasting. Although no exact minimum for the number of columns per critic was set, the author kept this rough consideration in mind: to qualify as a regular writer, the critic should have been on the staff of a daily for six months, of a weekly publication for a year, and of a monthly for a year and a half. Eliminated from the study were regular commentaries in publications of the entertainment or broadcasting industry, in academic journals, or in "fan" magazines. As has been previously indicated, the term broadcast refers either to radio or television and often it is used as a collective noun.

Defining the term critic was a more complicated matter involving a consideration of standard definitions from the traditional arts, of definitions devised by those who had studied the writing of journalistic appraisers of the theater and films, and of subjective, qualitative factors derived from previous acquaintance with a few commentators about broadcasting.

It required very little imagination to apply to broadcasting, S. Stephenson Smith's dismissal of the movies as an area for serious criticism:

> Unluckily for their progress as an art, the movies are also a craft and a business. . . . Those who have no appetite for the study of low life in commercial circles, and who scorn the tastes of the pit, had better keep aloof from the movies, at least until the process of sifting is over.[7]

If the cinematic form, which was some thirty years old at the time of Mr. Smith's observation, was still too unsettled for the serious critic, and if its connection with business made it suspect, what, indeed, would have been his reaction to the presumptuousness of writers about broadcasting daring to call themselves critics! At the moment, comments more pertinent to this study might be found by turning from the austere practitioners of literary, music and fine arts criticism to observers in those lesser temples of the arts, the playhouse and the movie palace.

After an analysis of the procedures and pronouncements of some of the most renowned drama critics, Edna West and Jerry McNeely arrived at these general definitions of criticism: (1) Criticism is an expression of point of view involving a careful judgment of values, based on knowledge and characterized by propriety.[8] (2) Criticism is a carefully considered judgment of the merits and faults of a work of art with the purpose of improving and stimulating interest in that direction.[9] Here, it seemed, were characteristics applicable to some of the writing about radio and television. To be sure, there is a question as to whether the products of broadcasting are works of art. However, no general condemnation is valid, and there are many programs approaching art which need careful appraisal if similar ones are ever to become art in the future. In addition, the careful examination of environmental faults which keep a medium from becoming an art form still requires efforts of perception, of thought and judgment which can be equated with accepted practices in criticism.

Add to the theoretical definitions quoted above the following practical reminder from Richard Gibbs, who was concerned with motion-picture reviewing in the daily press, and the result points the way to a comparable working definition of criticism as it is applied to broadcasting. Said Mr. Gibbs, "This ephemeral criticism is a far cry from the classical criticism of the past, but it has a greater part to play in the world of today because it is addressed to guide the public, the consumer of art."[10] This statement recognizes the function of a critic who writes about a mass medium (the motion picture or radio) in a mass medium (newspaper or magazine). The broadcasting critic must somehow join the serious criticism of a semi-popular art form like the theater, to the judgments of a more casual, highly popular art form like the movies.

Unlike the critic of either of these forms, however, the critic of broadcasting does not have the responsibility of indicating where his readers should spend their entertainment money. His subsequent, mild connection with the "hit or flop" aspect of show business (so important to legitimate drama, in particular) is reflected in a weaker impact on the public and more especially on the broadcasting industry. He assumes, however, more complex responsibilities, in having to appraise an extreme variety of programs, in having to explain technical, economic, and governmental matters, and in trying to activate the silent public, who owns the airwaves, to assert some constructive control of them.

Whereas the student of journalistic theater or film criticism, moreover, has often concerned himself with the distinctions between a critic, a reviewer, and a reporter,[11] initial perusal of a cross section of regular writers about broadcasting indicated that for the purposes of this study, at least, there were just two relatively clear categories:

critics and non-critics. The difference between them is primarily a matter of function, though it may also be a matter of viewpoint, of style, and of skill.

The average columnist for a daily paper, and even for some magazines, lets his readers know about coming attractions in broadcasting, titillates them with a little gossip about a star, inserts a line or two of surface appraisal about a recent program and then concludes with a joke. He serves in a non-critical, utilitarian capacity as reporter-press agent. The critic, on the other hand, although he also writes for newspapers and magazines and may also inform or amuse his readers, does so in a broader, deeper context of constant evaluation. He seeks, always, to judge the significance of an event in broadcasting, to prognosticate its future consequences or to relate it to past events whether in broadcasting or some other area.

To the non-critic, broadcasting is a series of discrete programs making a moment either enjoyable or unpleasant. To the critic, broadcasting presents programs with interesting or hopeless roots in the past or with exciting or horrifying implications for the future. The critic adds artistic, philosophical, sociological or other dimensions to his reviews of programs and to his comments on industry, government or public action. The viewpoints of the critic are frequently conditioned by familiarity with the arts, wide reading in the classics and a genuine sympathy for affairs of the mind. Critics are inclined to be moralists, unafraid to preach standards, and idealists, untiring in their efforts to bring commercially subsidized mass arts into closer relationship with traditional arts, and to see that fringe functions of broadcasting, like education and public affairs, grow in importance. Unlike the non-critics whose column formats rarely change, the critics may alternate short but subtle reviews with thorough, detailed reviews, or long essays on important trends or problems.

In summary, the professional critics of broadcasting are informed, sensitive journalists employed by general publications to give radio and television steady, serious appraisal; and they share their conclusions based on facts, fused with evaluative opinion, with the industry and the public in the hope that the potentials they envision for broadcasting will some day come to pass.

The search for current critics who qualified under this restricted definition was not too difficult. Three columnists are writing for leading New York City newspapers, and the work of four critics appears in two of the small-circulation, quality periodicals. In addition, some of these seven critics have written books and articles in academic journals so that their opinions are readily available.

A more painstaking examination of two-week segments of fifty-nine metropolitan newspapers from 1955 by five year intervals back to 1920 (or to the year when they were first subscribed to by the University of Wisconsin Library) disclosed the work of two, current, non-New York critics and two early radio critics. Sources obtained from the <u>Readers' Guide to Periodical Literature (1920-1955)</u> indicated that an additional seven critics had written regular magazine columns dealing with radio or television at various periods during the thirty-five years.

From this total of eighteen newspaper and magazine critics, the work of fifteen was reviewed in detail, including the reading of every column and relevant longer works by twelve of the authors. Five of these twelve were interviewed. The remaining three critics, whose columns were not easily available for study, corresponded with the author, and one of them was interviewed.

In addition, an examination of popular, mass publication magazines indicated that a grocery chain-store monthly had for years carried a semi-critical column on broadcasting. These articles were read and the author was interviewed.

The columns of John Hutchens, Jack Gould, and John Crosby were too numerous to review individually. Eighty-five of Mr. Hutchens' one hundred sixty pieces for the New York Times were read in a sampling of his three year stint as radio editor. Approximately half of Mr. Gould's Sunday columns and many of his weekday columns for the same paper over a ten year period were read. The New York Times Index was, of course, a useful guide to the selection of particularly pertinent essays by these critics. Mr. Crosby provided a sampling of his columns from the Herald Tribune (New York) for the years 1946-1951, in the one hundred thirty-one pieces which appear in his book Out of the Blue.[12] Almost all of Mr. Crosby's remaining columns, which appeared approximately four times a week from 1952 to 1955, were then read.

Helpful information about the difficulty of professionalizing broadcast criticism was obtained from an interview with Robert J. Landry, managing editor of the trade journal, Variety, who has been intensely interested in this problem for over twenty years. In addition, interviews with Mr. Ben Gross of the Daily News (New York) and Mr. George Rosen, radio-TV editor for Variety, and correspondence with Miss Harriet Van Horne of the World-Telegram (New York) provided further material about the procedures and problems of the critic. An interesting letter about early radio criticism in the Christian Science Monitor was received from its former radio editor, Mr. Volney Hurd. And a delightful letter reminiscing about his articles in the old Forum magazine under a protective nom de plume was received from Mr. Darwin Teilhet.

Although most of the research for this study was conducted at the University of Wisconsin Library, the author wishes to acknowledge the assistance he received at the New York Public Library which provided volumes of early radio magazines and New York newspapers of the '20's, and at the Milwaukee Public Library which carried back issues of Woman's Day magazine.

The data thus collected was organized into four major blocks which shed light on the following questions:

1. What do we know about the personnel in this new area of criticism? (Who are the critics? When did they write? What are their procedures? What is their function?)

2. What are the critics' opinions about major broadcast forms? (drama, games and light entertainment, music, news, discussion and talks programs, documentary programs)

3. What have the critics had to say about three persistent, major problems in American broadcasting? (educational programing, advertising, various systems of operation)

4. What has been the response to the critics, and what suggestions have been made for strengthening criticism?

Material in each of these areas has, of course, been re-enforced by important contributions from many other sources in the voluminous literature on broadcasting, from academic critics and lay critics, and from historians and spokesmen within the broadcasting industry. But the controlling purpose in this study has been to let the professional critics speak for themselves. From their witness, the author has been enabled to trace the forces acting upon the development of a new profession, and to reconstruct major patterns of thought with respect to the product and the problems of American broadcasting.

The motivating force behind the study is the author's conviction that a body of regular, informed comment by skilled critics is a necessity, if the art and the industry of broadcasting is to fulfill its obligations to the public, and if the public is to improve in its ability to evaluate broadcasting.

The author wishes to thank the following members of the Department of Speech at the University of Wisconsin: Professor Henry Ewbank and Professor John Highlander for their interest in the initial planning of this study, and Professor Jonathan Curvin for his skillful guidance during the early stages of research and writing. Particular appreciation is extended to Professor Jerry McNeely for his careful, prompt advice and steady encouragement during the major phases of writing. Finally, the author acknowledges with deep sincerity, the assistance of his wife in many of the arduous tasks necessary to the study's completion.

Notes

[1]Peter Temple Whitelam, "The Critic in the Mass Media" (unpublished Master's thesis, School of Public Relations and Communications, Boston University, 1955).

[2]David Lyndon Woods, "The Criteria of the Radio and Television Criticism of Gilbert Seldes," (unpublished Master's thesis, Stanford University, 1955).

[3]Gilbert Seldes, The Public Arts (New York: Simon and Schuster, 1956).

[4]Charles A. Siepmann, "Further Thoughts on Radio Criticism," Public Opinion Quarterly, V (June, 1941), 308-12.

[5]Lewellyn White, The American Radio (Chicago: University of Chicago Press, 1947), p. 236.

[6]Edward R. Murrow, quoted in Giraud Chester and Garnett Garrison, Radio and Television (New York: Appleton-Century-Crofts, Inc., 1950), p. 515.

[7]S. Stephanson Smith, The Craft of the Critic (New York: Thomas Y. Crowell Co., 1931), p. 296.

[8]Edna West, "The Broadway Critics" (unpublished Ph.D. dissertation, Department of Speech, University of Wisconsin, 1952), pp. 5-6.

[9]Jerry Clark McNeely, "The Criticism and Reviewing of Brooks Atkinson" (unpublished Ph.D. dissertation, Department of Speech, University of Wisconsin, 1956), p. 2.

[10]Richard Leslie Gibbs, "Motion Picture Reviewing in the Daily Newspaper" (unpublished Master's thesis, Department of Journalism, University of Illinois, 1950), p. 2.

[11]See as one example, John Mason Brown's definitions of these three catêgories in his Upstage (New York: W. W. Norton and Co., 1930), p. 215.

[12]John Crosby, Out of the Blue, (New York: Simon and Schuster, 1952).

TABLE OF CONTENTS

CHAPTER I

THE COURSE OF PROFESSIONAL BROADCAST CRITICISM IN THE UNITED STATES

If criticism is a parasitic activity, depending for its life upon the organism it is attempting to interpret, no apologies need be offered for surveying the history of a critical form which is a mere third of a century old; the life of the host itself dates only from 1920. Indeed, it redounds to the credit of the first professional critics that they sensed exciting potentials in the uncertain mewings delivered to them from an instrument picturesquely described by the term "cat's whiskers." Strangely enough, however, as the fortunes of the host waxed, the health of the parasite waned almost unto death, having been revived only within the last ten years. As a result, broadcast criticism, which should be entering a phase of vigorous maturity, has gained merely a youthful confidence. Our story, then, is one of arrested development -- a matter which cannot be explained adequately by the simple pronouncement that an adolescent industry fosters adolescent criticism.

A complex environment composed of five interacting forces has been in operation to shape the history of broadcast criticism in this country: the internal development of the radio industry, external economic and political events, the editors and publishers who employ critics, the reading public, and the critics themselves. It is not my purpose to discuss each force in isolation, except for a treatment of the background and procedures of outstanding critics in a succeeding section. Instead, I shall focus my attention on the chronological pattern of criticism, describing qualitative as well as quantitative shifts, and emphasizing the particular forces which were operative at any given time.

The ages of radio and television criticism have thus far been seven, with no intended parallel to Jacques' famous observations, although it is conceivable that the age of "the whining schoolboy" or of "a soldier full of strange oaths" or even of "second childishness . . . sans taste" might be fairly apt descriptions for certain periods. However, it will be more accurate to pass up poetic labels in favor of items which derive from the evidence at hand. That this evidence is unwieldy, that some of the ages overlap, that the depth of evaluative opinion about the new media ranges from a few shallow phrases inserted into a scientific article on grid circuits, to a perceptive volume on the public arts is to be expected. We are dealing with the history of comment about a form of communication which is bewildering in the complexity of its structure and the ubiquitous subtlety of its impact.

Focus on Science

Wireless communication was born simultaneously about the turn of the century in the laboratories of scientists in Europe and the United States. It emerged as a reliable courier for industries like shipping and was perfected under pressure of the First World War. Several years before studios were opened in the downtown theater districts of large cities, all the tools of the amazing invention — the batteries, the crystal detectors, the earphones — were to be found under the attic rafters in the homes of thousands of amateur physicists. Here was an eager group unconsciously destined to become the first audiences for a new form of public communication. It is of particular interest for us to note that they were already enthusiastic readers of a few popular technical periodicals, and that they searched their daily newspapers to stay abreast of the latest developments in this scientific hobby. The seriousness of these "hams" has even earned them recognition as broadcasting's earliest critics. They were the listeners "who tuned in to Dr. Frank Conrad's transmitter in 1912 and wrote him in Pittsburg, 'Why do you play the same records over and over again?'"[1] This question, coming eight years before the official inauguration of audience broadcasting, emphasizes the intense laymen's interest in radio.

By late 1920, when WWJ in Detroit and KDKA in Pittsburgh had inaugurated a series of regularly scheduled daily programs it was estimated that 15,000 receiving sets were in operation with a listening audience of 20,000 persons.[2] Four years later the infant enterprise had surpassed the growth record of any other industry in the history of the United States.[3] Five hundred and sixty-three stations were on the air, three million receiving sets had been sold, and listeners numbered ten million.[4] What their patient and endless adjustments of an array of dials finally brought them for a few static free seconds every night was immaterial. The important thing was that they had tuned in on the invisible, unfathomable ether. They had actually heard Vaughn De Leath "crooning" (a style imposed by the fragile early microphones),[5] or they had listened with wonder to a sober talk on hygiene of the mouth.[6]

This was not the time for the artistically critical mind to function, but it was highly appropriate for the journalist with a scientific background to offer his opinions on the state of affairs in the new empire which had mushroomed to such enormous proportions. As a matter of fact, such a journalist found that his offers were readily accepted. To serve the public appetite for technical information sprinkled with program comments, the number of radio periodicals had increased from three in 1920 to twenty by 1924.[7] The magazine, Radio Broadcast, first published in May, 1922, is not only the outstanding example of a technical journal which attempted to provide early critical leadership for the programing phase of the new industry, it is (with the exception of a few single tattered copies) almost the only available evidence left from that rash of early publications. An excerpt from an article by Perce Collison in September, 1922, will illustrate the technical critic's primary concern with the quality of transmission and reception of programs and his relative neutrality concerning content:

> [The broadcasting stations'] main fault lies in imperfect modulation and wrong methods of recording. As a general rule a single voice gives much better results than a chorus. Likewise a few stringed instruments sound better than an entire symphony orchestra. Jazz bands are an abomination and should be absolutely eliminated not because the public does not like jazz but because the scrambled mess of disjointed harmony that is jazz just cannot crowd into a telephone transmitter . . . . What the public wants is music not excitement. . . . Canned music is not wanted. In many [piano] compositions softly played portions are hardly audible and then when the artist crashes into a grand finale, the telephone diaphragms go crazy.[8]

The only important non-technical magazine focusing enough attention on broadcasting to warrant a separate department was the Literary Digest. For ten months, from April 1, 1922 to February 3, 1923, approximately two pages of varied information appeared three or four times a month. The section was not by-lined and contained, primarily, résumés of articles from other journals concerning the wonders of the new invention. For example, readers noted with interest that a grocer could talk to his customers all at one time by radiophone,[9] or that they could tune in to a series of lectures on wireless broadcasting by Tufts College, "of a popular nature and not beyond the understanding of the thousands of young men and boys between the ages of 15 and 25, who are especially interested."[10]

In a process which might be called indirect criticism the Literary Digest chose to assess current programing for "simultaneous audience listening" by concentrating on glories which would come to pass. A June, 1922, issue quoted a statement by M. P. Rice, manager of the General Electric Company station at Schenectady: "Public taste will be educated, and it will be more critical. It will demand higher standards. There will be a beneficial evaluation of press, pulpit, school and theater, in which the inferior and the mediocre will be eliminated. Radio broadcasting carries with it responsibility. It is to be hoped that the power to say something loud enough to be heard by thousands will give rise to a desire to say something worth while, and to say it well."[11] Almost every issue contained at least one optimistic statement of this sort. Shortly before the "Radio Department" was absorbed into a section entitled "Science and Invention," we were informed that the term "radio broadcasting" would be added to Funk and Wagnall's Dictionary in December, 1922.[12]

Obviously, the medium had arrived. And, if we are to believe another statement from the Literary Digest, the role played by the daily paper had been particularly significant. "Much of the radio's popularity is due to the way newspapers have been playing it up . . . devoting whole pages and in some cases entire sections to radio developments. [The program log] . . . which the newspapers publish is of inestimable value to radio users, and broadcasting stations."[13] Science stories about radio, about the newest receiving set circuits, about the latest tubes and aerials flooded the newspaper offices of recently appointed radio editors. They frequently collected them for weekly publication in special sections supported by the advertising of hundreds of manufacturers of radio parts and sets. With the exception of printed program schedules of the major stations around the nation, this technical emphasis on the part of newspapers continued well into the late 1920's when, as we shall see, it was gradually replaced by other material. The <u>New York Times</u> was listing programs in Newark, New York City, and Pittsburgh in 1923 with a Sunday column of technical news. By 1925, its Sunday section consisted of five pages containing a program log for the week and more technical material. Similar newspaper sections appeared in other cities. The <u>Boston Transcript</u>, in 1925, published a daily radio log and every Friday had a page devoted to answering technical questions. On Saturday nights in Chicago the radio enthusiast could find a full page of scientific comment in the <u>Herald and Examiner</u>. Whereas in 1920 not a single newspaper was listing program schedules, by 1924, fifty papers included them.[14] The <u>Editor and Publisher Yearbook</u> for the first time in 1925 counted thirty-four newspapers which had separate radio departments.[15]

In this plethora of information about broadcasting, it is not fair to assume that no serious critical comment can be found. Many observers voiced opinions over basic issues facing the new industry and expressed idealistic hopes for its future. The radio "bug" of several years experience worried about the new stations interfering with his "ham" broadcasting, while the new station operators began to wrestle with solutions to the problem of overlapping frequencies and interferences from all sources. As unlimited possibilities for bringing culture and enlightenment into every home were envisioned, realistic questions of limited finances were beginning to be explored. But in the main, the first age of broadcast criticism was technical in nature. It was dominated by the scientific journalist who not only met the needs of those readers with a specific interest in the operation of a new invention, but titillated the imaginations of the average laymen who were understandably curious about what seemed like a near miracle. Their comments on programs were generally used to illustrate quality of reception or uniqueness of production details. This type of criticism did not repeat itself (at least in any quantity) a generation later in the popular press for two reasons: the transition to television was accomplished with relative technical smoothness under the tight control of the parent radio companies (television was not an amateur hobby), and there was, by the late 1940's, a young but, nevertheless, respected pattern of professional program criticism.

Fan Fare

It is interesting to conjecture what the fate of broadcast criticism might have been had the sober sections of technical advice in the newspapers and periodicals been supplemented with the more sprightly style but equally serious purpose of essays by a corps of writers interested in developing criticism as a profession. However, this was a period of increased emphasis on mass circulation of newspapers and magazines, which encouraged the activities of promoters and publicity experts. What was more natural than that radio, the entertaining new toy, should command the attention of energetic press agents and derring-do reporters instead of serious critics? Indeed, who could be serious about an upstart in show business which was so desperate for talent to fill its lengthening hours of operation that it picked artists up in black limousines, whisked them to a loft in Newark, confronted them with a tin can on a pole and told them to perform![16] It was all a lark — albeit one which the performer had been told would publicize his talents in thousands of homes. As Mr. Landry, the founder of <u>Variety's</u> radio section, indicated, "Broadcasting, in particular, has always been inflated, razzle-dazzle, wide-open for press agents and promoters."[17]

An invention which had been steadily supplying science news items for years suddenly became allied with the entertainment world and found itself the darling of publicity agents and gossip columnists. Not that it minded the spotlight of glamour — any new broadcasting station had to be talked about, had to attract an audience, had to be able to entice quality performers to either offer their services gratuitously or accept only a token fee. Consequently, instead of publishing an erudite report about its attenuated ground waves, the station would advertise the fact that its listeners would be able to hear bullets being shot into a man wearing a bullet proof vest, if they would tune in at a specified time.[18] Not only did they have to publicize unknown performers, who had been only too glad to entertain an invisible audience, but they willingly entered into wild conspiracies with famous vaudevillians and their agents.

The daily press usually listed news of this type in a separate column adjoining the radio program log. Later, these exciting items were incorporated, along with gay bits of chit-chat, into a gossip column which was often by-lined. For example, in 1925, the Milwaukee Journal offered a daily column called "The Listener In" by a mysterious B. C. L., while its sister newspaper, the Wisconsin News, took readers "Around the Radio Dial with Mike." The Globe Democrat (St. Louis) in the same year discussed weekly events "In the Broadcast Realm" written by John Estes. And readers of the Atlanta Constitution in 1928 could go "Radioing the Air Waves" with Will Smith. Scores of other daily and weekly columns remained anonymous, and properly so, since they were more often than not simply a listing of press agents' items.

It was unfortunate for the development of criticism that the scientific journalist seemed interested only in opinions about the electronic functioning of a program and was unable to cope with non-technical criticism; it was equally unfortunate that the dealer in chit-chat emphasized only the "personalities" appearing in a show and was inept at any more profound analysis of it. He could write long feature articles about famous figures like "Amos 'n' Andy" for the Sunday radio section of his paper, but his brief evaluative vocabulary for any particular program was often limited to the standard, unimaginative adjectives "beautiful," "colorful," "cheery." In the three-year period from 1924-1927, when the die was being cast for our sponsored system of radio, when a new federal regulatory agency was trying to stem the chaos of interfering stations, when two great networks were born, most of the regular coverage in the popular press concerned itself with intimate details in the lives of rising stars. Events in the following three decades of broadcasting could not have warranted any more serious commentary than these momentous decisions of the twenties which actually established our structure of public radio.

Even periodicals which had been initiated as a technical service were not immune to the blandishments of inflated, press-agent copy and profusely illustrated feature articles about radio personalities. Radio Age, a publication older by two months than Radio Broadcast, had added eight pages of "Studio Land" features by 1924. In it one could find a detailed description (but no critical comment) of Roxy's (S. L. Rothaphel) famous variety program broadcast from a second floor studio every Sunday night while the movie in his elaborate Capitol Theater was being shown downstairs.[19] Radio Age also ran a popularity contest among its readers to determine the best announcer each month. Radio Broadcast, itself, changed character over the years. By 1930, it was absorbed by a magazine called Radio Digest. It had lost its technical emphasis completely and was now billed as "the oldest and greatest of all radio fan magazines."[20] Its metamorphosis was complete from a hardworking technical grub containing an excellent column of criticism to a fashionable, brainless butterfly, content to repeat endless stories about the stars.

The reasons for these shifts are understandable. The listeners, who now purchased ready-made sets, far outnumbered the technical enthusiasts, and reader interest in these periodicals began to decrease. In the early years of the depression, many of the publications dependent on describing the world of broadcasting were wiped out, and the others had to convert to more popular reading material in order to stay in business. From nineteen radio magazines of general circulation in 1927, the number had dropped to four in 1936.[21]

The depression, of course, even affected the amount of radio gossip copy being written for newspapers, but not to the extent with which it discouraged serious criticism. Radio, contrary to the publishing and other industries, continued to grow and to make news. Its economic base, by now firmly established on advertising, fostered the kind of ballyhoo which so easily finds its way into a gossip column, and the New York-Hollywood axis, possible since NBC had developed a coast to coast network in 1928,[22] provided an unlimited source of copy. These notes were avidly read by radio's vast audience which had also developed during the "stay-at-home" depression days. In the mid-thirties, some six hundred stations were transmitting programs to approximately 25,000,000 receiving sets. Four networks were busy broadcasting the slick comedy shows, the formula half-hour dramas, the amateur and variety shows, and the serious music programs through which they achieved their fame and for which sponsors were paying an annual bill of over $50,000,000.[23]

During all of this furious studio activity in the mid-thirties, the number of magazines and newspapers employing persons who could claim even the title of "semi-critic" totaled perhaps a dozen or so. To be sure, each year since 1931, Alton Cook, radio editor for the World-Telegram (New York), had conducted a favorite program poll in which as many as four hundred radio editors from all over the United States voted.[24] Surely, a group that size would seem to have some critical impact even though it has fluctuated in numbers over the last twenty years.[25] However, Lewellyn White in summarizing a study made of these men by Variety magazine in 1946, indicated that almost 85% of them were "'mostly office boys or old men' who simply print the daily radio logs, now and then 'highlighting' a few programs in boxes, and for the rest, relying on broadcasters' 'handouts' for filler."[26]

The atrophy of most professional broadcast criticism at this second stage in its development has been a serious cultural blight. The average reader of a column called "The Dial Twister," "Ray De O'Fan," "Behind the Mike" or "Radio and TV" assumed thirty years ago, and does today, that a paragraph or two of review and personality chatter constitutes broadcast criticism. He may select a program from "The Best Today" box, nod his head in agreement with an editor who takes Arthur Godfrey to task for an off-color remark and rest assured that he and his newspaper are doing all or even more than is necessary to keep up with broadcasting. The role of the newspaper publisher in this state of affairs will be described a little later in the chapter, but for the moment let us turn our attention to a third stage in the history of criticism -- one which seemed to imply a more promising future.

A Serious Start

As early as June, 1922, radio had a "real" studio which was a "real" showcase at WJZ, Aeolian Hall, New York. Those pleated draperies made of monk's cloth, those heavy rugs, padded chairs, and artificial ventilation indicated an earnest, professional concern for the new, public art of broadcasting.[27] Of course the problem of paying for plush and programs was still not satisfactorily solved; but audiences had to be built, and radio had to demonstrate its potential for providing respectable entertainment or it would never succeed. So the broadcasters plunged in. Several complete stage productions were presented directly from New York theaters in 1923. A national radio playwriting contest was sponsored by WGY, Schenectady, in 1925.[28] "Of talks, interviews, and exhortations to repent there was no undersupply . . . . Radio was, perhaps, safest in the area of classical, and dance music, in sporting events, and in pickups from banquets."[29] By January 1, 1925, when John McCormack and Lucrezia Bori sang over WEAF, symbolizing the ability of radio to attract the world's greatest talent, the "Eveready Hour" and the "Atwater Kent" series had already been broadcasting for several months.[30]

The increase in worthwhile programs and the vigorous development of the industry was enough to convince the editors of some newspapers and technical magazines that departments of serious review and criticism were necessary. Having little in the way of criteria for selecting critics, it was only natural that they ask the scientific journalists, who already had experience in writing about the medium, to turn their attention to programing.

The <u>New York Sun</u> published a separate "Saturday Radio Magazine" section, and as early as January, 1924, Mr. Zey Bouck was conducting a weekly column called "What the Air Waves Are Saying." This alone would not qualify him as the earliest regular critic, since it was primarily a series devoted to technical comment written in a humorous vein. However, he followed each "Air Waves" strip with a special box containing a brief three-hundred-word essay on some phase of programing. Even these were apparently written more to be clever than critical. By 1925 the separate box was gone, and his critical comments, which continued through 1928, were interspersed with technical information. They frequently were in the nature of editorials in which, for example, he took issue with someone for trying to place the importance of the amateur operator above that of the regular broadcasting stations[31] or predicted that radio would eventually improve the other arts because "only the best will then tempt us away from our homes." [32]

An important daily column made its first appearance when Raymond Francis Yates started writing for the New York Tribune on Monday, February 25, 1924. By-lined as the "Pioneer," he discussed "Last Night on the Radio" for over two years. As its title implies, these pieces consisted of a strip of brief reviews. They, too, contained frequent technical comments such as the suggestion that by putting a high resistance across a microphone, the applause at a concert could be controlled in volume.[33] And much of his concern was with the microphone as it affected the mechanics of delivery on the part of performers. Mr. Yates must have been immediately popular with his readers, for the paper which had merged with the Herald only a month after he started writing, shifted his column to the entertainment section where it appeared opposite the theater reviews of Percy Hammond. The move was highlighted in an advertisement in the paper headed "A Treat for Radio Fans," which went on to indicate that "Now the daily criticism of Radio Programs is given the recognition they deserve in this original Herald Tribune feature."[34]

It is not uncharitable to state that the "Pioneer" actually did very little more than recognize programs. True to his name, he was beating out a new path in journalism. That he probably took too many interesting but insignificant detours is understandable, since the medium about which he was writing was a fascinating wilderness of endeavor. For every serious comment on the new drama or a thoughtful suggestion about staggering the superior programs on different stations to prevent overlapping,[35] there were a dozen amusing discussions of such topics as the advantages of the word "broadcast" over "radiocast,"[36] or how to dress for the publicity stunt radio-wedding of two early songbirds, Wendall Hall and Marion

Martin.[37] Nevertheless, his brief statements of evaluation were helpful, and I believe it is fair to say that from Yates' writing emerged a concept of criticism and review which was freed from the limiting technical perspective of Zey Bouck.

The first "Pioneer" relinquished his post to a more polished but less adventurous second "Pioneer," Stuart Hawkins. This change in columnists on July 12, 1926, brought a significant change in purpose with Hawkins' initial statement that a considerable portion of the space formerly devoted to reviews would now be concerned with pre-views. Even though the new critic did deliver quick jabs of constructive comment and occasional longer discussions of serious issues, the six-days-a-week column became more and more a collection of cleverly written, informative paragraphs. The paper dropped its important experiment in radio criticism on June 16, 1928. It was not revived until eighteen years later when the _Herald Tribune's_ John Crosby burst on the scene in the vanguard of a new era of criticism. In 1935 Ted Husing, by now a famous announcer and sportscaster, remembered the two voyageurs of the _Tribune_ and dictated an epitaph to their memory:

> The _Herald Tribune_, for a while in the mid-20's, showed the way to the whole country in radio criticism . . . . These two men were the forerunners of modern radio criticism, which has, however, now retreated largely to the pages of the radio and entertainment magazine. They told the truth about radio. Radio itself didn't like it. Every morning the _Herald Tribune_ radio page lay on every executive desk in New York broadcasting. The alleged experts of the studios pooh-poohed 'Pioneer's' cracks, but nevertheless they were gospel with us.[38]

Perhaps there would have been more pioneers producing regular critical gospels, if the editors of radio pages in newspapers all over the country had shared the tardy but growing conviction of Mr. Volney D. Hurd, who instituted the first radio section in the _Christian Science_

Monitor in May, 1924. He, again, was a scientific journalist, more interested in keeping his readers informed about refinements in radio, about the progress being made in primitive television, and about early high fidelity reproduction. Rapid developments on all of these fronts occupied his allotted space in the Monitor for several years. However, he realized that art forms carried by the new transmission medium were reaching millions of people. Was it not now reasonable to assume that a radio drama received by such a vast audience required at least as much critical attention as a theater performance, which, even though it ran for many weeks might ultimately play to only one hundred thousand people?[39] Acting on this logic, Mr. Hurd employed in January, 1930, a young free-lance writer, Leslie Allen, who started a weekly column of criticism in the Monitor which continued until the end of 1931. Mr. Allen's critical offerings represented the high point of responsible, informed comment to appear in the newspapers of this period. They will be discussed in more detail later in this study.

Finally, mention must be made of one other writer who started a daily column in the summer of 1925, Ben Gross of the Daily News (New York). Today, on a less demanding schedule, Mr. Gross is still the radio editor of this paper. He is more accomplished as a chronicler of events than as an interpreter of their significance, although he, too, has contributed serious reviews and criticism to the press literature about radio-television.

Realizing the inaccuracy involved in categorizing the daily critic with his weekly colleague, it still might be of some help to suggest the following evolutionary progression in early, serious newspaper criticism. Zey Bouck, with his strong technical bent, gave way to Yates and Hawkins, who practiced brief but less technical and more sophisticated program reviewing. They, in turn, were replaced by Leslie Allen, who represented a sturdier critical mind which was able to focus attention on the more significant aspects of the problems and programs of early broadcasting. The columns of these four men, along with the minor criticism of Ben Gross, comprised the pitifully meager contribution of the American newspaper to serious broadcast criticism during the formative years of radio.

Nor was the technical periodical any more successful in this respect. The scientific radio magazine quite naturally began to outlive its usefulness as the twenties drew to a close and as an interest in electronic matters was supplanted by curiosity about radio show business. Nevertheless, these early monthlies devoted to helping listeners "tune in" might have felt some obligation to initiate sections on criticism. As far as I have been able to discover, only two of them did: Radio Broadcast and Popular Radio.

The former magazine, which spanned the decade, is undoubtedly the most complete source of information about all phases of early radio. The publication entered the area of program review and criticism in April, 1924 (two years after its founding) with a department conducted by Miss Jennie Irene Mix. That it was not entirely successful, in my opinion, may have been the result of her background as serious music critic for fourteen years for the Pittsburgh Post. It was somewhat too limiting for her new responsibilities, even though, as Landry reminds us, "During the twenties the radio 'musicale' . . . dominated the program-popularity ratings."[40] However, for fourteen months she did fulfill the claims of the magazine that "'The Listener's Point of View' was the first attempt to present sound radio program criticism in any magazine."[41]

Her series varied from feature articles on rising young singers, to reviews of classical music programs, to dignified chit-chat about conductors, composers and occasionally about non-musical programs. After her sudden death in April, 1925, Kinglsey Welles, one of the editors of the magazine, continued "The Listener's Point of View" for five months until a new critic could be found. In the interim, he provided primarily informative material about new stations, new programs and receiving-set surveys but relatively little critical comment. With the arrival of John Wallace as critic, in the issue for January, 1926, Radio Broadcast reached and maintained, for three years, a high level of criticism very similar to that of Leslie Allen's future writing for the Monitor. As with Allen's work, Mr. Wallace's material will be analyzed in later chapters.

"Pioneer" was obviously a vigorous fellow, since a little over a year after he started his daily column in the Herald Tribune, Mr. Yates undertook the simultaneous preparation of a three-page monthly department called "The Broadcast Listener" for the magazine Popular Radio. This publication was very much like Radio Broadcast, although, perhaps out of deference to its title, it was less dignified in its general tone. It had started in 1922 purely as a technical magazine. Two years later it was carrying occasional articles which gave serious discussion to such matters as a proposed "University of the Ether"[42] and the effect of radio on the small newspaper. By July, 1925, Yates was contributing his monthly comments in the form of two-hundred-word squibs on a wide variety of topics. The column was brightly written, sprinkled with sarcastic observations and serious suggestions--a frank extension of his Tribune feature. This department continued until 1928 when Popular Radio reverted to its earlier strictly technical format. These monthly journals can be justly proud of their contributions to professional criticism. However, Kingsley Welles' belief that after Radio Broadcast began "The Listener's Point of View," "it seemed as if newspaper and magazine radio critics increased even as beasts of the field,"[43] is something of an exaggeration.

Certainly any increase of critical fauna in the field of general magazine publishing was not discernible. The "beasts" simply were not employed on a regular basis. There were the usual, popularly written and illustrated, informative pieces on the industry in magazines like the Saturday Evening Post, while a spirit of gentle debunking (which was to grow more severe as the years passed) combined with grave social concern infused the occasional critical articles of the "serious" magazines. For example, Joseph K. Hart sounded an amused alarm in Survey magazine in 1922:

> This all pervasive medium [the ether] has been pressed into the service of an all pervasive culture, near-culture and pseudo-culture. If anyone remains uncultured today, it will be against the combined efforts of the world. . . .If ever in history civilization needed to take account of stock, and to make sure of having something worth communicating to all the world, now is that time.[44]

One year later, the Atlantic Monthly recognized the new medium by printing the humorous experiences of a lecturer who gave his first broadcast from a station in Los Angeles. He was met at the studio door by a page boy with this greeting: "'You're one of those broadcasting guys, a regular scientific gent that comes up here to give the radio fans highbrow stuff.'"[45]

And only four years after the inauguration of public broadcasting, Bruce Bliven was able to observe in the Century that:

> Radio is fast becoming an institution; and institutions are

> built by and run for the majority against whom the minority must always fight for a hearing . . . radio will develop, as press and church and school . . . into an organ of orthodoxy.
>
> . . . .
>
> The real danger for radio is not that it will destroy other means of communication but that its users will fail to live up to the magnificent opportunities it creates. Here . . . this magic toy is used in the main to convey outrageous rubbish, verbal and musical, to people who seem quite content to hear it.[46]

Thus we see that contributors to serious magazines were already taunting the new showmen with the rebuke of the elevated brow. In fact, the jibe "low brow" was to become the most popular battle cry in what Gilbert Seldes in 1953 called "the Thirty Years' War between the broadcasters and their critics."[47] Regrettable as was the response of the general magazine, intelligent criticism on a systematic basis had become an attractive feature of at least four newspapers and two specialized periodicals during this first decade of broadcasting. It was an exciting time. A new profession for the journalist, which might have helped both the broadcaster and his listeners, could have been firmly established. That this never happened, that the transition from regular scientific writing to regular critical writing about radio never took place, was primarily the result of two factors to which we have alluded before: the development of sponsored programing and the financial debacle of 1929.

A Serious Setback

"Who is to pay the artist?", asked the New York Times in an article in their radio section for May 18, 1924. "Can singers, players, speakers of quality be expected to go on forever providing free entertainment for the radio audience?"

Here, indeed, was the great question confronting broadcasting in the mid-twenties. It was constantly being raised not only by the entrepreneurs in the new medium, but also by the public, the government, the journalists, even by the gossip-columnists. William H. Rankin, head of the advertising agency bearing his name, had been suggesting the answer to the problem ever since he had tested the mail "pull" of radio in a fifteen-minute talk on the subject of advertising by radio over WEAF, December 22, 1922. Even though he had brought the makers of "Eveready" batteries to radio, and even though the Goodrich Company sponsored tenor Joe White over eight stations for $1600 an hour in 1923,[48] the alliance between business and radio entertainment was still an uncertain solution. Two years later Mr. Sarnoff's corporation announced the formation of the National Broadcasting Company. They would sell time over twenty-four stations to advertisers who were also willing to pay for the cost of programs. After NBC's four and one-half hour inaugural program sponsored by the Dodge Automobile Company, November 15, 1926, everyone agreed that the question was answered.[49] Although a chorus of grumblers continues to the present day, the sponsor system has never been seriously threatened. Conclusive proof of its economic vitality, at least, can be seen in these figures which span the years of the stock-market crisis and its aftermath. In 1927 national network advertising billings totaled $3,832,000. By 1932 the amount had jumped to an amazing $39,106,000.[50] Robert J. Landry, for one, also believed that radio demonstrated program vitality from this time on: "After 1927 broadcasting gradually became an art — before that it was half miracle and half nuisance."[51] "The networks have supplied the driving force and the creative talent."[52]

This seemingly happy answer to the broadcasters' difficulties, which even enabled them to ride out the depression with comparative equanimity, had a deleterious effect on the infant profession of criticism. The technical magazines, whose critical departments might conceivably have been least affected by commercial broadcasting, were, nevertheless, either forced out of business by the depression or forced to shift to more popular "fan" material.

The serious, non-technical magazines were horrified by radio's new but tainted partnership. (Little attempt was made to search for a new critical approach to a medium which not only brought public entertainment privately into the home, but financed the transmission by selling time.) As one writer commented, "[What became] bait for advertisers [was now] poison to the intellectuals."[53] Magazines which should have been sources for responsible, critical leadership on a regular basis became, instead, oracles of sporadic comment, some of which was wise, more of which was uselessly vitriolic. Henry Volkening, writing for the magazine Current History in December, 1930, provides a representative sample of the kind of critical article which appeared during the shaking down period of the commercial radio system:

> Listeners have without protest, and in many cases with positive pleasure, come to think of entertainment and advertising as being practically one and the same thing.
> . . . .
> The ultimate dictators of programs will always be that majority of listeners whose support, as one radio advertising man put it, can best be won by programs appealing to a fifteen year old intelligence.
>
> Thus the whole great commercial system of broadcasting has brought us programs that, for the most part, tickle the tastes of the mentally deficient. . . . To date, radio broadcasting has principally its gargantuam size to be proud of.
> . . . .
> Indirect promotion can be even more annoying because of the very transparency of the attempt to hide its commercialism. A series of songs about eyes is sponsored by an optician . . . . This is the sort of vulgarity the public loves, or at least says the advertising agent. But this same vulgarity may also account for the fact that a great many Americans choose to

forgo some real pleasures of the air rather than [hear ads].[54]

The aesthetic disillusionment expressed in the serious magazine was mild compared to the sense of anguish and outrage experienced by the newspapers for an entirely different reason. Here was the new medium, to which they had devoted mountains of Sunday supplements and miles of press agents' bally-hoo, brashly asserting its right to a portion of the advertiser's dollar. In the face of what they considered to be a serious economic threat, editors acted to boycott radio. Early in 1927, the New York dailies insisted that no radio time-tables would be published unless stations paid for the space at regular advertising rates. For two days only one paper carried a time-table, but the _Telegram's_ defection, which was immediately supported by the public, ended this scheme.[55] A short time later another agreement was reached in which the log would be printed but no mention of the sponsor's name would be included. Thus the "Eveready Hour" would simply be listed as "concert."[56] Although apparently none of these agreements was ever thoroughly enforced on a nationwide basis, they did indicate the common determination of the newspaper industry to try to ignore broadcasting just as completely as its readers would allow. As late as 1944, _Printer's Ink_ surveyed the radio log situation and reported that 563 newspapers published radio programs free (493 of the group omitted trade names) and 271 papers published logs as paid advertising.[57]

In fairness to the press, it must be admitted that competition for advertising revenue during the early thirties was a serious matter. For example, from 1928-1934 radio advertising increased by 316% while newspaper advertising dropped by 30% and magazine advertising dropped by 45%.[58]

Also, during the period 1930-1933, 246 daily newspapers had ceased publishing.[59]

When editors were not worrying about the advertisers being won to radio, they were in turmoil over the very news itself, which was leaping from the transmitters before their own dailies could reach the street. Again boycotts were tried. In 1933, the Associated Press and other news services were forbidden to give news to radio stations. When the broadcasters established their own Radio Press Bureau in 1934, the boycott was weakened, and by the end of the thirties, the wire services were once more supplying both customers.[60]

Obviously, this unpleasant estrangement between two competing media did not provide conditions favorable to journalistic criticism of radio. If an editor would print a program log only with great reluctance and only upon an insistent demand from his readers, what would ever force him to hire, during an economic slump, a competent writer of criticism who might lose him further advertising? And, of course, he was not troubled by reader demand, because the average person did not realize such a feature as broadcast criticism existed. Ted Husing, in 1935, breezily summed up the situation:

> On most newspapers the radio critic is simply a bum reporter who couldn't make good on any other job. . . . Why? Because radio is the only national entertainment hooked up with commercial advertising. If a news rag pans a show or picture, the most it can lose is a little amusement-page advertising. But let the radio critics take a fall out of the Pond's Vanishing Cream program or the Camel Cigarette hour, and he hears from the Business Office in a hurry . . . . If they dared, the rags would drop radio out of their columns altogether. Let 'em try that though, and see how circulation takes a nose dive! Yet every word of radio publicity they print helps build up their most dangerous business rival. So they compromise. They print the bare program news, and the radio editor's job consists of clipping and pasting publicity releases from the studios."

. . . .
It's too bad, because radio entertainment would be the better off if it had to stand up to fearless criticism. In the beginning, it looked as if it would get just that. Before the Advertising Managers woke up, all the papers were saying their say about the programs.[61]

Almost two decades went by, from the time of the boycott of 1927, before newspapers began to "say their say" again. Even though the period of the thirties saw a tremendous increase in the number of newspaper-owned stations (evidence of another competitive maneuver), the tradition of newspapers not printing a critical column was still enforced. There were 269 such stations by 1940—comprising almost 33% of all broadcasting outlets in the United States.[62] It would have been too much to expect that they would criticize their own programs or give aid to another station by mentioning its programs.

Professional broadcast criticism had thus far led a disorderly and hectic life during these first four stages covering the period 1922 to 1932. If it did not receive direct assistance, it at least received encouragement from its scientific confreres in the early twenties. All but smothered by the flamboyant activities of publicity journalism, it could have achieved an uneasy compromise (as it did in some instances) by appearing as a single column combining serious comment with chit-chat. In general, however, it was the gossip column which thrived and continues to this day as a separate form of adolescent commentary on broadcasting.[63] The experiments in regular criticism during the period from 1924 to 1932 were few in number but worthwhile in quality. They were just beginning to exhibit confidence and purpose when the daily press and the serious magazine decided to ignore the new medium, the one as a result of economic fear, the other from a misguided desire to remain intellectually pure. Criticism might have ignored the bally-hoo column and continued to grow.

It could not ignore the fact that the technical magazines had disappeared and that "no help wanted" signs were being displayed by the daily papers and the general magazines.

The Reign of the Lay Critics

A comparison has already been made (see p. 11) between the remarkable activity of the radio industry and the desultory comment about that activity by radio editors during the period of the thirties and early forties. Regular professional criticism was undeniably feeble, but criticism itself was far from dead. It led a vigorous, if sporadic life at the hands of well-meaning citizens and network officials who were enough concerned about the medium to submit their opinions for publication. Their contributions lacked the regularity and the sense of informed detachment which characterize the writing of the professional critics, but they did provide lively debates on important issues. In order to understand the background against which such criticism was written, it is necessary to examine this section of radio's history more carefully.

Merlin H. Aylesworth, the president of NBC from its inception until 1936, once described the snaring of sponsors as the most difficult of all radio sciences.[64] It was to this science that the industry primarily dedicated itself, and as a result, radio achieved no small measure of commercial success. By 1933, the main patterns of radio programing were clearly enough defined to enable the show business trade paper, Variety, to prepare a list of program types and the advertising agencies most skilled at executing any one type for a particular sponsor. For example, the J. Walter Thompson Company had become the specialist in comedy-variety programs using stage and screen stars. Lord and Thomas developed human interest script serials such as "Amos 'n' Andy," "The Goldbergs," and

"Clara, Lu, 'n' Em." Benton and Bowles were famous for the "Maxwell House Showboat" and also for a number of children's shows like "The Story Man" and "Captain Diamond's Adventures."[65] The science of snaring sponsors had, in reality, created a highly mechanized show factory which operated on a carefully calculated, assembly line basis to produce quarter-hour, half-hour and a few hour segments of shiny, smooth, professional entertainment with mass appeal. In one sense the Red and Blue networks of NBC, the Columbia, and the Mutual Broadcasting systems were a subsidiary agency of the show factory. They simply distributed to the public, the programs produced in the advertising plants. In 1929, one third of all sponsored programs had been prepared by advertising agencies, but by 1934 the figure had risen to eighty percent.[66]

While acting as distributors for sponsored programs, however, the networks also earned enough money to finance some excellent sustaining programs. As a matter of fact, NBC indicated that in 1934 seventy-two percent of its programs were sustaining, and twenty-seven and eight tenths percent were sponsored.[67] This period saw the establishment of regular, classical music hours, like the Damrosch Children's Concerts, the Metropolitan Opera broadcasts, the New York Philharmonic series, and the NBC Toscanini concerts. Interesting strides were made in dramatic form, ranging from a "Great Plays" series, to a documentary series like "Americans All -- Immigrants All," to the high point in all radio drama, the Columbia Workshop productions. Informational programs, along with serious drama and music, were also placed largely on a sustaining basis. Exciting forums like "America's Town Meeting of the Air" were matched by equally exciting reports from the networks' own correspondents, who let Americans know what was happening in Europe during the years of crisis preceding World War II.[68] In terms of income, in terms of prestige, in terms of bigness, commercial radio was indeed a success. By 1938, Fortune magazine was able to announce that eighty-eight percent of all homes in the United States had radios and that listening to them was this country's favorite form of recreation.[69]

Meanwhile, sniping at radio from the sidelines seemed to be a favorite form of recreation for those who listened infrequently. As a matter of fact, the majority of critical comments during this period is to be found in occasional articles in the serious magazines and in statements issued by various pressure groups. Part of the basis for this response lay in the acknowledged dislike by many well-educated observers for the laissez-faire manner in which broadcasters and advertisers in the twenties were permitted by the government to establish one more medium of Babbitt-like culture. This opinion about broadcasting was only strengthened when laissez-faire fell generally into disrepute during the tragic economic and political situation of the early thirties. Thus, the coupling of a traditional dislike for mass entertainment with a temporary righteous indignation at the mistakes of a free enterprise system produced some strong critical protests about American broadcasting.

One of the first targets of attack was the rapid acquisition by commercial stations of frequencies which had been originally assigned to educational institutions. Without judging the bases for provocation, suffice it to say that the combined propaganda of many educational groups resulted in a series of bills and resolutions being introduced into Congress, at one time or another, from 1931 to 1934. Proposals ranged all the way from a demand for educational reservations of a percentage of all frequencies, to a request that twenty-five percent of all commercial air time be devoted to religious and educational programs.[70] One Senate resolution in 1932 even asked the Federal Radio Commission to investigate the feasibility of complete government operation of our radio system.[71] This agitation by educators and spokesmen from other professions found its way into many publications to form a considerable body of critical writing about radio. These particular protests gradually diminished when the seven-year-old Federal Radio Commission was reorganized into the Federal Communications Commission with the passage of the Communication Act of 1934.

Another, more constant irritant which stimulated the flow of non-professional criticism was the sponsor's commercial message and the level of taste of some programs, particularly those for children. The idea of a brief, dignified, institutional announcement was never seriously considered by more than a handful of advertisers even during the prosperous days before 1929. It was almost completely ignored during the "hard sell" days of the depression when time limits were sometimes violated and bodily nostrums were increasingly hawked from the loudspeaker. These breaches of good taste were not enhanced by the crime, violence and heart-throbbing suspense which clever talents had devised to grip an enormous children's audience. The non-professional grew indignant.

In the spring of 1935, an amalgam of a score of women's clubs called the Women's National Radio Committee started the publication of Radio Review, a monthly bulletin which singled out specific programs for brief statements of either commendation or castigation. Forty thousand copies of the first issue were distributed free. Their pamphlet, which appeared for at least two years, was supplemented by annual awards which the WNRC bestowed on deserving programs.[72] Responding to criticism of this type and also under urging from the F.C.C., certain reforms were adopted by the networks and by the National Association of Broadcasters (the most important industry organization). Time limits on commercials and restrictions on types of copy and products were tightened. A famous psychologist, Jersild, was retained by CBS as consultant on children's programs, and the N.A.B. drafted a new code of practices.[73]

Although the writing of the disillusioned intellectuals and the aroused reformers, who disliked what they heard on the air, did not appear on a regular basis, it was quite abundant. Contributing to this stack of literature were some articles by frustrated professional radio people who felt that the combination of commerce and art was not in the best interests of the listening public. Merrill Denison, who had come to network radio in this country after experience as a writer and producer of dramatic programs in Canada, was one of the more outspoken critics of radio writing:

> That the level of the broadcast play in this country should be so lamentably low is quite understandable. So far as I am aware no practicing dramatist has ever turned his attention to the radio or interested himself in it as a possible medium for the conscientious dramatic craftsman. . . .There is little or no opportunity in the field of the commercial program. Advertising agencies are developing a new and highly specialized type of hack writer. Rewards are poor. Pay is indifferent and the writer's identity is sunk in anonymity.[74]

The industry, of course, did not remain completely silent during these attacks from within and without. Whenever the needling hurt too much, an article defending the medium would appear, usually in the serious publications. For example, Richard Ames, an NBC news editor, wrote a piece in 1936 for the Atlantic Monthly entitled "The Art of Pleasing Everybody" in which he said, among other things, "At the present time radio people probably possess more tangible proof of likes and dislikes than their voluble critics. Generalizations about popular taste are likely to camouflage private pleading."[75] Mr. Ames' employer, in 1935, published four little volumes emphasizing the point that our system of competitive broadcasting was the "American Way."[76]

However, articles in defense of radio were in the minority, and an impartial observer of this period of broadcast criticism would have to conclude that the debunking spirit -- that generalized intellectual contempt for popular entertainment and art, which was at its height in the twenties -- continued to infuse most of the critical writing about radio in the thirties and early forties. Any attempt by supporters of the medium to correct this imbalance in viewpoint was usually based on the facile and somewhat irrelevant boast that the people were getting what they liked. The idea was to meet all complaints with popularity statistics, a strategy certain to convince a sponsor and to arouse the attention of the public but hardly the method for leading to a better understanding of broadcasting. Often the radio editors of the large dailies (for example, the World-Telegram [New York], and the Hearst papers) were busy drumming up interesting copy by polling their colleagues about their favorite radio shows. A national magazine also provided this kind of criticism by "statistics." The Literary Digest (destined for oblivion as the result of a political poll in 1936) told us that in a radio poll of its readers, Rudy Vallee and Walter Damrosch shared popularity honors with Baron Munchausen and Ed Wynn, and that "Myrt and Marge" drew mixed reactions.[77]

One reason the radio industry could shrug off so many barbed attacks was because it could retreat quickly behind its own sturdy armor of ratings. Starting with information on audience likes and dislikes from the

Crossley organization in 1929,[78] broadcasters grew increasingly dependent on the statistics furnished them by a new service called audience research.

Buffeted by angry denunciations and buried under mountains of statistics, broadcasting needed the voices of some regular, professional critics. A few did rise to the challenge -- a challenge which was complicated not only by the need to strike a balance between realistic praise and blame, but also by the framework of programing which, by this time, had become firmly fixed. As Ben Gross put it, "Radio operated by format, week after week, through an entire season which started in September and ended in June. The regular critics seldom covered a show after its premiere and there were not enough new openings to keep him busy. This helps explain why so many radio columns dealt with bits of news and gossip as well as with criticism."[79]

Two writers, in particular, (whose work will be discussed in succeeding chapters) managed to escape the bug-a-boo of complete absorption in trivia. One was already famous as an artistic observer of American society, and it was a triumph for radio criticism that his name headed a regular column of comment. The other, interestingly enough, was a relatively unknown writer who, nevertheless, felt compelled to disguise his critical career. Ring Lardner wrote a column called "Over the Waves" which was published every three weeks in the New Yorker, from June, 1932, until August, 1933. And Darwin Teilhet, who wrote under the nom de plume of Cyrus Fisher, prepared a monthly section on radio from May, 1932, to March, 1934, for Forum magazine.

Of less permanent interest as far as critical comment goes, but of some significance for the future of this type of journalism in the popular magazine, was the attention given to radio by Woman's Day. Between March, 1934 and April, 1939, not a single national magazine of any importance instituted a regular section on broadcasting review and criticism. (Perhaps a partial exception can be made for a periodical like Time which started a radio page with the issue of May 16, 1938. The column, however, like that in the old Literary Digest, was not by-lined and consisted almost entirely of news items about radio. It was of no more importance, critically speaking, than was Newsweek's similar department which had been initiated June 9, 1934). However, Woman's Day, a publication for housewives sold through the A&P chain stores, made a beginning in the direction of regular criticism by printing, between April and August, 1939, four monthly articles called "Radio in Review" by Weldon Melick. A half year later a column by Raymond Knight, who had been on the staff of NBC for eight years, made its first appearance and continued to run with fair regularity as a monthly feature until 1944. The aim of this department seemed to be that of providing readers with some behind-the-scenes information, some reviews, and a little social comment about the medium all couched in terms of lively humor. During 1944 the column passed into the hands of Jack Cluett who is still conducting it. This is the record for longevity in magazine criticism. Even though it seems to be primarily a section of comment which is more amusing than profound, it will receive later discussion in this study.

The newspapers, of course, continued their policy of indifference to broadcasting with only an occasional radio editor asserting himself as more than a proof reader for the daily log, an arranger of items, or a contributor of an occasional personality piece for the Sunday section. Leonard Carlton of the New York Post wrote some fairly solid program reviews during the late thirties, although they usually consisted of single, short paragraphs much in the style of Stuart Hawkins' work. Robert Stephan of the Plain Dealer (Cleveland) was, perhaps, the outstanding example of a responsible newspaper critic outside of the New York area. Starting with that paper as radio editor in 1929, he continued in the post until his death in 1949. Most of that time his daily material was informative rather than critical in nature. But he did editorialize about some important radio issues in his Sunday columns, and he continually urged his readers to write him and the broadcasters. He encouraged locally produced shows and acted as the conscience for Cleveland's stations. It was unfortunate that not until a few years before his death did he seem to realize the need for what he called more "formal criticisms" which he proceeded to include in his news column.[80] A further example of the seriousness with which Stephan accepted his responsibility to the Ohio community was his participation in many of the annual conferences of the Institute for Education by Radio at Columbus. He was also instrumental in organizing the Greater Cleveland Listening Council, one of some fifty local groups scattered over the nation devoted to developing discriminating audiences.[81]

A further word of comment might well be added here about these councils which were an interesting development in lay criticism coming out of the late thirties and early forties. The original motivation for their formation was a growing concern over the effect of radio on young people. Women's groups in several communities undertook a pioneering job of monitoring programs, constructing criteria for their evaluation, and promoting those which were deemed worthwhile. This promotion took place primarily by working through the public schools. It included publishing regular lists of acceptable programs and encouraging teachers to include units of instruction on discriminating listening. In addition, some councils enlisted industry aid in helping community service groups produce less amateurish broadcasts.

It was not long before the interest of the National Association of Broadcasters was aroused, and in the early forties an outstanding woman's club leader, Mrs. Dorothy Lewis, was employed by them to develop more listener councils which would serve as liason groups between communities and radio stations.[82] The councils, which were probably at their peak around 1946, have had some influence on local and network programing, although the pressure they were able to exert fluctuated widely because of organizational weaknesses. Within the last few years concern over television programing has strengthened the councils which are loosely organized into two national groups, the American Council for Better Broadcasts and the National Association for Better Radio and Television. Although listener councils have never been a major force, they represent a unique attempt to encourage lay criticism, and could, conceivably, become the source of a strong, intelligent public voice which would improve American broadcasting.

As we have seen, this approximately ten-year period, from 1932 to 1942, was scarcely one of great accomplishment for professional criticism, at least as directed to radio's listeners. The industry itself, however, was fortunate in having to contend with a few critical departments which had been established in trade papers and magazines during the same period. Although this study will not be concerned directly with these efforts, they have had an effect on criticism prepared for the general reader. Any serious commentator on broadcasting will have absorbed some of the ideas which appear in the trade journals, and it will complete the historical record to list the important trade publications which carried and are still carrying broadcast criticism. I quote from Robert J. Landry, the former radio editor of Variety, who, for a generation, has probably been the most consistent crusader for the cause of more and better criticism: "Variety, Billboard, and Radio Daily have catered necessarily to the inner circle of the initiated. The quality of their criticism was distinctly uneven but on occasion healthily jolting to the complacency of program makers."[83]

Several years of inactivity on the critical front were enough. Radio was still young in wisdom, but it was full grown in power. It had proved to be a terrifying tool for stunting men's minds in Nazi Germany and a genial necessity in the households of America. Heywood Broun, early in 1936, observed that "the development of the medium lags. Radio needs critics. Fan letters do not suffice."[84] His plea was taken up again in 1940, this time by Mr. Landry who had been proving since 1932 that Variety's critical efforts could be a helpful force in the industry. In an article abruptly titled "Wanted: Radio Critics," Landry surveyed the critical scene, analyzed its shortcomings and joined the issue to the fearful foreign emergency: "I urge the point that radio channels are so important to democracy that as a nation we would be much better off to have, rather than not have, a widespread corps of professional radio watchmen."[85] Had this article been only a condemnatory post mortem over the corpse of criticism, it would not have been important. But it contained so much of constructive value that it serves, at least figuratively, as the rallying point from which it is possible to describe a new stage in the history of criticism — a stage characterized by an intelligent determination to rouse a dormant profession into action and, more important, to define its services to a mass medium with greater specificity.

Reveille for Professional Critics

With the entry of the United States into the Second World War, the broadcasting industry was able to offer the country a generally responsible structure for public service programing. The networks, one of which was soon to change its name from "Blue" to American Broadcasting Company, had been developing an excellent corps of news reporters ever since the Munich crisis in September, 1938, indicated the eagerness of the American public for that kind of information. For the building of unity and morale, radio was able to command the talents of the few writer-producers it had encouraged during the thirties -- Norman Corwin, Arch Oboler, Orson Welles. These men were able to swing quickly into action, using the spoken voice, sound effects, and music to create, within the documentary framework, programs of comparatively good literary quality, emotional impact and informational soundness.[86]

The glittering show-pieces of the mass medium, the masterfully polished, ingeniously timed comedy shows were also indispensable to maintaining popular morale. Fred Allen, Jack Benny, Bob Hope, and Edgar Bergen with "Charlie" pepped up the spirits of the nation during those anxious evenings, while the standard fare of daytime radio, the fifteen minute serial, proceeded along its ponderous way, at least dispensing the feeling that if "Ma Perkins" could keep her chin up so could the listener.

Add to these programs all of the special efforts of broadcasting, the camp shows, the pickups from submarines, battle ships and foreign bases, the war bond announcements with Kate Smith's fantastic record of

$105,000,000 in a single twenty-four hour bond drive,[87] and it is easy to see why the industry achieved tremendous status during the years 1941 to 1945. For a great many people, radio was their most important contact with a world at war. Even the intellectuals, who had so studiously ignored the medium during the thirties, could not deny that it was satisfying to be kept in touch with the world. Attention was focused on broadcasting as never before. The result was a quiet but earnest demand for an intelligent scrutiny of the medium in all its aspects. A need was felt, not only to point out the glaring failures of the industry, but to commend it for its displays of maturity; and most important of all, to try to assess its unique impact on society.

As has been indicated, the demand for more and different criticism seemed to begin with Landry's article in 1940. He admitted there was a general lack of respect for radio as an art, but he also emphasized that the days of the "early purge-urging advertising excesses of cheap-tinsel-and loud-music, red flannel and hillbilly stuff" were over. He deplored the fact that "the only art medium with a universal audience, the one conduit for ideas that must be kept unclogged if democracy is to survive is without any organized, extensive, general criticism."[88]

In the same year Max Wylie, a radio writer, edited Best Broadcasts of 1939-40 which included the radio scripts he thought were deserving of more permanent form. In the forward to the collection he reiterated Landry's theme:

> Radio hears much squawking. . . . But thus far its millions of listeners have not yielded a true critic of the industry.
>
> . . . .
>
> Few discerning men within the industry itself would claim that broadcasting as a whole is an art . . . . But it can never reach its peak of self-realization without the assistance of intelligent and sympathetic public review.

> . . . Sooner or later adventuresome spirits will begin to perceive the challenge that the immensity and heterogeneity of radio offer to the restive and exploring mind. People will begin to dissect its social implications.[89]

Mr. Wylie was joined by another member of the radio profession, Albert Williams, who wrote some pieces for the Saturday Review of Literature in the early years of 1940. Firmly convinced that a medium which could now produce writers of stature accepted "for their own worth rather than for the glory reflected from their accomplishments in other fields,"[90] Mr. Williams urged that radio be given the leadership it so sorely lacked from "the serious thinkers and writers who have been scorning it."[91]

One of the most astute critics of broadcasting, a man who had been with the British Broadcasting Corporation and who was to assist the Federal Communications Commission in the preparation of its important critical document, the 1946 "Blue Book," also recorded some thoughts on the subject, which he indicated were inspired by Landry's article. Charles Siepmann, in 1941, drew up a careful outline of the types of criticism which were needed, what journals should carry criticism, who should write the pieces, and other steps which would strengthen the field.[92]

The causes for this searching into the status of professional criticism are difficult to determine. One factor has already been suggested: the increased importance of radio during the war emergency which called attention to the need for criticism. Another factor might be that the general rationalization of many of our American institutions which infused the patriotic writing of the period, also resulted in a mellowing of intellectual opinion about broadcasting. Radio, even with its singing commercials, had been able to state America's interest in world freedom with undeniable eloquence. Our system of broadcasting was as American as the hot-dog, the capitol dome, and the little, red school-house. The debunkers turned another ear to the loudspeaker and decided to give the medium more sympathetic, critical attention. A third factor might have been the amount of scientific attention radio had been receiving as a purveyor of anti-democratic propaganda before the war and of enemy propaganda during the war. Sociologists, psychologists and specialists in communications were busy analyzing programs and devising methods of testing radio's effectiveness on civilian and military populations. More esoteric in symbols than even _Variety's_ trade language, these media studies never appeared directly in popular magazines. But their conclusions, which did circulate in professional journals, were interesting and important. They were convincing evidence of the role radio had been playing in our society as more than just a mover of advertised products or a mere dispenser of mass entertainment. Radio was now a measurable force in a society which was not even aware of its power. Where were the professional critics who should have been alerting the people?

It may have been with feelings somewhat akin to those of the atomic scientists who suddenly realized the moral implications of their research that the mass media scientists began to recognize the public need for a type of guidance for broadcasting which only professional critics can give. The manager of radio research for the advertising firm of McCann-Ericson, Incorporated, Dr. Herta Herzog, surveyed the first post-war year of radio in 1946. She noted with pleasure that "the press has been devoting more and more space to the publicity and criticism of radio, notably through the creation of radio columns in the _Saturday Review of_

Literature and several metropolitan newspapers."[93] Lewellyn White (another social scientist who had just completed a report on broadcasting in the United States for the Commission on Freedom of the Press) acknowledged that gains had been made, but he was more aroused by Variety's discouraging 1946 survey of radio editors. He stated that "the other media of mass communication, and especially the newspapers and magazines, need to recognize radio as a coequal partner entitled to both support and honest criticism."[94] Their voices were joined by that of Paul F. Lazarsfeld, one of the great pioneers in communications research, who had helped conduct the first, large-scale, impartial study of the American public's reaction to radio in the middle forties.[95] In 1948, he examined the role of criticism of the mass media and concluded that it needed to be placed on a more formal and regular basis, conducted by a new breed of critics who understood how to separate fact from judgment and who could refrain from applying nineteenth century literary standards to a mass art.[96] This agitation by a few professional critics and by a few radio researchers would probably never have resulted in a revival of regular critical comment had not other important events occurred during the mid-forties within the government, within the publishing business, and within the industry.

The Federal Communications Commission, busy with a re-allocation of FM channels (a new form of radio transmission first authorized in 1939), and with technical matters pertaining to television which had been in very limited operation since 1942, still found time to examine the program promises and operations of existing radio stations and the qualifications of the tremendous flood of new post-war license applicants. They were concerned about the lack of broadcasters' responsibility to the public revealed by their studies, and they issued a strong criticism in March, 1946.[97] The "Blue Book," as the report came to be known, dealt primarily with advertising excesses, the lack of local programing, and the lack of programs dealing with public affairs. It was the first time in the history of the twelve-year-old government regulatory body that they had concentrated their attention on programing.[98] The report received wide publicity, was heatedly denounced by the industry, and was discussed in a great number of popular publications. No less an observer than Jack Gould, distinguished broadcasting critic for the New York Times, gives a great deal of credit to the appearance of the "Blue Book" for stimulating interest in professional criticism.[99]

In a July, 1946 issue of the Saturday Review of Literature, Albert Williams wrote an article entitled "A Ghost Is Laid," in which he described a new series of public affairs programs over the Mutual Broadcasting System prepared cooperatively by leading magazines and the network. He cited this as evidence that the deadly competition between radio and the printed page was coming to an end.[100] Even as he wrote, more evidence was accruing to prove his point, and by the end of the forties the press was paying more attention to the criticism of broadcasting than ever before. The immediate reasons for this change in attitude will be discussed in the next section, but there were earlier, more general indications that the jealous rift was disappearing. For one thing, it is likely that newspapers were beginning to admit that the economic slump fifteen years before was a major, industrial catastrophe which they could not have avoided even if radio had stayed out of the advertising field. For another, the decrease in daily papers was financially offset by the growth in circulation and prosperity of those which were left.[101]

They could afford to be more indulgent toward broadcasting. Finally, the place of news in the two media was coming into clearer perspective. The war had indicated that although people wanted the major facts as quickly as they could be delivered, they would still purchase a paper in order to read the details.

These practical considerations helped editors and publishers examine with more objectivity some of the fine programs radio had been producing during the war. As if reluctantly agreeing that the medium deserved more thoughtful comment, a few excursions in regular criticism were made, or at least contemplated, in the early and mid-forties. The New York Times, for example, installed as radio editor a former drama critic, John Hutchens. From mid-summer 1941, for three years, he was responsible for a weekly column on broadcasting. His career will be examined later in greater detail. In the issue for September, 1944, the Atlantic Monthly seemed about to change its policy of printing only occasional articles on radio by introducing a short column of criticism signed with a pseudonym, "The Listener." Apparently unwilling to make this a regular monthly event, the magazine simply indicated that this "well-known authority" would report "from time to time."[102] After three or four irregularly spaced contributions which could have developed into a thoughtful department of criticism, "The Listener" stopped listening. The erudite Bernard De Voto, who assayed the world from his "Easy Chair" in Harper's Magazine, also deigned to turn his critical gaze on broadcasting in two articles in 1945.[103] The pieces were caustic but truly profound. The medium would have profited had more such criticism been written.

So unmistakable were all the signs that a sleeping profession was stirring that radio itself, for the first time in its brash, successful life, actually took to the air in a modest, quite commendable defense. The term "radio" can justifiably be used since the spokesman was not a small town, educational station, but a powerful network with as many of its affiliates as it could commandeer. For twenty-seven Sundays, from December 1, 1946 to June 8, 1947, Lyman Bryson of the Columbia Broadcasting System presented a fifteen-minute discussion entitled "Time for Reason About Radio." The series was inaugurated by William Paley, chairman of the board, who stated that he was not against criticism as such but simply wanted intelligent discrimination on the part of critics.[104]

Robert J. Landry's call to action in 1940 was selected as the start of a new period of agitation for more criticism and as a time for a more thorough examination of what broadcast criticism actually should be. It is interesting that just as these efforts, which continued for seven or eight years, had started to produce results, Mr. Landry again wrote an article which he despairingly called "The Improbability of Radio Criticism." Whether he wanted to stimulate more action or simply bid for more personal understanding, now that he had left Variety and was in charge of program writing at CBS, it is impossible to tell. But the article provides a fitting contrast to the end of this phase and the start of the next and last stage in criticism's development. After lamenting the fact that several magazines rumored to be preparing departments of criticism had not published them, Landry sums up the critic's plight:

> The critic cannot write in his own way. Hardly a magazine is temperamentally receptive to even inferential praise of radio. If he wishes to make a sale the critic must cater to the typical editor's slant that radio can be pictured only as moronic or melodramatic but never heroic . . . . This isn't criticism but editors having fun.[105]

He makes one more effort to describe what criticism should be like and then concludes morosely that: "The ideal radio critic might well be a bedridden genius forced to listen to radio days on end, inured to hardship and patience undaunted by 65,000 units of fifteen minutes every day."[106]

A Firm Revival

John Campbell Crosby is not a bedridden genius, nor is he the ideal radio critic, but there is common agreement among professional critics that the appearance of his first daily column in the Herald Tribune (New York) for May 6, 1946, marked the beginning of a new era of criticism. As we have indicated in the last section, the time was ripe for action; Crosby's success served to arouse competing publications. The Herald Tribune noted the important event in a prosaic way: " John Crosby begins today, a column of comment on radio programs." But five months and four salary raises later, the syndication of the oolumn was announced, and within a year, it had been moved from the classified advertising section to the entertainment pages.[107] Crosby's critical contributions will, of course, be considered later in this study. For the moment his significance can be described in this opinion from Newsweek magazine:

> Possibly what gave the greatest importance to the Tribune's venture was its imitators. Previously radio editors were inclined to use their columns for a display of corny and irrelevant wit. But Crosby's followers were learning fast that radio deserved the same adult criticism as music or the theater.[108]

Within a few years there was no doubt that professional criticism had made a strong return. Albert Williams became a regular monthly writer for the Saturday Review of Literature from June 8, 1946, until October 4, 1947. Saul Carson started a five-year association with the New Republic on March 31, 1947. The Nation, at least, made an effort to publish a regular column when Lou Frankel wrote weekly for six months from October to April, 1946. And even more important, Jack Gould, who had replaced Hutchens of the New York Times in 1944, was just beginning to acquire an outstanding critical reputation.

The new group started in with vigor and dedication to provide responsible comment on the broadcasting scene. There was much to write about. Radio had undergone something of a revolution in physical growth after the war. "While on October 8, 1945, after a history of twenty-four years, there were 909 commercial standard broadcast stations authorized in the United States, by February 7, 1947 . . . approximately 600 new stations were either on the air or under construction, and more than 700 applications were still pending for new stations."[109] This expansion of the number of standard stations was to increase to 2771 by January, 1956.[110]

Programing, at least on a network basis, simply reverted to peacetime themes. No revolutionary patterns were established, although, as Sydney Head states:

> The emphasis on selling led to an emphasis on program popularity ratings which amounted to a fetish. Reciprocally, there developed a tendency to devise programs which would "buy" audiences and thereby inflate ratings artificially, i.e., the "giveaway" program which reached a zenith in radio in 1948. On the local level, the narrow margin of profit of the smaller, independent stations [saw] . . . . a resurgence of some of the . . . . patent-medicine-show atmosphere of the earliest days.
> . . . .
> On the other hand competition . . . stimulated . . . more imaginative, creative programing. For instance the documentary program . . . came into prominence in 1947. . . [also there] had been an extensive development of classical-music stations, foreign-language or racial-minority stations, sports stations, and the like.[111]

Industry problems, government censorship, FM channels, the soap operas, the United Nations -- all were providing grist for the new critical mill, which, even though Crosby had given it a mighty push, could have stopped turning had not a more exciting medium appeared.

There is strong irony in the fact that the revival of critical attention to radio occurred just two years before the advent of television, an event which was eventually to send network radio into a decline. Nevertheless, in addition to giving the public informed opinion on immediate radio programs and new television experiments, these two years of critical activity were important because they enabled the profession of criticism to stake out a confident claim to future relationships with the new medium and its audience.

Television suffered a number of false starts. It had garnered a great deal of attention during the New York World's Fair at the end of the thirties, and it had even reached the stage of local, regularly-scheduled telecasts by CBS and NBC in New York when World War II prevented further growth. A controversy over the CBS color system in 1946 prevented an immediate boom when the war was over, but by 1948 the F.C.C. was busy processing station applications and television was on its way. By the end of that year twenty-three cities were providing service. Suddenly, in September, 1948, the F.C.C. called a halt to this expansion because frequency allocations needed more careful study, if station interference was to be avoided. For four years only 108 stations were permitted to operate, but the number of receiving sets increased to fifteen million in that time, and coast to coast network service became available in 1951.[112] Finally, it was decided to add a band of ultra-high frequencies to the original, very-high frequency allocations and permit more stations to start operating. From the time the "freeze" was lifted in June, 1952 to January 1956, 380 new stations were opened, including fifteen educational statibns operating on newly reserved frequencies.[113]

Three television networks, NBC, CBS, and ABC were now providing program service for some 37,000,000 receiving sets.[114]

Although the problems of color and of the financial insecurity of stations operating in the ultra-high frequency range are still unresolved, television has quickly supplanted radio as the more important medium of entertainment. Network radio has become primarily a daytime service providing serial stories, news, and music for the majority of people who are too busy to watch a television set. The local radio stations have turned largely to recorded music programs for the bulk of their air time. To some extent television programing has followed a course somewhat similar to that of early radio. Jack Gould, in a very succinct analysis of television's first nine years,[115] lists three main stages: first, the stage of technical novelty when the public would look at anything, although they were particularly excited by telecasts of sports events; second, the stage of the "personality" novelty, when, after most of the former star-comedians and entertainers of radio had settled into regular programs, the sight of a new face periodically refreshened interest in television; third, the present stage in which "with almost everybody and his brother having had a TV debut, the industry is confronted with the realization that it must rely on itself."[116] At the moment the demand for ingenuity has resulted in special events like the ninety-minute "spectaculars" becoming the most valuable assets for television. The medium's regular events are creating viewer restlessness, and Mr. Gould borrows a phrase from Gore Vidal as he expresses the hope that "in sheer desperation [the industry] may have to scrape the top of the barrel" for future programs.[117]

The two paragraphs above are an admittedly brief summary of a gigantic new force in American life, but many facets of the television industry are familiar patterns long since established by radio. It has not been considered necessary to comment on the commercialized, assembly-line productions of the new medium, the unstable position of educational television, the effects of video crime on children, all of which continue to be problems bothering both lay and professional critics, as they did in the days of radio's prominence.

Of direct significance at the moment, however, is the effect of television on professional criticism. After reviewing criticism's meager and scarcely distinguished course during the generation before the arrival of television, its status in the last few years seems as remarkable as the growth of the medium itself. Almost twice as many regular columns of professional criticism have appeared in non-trade publications during the nine years from 1946 to 1955, as appeared in the previous twenty-two years. (The writing of Bouck, Yates, and Mix in 1924 is taken as the starting date.) The author is aware that any effort to distinguish the true critic from the mere reviewer or informative writer is largely subjective, even though some rather strict qualifications were discussed in the preface to this study. At the risk of deleting some deserving names, however, the following categories of current critics are established: outstanding columnists whose major critical contributions have been surveyed from the time they started writing through 1955; competent critics, some of whom have either corresponded with, or been interviewed by the author, but whose complete writings it has not been feasible to survey; a few critics whose names have been mentioned by others in the profession, and who, upon very brief inspection, would seem to have made at least a minor contribution to the area.

Jack Gould of the New York Times and John Crosby of the Herald

Tribune (New York), whose writings span the period, 1946-1955, are the two leading newspaper critics in this field. The other major columnists write, or have written, for a variety of magazines. Mention has already been made of Saul Carson's 1947-1952 tenure with the New Republic. In addition, the New Yorker published a bi-monthly column by Philip Hamburger from 1949-1955, and the Reporter has presented Marya Mannes' comments in monthly articles from 1953 to 1955. The Saturday Review has probably contributed the most outstanding array of critical talent. After Albert Williams left the magazine in 1947 nothing appeared for three years. Then, in the fall of 1950, Robert Lewis Shayon (who also contributed quite regularly to the Christian Science Monitor from 1950-1951) and Goodman Ace started writing on an alternating weekly basis. They were joined in 1952 by Gilbert Seldes, and all three have continued their columns through 1955. Harriet Van Horne's brief connection with Theater Arts (1951-1952), and Jack Cluett's long-term stand on the staff of Woman's Day (1944-1955) complete the writers in this first category.

Another New York daily and a few papers in other parts of the country have also been publishing sound columns of criticism and review. Jay Nelson Tuck has been critic on the New York Post since 1954, while Donald Kirkley of the Baltimore Sun, and Paul Cotten of the Register-Tribune (Des Moines), have been serving their respective communities during the fifties.

Finally, in the third category, mention must be made of the following columnists: Paul Denis with the New York Post during the mid-forties, John Horn of the New York Star which was published for only a year in 1948-49, Ulmer Turner of the Chicago Sun during the late forties, and Stanley Anderson currently with the Cleveland News. In addition, worthwhile critical columns appear frequently, but with no absolute regularity in the Christian Science Monitor and the New Republic. Rod Nordell has been writing for the Monitor since 1952, while three critics, Wendall Brogan, David Ebbitt, and F. N. Karmatz contributed in 1955 to an irregular television department in the New Republic. It is primarily through the efforts of the people just mentioned that professional criticism has been placed on a more stable basis than it has ever enjoyed before.

Many of the reasons for the meagerness of criticism before 1946 and for its sudden increase after that year have already been discussed. All that remains is to analyze some of the unique reasons why television is able to command the critical attention which radio never received. One minor factor, which contributes to the general economic health of the daily newspaper and thereby insures some steady financial support for a critical column, is the increased amusement advertising being placed by sponsors and networks. The more revenue the press receives from producers who wish to advertise their television programs, the more willing they are to hire a critic to discuss the programs.

Of greater importance than the matter of advertising income, however, is the fact that newspapers and magazines realize how interested their readers are in television. According to Jay Nelson Tuck, "The medium has generated excitement in the viewer and he is anxious to read reviews and compare his opinion with the critic. The Daniel Starch and Staff research bureau has conducted a great many readership studies for newspapers which indicate how widely television columns are read."[118] More concrete evidence of this last point comes from Donald Kirkley whose position as critic was the direct result of a survey. "A readership survey showed greatly decreasing interest in theater and movies. We abolished those two jobs (held by me) and turned to TV."[119] Ben Gross further confirms the point: "Readership studies indicate that the television column has three to five times more readers than either the drama or the movie columns."[120] Nor are the serious magazines unaware of this matter of reader interest. Robert Lewis Shayon "started writing for the Saturday Review under the editorship of Norman Cousins when he decided to broaden the market for the magazine by including material on TV."[121]

Finally, the matter of the worth of the new medium is seen by some critics as the reason for more attention being paid to television. Ben Gross states the situation very abruptly: "A premier on television is costly and important enough to warrant criticism."[122] The theme is expanded by George Rosen, present radio-TV editor of Variety:

> During the years of radio's heyday it was still regarded as a "B" medium by many people, and this attitude affected the type of critical writing about radio. However, television cannot be brushed off so easily. It is a wealthy medium. It can afford top talent, and it has become the incubating ground for films and the legitimate theater. Television is beginning to create its own talent. All of these factors mean that TV is worthy of criticism.[123]

Indeed, television is worthy of regular professional criticism. So was radio. It is important to remember, however, that this worth does not lie in the publisher's practical conclusion that since people are interested in television, they will buy a paper to read a columnist's remarks. Broadcasting is worthy of criticism because of the powerful impact which it has made and continues to make on our values and our mores, our art and our leisure. The impact demands examination and comment by trained critical observers, if only to guide the intense concern of parents, teachers, ministers, and other lay critics who have organized so many committees for better television.

Much in current television reading fare is the familiar gossip copy.

(Over twenty "fan" magazines were published in 1954.)[124] Even today most of the reading public is treated to no more serious comment than the pallid, capsule criticism of "best" awards -- whether Peabody, Christopher, or Look. John Crosby and Jack Gould refused to join a radio and television critics circle, which met for two seasons in 1948 and 1949, primarily because it seemed to them simply one more aimless award-granting body.[125] Their action indicated an encouraging growth in seriousness of critical purpose. And this trend in particular, notwithstanding the important increase in number of critics (The Nation and Holiday magazines have added television departments since January, 1956.) provides a most optimistic conclusion to the course of an erratic phenomenon.

Broadcast criticism is a profession which was conceived in the "jazz age," aborted by the depression, and reborn at mid-century. From this general historical review, we shall proceed to examine the backgrounds, procedures, and ideas of its leading practitioners.

Notes

[1]Ben Gross, I Looked and I Listened (New York: Random House, 1954), p. 51.

[2]David Sarnoff, quoted in Rixey Hobson, "Radio With the Romance Tuned Out," Journal of the American Bankers Association, XVI (February, 1924), 480.

[3]Henry Volkening, "Abuses of Radio Broadcasting," Current History, XXX (December, 1930), 396.

[4]Sarnoff, loc. cit.

[5]E. P. J. Shurick, The First Quarter-Century of American Broadcasting (Kansas City: Midland Publishing Co., 1946), p. 69.

[6]"Radio Department," Literary Digest, April 15, 1922, p. 28.

[7]Sarnoff, loc. cit.

[8]Perce Collison, "Shall We Have Music or Noise?" Radio Broadcast, I (September, 1922), 434-35.

[9]"Radio Department," Literary Digest, loc. cit.

[10]"Radio Department," Literary Digest, May 13, 1922, p. 28.

[11]M. P. Rice, quoted in "Radio Department," Literary Digest, June 24, 1922, p. 24.

[12]"Radio Department," Literary Digest, December 30, 1922, p. 22.

[13]"Shall We Advertise By Radio?" Literary Digest, May 26, 1923, p. 27.

[14]Sarnoff, loc. cit.

[15]"Radio Departments Are Now Fixed Feature in Many Newspapers," Editor and Publisher Yearbook, January 31, 1926, p. 202.

[16]Interview with Mr. Gilbert Seldes, critic, Saturday Review, April 5, 1956.

[17]Interview with Mr. Robert J. Landry, managing editor, Variety, April 3, 1956.

[18]Gross, op. cit., p. 252.

[19]Radio Age, IV (April, 1925), 24.

[20]Radio Digest, XXX (February, 1933), 3.

[21]Directory: Newspaper and Periodicals, Vols. 1927, 1936 (Philadelphia: N. W. Ayer and Sons). These numbers were derived by counting what seemed according to title to be non-technical radio magazines.

[22]Shurick, op. cit., p. 53

[23]The figures mentioned are an approximation by the author of this paper based on statistics found in these two articles: Herman S. Hettinger, "Broadcasting in the United States," Annals of the American Academy of Political and Social Science, CLXXVII (January, 1935), 1-13, and Paul F. Peter, "The American Listener in 1940," also in the Annals, CCXIII (January, 1941), 1-8.

[24]"Radio Editors' Annual Poll," Newsweek, February 17, 1934, p. 34.

[25]1937 - approx. 260 radio editors listed in Radio Directory 1937-1938, ed. Edgar A. Grunwald (New York: Variety, Inc., 1937), pp. 837-50.
1946 - 324 radio editors mentioned in Variety survey published in Variety, January 23, 1946, p. 25.
1950 - approx. 350 radio and television editors listed in The Working Press of the Nation, ed. Tom Farrel (New York: Public Relations Press, 1950), pp. 327-30.

[26]Llewellyn White, The American Radio (Chicago: University of Chicago Press, 1947), p. 123.

[27]Shurick, op. cit., p. 50.

[28]Shurick, op. cit., p. 81.

[29]Robert J. Landry, This Fascinating Radio Business (Indianapolis: Bobbs - Merrill Co., 1946), p. 82.

[30]Shurick, op. cit., p. 67.

[31]Zey Bouck, New York Sun, January 30, 1924.

[32]Zey Bouck, ibid., January 10, 1925.

[33]Raymond Yates, New York Tribune, February 25, 1924.

[34]Raymond Yates, Herald Tribune (New York), June 3, 1924.

[35]Raymond Yates, ibid., June 1, 1925.

[36]Raymond Yates, ibid., February 6, 1926.

[37]Raymond Yates, ibid., June 3, 1924.

[38]Ted Husing, Ten Years Before the Mike (New York: Farrar and Rinehart, Inc., 1935), pp. 264-65.

[39]Letter from Mr. Volney D. Hurd, Chief of the Paris Bureau, Christian Science Monitor, May 29, 1956.

[40]Landry, op. cit., p. 84.

[41]Editor's Note, Radio Broadcast, VII (July, 1925), 310.

[42]Mackaye, Percy, "The University of the Ether," Popular Radio, V (January, 1924), 37-40.

[43]Kingsley Welles, The Listener's Point of View" Radio Broadcast, VII (August, 1925), 472.

[44]Joseph K. Hart, "Radiating Culture," Survey, March 18, 1922, pp. 948-49.

[45]Ford A. Carpenter, "First Experiences of a Radio Broadcaster," Atlantic Monthly, CXXXII (September, 1923), 386.

[46]Bruce Bliven, "How Radio is Re-making Our World," Century Magazine, CVIII (June, 1924), 153-154.

[47]Gilbert Seldes, "Radio, TV and the Common Man," Saturday Review, August 29, 1953, p. 11.

[48]Gross, op. cit., pp. 62-63.

[49]Ibid., p. 101.

[50]Hettinger, loc. cit., p. 2.

[51]Robert J. Landry, Who, What, Why Is Radio? (New York: Stewart, Inc., 1942), p. 24.

[52]Ibid., p. 27.

[53]Lou Frankel, "In One Ear," Nation, November 9, 1946, p. 528.

[54]Volkening, loc. cit., pp. 397-98.

[55]Frank A. Arnold, "Radio and the Newspapers," Editor and Publisher, February 20, 1937, p. 22.

[56]John Wallace, Radio Broadcast, X (February, 1927), 375.

[57]"Results of Recent Survey," Printer's Ink, January 21, 1944, p. 38.

[58]George Fernand Gerling, "Trends in the Early Relationships Between Newspapers and Radio Broadcasting" (unpublished Master's thesis, Dept. of Journalism, University of Wisconsin, 1946), p. 260.

[59]Directory: Newspapers and Periodicals, op. cit., Vols. 1930, 1933.

[60]Gerling, op. cit., pp. 261-94.

[61]Ted Husing, op. cit., pp. 263-64.

[62]Herman S. Hettinger, "Organizing Radio's Discoveries for Use," Annals of the American Academy of Political and Social Science, CCXIII (January, 1941), 185.

[63]TV Guide (very similar to Radio Doings, a 1922 publication) had the second largest newstand sale in the United States in 1954. It is a calendar of broadcasting events to which a few pages of news and gossip have been added. See Gilbert Seldes, The Public Arts (New York: Simon and Schuster, 1956), p. 231.

[64]Merlin H. Aylesworth, "Men, Mikes, and Money," ed. Ben Gross, Collier's, April 17, 1948, p. 66.

[65]"Variety Tells All," Printer's Ink, August 24, 1933, pp. 90-91.

[66]Robert J. Landry, Who, What, Why Is Radio?, p. 37.

[67]Broadcasting to All Homes, (New York: National Broadcasting Company, Inc., 1935), p. 51.

[68]See E. P. J. Shurick, op. cit., for a complete survey of programing during the first twenty-five years of broadcasting.

[69]"Radio Favorites," Fortune, XVII (January, 1938), 88-89.

[70]"Air Uplift," Newsweek, October 27, 1934, p. 36.

[71]"Two Exciting Decades," Broadcasting-Telecasting, October 16, 1950, p. 73.

[72]"Second Annual Awards of WNRC," Literary Digest, May 2, 1936, p. 34. "Radio Critics: Seven Programs Attacked by WNRC," Business Week, August 10, 1935, p. 23.

[73]Broadcasting-Telecasting, op. cit., p. 91.

[74]Merrill Denison, "The Preparation of Dramatic Continuity for Radio," Education On the Air, 3d. yrbk., ed., Josephine H. MacLatchy (Columbus: Ohio State University Press, 1932), p. 120.

[75]Richard Sheridan Ames, "The Art of Pleasing Everybody," Atlantic Monthly, CLVIII (October, 1936), 445.

[76]Broadcasting-To All Homes, Broadcasting-Music, Literature, Drama, Art, Broadcasting-Religion, Education, Agriculture, Broadcasting-Public Affairs (New York: National Broadcasting Company, Inc., 1935).

[77]Literary Digest, December 23, 1933, p. 8.

[78]See Radio Directory 1937-1938, ed., Edgar Grunwald (New York: Variety, Inc., 1937), pp. 18, 29-31 for an interesting discussion of early polling techniques.

[79]Interview with Mr. Ben Gross, radio-tv editor, Daily News, (New York), April 5, 1956.

[80]"Radio Critics Talk to Program Directors!," Education on the Air, 16th yrbk., ed., I. Keith Tyler and Nancy Mason Dasher (Columbus: Ohio State University Press, 1946), p. 413; Robert Stephan, "Informing the Listener," Education on the Air, 9th yrbk., ed., Josephine H. McLatchy, (Columbus: Ohio State University Press, 1938), pp. 60-64.

[81]White, op. cit., p. 114.

[82]White, ibid., (see also Judith C. Waller, Radio, the Fifth Estate 2d. ed., Boston: Houghton Mifflin Co., 1950 , Chap. 20.)

[83]Landry, This Fascinating Radio Business, p. 98.

[84]Heywood Broun, "Radio," Nation, May 27, 1936, p. 686.

[85]Robert J. Landry, "Wanted: Radio Critics," Public Opinion Quarterly, IV (December, 1940), 621.

[86]William C. Ackerman, "U. S. Radio: Record of a Decade," Public Opinion Quarterly, XII (Fall, 1948), 440-54.

[87]Ibid., p. 446.

[88]Landry, "Wanted: Radio Critics", Public Opinion Quarterly, IV (December, 1940), 620.

[89]Max Wylie (ed.), Best Broadcasts of 1939-40, (New York: McGraw-Hill Book Co., Inc., 1940), preface.

[90]Albert Williams, Listening (Denver: University of Denver Press, 1948), p. 150.

[91]Albert Williams, "Radio and the Writer," Saturday Review of Literature, October 24, 1942, p. 44.

[92]Charles A. Siepmann, "Further Thoughts on Radio Criticism," Public Opinion Quarterly, V (June, 1941), 308-12.

[93]Herta Herzog, "Radio-The First Post-War Year," Public Opinion Quarterly, X (Fall, 1946), 311.

[94]White, op. cit., p. 231.

[95]Paul F. Lazarsfeld, and Harry Field, The People Look At Radio (Chapel Hill: University of North Carolina Press, 1947), p. 217.

[96]Paul F. Lazarsfeld, "The Role of Criticism in the Management of Mass Media," Journalism Quarterly, XXV (June, 1948), 116, 124.

[97]William C. Ackerman, loc. cit.

[98]White, op. cit., pp. 182-99.

[99]Interview with Mr. Jack Gould, critic, New York Times, April 2, 1956.

[100]Williams, Listening, pp. 42-46.

[101]Harvey J. Levin, "Competition Among the Mass Media and Public Interest," Public Opinion Quarterly, XVIII (Spring, 1954), 73.

[102]"The Listener," Atlantic Monthly, CLXXIV (September, 1944), 115.

[103]Bernard DeVoto, "The Easy Chair," Harper's Magazine, CXCI (July, 1945), 33-36; ibid., (October, 1945), 325-28.

[104]William Paley, quoted in Lyman Bryson, Time For Reason About Radio (New York: George W. Stewart, Inc., 1948), p. 13.

[105]Robert J. Landry, "The Improbability of Radio Criticism," Hollywood Quarterly, II (1946-47), 68.

[106]Ibid., p. 70.

[107]Marjorie Cordee, (ed.), Current Biography, 1953 (New York: H. W. Wilson Co., 1954), p. 134.

[108]"Crosby's First Birthday," Newsweek, May 19, 1947, p. 66.

[109]"An Economic Study of Standard Broadcasting," F.C.C. mimeo., 1947, p. 1, quoted in, Sydney Head, Broadcasting in America (Boston: Houghton Mifflin Co., 1956), p. 150.

[110]Variety, January 4, 1956, p. 152.

[111]Sydney Head, Broadcasting in America (Boston: Houghton Mifflin Co., 1956), p. 151.

[112]Ibid., pp. 158-61.

[113]Variety, loc. cit.

[114]Jack Adams, "Proposed FCC Policy," Capital Times, (Madison, Wisconsin), June 27, 1956.

[115]Jack Gould, "Television Today," New York Times Magazine, April 8, 1956, pp. 12-13, 36, 38.

[116]Ibid., p. 12.

[117]*Ibid.*, p. 38

[118]Interview with Mr. Jay Nelson Tuck, critic, *New York Post*, April 6, 1956.

[119]Letter from Mr. Donald Kirkley, critic, *Baltimore Sun*, April 16, 1956.

[120]Interview with Mr. Ben Gross, *loc. cit.*

[121]Interview with Mr. Robert Lewis Shayon, critic, *Saturday Review*, April 4, 1956.

[122]Interview with Mr. Ben Gross, *loc. cit.*

[123]Interview with Mr. George Rosen, radio-tv editor, *Variety*, April 5, 1956.

[124]*Broadcasting-Telecasting*, November 22, 1954, p. 54.

[125]Jack Gould, *New York Times*, January 25, 1948.

CHAPTER II

THE CRITICS AND THEIR PROFESSION

> Radio Critic Wanted—Must be gentle, understanding, fond of children's programs, devoted to finer things yet capable of listening to claptrap for hours at a time. Should be socially conscious but no business hater, should have working familiarity with classics, the lower middle class, the consumer movement and the Crossley Report. He must be highminded, yet possessed of humor; he must modify his boldness with discretion; he must know acting, directing, advertising, merchandizing, and orchestrating and should know about public interest, convenience and necessity. Finally, he should be free of bias, a master literary stylist and willing to work for small wages: also willing to arrange free talent for publisher's pet charity and relieve switchboard operator at lunch hour.[1]

This remarkable assemblage of contradictory qualifications and dubious duties never really found its way into the classified section of a newspaper or a trade magazine. However, had Mr. Landry's mythical request appeared, there would have been a surprising number of promising applicants. None of them, of course, matches the unique professional image described above. Nevertheless, drawing on a wide variety of experiences, and helped as well as hampered by the lack of relevant critical patterns, the broadcasting critics have explored a fresh area for the journalist, established certain procedures and wrestled with problems never encountered in other forms of criticism. The present chapter examines in somewhat closer detail the professional activities of those journalists whose careers in criticism are most noteworthy. We shall concern ourselves first with a record of the critics' vocational experience, second, with an account of the procedures they have developed for criticizing radio and television, and last, with an examination of the more important problems a new branch of criticism has posed for them.

Vocational Backgrounds of the Leading Critics

It is not the purpose of this section to develop complete biographical profiles of these writers. For one thing, information not only about former critics but even about present day writers is meager. And for another, this study will emphasize primarily what the critics have had to say, not the indirect experiences which led them to say it.

The paucity of information about broadcast critics is understandable. Of all critical writing, the column about a program which will be seen or heard only once is by nature an ephemeral affair, which tends to carry its author along with it into obscurity. This state of semi-anonymity is even more understandable when we realize that the struggling, new profession has only one tradition: lack of prestige. Broadcast critics have often deserved the epithets, "bums"[2] and "paste up guys."[3] Although the situation is slowly changing, newspaper editors are apt to make critics responsible for so many jobs that they can perform none with distinction. For example, it is not unusual to discover that theater reviews, garden information, and radio-television are assigned to one reporter.[4] His only defense is to use clippings from other sources to fill out his columns.

However, editors need not bear the complete onus for the feeble reputation of broadcast criticism. Even competent and successful critics are responsible, in part, for not calling more attention to their profession. They may not be consciously ashamed of their positions, but there is no question that many of them acquiesce only in lieu of finding more "respectable" work.

> "Gross, you're it," said the Boss. [Colonel Frank J. Hause.]
> "I don't like radio," I said. "I want to be a drama critic."
> "You'll be a radio critic," he insisted. "It's not a full time job; you'll also cover other stories and continue writing that labor column you're doing."
> "But I'm not qualified," I protested. "I don't know a thing about radio."
> "Oh, yes you do!" There was ice in the Colonel's voice and a determined glint in his eyes. "From now on you're our expert -- our great authority. And do you know why? Because you're the only guy around here who knows how to turn one of the damned things on!"[5]

This account by Ben Gross of how he became a radio critic in the summer of 1925 is, of course, humorous as a retrospective anecdote. His reluctance was only natural since broadcasting itself was new. Apparently, however, similar scenes were repeated some fifteen years later when broadcasting was a full grown industry. If we are to believe the knowledgeable editor of <u>Variety</u>, other critics, who, like Gross, could turn "the damned things on," were equally unenthusiastic about fulfilling the rest of their responsibilities. George Rosen tells us that John Hutchens, former radio editor of the <u>New York Times</u>, "considered book reviewing a promotion, although he may not admit it."[6] He reveals in the same article that Alton Cooke of the <u>World-Telegram</u> (New York) "was eager to get out of radio." "He now does film criticism."[7] And says Rosen, "Van Horne [Cooke's replacement] . . . is said to be ambitious to be a 'real writer' rather than a radio columnist. . . . she's young (26), good looking, bright, and building a reputation as a writer -- that's what radio columning is good for sometimes."[8] As it turned out, Miss Van Horne was still with the <u>World-Telegram</u> ten years later and still enthusiastic about the profession of criticism. "You've got to love it with all your heart to stay in it."[9] Nevertheless, Mr. Rosen's thesis has validity.

Such lack of enthusiasm helps to explain the comparative obscurity of the practitioners of the new form of criticism. Although broadcast critics write for the public, they lack the potent influence of the Broadway theater critics, the aura of profundity associated with literary arbiters, and a critical tradition which could command respect from employers as well as readers. Consequently, they have not publicized themselves widely, nor have they received wide publicity about their professional careers. However, if we are to understand more completely the development of this field, we must know a little about the vocational experience and qualifications of critics who helped and are continuing to help interpret the events described in the preceding chapter. By utilizing facts which have been discovered, we can compile a rudimentary "Who's Who" of broadcast criticism.

Newspaper Critics

Dalton Trumbo once referred to newspaper critics as a "gang,"[10] and, I suppose, if we were to distinguish a "professional group" from a "gang" on the basis of important academic qualifications, the latter designation might be more accurate for many of our most prominent critics of broadcasting. They would be the first to admit their unorthodox scholarly backgrounds and the last to deny the tremendous value of general newspaper work as preparation for criticism. Consider the following writers who did not assume posts as broadcast critics until they had served a considerable apprenticeship in various reportorial assignments for metropolitan newspapers.

Until Mr. Gross was victimized by his knowledge of the switches on a primitive radio set into becoming radio editor for the <u>Daily News</u> (New York), he had served as general reporter for the <u>Birmingham News</u>

(Alabama) and the Bronx Home News.[11] Volney Hurd, who hired Leslie Allen for the Christian Science Monitor in 1930, contributes this comment about him: "Leslie Allen had been on the Monitor copy desk before World War One. I had known him when a boy, ran into him in 1929, found he was free-lancing in New York and had critical talent and so engaged him to do my column."[12] Mr. Allen, himself, referred rather vaguely, once or twice in his columns, to having been a sports reporter. With disarming frankness, Jay Nelson Tuck, perceptive critic for the New York Post since 1954, admitted that his background had been completely in the field of news reporting. For several years he had been night editor for the Post and "as a matter of fact I did not even have a TV set when I was asked to take my present job."[13] It is now legend, of course, that John Crosby, who has been called "one of the most astute critics of radio and TV,"[14] knew nothing about broadcasting when he started his column for the Herald Tribune (New York) in 1946. Like the others, he had served as a reporter for over ten years. In 1933 he was a police, news, and political reporter for the Milwaukee Sentinel. From 1935 until World War II, he was a police reporter and then an amusement reporter for the Herald Tribune (New York).[15]

It is significant that three of these four men who worked as straight reporters all admit having a more than casual interest in the theater. If Mr. Gross had once entertained hopes of becoming a drama critic, he had doubtlessly been preparing himself for such a job. And Mr. Crosby, who had done some writing in the drama department of the Herald Tribune before serving in World War II,[16] actually wrote a play, "The Mirror Cracked," which attracted the attention of no less a person than Theresa Helpburn of the Theater Guild.[17] Even Mr. Tuck, who insists he received his experience at the city desk, indicated he had long been a Broadway theater goer and had done wide reading in the field of drama.[18] None of them was completely ignorant of a critic's responsibilities.

Two other prominent writers of broadcast criticism for the newspapers had thorough backgrounds in drama criticism before entering the new field. John Hutchens had long experience as a drama critic before becoming radio editor of the New York Times in 1941. He was with the New York Post in 1927 and 1928, served as assistant editor and drama critic for Theater Arts magazine during the early thirties and was assistant dramatic editor for the New York Times until assuming the radio post.[19] When he left to engage in book reviewing, his position was taken by Jack Gould, who had been a reporter for the Herald Tribune (New York) during the mid-thirties, a member of the New York Times' drama department from 1937-1942, and a member of the radio department under Hutchens until he assumed the editorship in 1944.[20] Mr. Gould has made frequent references to his early work as reviewer of night club acts for the Times, which he feels "provided an essential background for the position of radio editor."[21]

When we consider the vocational backgrounds of the newspaper "gang" it is apparent that we cannot dismiss the importance of reportorial training as part of a critic's qualifications. This is particularly true when we realize the unique similarity between the coverage of a newspaper and the programs of a broadcasting station. Broadcasting, unlike the theater, the film, the music world, is not restricted to the presentation of discrete units of entertainment alone. During its long hours on the air, a station represents a microcosm of education, politics, commerce, as well as entertainment. Radio and television programs have aspects of "assignments" similar to the wide variety of events a good reporter is expected to be able to handle. This ability to interpret a kaleidoscope of daily programs is a prime asset for the broadcast critic, an asset which is further enhanced by two basic reportorial skills which, Jack Gould feels, are particularly important: judgment and speed.[22]

Paul Cotton, of the Register and Tribune (Des Moines), was asked about the qualifications for criticism, and his reply is an excellent final comment about the worth of a newspaper background:

> The more experience a critic has had with the human race the better he will be able to do his job. Specifically, because much broadcasting is entertainment, I think a critic has to have some knowledge of drama and the theater. I did theater criticisms years ago, when there was a substantial road theater. On evaluating public information programs -- deciding how well they are presenting an educational or informational subject -- I think long newspaper experience is very valuable.[23]

Magazine Critics

More can be said about the vocational backgrounds of the leading professional magazine critics. They have not only been given at least a modicum of publicity in the "editor's note" appended to a column, but the greater permanence of a magazine article as contrasted with the highly expendable newspaper column seems to give their authors more prominence. (Perhaps the notable exception is John Crosby whose newspaper career has stimulated several biographical articles.) At any rate, the only important magazine critic whose background remains entirely unknown is John Wallace of Radio Broadcast, that important journal of the 1920's. A perusal of the experiences of the remaining major writers indicates that they fall into two groups: six of them have the interesting qualification of having held positions in broadcasting so that they write with first-hand knowledge of the radio-television industry. The other four, like the newspaper critics, are professional authors and journalists.

Let us consider first some pertinent facts about those critics who have had studio experience. Darwin Teilhet was perhaps the first radio producer who also accepted responsibility for writing a monthly feature on broadcasting. His articles appeared in the Forum magazine from 1932-1934 while he was in charge of radio production for the west coast office of N. W. Ayer & Son, an advertising agency. He had no sooner started his critical articles than their propriety was questioned by his employers. So for several months he continued them under the pseudonym Cyrus Fisher. During this time, he became an account executive in charge of the Hawaiian Pineapple Company's advertising which, fortunately, did not utilize radio, thus leaving him free of further concern over any conflict of interest arising from his critical avocation.[24]

It was not until a decade later that another radio producer turned critic. Albert N. Williams, who had been associated with NBC from 1937 to 1941, projected an occasional article for the Saturday Review of Literature into a monthly series which ran from 1946 through 1947. Of longer duration has been the association of Robert Lewis Shayon with the Saturday Review. Mr. Shayon served as a producer-director for the Mutual Broadcasting System from 1938-1942 and as an executive producer for CBS from 1942-1949, where he received particular acclaim for a series of historical programs entitled "You Are There," and for several outstanding documentary programs including the famous report on juvenile delinquency entitled "The Eagle's Brood." He has guided the production of some educational programs at WOI-TV at Ames, Iowa and is currently an executive of Pyramid Films, Incorporated, which specializes in industrial films for television. Drawing upon the knowledge gained from these positions, Mr. Shayon has been able to combine authoritative information with criticism in columns written, first, for the Christian Science Monitor from the spring of 1950 through 1951 and then in the fall of 1950 for the Saturday Review.[25] This last column has been appearing approximately every three weeks since that time. The chronological pattern followed by Teilhet, Williams and Shayon would also seem to be a logical procedure. These men had first been confronted in the studio with the problem of broadcasting. Certainly, they were well equipped, then, to criticize radio and television on the basis of practical experience.

Two other magazine critics, however, reversed the pattern; they were invited to put their theories to the test and entered the broadcasting profession after publishing critical articles. Gilbert Seldes is probably the only American critic who has devoted the major portion of his life to a deliberate, serious, yet eager examination of the popular as contrasted with the fine arts. His career began with solid orthodoxy when, upon graduation from Harvard, he became music critic for the Evening Ledger (Philadelphia). After the first World War, he entered upon a phase of drama criticism for Dial magazine and the Evening Graphic (New York). His versatility was established by two outstanding publications during this period: The Seven Lively Arts, a thoughtful paean to vaudeville, the silent movies, jazz, and the comic strips, and a highly successful translation of Aristophanes' uproarious comedy Lysistrata. The new mass art of radio attracted his critical comment as early as 1927. For several years he contributed articles on films and radio to various publications until 1937, when he dropped a column which had been appearing for several months in Scribner's in order to work with CBS in developing television programs.[26] Mr. Seldes left the network in

1945 and since that time has devoted most of his time to interpreting the mass media in campus lectures, magazine articles and books. In 1952, Mr. Seldes joined Mr. Shayon on the staff of the Saturday Review, contributing a monthly column on broadcasting.

Saul Carson, who is perhaps best known for his critical columns in the New Republic from 1947 to 1952, cut his critical teeth while serving as assistant radio editor under George Rosen on Variety magazine in the early forties. In addition to his New Republic column, Mr. Carson contributed regularly to Radio and TV Best magazine and occasional articles to other journals.[27] He had an opportunity to develop a working knowledge of radio when he wrote and assisted in the production of several documentary scripts for the "New World A-Coming" series over WMCA, New York, in the late forties.[28]

One critic achieved early fame, not for his commentary about radio, but for his masterly performance in radio. Goodman Ace, with his wife Jane, was a leading network entertainer for about twenty years. He had been film and drama critic for the Kansas City Post when, in 1928, he started reading his column over station KMBC. This developed into a fifteen-minute nightly, domestic travesty which attracted the attention of CBS in 1931, and from that time until 1947 his light satires delighted large audiences. He has since supervised comedy and variety shows for CBS[29] and has, within recent years, been praised by professional critics for revitalizing Milton Berle's comedy television hour. The general public has enjoyed regular columns of Mr. Ace's critical humor about television in the Saturday Review from 1950-1955. As a matter of fact, from 1952-1955, this small but important publication made the single most significant contribution toward elevating broadcast criticism to a serious position in American letters. Week after week several thousand readers were amused, provoked, and inspired by the alternating columns of Ace, Seldes and Shayon.

As meager as the professional diet of criticism has been in this country, the public can at least be grateful that the fare is balanced between the layman's viewpoint as represented by the newspaper critic and the industry-informed viewpoint of the critic who worked in broadcasting. The general reader can also be grateful for the columns of the second group of magazine critics whose backgrounds are to be discussed here. These are the professional writers, akin to newspaper critics, who have included broadcast criticism among their other assignments in the novel, the short story, and other types of literature.

Very little has been made of the fact that one of America's most important literary figures wrote a monthly column for the New Yorker from 1932 to August 1933. That these were, in tragic fact, deathbed pieces should have focused even more attention upon them. Ring Lardner, won wide fame as a sports reporter and sports writer during the World War I era; however, his ear for colloquial speech, which was sharper than any other native writer, won him even greater literary acclaim as the author of satiric short stories about lower-middle class Americans. He collaborated on two plays, Elmer, the Great and June Moon, which had good runs on Broadway in 1927.[30] Forced to a hospital bed in 1932, Lardner occupied his time by listening to the radio. We are told by his biographer, Donald Elder, that "for him music and theater became a single interest," and that "in music, as in writing, being a popular artist was the condition of his being an artist at all."[31] Radio, of course, was just beginning to take a commanding lead as the great medium of mass entertainment, the most popular purveyor of the popular arts. Naturally, Lardner was interested, and out of his sardonic musings about the new entertainment form came the New Yorker columns. Gilbert Seldes has this to say about them: "In these special articles, with the pressures removed, Lardner seemed to set himself the strictest standards; free from the restrictions of time and space, he worked under the laws of his own integrity; I think he took vast satisfaction in doing them."[32]

Mr. Lardner's biting humor was, of course, his trade mark in criticism as well as in his other work. Another less acrid humorist, who has been practicing his profession both in defense and at the expense of broadcasting, is Jack Cluett, monthly columnist for Woman's Day magazine since 1944. Mr. Cluett has been variously a columnist for the Brooklyn Eagle, an associate editor of Judge (well-known humor magazine of the thirties), a contributor to the New Yorker and Vanity Fair and a writer of "Post Scripts" for the Saturday Evening Post. In addition, he spent five years in Hollywood writing movie scenarios and dialogue for comedians like Jimmy Durante.[33] Because his columns include so many things, from news items, to feature pieces, to program reviews, to very occasional critical comments, Mr. Cluett cannot be labeled strictly a critic. However, he has successfully managed to entice a wide audience into thinking about broadcasting. He, Ring Lardner, and Goodman Ace could, with some justice, be called the comic spirits of broadcast criticism.

The editor of the New Yorker had at one time considered having

Dorothy Parker revive the humorous radio column popularized by Ring Lardner,[34] but it was not until 1949 that the magazine started publishing an approximately bi-weekly column on television. Its author was Philip Hamburger, who had been on the staff since 1939 and had served as a music critic part of that time.[35] Mr. Hamburger did not attempt to compete with the kind of comic writing which came from Lardner and might have come from Dorothy Parker. Most of his reviews, during the years from 1949 to 1955, were urbane and thoughtful pieces about television drama, although he did comment on informational programs too.

One of the more recent magazine broadcasting critics to receive respectful attention from her readers is Marya Mannes, who started writing regularly in 1953 for a comparatively new publication, the Reporter. Like Mr. Tuck, Miss Mannes did not even own a television set. Her editor, Max Ascoli, sent her a second-hand receiver and told her to try writing a few pieces. He was not asking for the impossible, however, because Miss Mannes had a thorough background as a critic. She had been, during the thirties and forties, an art critic, a book reviewer, and a contributor to Vogue on the theater. This knowledge of many artistic media has given Marya Mannes a general frame of reference within which she fits her comments about broadcasting.[36]

These, then, are the vocational backgrounds of the critics who would be most qualified to answer the advertisement heading this chapter. Their experiences vary from years in professional broadcasting to a few hours wandering around a studio; from an extensive knowledge of the arts to an average layman's familiarity with them; from scholarly writing in thoughtful journals to popular writing in the daily paper. But they do have these qualities in common: they are skillful writers who can meet a deadline, who are emotionally and intellectually responsive to an unusual variety of programs, and who are concerned about broadcasters and their audiences. They, after all, are the ones who have attempted to give the newest mass media some honest guidance. That their efforts have not yet led them to experience the success and prestige of critical colleagues in other departments is attributable primarily to the youthfulness of the profession. Broadcast critics have not written steadily enough to have developed completely adequate procedures for the task, and they are beset with peculiar problems for which solutions are still being sought. Let us turn now to a consideration of these matters, with which any of the critics, no matter what his qualifications, is faced.

Procedures of the Critics

The temptation is strong to answer the question, "What does a critic do?" very simply and let it go at that: "He writes about radio and television." But our purpose in these next few pages is to discover how he goes about the job -- to discover the different kinds of columns he writes, how he organizes his columns, his activities corollary to the writing, and finally, his writing style. Needless to say, each of these points is intimately related to the fundamental concepts the critic holds about the nature and function of criticism. The importance of these concepts, however, calls for a separate emphasis which will be given them in the next chapter. We will concern ourselves at present with an arbitrary, more mechanical description of the critics' procedures.

Kinds of Columns

While the austere world of letters may regard the journalist with some disdain, there is one, admittedly partial, observer who has these kind words to say -- words which admirably characterize our professional critics:

> Journalists are among the very few generalists left in a boringly specialized world. You are in touch with everything [underlining mine] from the local grass roots to the most complicated international thing. You rub up against so many things that you have an opportunity to be decent, constructive and half intelligent about some of them.[37]

Redefine "everything" in terms of the world of broadcasting, as Jack Gould does, and it is evident that critics have a wide range for their talents: "The problems of the video art fall roughly into three different, if overlapping classifications: the technical, the programmatic and the economic."[38] The leading critics comment on all three categories at one time or another, employing a variety of techniques to do so.

Ever since the days when "Pioneer," the 1924 critic for the Herald Tribune (New York), described clamping earphones on his head in order to write more accurately about classical concerts,[39] program reviewing has occupied most of the wordage devoted to radio and television. "Selectivity," a technical term denoting the ability of a radio to discriminate between frequencies on the broadcast band, might also be used to designate a principle followed by the critics as they decide which programs to review. Mr. Landry, even though he speaks for the trade journal, Variety, breezily summarizes the determinants employed by most critics as they practice selectivity. A program is certain to be reviewed, if it "has a big star, a big budget, the guidance of a big agency, and the appearance on a big network at an important time."[40] Critics on the daily papers state the matter even more succinctly. They review the "newsworthy" programs. "The doings of a prominent individual naturally attracts more attention than the activities of a pedestrian figure."[41]

In this country, where an around-the-clock flow of programs from several networks and hundreds of stations is taken quite for granted, the critic is confronted by a constant dilemma as he tries to decide which "newsworthy" program, of several broadcast at the same time, is to receive priority. Frequently critics resorted to listening to transcriptions of a radio program when they were unable to hear the various broadcasts, and, of course, as home tape recorders became available in the forties, the critics found it easier to schedule listening sessions at their own convenience. Today, kinescope recordings of television programs can serve the same function as radio transcriptions, although the time has not yet come when inexpensive video tape recordings will assist the critic in his reviewing of television programs. A few of the large Metropolitan papers, like the Daily News (New York) and the New York Times, are fortunate in having two or three people[42] who can review the increasingly important "special" television programs, which are broadcast only once and often at competing hours.

The concept of a series of regular weekly programs was an outgrowth of the economic theory that audiences needed regular exposure to an advertised product. It was a new idea to the entertainment world and, consequently, required a new critical procedure in program reviewing. Most critics try to review the first program and occasionally will come back to a series later on in the season to see how it is faring. In addition, their September and October columns are frequently concerned with the first show of each major series carried over from the previous year. (The regular season in broadcasting starts in September and runs for thirty-nine weeks through May.) Although commenting on the major programs alone is an arduous job, the leading critics usually find time to comment about programs which may be less well-publicized but which they feel are particularly noteworthy or abhorrent as the case may be.

The common description of broadcasting as an "industry" is particularly appropriate when considering another kind of column which the critics prepare. Broadcasting is an entertainment factory, and, unlike other branches of the amusement arts, the public is not only a consumer of programs but the owner of vital channels over which the programs are distributed. As shareholders in the enterprise, the people are entitled to reports about its operation. At this point the program reviewer becomes reporter. His column, which last night may have carried an artistic appreciation of "The Saddler's Wells Ballet," turns tonight to a probing discussion of a new Federal Communications Commission dictum. Jack Gould, for one, is particularly skillful at condensing a complex technical and economic issue into a well-balanced presentation written for the layman. The entire radio-television page of the Times for June 19, 1955, was devoted to his explanation of toll television -- its legal and social implications, its advantages and disadvantages. Most of the critics have taken their readers on lively studio and control room tours calculated to impress them with the intricacies of radio and television production. If they tarry at all in the dressing rooms of the stars, the leading critics concentrate on skillful dissections of an artist's technique in contrast to the revelatory feature stories of the stars composed by lesser journalists. Major decisions of the Federal Communications Commission, such as the allocation of television channels for education, are explored, and technical advances like color-television are discussed. The critics frequently expose the statistical mysteries of the Nielsen and Trendex deities or take time to comment on the sociological impact of the electronic media. As new books about broadcasting are published, a critic will often call them to the attention of his readers. In these columns, journalists are not unlike teachers in their desire to give listeners and viewers an accurate background in broadcasting.

The objectivity of the pedagogue may, however, be swept aside by the passion of the journalist engaged in a crusade. Column after column of the critics' most vigorous writing is thrust into print as he demands that sinners (frequently brash ad men, and timid broadcasters) mend their ways; or as he urges the industry to adopt a new plan. For example, in 1926 John Wallace appealed to broadcasters to establish networks which would specialize in specific types of programing rather than weaken themselves by trying to compete in all of radio's forms.[43] Some of Ring Lardner's wittiest pieces were concerned with his deadly serious desire to purge the air of "off color" lyrics in popular songs. The battle of the educators in 1951 for television channel reservations received much of its strongest support from the alarums echoed by many of the outstanding critics. Without a doubt, these critics feel they would be failing their readers, if they were unable to establish firm points of view on significant issues, and if they were unable to engage in the persuasive writing necessary to influence others toward that point of view.

There may come a lull in the critic's deadline dash from one review to the next, or a quiescent period when the need for informational and persuasive pieces is not so pressing. These are the times when he may choose to toss off a lightly sarcastic column, or at the opposite extreme, compose a tightly organized, philosophical essay upon which his readers can cogitate. John Crosby, who has probably achieved most of his fame for the sheer entertainment value of his newspaper columns, delightfully states a critic's justification for the humorous piece:

> Today is our day for small trends, the smaller the better, for little happenings in radio of minute consequence and virtually no significance. A man gets tired of handing down sweeping judgments every day; every man should have a day of rest devoted exclusively to any minutia he happens to have lying around.[44]

These odds and ends, shaped by the journalists into an amazing variety of forms, are limited in their comic and critical values only by the wit of the writer. In a gesture, typical of many a present day critic, John Wallace threw caution to the winds in an article entitled "Why There Should Be More Vice in Radio." There he was, in 1927, decrying the dullness and blind conformity in radio programing which gives "the poor radio reviewer . . . no scandals to wax eloquent on."[45] Leslie Allen enlivened his column for the Christian Science Monitor, in 1931, by compiling an amusing glossary of derogatory adjectives to be used by the critic of radio. He defined such terms as "vapid," "insipid," "jejune," "silly," and "fatuous," illustrating them, of course, by reference to current programs.[46] Mock commercials, burlesque scripts, hilárious, imaginary conferences at top network levels fill the paper funhouse which critics over the years have built.

Not all of the critics attempt to turn from laughter over the trivial and the profound to an utterly sober contemplation of the broadcasting media. Certainly Lardner and Ace, whose forte lies in satire, never do. Nevertheless, there is an increasingly rich supply of sagacious "think pieces," as Jay Nelson Tuck calls them,[47] to be found in the literature of the critics. These are the essays which, more than any other, have helped to provide a disciplined method for considering the aesthetic and sociological principles of a vague and overwhelming new phenomenon. Just as they form the main body of critical writing by

Seldes, Shayon, and Mannes, the results to be derived from analyzing such essays will form a fundamental part of this study. It can be seen from this brief résumé of the kinds of columns produced by the critics, that broadcasting offers a variety of challenges to the skillful journalist who is willing to give it steady, thoughtful attention.

Column Formats

It is easy to see why the journalist jack-of-all-trades became an experimenter in column format in his attempts to impose structure on reviews, essays, and miscellany. One natural solution to the problem, which has been accepted by many critics from the earliest days of radio, is to divide a column into segments. A 1926 reader, for example, could look forward each month to one long essay, two or three short reviews, and a number of brightly written tid-bits in John Wallace's section of Radio Broadcast magazine. A clever twist to this format was provided in the October, 1942, issue of Woman's Day, when Raymond Knight set up his material in newspaper form. "The Radioville Chronicle" contained an editorial (review of a program), a local gossip column, a classified section of "Good Buys" (short program recommendations), and amusement ads (notices of new shows). Darwin Teilhet's columns in the Forum magazine of the early thirties, although divided into segments, were unified by his selection of a theme around which to build program reviews. In the September 1932 issue, for example, he headed the review section "Political Static" and proceeded to draw up a talent list of campaign broadcasters for that presidential election year. The reviews in another issue were labeled "Lady Nicotine's Children," and there followed brief comments on the various musical programs sponsored by Lucky Strike, Camels, Chesterfields and other tobaccos.[48] Jack Cluett's columns for

Woman's Day usually consisted of short, humorous essays followed by ten or twelve brief reviews, until he started writing previews of programs in 1956.

Another type of organization employs a program or some other event upon which a critic can build a series of comparatively profound ideas about broadcasting. The critics for the serious magazines tend to use this method. Marya Mannes of the Reporter states her "approach to criticism is to write articles covering one phase of television at a time, such as, acting, commercials, news."[49] And Robert Lewis Shayon says that in his Saturday Review pieces he seeks "to illuminate an entire area in one article." "A particular show is simply a touchstone leading to comments about sociological trends, cultural plateaus, and other broad matters."[50]

Many of the newspaper critics, who write several times a week, vary their column formats from time to time. For several years in the forties, Jack Gould confined his radio reviews to several short, separate items in a Sunday column. During the week, occasional news columns about radio would appear. Other Sunday pieces included editorials and informative essays. During the 1948-49 season, as television grew in significance, he followed a hectic schedule of reviewing every important show in the following morning's paper. Then he shifted to writing three columns a week only to discover that reader interest waned during the interval between programs and their reviews. At present, Gould usually divides his week-day columns into a review and news sections, reserving his Sunday column almost exclusively for the essays which deal with broader, more complicated issues.[51] Jay Nelson Tuck describes his procedures in organizing a daily column for the New York Post.

> My old division was one short item column, one hard news or feature piece, two pieces of criticism, and one "think piece" --- an opinion column on some phase of the business but not necessarily related to any particular program --- per week. Since the paper's request for more criticism, it has been one short item column on Fridays, plus an average of three critical pieces and one hard news or feature piece. (This doesn't mean I've really lost the think pieces; simply that I wait until the material can be tied into a critical piece on a particular show, adding a feeling of timeliness.) But even this formula is flexible. Some weeks there may be as many as four critical pieces; last week there was just one, with the other four pieces as a series examining the current state of color TV.[52]

Almost all of the critics stand off from the chaotic broadcasting scene to get an occasional long view. These are the times when they shuffle through their unused program notes and other jottings and come up with a summary column. Such pieces are valuable because they help the reader take stock of broadcasting's progress, retrogression, and future. As for the future of professional criticism, it need scarcely be emphasized that clear, interesting formats are particularly necessary for the author who would write about a medium which is both complex and voluminous in its output.

Associated Activities

Up to this point the discussion of the critics' procedures has dealt with the actual writing of the column. This activity is preceded and succeded by other activities which will be touched upon briefly. No critic can write perceptively about broadcasting unless he has an authoritative background in the area. This does not mean that he must necessarily have been a broadcaster himself, although, as we have seen, some of the critics were. It does mean that he must be continually aware of what is happening in this field. And he will, of course, be a more valuable critic if he can discuss causes as well as effects.

The critics may go directly to industry sources for information; they are invited to rehearsals and previews of programs; they interview actors, producers, and network executives; they keep in touch with union officials and advertising agency personnel. More than just reporting the news they have gathered from behind the scenes, they often utilize particular comments from industry workers as the basis for an entire column. Important as associations of this sort are, the critics, to a man, are conscious of the danger of losing a sense of objectivity by becoming too intimate with broadcasting's practitioners. John Crosby is notorious for his aloofness. Only a few months after he started his column in the *Tribune*, he bluntly stated, "I've never gone to a broadcast. I find that people in radio can be awfully damned convincing. . . . [My] column is written by a listener for other listeners."[53] Years later the same attitude persisted. It was reported that "he refused to answer his telephone, read his mail, or see visitors." "So effective is this barrier that the Mutual Broadcasting System bought a large ad in a newspaper and addressed it to him."[54] While this represents the xtreme, most critics would approve Jack Gould's directive that, "It is etter for the critic if he does not become a close friend of many rtists."[55]

First hand contacts, of course, are not the only available means f getting background information. The critics read widely, particuarly in the current literature on broadcasting. Frequent references n their columns indicate that they are familiar with industry publicaions like *Broadcasting-Telecasting* and *Sponsor* as well as with the tertainment papers, *Variety* and *Billboard*. They are among the first analyze government releases pertaining to broadcasting and to call attention to studies in the mass media. Saul Carson's New Republic column for October 16, 1950, expressed the following desire:

> We wish we could crowd broadcasters into one armory and keep them there until they have mastered every chapter of C. A. Siepmann's book on Radio, Television and Society . . . the most responsible, most provocative criticism of broadcasting that we have had.

When a critic is not involved in collecting information for a regular report to his readers, he frequently is busy with special writing assignments. Sometimes this may be no more than editing a number of columns for book form as Crosby, Shayon, and Ace have done. However, Gilbert Seldes and Jack Gould have published separate books on broadcasting.[56] Many of the critics find a ready market for occasional articles in other publications than the ones for which they regularly write. Life, Collier's, the Atlantic, Harpers, and educational journals like the Quarterly of Film, Radio and Television have carried pieces by the leading critics.[57] The critic who is radio-television editor of a newspaper has an additional responsibility for the makeup of the broadcasting page and for preparing special sections when the need arises. For example, the dedication of a new station in a city, or a new allocation of stations by the Federal Communications Commission may be announced in a separate feature section of a newspaper. Jack Gould writes several articles a year for the New York Times Magazine, which appear concurrently with his regular Sunday column.

It is quite natural that these authorities should receive many invitations to speak before various civic and educational groups. A representative example of such activity is seen in a symposium which was arranged by Saul Carson with the cooperation of the National Association of Educational Broadcasters in January, 1951. Mr. Carson chaired the meeting which was held in Washington, D. C., when F.C.C. hearings on educational television were in progress. Later, a transcript of the proceedings, at which prominent government officials and educators spoke, was published in the February 26, 1951, issue of the New Republic. Civic helpfulness of this sort is not unusual. Most of the prominent critics are concerned enough about the impact of broadcasting to accept innumerable engagements to share their enthusiasm with lay groups. Concentrating on programs, on books, on writing and speaking, it is obvious that the professional critic's life can be a very full one indeed, although, as we have seen many of them combine criticism with other journalistic endeavors, or with actual work in the broadcasting industry.

Writing Style

Basically, a journalist writes in order to get a response; this, in turn, permits him to exert a measure of social control over the activities of man. It is appropriate, therefore, to examine some of the writing traits of the professional critics. The eminence, and consequently the social control, they have achieved is due in part to their attractive use of language. However, it is not necessary to become deeply involved in the complex subject of style. Critics, themselves, admit the transitory nature of their columns and would, I believe, be reluctant to have this kind of fluid, journalistic output forced into a rigid classificatory scheme. It is sufficient to recall that the style of a man's writing reflects, to some degree, his spirit and personality; it indicates the manner in which he holds the attention of a specific group of readers; and it includes a consideration of two fundamental devices necessary to successful communication : clearness and impressiveness.[58]

To take these last qualities first, two brief comments from the experiences of Ben Gross and John Crosby testify to the critics' general awareness of the need for clarity in writing. Captain Joseph Medill Patterson, one time publisher of the Daily News (New York), once sent Ben Gross out on the street to ask ten people what the words faux pas meant, which Gross had just used in a radio column. When only two people recognized the phrase, the Captain nodded, "You fellows could learn a lot if you talked more with truck drivers. . . .Anyone who uses foreign words when there are good English ones to express the same thought is either a show-off or doesn't know his own language."[59] This kind of direct object lesson may never have been part of John Crosby's experience. Nevertheless, he implies in a tribute to the late Charles Ross that the writing standards set for the New Yorker magazine affected his own style, which is acknowledged to be a model of polished, critical clarity:

> The hatred of bunk, of which the New Yorker and especially Ross was a personification, left its mark on everyone who writes or edits or publishes. An awful lot of malarkey disappeared from journalism in the twenty-five year history of the New Yorker.[60]

To eliminate "malarkey" and to express ideas accurately and clearly, does not mean that the professional critics have had to sacrifice another aspect of style: impressive language. All of them have their quotable phrases as abundant illustrations in later chapters of this study will prove. For the moment, the following examples of imaginative writing can be cited: (1) Philip Hamburger's reference to television authorities as "the most misguided and sadistic group of noodles in the entire history of show business"[61] or to Fred Waring's troupe as "healthy and refreshing as a 4-H marshmallow roast,"[62] (2) Jack Cluett's reference to the network "habit of treating a new found comedian like a roulette wheel -- whirling him continuously around into so many slots that he doesn't know where he belongs,"[63] (3) John Hutchen's comment about the popular radio program "Easy Aces" - "The general atmosphere is one of pleasant existence in an amiable asylum,"[64] (4) Marya Mannes on the passivity engendered in the television audience: "We are becoming sponges in urgent need of squeezing."[65] The leading critics' columns are sprinkled with allusions and crisp metaphors. They bring to their procedures as professional journalists an enviable talent and skill in the use of fresh, affective language.

As readers are regularly exposed to a critic's highly seasoned opinions about the manners and machinations of the fifth estate, they come to know him not merely as a writer but as a person with a particular personality and particular crotchets. This kind of professional recognition is a natural concomitant of a critic's style. Both the critic and his audience join in creating his personality. He writes in a style which will hold their attention, and they continue to read his essays because they like that style. Consequently, it is possible to risk, at least, a loose classification of the major critics based on their stylistic response to particular audiences.

The Wits

There is a small company of critics who use the broadcasting scene as a whetstone on which to sharpen their witticisms. They entertain their readers by treating both the genuinely risible as well as the genuinely serious with an audacious humor; and their style of writing largely depends on various degrees of irony. Jack Cluett is, perhaps, the most affable of the group. He views the vulgarities of broadcasting merely as a "springboard for humor" and sees his responsibility as an attempt to "kid radio and television out of their clichés" by keeping his comments "amusing not bitter."[66] One of his most successful techniques is to muse about the possibilities of a popular program whirling off on an insane tangent. He once suggested that the sentimental, domestic, give-away show "Queen for a Day," on which an average housewife is given the glamour treatment, have its title changed to "Grandma for a Day" and feature four "dolled-up glamor pusses" whose deepest desire is to be conservative grandmothers.[67] Cluett's humor, gay and flitting, appeals to the young housewives who purchase Woman's Day.

The humorous essays of Goodman Ace would seem to be on a middle-plane of contrived joking and punning about broadcasting, interwoven with occasional acidulous jibes about important problems. In a column entitled "Writer Is a Dirty Word," Ace comments on the fact that Jackie Gleason omitted giving credit to his writers:

> It's possible he didn't know their names. It's possible that when he received his mimeographed script each week he visualized dozens of tiny, unshaven elves in leather aprons and fools caps, their hands and faces smeared with printers' ink and perspiration, crawling in and out of a huge typewriter, dragging the pages after them and whistling while they worked.[68]

In general, Ace is a straight comedy writer, read for the laughs in his criticism.

There is still a third degree of ironic style which is evident in the satiric writing of Lardner, Hamburger, and to some extent Crosby. They are idealists who have a vision of art and culture as it might be and whose reaction to the gap between the real and the ideal is amused scorn rather than heavy indignation. They are masters of sarcasm and the derogatory phrase. They require readers who are sophisticated enough to recognize that intellectual needling can stimulate its victims into renewed creative activity. John Crosby somewhat ruefully summarizes the judgment such critics pass on their own writing:

> The most agreeable columns -- to me, at least, in retrospect -- have been the most savage ones. I find this deplorable. . . . I find that I -- and most critics -- are incoherent in our admiration, but afflicted with a formidable coherence when we disapprove.[69]

So skillfully does Mr. Crosby disapprove that a sixth grade girl once informed him her class read his columns for "styles of sarcasm." Crosby asked if she took "irony" in seventh grade and "invective" in her senior year. He then went on to suggest that she read Beerbohm-Tree, Ring Lardner, Samuel Johnson, and Wilson Mizner for their superb sarcasm.[70]

Readers of the keen-witted broadcasting critics are treated to retorts like these: (1) Lardner on Rudy Vallee - "I heard Mr. Vallee sing the 'Barcarolle' . . . I hasten to apologize for anything I wrote of him that may have seemed captious, and I hereby vote him the Olympic and All-American, Intercollegiate and A. A. U. medals for nerve."[71] (2) Crosby referring to a program called "Okay, Mother" - "The brightest particular star of this hideous firmament is Dennis James, a man of many faces, none of them especially edifying."[72] (3) The left handed praise of Philip Hamburger - "There have been some good dramatizations on television recently . . . and I am almost inclined to believe that there is still some hope for the basement of the arts."[73]

An interesting stylistic device used by both Lardner and Hamburger is the letter. It permitted them to write a seemingly straightforward chronicle of what they had heard on radio or seen on television. However, by the very selection of particular events, described with a skillfully assumed naïveté, they could reach an unusual depth of derisiveness. All of Lardner's columns were letters to his editor, written with his famous grammatical ineptitude, which created a deliberate illusion of "the wise boob."[74] Hamburger's confidante was Aunt Pauline who lived in West Virginia and was an avid television fan. Crosby uses a similar technique when he occasionally records a chat, in appropriate Madison Avenue lingo, with Mr. Y, a mythical neighbor, who just happens to be in the advertising business. There is no denying that the humorous columnist is apt to be the most successful. Readers will chuckle over his rapier thrusts, recall them, and pass them on. But the wit, as we are reminded by the biographer of Ring Lardner, creates a frustrating occupational hazard for himself. Mr. Edler is discussing F. Scott Fitzgerald and Lardner:

> Both of them had reason to be skeptical of the role of the satirist in society. They knew that a satirist plays a dangerous game; he is tolerated only so long as he makes people laugh, and he is tolerated not as a critic of society, but as a funny man.[75]

Regardless of the ultimate worth of these journalists, their style of comic writing lends a brilliance to the entire body of critical literature on broadcasting.

The Reporters

As far as style is concerned, the columns of this next group of critics can be treated with greater brevity. They reveal more concentration on reportorial brilliance than on verbal brilliance. The writing of Jack Gould, Saul Carson, and Darwin Teilhet is representative of a reportorial style. The expression of their ideas is clear in structure, in logic, and in proof, but they lack the scintillating phraseology of the wits.

The following quotation from an early column by Jack Gould illustrates his frank but carefully balanced comments, couched in plain, effective words. He is discussing a radio play called "The Land of the Lost:"

> Cyril Armbruster's direction is generally fluid and takes full advantage of sound effects. Now and then, however, it reflects a trace of carelessness, with crowd noises sometimes blasting out the dialogue and the musical cues not always being introduced as promptly as they could be.[76]

Saul Carson's appraisal of the state of television in 1948 reflects a similar style. It is honest in its idea and unspectacular in its wording:

> Television is taking much of the sting out of the old line radio reviewer's acidity. In the face of real progress he has to become sweeter, even if by so doing he runs the risk of accusations that he has sold out to "the interests" . . . TV, on the whole, may not yet have arrived, but it is certainly on the way.[77]

A final sample of this writing style is evident in a brief quotation from a column by Darwin Teilhet in which he is appraising the state of radio in 1933:

> Many honest citizens are clamoring for the millenium in the form of government control of radio . Perhaps we are ready to consider a change or at least improvements for our creaking system. . . . We are not prepared to be thrown pell-mell into government control -- think of the Nazis.[78]

The moderation and basic good taste reflected in the language of these writers has helped them to earn deserved accolades for critical responsibility. Their columns represent a steady, thoughtful approach to a new kind of professional writing.

The Social Philosophers

Standing in marked contrast to the style of the wits, who can always manage to view broadcasting with amusement, is the usually serious, even somber, complex style of critics who write for periodicals which are low in circulation but high in ideas. Marya Mannes, Gilbert Seldes, and Robert Lewis Shayon meditate about the significance of broadcasting; they enjoy discovering first causes and speculating about future effects. Their writing is apt to be subtle in thought, rich in allusions, varied in vocabulary. Gilbert Seldes has the least polish of the three. He seems to be bursting with ideas which must be jotted down quickly, as if he were conversing with his readers. In the following passage Mr. Seldes is trying to probe his reactions to broadcast programs:

> More and more I am aware of a factor beyond my instant response, of like or dislike, laughter or boredom, excitement or disturbed slumber as a program proceeds. What I am aware of is satisfaction, and it is my fundamental belief that the audience which isn't critical, not being paid to be critical, has also this secondary abiding response. . . .The way people express their residual satisfaction, the way x or y or z lives in their memory and their affection is the real test.[79]

Robert Lewis Shayon writes with dignity and with high verbal fluency. Consider part of his definition of feature journalism, which he hoped would distinguish more news broadcasts:

> Reaction is what distinguishes "feature" journalism from straight news — the reaction of a gifted, trained observer to an event. His response to what he sees and hears becomes the lens by which we focus meaning. Without reaction there is mere chronology, position in time and space, but no relatedness, light or understanding.[80]

The articles by Marya Mannes are exceptionally articulate. They are models of skillful composition, illuminated by a sensitive, emotional warmth. One review of several fine programs was organized around her thesis that "truth could be called the oxygen of the spirit without which the spirit cannot live." Developing the metaphor further, she said of one program, "In this half hour oxygen again circulated in the blood and awoke the mind so that one wanted to read and read and talk and talk as one used to do out of hunger for wisdom."[81]

The social-philosopher critics are steeped in the humanities, yet responsive to the modern milieu. They are scholarly sophisticates with an abiding interest in the arts. All of these traits are reflected in their style of writing and are admired by readers of the Saturday Review and the Reporter.

In summary, there would seem to be critical styles for every taste. Audiences may have their sensibilities tickled or agitated or disciplined, depending upon the particular columnist they choose to read.

The survey of the last several pages has attempted to analyze the mechanics of the critical profession. The broadcast critics' occupational procedures are similar in many respects to the procedures of the rest of the critical fraternity. However, broadcasting has posed some unique problems for the critics, and these are to be discussed in the next section.

Problems Peculiar to Broadcast Criticism

Program Variety

Radio and television are fundamentally media for the transmission of audio and video signals. Wherever a microphone is placed or a camera trained, that location becomes the origination point for a broadcast. In theory, then, any sounds and any sights which can be transformed into electronic impulses become the subject matter of a program. And, although in practice, public broadcasting is limited in content, the overwhelming variety of programs has created a continuous problem for the critic.

John Hutchens was not the first person to assess this critical burden, but he is one of the few to express himself so forcefully on the issue:

> . . . There is no such person as a radio critic. Not in the sense that there are drama, film, book, music and art critics. The reason is, of course, that no one has yet lived who knew enough to be a radio critic, and sooner or later, he who naively aspires to be one is going to experience a sharp and rather appalling embarrassment. It is going to occur to him in a withering burst of introspection, that to be a first rate or even an adequate radio critic, he would have to know a good deal about--indeed, be an expert on--music (all kinds of music), world literature, sports, economics, politics, international affairs, history, education, science, household management, psychology, agriculture and the drama. [And now, with television, the critic must also have a background in the visual arts.][82]

Hutchens realized, of course, that even though the ideal critic did not exist, many "compromise critics" did exist. These were (and are) the responsible writers who tread lightly in realms where they have little background. Their comments are restricted to those programs about which they feel competent to express an opinion. If the critic is a Jack Gould, employed on a large metropolitan newspaper, he can either enlist the aid of an appropriate fellow-critic of ballet or music, for example, or that specialist critic will write the entire review.[83] Sometimes a critic will admit, as Jack Cluett does, that he can deal only mechanically in a review, for instance, of a television opera.[84] As a matter of fact, Cluett sees the problem of variety as one covering wider scope than the field of broadcasting alone:

> Never in all history have the various media of the entertainment world been so confused. The legitimate theater, movies, recordings, opera, music, television and radio have gradually evolved into one giant, overlapping mass . . . .

> Maybe the best solution is for the critics to sit down and pull straws. Long one gets the review. Otherwise, we're faced with a flood of conflicting opinion.[85]

Program Quantity

The problem presented by the vast range of programs is nothing, however, to the problem of sheer quantity of material which is broadcast daily. Actually, this concept of continuous broadcasting is the single most striking fact of American broadcasting, and it poses additional difficulties for the professional critic. As early as 1934, Darwin Teilhet struggled to devise a system for listening to as many programs as possible. Even though he was employed simultaneously by an advertising agency, he chose to complicate his reviewer's duties by trying to evaluate regional programs from all over the nation:

> I had installed in my home one of the finest Scott radio receivers probably built in the thirties. I could pull in New York by long-wave; and, even in the day time by switching to short-wave could pick up almost any program in the country of sufficient importance to go out both long and short-wave.
>
> My problem was to get the hell away from my San Francisco office at odd hours to listen to the daylight programs as well as evening programs.
>
> In the bad days of 1932-33 we weren't very busy and I could get away without too much trouble. However, by 1934 my own business responsibilities were heaping on me. For many years I have collaborated with my wife, Hildegard Tolman Teilhet. As an expedient, in late 1933 and early 1934 she would listen to a program for several weeks, clocking it, getting background for it, while I would manage to make a dash to get it at least once.
>
> As a consequence, we did get quite a spread of programs in the final ten reviews; but it was very tough.[86]

It was just as tough years later in 1951, when Saul Carson described the plight of the critic at the opening of each new broadcasting season:

> My friends in the trade press walk around bleary-eyed from looking, woozy from listening. And we in

> the more privileged general magazine class, who theoretically practice on a selective basis, stumble around between the hazy guide-posts, reduced to a catch-as-catch can twisting of the dials.[87]

As has been mentioned earlier in this chapter, by obtaining transcriptions and tape recordings, a critic was able to schedule programs efficiently, thereby permitting a broader coverage. It is true that the lack of accessible video recordings has denied the present-day critic this partial solution to the avalanche of television programs, but a decrease in network radio and the development of steady music programing on local radio has actually given him more time to concentrate on television. Thus, it is some small comfort to a critic to realize that, although program quantity is a persistent problem, it is not necessarily a growing problem. In fact, he may feel that he suffers more from a corollary difficulty: lack of space in which to print his opinions. Robert Stephan touched on this point several years ago in a discussion of radio criticism: "Newspaper criticism is spacebound. Often criticism must be confined to two paragraphs. There are ten stations in Cleveland, which leaves me little room for extended criticizing."[88]

The volume of programing in this country, however, has a still more serious aspect for the critic than either the utilization of time or space. It would seem to be the first law of broadcasting that quantity production results in a preponderance of mediocre programs. This is not to deny the fact that excellence exists; it is merely a statement of the fact that dullness exists in greater supply, or if not actual dullness, at least assembly-line programing about which most critics find it difficult to say very much. Almost all of the leading critics, at one time or another, have bemoaned a situation in which hour after hour of broadcast signals can with accuracy and integrity be evaluated by the simple word "trivia."

Once again John Hutchens has analyzed the matter very clearly:

> "The trouble is the reviewer discovers with a start, that radio's successful people and programs have found formulae and stayed with them.. . . . He realizes with dismay that radio is at once overwhelming in its variety and deadly in its repetitiousness.[89]

The specific difficulty such a situation poses for the critic is frustratingly described by John Crosby:

> The persistence of Mr. Godfrey (as well as everyone else who hits the big time in radio or television) is the worst obstacle in this business. Radio entertainers never retire and there are grounds for suspicion that they never die. They don't--like General MacArthur--just fade away, either. They just go on and on and on--defying the columnist to find something new to write about them. After you have poured out your innermost thoughts about Arthur Godfrey (or Faye Emerson or Jack Benny or Burns and Allen) four or five times, you find you have exhausted the subject.[90]

Most critics confronted by the problem would probably prefer to solve it by remaining mute. "My drawers are stuffed," says Crosby, "with notes about programs which are neither bad enough nor good enough to warrant comment of any sort. They hover, these programs, in a sort of nether world of mediocrity and defy you to compose so much as a single rational sentence about them."[91] Interestingly enough, this critical hazard inherent in mass entertainment was recognized by Gilbert Seldes in his first book on the popular arts, written before audience broadcasting had become a reality. He is referring to the circus, but the comparison is evident: "This extraordinary mixture of good and dull things, this lack of character, makes the circus easy to like and useless to think about."[92]

Unfortunately, however, if critics are to retain their titles, they cannot remain silent and they cannot stop thinking. They can, instead, employ their intellectual talents in poking clever fun at unexciting programs and in becoming bitterly sarcastic about the really bad ones. Those who, according to Goodman Ace, "want to indulge in smart-alecky causticism" find TV "an easy target."[93] "Cynicism," says Robert Lewis Shayon, "is perhaps the greatest danger for the critic of television. He can't say much about most shows and yet to function as a writer, he must be excited by a show. Since input on the part of the producer of a program is not creatively serious, the response of the critic cannot be serious. Mediocrity invokes mediocrity. Critics get tired of being negative. They yearn for something good to say."[94] His theme is echoed by Marya Mannes:

> One of the problems faced by the television critic arises from the fact that bad shows are so frequent they do not test the critic's skills enough. They are too easy to write about—like sitting ducks. It is difficult to be constructive and yet, of course, that is what the medium prefers.[95]

Perhaps the ultimate in cynical frankness is the following statement by John Crosby, who has aptly demonstrated his solution to the problem of what to say about mediocre and poor programs:

> Some of the worst programs ever broadcast—many of them long since departed—are described in agonizing detail while some of the best programs are not mentioned. That's because bad programs make fairly entertaining copy. Therein lies the secret of the success of any radio or television columnist. If every program was a good program, I greatly doubt whether anyone would read us.[96]

Immersed daily in the great sea of radio and television programing, it is small wonder that the critics become weary of struggling to discern differences significant enough to provide perspicacious columns. It is small wonder that they fall prey to either an overt or covert attitude of condescension and cynicism about the media they should be examining with clarity and objectivity. The major critics, by their very awareness of these tendencies, consciously strive for balance and perspective in their writing.

Evaluating Socio-Economic Issues

The quantity of programs carried by American stations is the result of a unique alliance between commerce (advertising) and the broadcasting arts. The founders of this cooperative system established it because radio could be received by a mass audience, and they soon found that their primary function was to create that audience. This, the business men and the communication artists proceeded to do with a success that has had a profound effect on our culture. The ensuing relationship between art, commerce, and the masses constituted a major problem for the early critics - one which exists to this day.

Some of the difficulty revolves about definitions as to what broadcasting really is. It is obviously more than a medium for entertainment, or more than a medium for the dissemination of information, or more than a medium for selling commercial products. For the critic, who must write from some view point which has a modicum of consistency, broadcasting is an enterprise of enormous complexity. He would be only too willing to agree with Gilbert Seldes that it is a popular art for which "no firm rules have ever been laid down," and for which "there are virtually no traditions."[97]

In the absence of established guides, the critics have asked and continue to ask themselves at least four questions which attempt to define crucial areas for investigation: (1) What degree of leadership in programing progress can reasonably be expected from communication artists who are subsidized by firms wishing to advertise over radio or television?

(2) If, as Sydney Head states, "Broadcasting requires popularization of the arts on an unprecedented scale.",[98] what new critical standards are required for program evaluation? (3) To what extent should the purveyors of entertainment and information to mass audiences be required to serve minority interests, since all of the people own broadcasting's channels? (4) What are the social effects of radio and television?

Answers to questions like these are not easy to find. As a matter of fact, part of their elusiveness can be attributed to the fact that the medium and public response to it has been in a state of flux ever since broadcasting began. We can expect that the new communication arts will continue to challenge the critics for years to come, certainly as much, perhaps even more, on this sociological-economic level as on the more familiar aesthetic level. Some of their answers, to date, will be presented in later chapters.

The Transitory Nature of Broadcast Criticism

A final problem, unique to the critic of broadcasting, is a minor one. It concerns the transitory nature of the broadcast program and the possible indifference with which comments will be written by the critic and read by the public. Goodman Ace states the matter abruptly when he reminds us that there is "nothing deader than yesterday's television column, to say nothing of yesterday's television."[99] However, such a deprecatory attitude would be accepted by most of the critics for its humor alone. They recognize the shortcomings of the review after the fact, but they also realize that American audiences, who have quite automatically become astute appraisers of entertainment, enjoy matching opinions with the critics. Therefore, it is not likely that the professional critics would be content to turn in thoughtless, ragged pieces of writing. Critics also have the incentive of knowing that the broadcasting industry is anxious to read their comments. In addition, broadcast criticism, as we have seen earlier in this chapter, is not composed solely of program reviews. Long range trends in programing and problems of economic, governmental or social concern supply important, less fragile topics for the versatile commentator. No, evaluating events which vanish into the ether as quickly as they arrive from it constitutes less a problem of morale for the critics than it does a problem of convincing publishers and readers that criticism is a worthwhile activity. Fortunately, today, even this problem is less acute.

It should be evident from the preceding analysis of the leading critics' backgrounds and procedures that they are competent writers whose sensitive curiosity about a new medium has enabled them to create a new branch of journalism. Largely through their efforts in wrestling with the problems just described, broadcast criticism has become a respectable profession. To understand its present practice even more clearly, and to appreciate its future value even more forcefully, it is now necessary to investigate the basic functions which the critics feel their profession performs.

Notes

[1]Robert J. Landry, "Wanted: Radio Critics," Public Opinion Quarterly, IV (December, 1940), 629.

[2]Ted Husing, Ten Years Before the Mike (New York: Farrar and Rinehart, Inc., 1935), p. 263.

[3]George Rosen, "Appraising the Radio Editors," Variety, January 23, 1946, p. 25.

[4]See listing of newspaper department editors in any volume of Editor and Publisher Yearbook between 1925 and 1942.

[5]Ben Gross, I Looked and I Listened (New York: Random House, 1954), p. 56.

[6]Rosen, loc. cit., p. 30.

[7]Ibid.

[8]Ibid.

[9]Letter from Miss Harriet Van Horne, critic, World-Telegram (New York), May 7, 1956.

[10]Dalton Trumbo, "Frankenstein in Hollywood," Forum, LXXXVII (March, 1932), 142.

[11]Gross, op. cit., p. 13.

[12]Letter from Mr. Volney D. Hurd, Chief of the Paris Bureau, Christian Science Monitor, May 29, 1956.

[13]Interview with Mr. Jay Nelson Tuck, critic, New York Post, April 6, 1956.

[14]Current Biography; Who's News and Why, 1953 (New York: H. W. Wilson Company, 1953), p. 133.

[15]Ibid.

[16]Ibid.

[17]Ibid.

[18]Interview with Mr. Jay Nelson Tuck, loc. cit.

[19]Theater Arts, XXV (February, 1941), 154.

[20]Who's Who In America, XXIX (Chicago: A. N. Marquis, 1956), p. 995.

[21]Interview with Mr. Jack Gould, critic, New York Times, April 2, 1956.

[22]Ibid.

[23]Letter from Mr. Paul Cotton, critic, Register-Tribune (Des Moines), September 6, 1956.

[24]Letter from Mr. Darwin Teilhet, former critic, Forum, May 18, 1956.

[25]Who's Who In America, op. cit., p. 2327.

[26]Who's Who In America, op. cit., p. 2305.
Stanley J. Kunitz and Howard Haycroft, Twentieth Century Authors (New York: H. W. Wilson Company, 1942), p. 1261.

[27]Editor's note to an article by Saul Carson, "Notes Toward an Examination of the Radio Documentary," Hollywood Quarterly, IV (Fall, 1949), 69.

[28]Interview with Mr. Saul Carson, former critic, New Republic, April 4, 1956.

[29]Current Biography: Who's News and Why, 1948 (New York: H. W. Wilson Company, 1948), pp. 6-8.

[30]Kunitz and Haycroft, op. cit., pp. 790-791.

[31]Donald Elder, Ring Lardner (Garden City, N. Y.: Doubleday and Company, Inc., 1956), pp. 243-44.

[32]Gilbert Seldes (ed.), The Portable Ring Lardner (New York: Viking Press, 1946), p. 8.

[33]Interview with Mr. Jack Cluett, critic, Woman's Day, April 4, 1956.

[34]Robert J. Landry, "The Improbability of Radio Criticism," Hollywood Quarterly, II (1946-47), 66.

[35]Who's Who In America, op. cit., p. 1071.

[36]Interview with Miss Marya Mannes, critic, Reporter, April 3, 1956.

[37]Philip Graham, publisher of the Washington Post, quoted in Time, April 16, 1956, p. 72.

[38]Jack Gould, "The Paradoxical State of TV," New York Times Magazine, March 30, 1947, p. 14.

[39]Raymond Yates, Herald Tribune (New York), September 1, 1924.

[40]Interview with Mr. Robert J. Landry, managing editor, Variety, April 3, 1956.

[41]Jack Gould, New York Times, May 26, 1957.

[42]The Daily News employs Ben Gross, Rudy Bergman, Kay Gudalla, and Sid Shalitt in its radio-television department. The Times, in addition to Jack Gould, employs Jack Shanley, and Val Adams.

[43]John Wallace, Radio Broadcast, VIII (March, 1926), 579.

[44]John Crosby, Out of the Blue (New York: Simon and Schuster, 1952), p. 191.

[45]John Wallace, Radio Broadcast, X (March, 1927), 474.

[46]Leslie Allen, Christian Science Monitor, March 28, 1931.

[47]Letter from Mr. Jay Nelson Tuck, critic, New York Post, May 14, 1956.

[48]Darwin Teilhet, "What America Listens To," Forum, LXXXVII (May, 1932), 275-76.

[49]Interview with Miss Marya Mannes, loc cit.

[50]Interview with Mr. Robert Lewis Shayon, critic, Saturday Review, April 4, 1956.

[51]Interview with Mr. Jack Gould, loc. cit.

[52]Letter from Mr. Jay Nelson Tuck, loc. cit.

[53]John Crosby, quoted in Time, August 5, 1946, p. 61.

[54]Dickson Hartwell, "John Crosby: Gadfly of Radio," Coronet, XXVIII (July, 1950), 112.

[55]Interview with Mr. Jack Gould, loc. cit.

[56]See bibliography for books by the critics. The Jack Gould book referred to is not pertinent to this study and does not appear in the bibliography. It is a book on technical television for children, How Television Works (New York: Longmans Green & Co., 1951).

[57]Many of these articles are listed in the bibliography. The perusal of the Readers' Guide to Periodical Literature (New York: H. W. Wilson Company, 1905--date), and the Education Index (New York: H. W. Wilson Company, 1929--date) will indicate the wide variety of publications for which the critics have written.

[58]See Lester Thonssen and A. Craig Baird, Speech Criticism (New York: Ronald Press Company, 1948), chap. XV for an interesting discussion of style.

[59]Gross, op. cit., p. 324.

[60]Crosby, Out of the Blue, p. 200.

[61]Philip Hamburger, New Yorker, April 28, 1951, p. 67.

[62]Philip Hamburger, ibid., June 30, 1951, p. 56.

[63]Jack Cluett, Woman's Day, XVI (March, 1953), 99.

[64]John K. Hutchens, New York Times, June 20, 1943.

[65]Marya Mannes, Reporter, March 24, 1955, p. 39.

[66]Interview with Mr. Jack Cluett, loc cit.

[67]Jack Cluett, Woman's Day, XVII (October, 1953), 10.

[68]Goodman Ace, The Book of Little Knowledge (New York: Simon and Schuster, 1955), p. 15.

[69]Crosby, Out of the Blue, p. 290.

[70]John Crosby, Herald Tribune (New York), December 27, 1953.

[71]Ring Lardner, New Yorker, March 18, 1933, p. 55.

[72]Crosby, Out of the Blue, p. 57.

[73]Philip Hamburger, New Yorker, June 2, 1951, p. 84.

[74]Elder, op. cit., p. 168.

[75]Ibid., p. 264.

[76]Jack Gould, New York Times, June 3, 1945.

[77]Saul Carson, New Republic, April 26, 1948, p. 34.

[78]Cyrus Fisher [Darwin Teilhet], Forum, XC (December, 1933), 382.

[79]Gilbert Seldes, Saturday Review, June 27, 1953, p. 32.

[80]Robert Lewis Shayon, Saturday Review, September 25, 1954, p. 28.

[81]Marya Mannes, Reporter, December 2, 1954, pp. 39-40.

[82]John K. Hutchens, "Same Time, Same Station," Saturday Review, May 4, 1946, p. 16.

[83]Interview with Mr. Jack Gould, loc. cit.

[84]Interview with Mr. Jack Cluett, _loc. cit._

[85]Jack Cluett, _Woman's Day_, XVI (February, 1953), 142.

[86]Letter from Mr. Darwin Teilhet, _op. cit._

[87]Saul Carson, _New Republic_, October 1, 1951, p. 22.

[88]Robert Stephan, panel member discussing radio criticism, _Education on the Air, 18th Yrbk._, ed. O. Joe Olson, (Columbus: Ohio State University Press, 1948), p. 122.

[89]John K. Hutchens, "Same Time, Same Station," _Saturday Review_, May 4, 1946, p. 17.

[90]Crosby, _Out of the Blue_, p. 289.

[91]_Ibid._, p.x.

[92]Gilbert Seldes, _The Seven Lively Arts_ (New York: Harper and Brothers, 1924), p. 292.

[93]Ace, _op.cit._, p. vii.

[94]Interview with Mr. Robert Lewis Shayon, _loc. cit._

[95]Interview with Miss Marya Mannes, _loc. cit._

[96]Crosby, _Out of the Blue_, p.x.

[97]Gilbert Seldes, _Saturday Review_, July 25, 1953, p. 29.

[98]Sydney Head, _Broadcasting in America_ (New York: Houghton Mifflin Co., 1956), p. 436.

[99]Ace, _loc. cit._

CHAPTER III

QUALITIES AND FUNCTIONS OF THE CRITICS

Down through history, the professional critics of any medium have been simultaneously condemned as cantankerous parasites and honored as significant contributors to man's cultural progress. Either response emphasizes the fact that they are a force which cannot be ignored. Such recognition is a testimony to their valuable qualities of mind and to their strong confidence in the purposes of criticism. Critics of broadcasting are part of this tradition even though they are recognized as operating not only in a fringe area of the conventional artistic domain, but also in the new territory of the mass media. Consequently, as we turn from the particular discussion about a critic's background and procedures to a more general discussion of his qualities and functions, it will be necessary to draw upon ideas from other branches of criticism as well as upon the concepts of the critics of broadcasting themselves. Since the preface to this study has already taken into account the definitional limitations involved in a term like critic, the primary concern of this chapter will be to examine the rationale for criticism in a broad sense.

A General Concept of Criticism and Major Qualities of Critics

Criticism itself implies an examination of and the development of a rationale for a particular field of activity. Although DeWitt Parker is discussing aesthetics and the fine arts, there is no reason why the following concept cannot be partially applied to the popular art of broadcasting:

> The science of aesthetics [which he feels is closely related to criticism] is an effort to obtain a clear general idea of beautiful objects, our judgments upon them, and the motives underlying the acts which create them--to raise the aesthetic life, otherwise a matter of instinct and feeling to the level of intelligence, of understanding.[1]

Granted that objects of beauty in Parker's sense are infrequently encountered in broadcasting, those which have made their appearance could profitably fall within the realm of the science he is describing.

Meanwhile, additional broadcasting activities can be studied within a framework described by the following paraphrase of Parker's statement:

> The science of broadcast criticism is an effort to obtain a clear general idea of programs, our judgments upon them, and the motives underlying the acts which create them--to raise public response to these programs, otherwise a matter of instinct and feeling, to the level of intelligence and understanding.

Joseph Wood Krutch, spokesman for the literary arts, is merely condensing Parker's concept when he says, "Criticism rationalizes and gives temporary form to our experiences with literature."[2] To substitute the word "broadcasting" for "literature" will provide a pithy restatement of the major reason for the existence of broadcasting criticism.

This matter of intellectualizing an experience, of imposing structure on a phenomenon whether it be a broadcast, a painting or a book, assumes the basic involvement of criticism with the expression of opinion. Criticism is built upon factual evidence, to be sure, but the facts serve as a point of departure for individual interpretations about the significance of those facts. The dean of American drama critics, Brooks Atkinson, has this to say about the importance of opinion in criticism:

> Criticism lives on opinions. Opinions are the electricity of the mind. "What do you think?" Is there a more profoundly social question than that? It assumes that we are all living together and have within ourselves the power to sort things out and create a civilization. No community is wholly alive that is not interested in art [Again, might not the art of broadcasting be included?] which is the mirror of human beings and that does not have vigorous opinions about art and artists. If it feels deeply about these things, it also has energy to look after other public affairs. It has a future. It is the function of the critic to pitch into the intellectual life of the community and express his opinions with force and clarity.[3]

Criticism is a high calling, indeed, if it assists in the creation of a civilization. Far from the glib and noisy chatter with which much critical writing about the popular arts is identified, criticism would seem to be a discipline based on thoughtful meditation and on a skillful analysis of cause and effect both in the passing artistic scene and in the more heterogeneous area of broadcasting. This is the type of criticism for which Lyman Bryson, long associated with educational programing for CBS, pleads in the following statement:

> To say that broadcasts are not worth serious criticism is begging the question in an especially shameful way. Who out of the world that constantly recreates and develops the criticism, the canons and the appreciations of the products of print or the stage (also a technological device) or musical instruments has ever suggested a list of cannons for any form of broadcasting? . . . The challenge to the members of the cultivated minority . . . is to criticize programs not mercifully but intelligently and with the slowly acquired expertness that makes criticism valuable. Vigorous, severe, and systematic criticism is needed. . . . Potential great audiences and potential great art come into reality together by interaction and by mutual stimulation in good faith.[4]

If the comments of these authorities are to be accepted, the serious criticism of any medium is an important, vigorous, intellectual activity -- an activity which can be further examined by considering the particular mental and emotional qualities which it demands of its practitioners.

Basic to valid criticism is the respect which the critic feels for the area under scrutiny. With no intention of suggesting maudlin sentimentality, such respect implies a sensitive, emotional pride or awe in the potentialities of the medium, at least, if not in its immediate accomplishments. The respectful critic is anxious to see his medium thrive. He may damn a poor product in that medium, or he may rail against some factor which stultifies its growth, but his faith in the medium itself remains unshaken. Robert J. Landry stresses the importance of this quality for the radio critic:

> He cannot function in a temper of constant dislike of the medium, the mass mind, and advertising. That way lies the intellectualized wisecrack and the clichés of condescension. Such a critic can have no real contact with the radio audience. He cannot share or interpret its enthusiasms. Indeed one wonders if he can even tolerate these enthusiasms.[5]

As far as Gilbert Seldes is concerned, this kind of respect is really a "matter of good manners." He feels that critics should "not use the broadcasters as whipping boys for all the faults they find with the capitalist system, and that the changes they suggest should all be workable within that system."[6] This initial quality can best be summarized by remembering that the critic must have "an intelligent hospitality of mind"[7] toward the object of his criticism.

Respect may provide some of the motivation needed for critical writing, but it can provide little in the way of purpose for writing. A mental quality which many critics refer to as point of view is needed for that task. One of the clearest explanations of the phrase has come from Robert J. Landry as he attempts to define criticism:

> By criticism is meant an essentially urbane approach to programs from any one of several possible or combined points of view [underlining mine] as for example, the sheer theatrical finesse, educational connotation, propagandistic character or social impact of programs.[8]

It is obvious that the broad term "point of view" must include associated qualities, some of which defy exact definition. For example, Mr. Landry feels that the most important quality for a television-radio reviewer is the possession of a critical mind. This implies more than a background in theater, or a knowledge of broadcasting production techniques, helpful as these are. The ability to marshall facts is less important than the ability to analyze.

The critic who can explain why a show is good has a special type of mind. He is not impressed by success or failure, although he sees the correlation between success and popularity. He is, instead, impressed by a show's goodness (The industry defines goodness in terms of success.) or badness.[9] Mr. Landry's definition, the conclusion of which suggests that the critical mind is one receiving significant impressions, can be reinforced by Henry Seidel Canby's contention that the critical mind must be open to ideas.

> The [book] reviewer must also have ideas--a flash in which comprehension of what essential must be known and understood breaks upon the mind of the critic--the idea may be the author's <u>real</u> purpose, his <u>real</u> achievement, an explanation of excellence a reason for <u>failure</u>, a coordination which places a new work into its place in history.[10]

Another quality associated with a critic's ability to write from a particular point of view is that of the inquiring mind. This is characterized by a critic's constant search for information to help him in making judgments which "avoid merely effective or volitional exclamation."[11] In other words, the critic must not be content with a mere "aye" or "nay," but must surround his decision with knowledge. As far as Harriet Van Horne is concerned, the breadth of that knowledge is positively encyclopedic:

> Critics, broadly speaking, should be better informed and that probably includes me. They should have a good working knowledge of such subjects as literature, the stage, the dance, music, history, sociology, psychology, and the folkways of advertising.[12]

Interestingly enough, most of the critics agree with Mr. Landry that a knowledge of production techniques is helpful but of secondary importance. Typical comments include the following:

> Although the critic does not have to have technical knowledge, an association with people in the industry helps him to learn more about production problems which in turn enables him to bring more substance to his pieces.[13] (Saul Carson)

> Some knowledge of production techniques is important. As a matter of fact, the average layman is a remarkably good technical critic of television.[14] (Jack Gould)

> Since the critic is concerned about the end product, he does not have to be too knowing about technical matters.[15] (Marya Mannes)

> A knowledge of the technical side of the medium is not essential to good criticism since the critic must make his judgment on the basis of what he sees, not on what he knows of the medium.[16] (Gilbert Seldes)

While they would not require the critic to have a profound knowledge of technical broadcasting, present-day writers do not hesitate to underscore the value of economic information. They would, in all probability, endorse the view that "the critic who fails to appreciate the financial problems imposed on radio by its competitive nature, is reasoning from faulty premises no less than the broadcaster who looks upon his station solely as a means of making a personal fortune."[17] For example, Jay Nelson Tuck insists that "the critic must know something about the economic background of television, and must be aware of the financial pressures under which the networks operate."[18] A similar consideration is recognized as necessary by Jack Gould:

> The critic must have some knowledge of the economic base of the industry. His job includes reporting not only broadcast

programs, but also the progress which a brand new industry is making.[19]

These, then, are some of the areas into which the inquiring mind of the critic must venture. The nature and extent of those explorations, however, are matters to be determined by his own interests and the interests of the audience for which he writes. Suffice it to say that the professional critic must utilize his critical and inquisitive faculties in a manner which will enable him to comment on broadcasting from viewpoints described by Mr. Seldes as being those of the "intellectual, aesthetic, and social critic at one and the same time."[20]

A final valuable critical quality is indicated in the broad term "sense of responsibility." Generally defined, this would mean that the critic is committed to serving the broadcasting arts, his craft, and his public to the best of his ability. If he possesses the other qualities previously discussed, a critic of the fine arts at least, no doubt engages quite automatically in what S. Stephenson Smith calls the critical process. It consists of five basic steps; (1) apprehension of the work by means of sense impressions, (2) analysis of the work which puts it in perspective and corrects unbridled impressionism, (3) interpretation of the work to the reader of the criticism, (4) orientation of the work to its place in the history of similar works, (5) valuation or the determination of the peculiar as well as general essence of the work.[21] This process may seem somewhat pretentious and even irrelevant as far as criticism of a popular art like broadcasting is concerned; but it does have relevance for some of the programs of high excellence on radio or television.

In addition, however, the critic of broadcasting must fulfill his responsibility to the new branch of the craft by searching for other processes by which to evaluate the major output of the studios. For example, Paul Lazarsfeld has suggested:

> We must revise our standards and judge products of mass art according to their effects on the audience. This is a return to classical standards [The Greeks felt that art should make a man a better citizen in his community.] but we need audience research to carry it out. . . .The entire question of judgment of mass media is wide open because nineteenth century literary standards [which considers the relationships between the artist and his product, rather than between the product and the consumer] cannot be applied to it.[22]

It is Gilbert Seldes' sense of responsibility which prompts him also to speculate on the need for a different approach to broadcast criticism:

> But I cannot set up my critical standards . . . as correct for mass entertainment. I cannot feel that the programs I find wanting are all of low quality. And the more I hear people say, "Of course we haven't got a TV set," as if that alone conferred an honor on them, the more I am reminded of those who never turned on the radio "except for music and the news." These people are refusing to separate the better from the worse. . . .They are being austere in the presence of good clean fun--and that is the road to the great sin of intellectual snobbery.[23]

There is little doubt that the responsible critics will evolve appropriate, if not unanimous, methods for treating the mass arts. Further awareness of this necessity will be indicated shortly, when their ideas about the specific functions of broadcast criticism are discussed.

Not only does the critic with a sense of responsibility seek to learn more about his craft, but he attempts to practice what he already knows with rigorous honesty. His intention, as Donald Kirkley, critic for the Baltimore Sun, states, is "to tell the truth as he sees it."[24] A critic must develop the discernment to select with accuracy those occasional items from the torrent of publicity material tumbling across his desk which can be of real help in the preparation of a column. He must also remain unaffected by a hazard which Jay Nelson Tuck describes as "the constant wooing by networks and agencies--the free samples, Christmas presents, advertising nick-nacks, and invitations to dinners and cocktail parties to meet talent."[25] Jack Gould warns against still another material threat to a critic's independence:

> A professional critic is in a very real sense a quasi-public official. In being privileged to have access to the columns of a publication, he is charged with a trust to serve to the best of his ability the readers of those columns and no one else. A critic cannot serve two masters. He should not have financial interests in the radio business.[26]

Lest a critic feel too confident in having met all these tests of his sense of responsibility, Robert J. Landry emphasizes a more subtle deterent to independence of judgment:

> One of the factors which has prevented the development of honest criticism is the fact that editors and publishers play their hobby horses. Instead of realizing the power of honest statement to produce wonders, they encourage their writers to use the idiom of their magazines . . . the critic finds himself frequently writing to entertain the publisher.[27]

Finally, as much as the critic may be subjected to pressure from the outside, he is still his own worst enemy. Criticism is not an activity which can be practiced by the dull or unresponsive person. By nature, the critic is someone who can be excited enough by an experience to concentrate full mental and emotional powers upon it. Because of this, he must be aware of two dangers: the distortion of his point of view by extreme personal prejudice, and (what is less forgiveable) his temptation as a professional writer to turn a witty phrase at the expense of an honest statement. The inherent subjectivity of criticism must still produce an eminently fair interpretation of an event. Critics must find within themselves that proper amount of objectivity which can serve as an antidote to the "lack of subtlety and variety" which, according to

Henry Seidel Canby, is the "disease of journalism."[28] The critic's sense of responsibility should prohibit the occurrence of a situation where "one reads a clever remark and feels what a good remark it would be if it were only true."[29]

A summary of these last few pages discloses that professional critics are called to a high purpose requiring mature talents and qualities and that such demands are no less relevant for critics of broadcasting than for the critics of any other medium. It is now time to examine the specific purposes of criticism for the field of broadcasting. These purposes, after all, combine to justify and motivate the participation of critics in what has all too often been a difficult and thankless task.

The Functions of Broadcast Criticism

Admission must be made at the outset of the dearth of published material either by radio-television critics themselves or by students of broadcasting bearing directly on this topic. It is probably a reflection of the uncertainties attending the criticism of a mass medium which is so young. However, the information obtained in scattered references and from interviews with current critics does permit some authoritative answers as to the purpose of criticism in the area.

Basically, the criticism of radio and television would seem to have two interrelated functions: a concern with upholding qualitative standards in programing, and a concern with interpreting socio-economic aspects of the medium to the public and to the broadcasting industry. Both functions have as their ultimate purpose the improvement of public broadcasting. Both functions imply a continual process of evaluation on the part of the critic, and ideally they unite to give control and direction to radio and television.

Upholding Program Standards

For critics to be concerned about standards in broadcast programs is a normal enough function. Criticism involves judgment, and judgment involves comparison between any number of important abstract standards: good and bad artistry, tasteful and tasteless content, true and false ideas, expedient and principled action. No critic, worthy of the name, can ignore this aspect of his job. In fact, he will usually attack problems in this area with gusto because he is convinced of the necessity for program evaluation.

Jack Gould, in a rare defense of his profession, stated with persuasive dignity what he conceived to be a justification for and the basic function of video criticism:

> A medium which daily pre-empts the attention of millions of adults and children surely cannot be ignored. Television is not a static or passive force. It can either elevate or lower national tastes and standards; it cannot operate and leave them entirely untouched. The context in which television must be placed therefore determines itself. Television cannot be judged only by rules and mores of its own making; it also must be weighed in the light of contemporary life as a whole, just as the theater, movies and books are. . . . Television should be hailed . . . for widening the horizons of the public . . . it also must be mindful of . . . its narcotic ability to deaden the national awareness of important standards and serious issues. TV is so powerful it can move up or down and take much of the country along with it either way. That is everybody's concern.
>
> Broadcasters and sponsors make their views felt; viewers are not so fortunate. Critics, in a sense, are the proxies of the viewers. This does not mean that viewers necessarily will agree with the reviewers. But it does mean that there is a common bond of independent opinion independently reached. . . .
>
> The set owner . . . doesn't give a hoot about mass tastes, ratings, or cost per thousand; he looks at the screen and makes up his mind. The critic is his stand-in.
>
> . . . .
>
> The most [critics] can do is urge and plead, encourage and reprove from the sidelines.[30]

Obviously, Mr. Gould is convinced of the necessity for the critic to uphold standards in broadcasting. Before examining this function in greater detail, however, another concept from Mr. Gould's statement needs emphasis since it actually forms the context within which many critics approach their work. It is the idea that the critic represents the voice of the people. Here are various expressions of that point of view. Robert Lewis Shayon feels that "actually the mass level desires cultural upgrading but it does not know how to articulate that desire. Here the critic can help."[31] During his stint with the New Republic, Saul Carson thought of himself as serving as a bridge between the transmitting and receiving portion of the medium. "It was my job to interpret the medium to the listener and to interpret the listeners' feelings and gripes to the originator of programs."[32] Jay Nelson Tuck states that his "main job is to be the voice of the viewer. I act as the viewer's representative to the broadcasters."[33] Gilbert Seldes concurs when he reminds broadcasters that "they are obligated to listen to the critics for substantially the critics represent the public (if not the audience), and the stake of the public in TV is even greater than that of the broadcasters."[34]

The reaction of the broadcasting industry to comments like this last one is mixed. As we shall see in Chapter X, many broadcasters tend to make a strong distinction between public desires and the critics' tastes. Saudek, who was at the time a vice-president of the American Broadcasting Company, would seem to support the critics in this concept of their function:

> Radio criticism gives a lead to many listeners who sit in a rather frustrated fashion at their radios. And while they don't like some of the programs they hear, they don't know

> exactly why. Without some expression of opinion by people who do know why, the listeners' frustration might increase to the point where they would stop listening. . . . [Upon reading criticism], the listener gradually becomes more articulate. He knows what he believes is good, why he thinks it is good, and gains an impression of the potentiality of radio. As listeners come to know more of these things, they become the final arbiters. The critic helps the audience to tell us broadcasters what is good and what is bad. We will take his word to an increasing degree as time goes on.[35]

The significance of the critic serving as representative for the people should not be understated. It not only suggests the important role that criticism may play in the future management of the mass media, but it also poses some interesting questions with relation to the critical function of upholding standards. As spokesman for the people, should a critic ignore their standards, concur with them, or guide them to an acceptance of other standards?

The implication exists, for example, that if a critic is a representative, then the standards of quality by which he judges programs must at least partially reflect the average taste. Gilbert Seldes feels that certain minimum standards must be upheld and that the critic must have an idea of the norm of taste of the average audience. Once this norm has been ascertained, the critic must make sure that a sponsor isn't going below this norm by fifty percent. "After all," warns Mr. Seldes, "sponsors will always play safe. It is up to the critics to make them take risks."[36] Mr. Seldes explains this interest in relative standards and average tastes by suggesting that the critic must more often be concerned with understanding broad program effects rather than program aesthetics. "If we were discussing aesthetics, the exceptions would count heavily; when we talk about effects, the general average alone counts."[37] He apparently feels that this is only a realistic attitude:

> If the major media are going to occupy so much of our time, they cannot prove their worth, their right to continue in their present direction by citing their few exceptional offerings. They can justify themselves only if they offer a balanced entertainment in their average product, if they interest the individual in as many ways as he is capable of being interested, and serve all significant groups instead of a single large section.[38]

Another reason for not losing touch with the norms of taste lies in Seldes' belief that "there grows up in critics a contempt for what the public likes, and this contempt is itself contemptible, for it is part of the duty of the critic to guide the public taste."[39] But Mr. Seldes is aware of a difficulty here: in the worthwhile effort not to appear contemptuous, the critic must not fall into the trap of embracing degraded standards. In an article called "Trash Is Where You Find It," Seldes takes John Crosby to task for implying "that no one knows what trash is exactly."

> The producers of mass entertainment are happy to have this gospel spread by perceptive and influential critics; and since the disciples of Irving Babbitt have been driven out of the critical field, it is fashionable to pretend not to know good from bad. Particularly in the popular arts . . . it is easy to say, "There are no right formulas," and make that an excuse for passing no judgments based on standards rising out of experienced taste. It is precisely the duty of a critic to be able to recognize inferior stuff, to make clear how he arrived at his judgments, and to impress himself upon the public so that in the end the managers of our entertainments will raise the quality of their output.
>
> . . . .
>
> The break between the intellectual and the average intelligent man is not going to be bridged by the intellectual's pretense of having a mind no better trained than that of the sub-average. Nor by pretending that taste and discrimination have no standing.[40]

What concrete suggestions has Mr. Seldes to offer by which a critic can recognize the norm and still remain true to his function of upholding and even raising standards? The answer lies in the critic's awareness that "orders of excellence,"[41] which he must respect, can be applied to several different categories of programing. "The critic must decide whether any particular program is below the tastes and standards of programs similar to it."[42] Certainly, this is an attempt to construct a workable system for judging the varying types of radio and television programs. The system is defended by Mr. Seldes in the following statement:

> The critic cannot require broadcasting, which serves all the people, to use nothing but pure gold, but he can ask that pennies and nickels and dimes should each have the legal minimum of their respective metals, that they should be genuine currency, not counterfeit.[43]

Mr. Seldes demonstrates this approach in the following comment about the dullness of Wednesday night television programing a few years back:

> The important thing is that in some four hours of broadcasting, the average viewer doesn't get a single fine example of the kind of thing he likes and wants. . . .That people want melodrama and amusing panel shows is true. That they prefer the third-rate in these categories is not true.[44]

One other critic expressed a parallel concept. Jay Nelson Tuck tries to keep in touch with audiences as a means of knowing about their tastes:

> A knowledge of various audiences helps me review shows in terms of what they are trying to do. I may not be able to stand some show, but it may be good <u>within its framework</u>. [underlining mine] For example, concerning hill billy shows, I can at least say, "If you like corn, here it is."[45]

Lest a critic, who includes average tastes and a wide range of program categories within the framework of his commentary, be accused of recognizing no specific standards, Mr. Seldes reminds him of a firm duty:

> The critic must attack the routine and repetitive. Whenever the broadcast program remains static, whenever the broadcasters think they have achieved a perfect thing, it is time for the critic to go to work.[46]

This is in accord with Seldes' optimistic philosophy "that whatever happens in television isn't fatal provided something else can happen. . . .

Only when whatever is current becomes permanent do we despair. For however good it is, if it cannot change, it carries the death of imagination with it."[47]

The flexible attitude of Mr. Seldes or Mr. Tuck is not subscribed to in its entirety by Jack Gould. He would require that broadcasters adhere somewhat more rigidly to traditional artistic standards. He describes this part of his function as a matter of "persuading the industry and its audiences to not settle for other than a reasonably good standard of taste. Any art form needs criticism, although the industry people do not realize they have an art form on their hands."[48] The strongly worded statement which follows exemplifies Mr. Gould's concern for maintaining quality programing:

> If there is a single most debilitating influence on the artistic standards of television, it may be the critical judgment almost invariably expressed in these words: "It wasn't so bad for television." or "Well, compared with most of the shows on TV . . ."
>
> This insidious process of rationalizing and excusing mediocrity or the second best is commonplace among the craftsmen of TV and, to be fair and candid, probably among many viewers as well. The nature of TV with its insatiable need for material tends to make it so. . . . [This is] the lazy man's way of criticism by comparison. Under such a code high standards of achievement need not be erected as a fixed goal to be pursued at all cost. Rather the standards can be conveniently allowed to fluctuate, invariably downward to accommodate a prevailing and expedient norm.[49]

This complaint by the present-day critic of the New York Times carries with it echoes of principles set forth three decades earlier by the first professional radio critics. Raymond Francis Yates' dream for the crackling crystal set included a vision of the critic as an agitator for culturally superior programing. On February 28, 1924, Yates, as "Pioneer," wrote the following in the New York Tribune:

> Progress comes through recognition of mistakes, and it is the object of the critic, however miserable his success may be, to point out fearlessly what he conscientiously believes to be mistakes. We simply want to be the ignitor of a little spark that will eventually fire the forces that will make radio the powerful, uplifting thing that it deserves to be.

Yates's comrade in criticism, John Wallace of Radio Broadcast magazine, replied with forthrightness to a letter calling critics "flies in the ointment." His answer not only justified criticism as the guardian of art, but reiterated the concept of the critic as a spokesman for the public. Nor was there any question in his mind that the public expected a critic to take the lead in demanding better broadcasts.

> By universal assent any and all of the products of the artist are open to criticism and he may not protest. . . .Art is not [the critic's] own private possession . . . but is . . . in the custody of the great unwashed public. . . .It is incumbent upon that public to weed out with vituperatives anything that threatens to cast a smirch on art . The commentary that the public makes is known as criticism.
>
> . . . .
>
> The fact that a majority of the listeners are perfectly satisfied . . . does not mean that any criticism on the part of a few of the minority is worthless.
>
> "Giving the public what it wants" is at best a phrase. . . . The public is not at all sure what it does want, seldom expresses itself on the subject, and finally, finds it the course of least resistance to take what it gets. The masses continue to be satisfied until something better comes along. . . . It is up to the minority kickers and mud slingers to secure for them these improvements. . . .Let there be more flies in the ointment![50]

Although the professional "critic-flies" (a metaphor attributed to Socrates by Plato in his Apologia) never increased to the point of becoming a swarm, Mr. Wallace would have been pleased at the response of those who did find their way into the ointment. A brief survey over the years confirms the wide acceptance of the critic functioning as a standard bearer, holding high the symbols of taste for others to see and learn therefrom. Ring Lardner's biographer, for example, tells us that the satirist brought to his criticism of radio "the standards which he had applied to his own work all his life: professional skill, good taste and decency."[51] An effective figure of speech was used by Mr. Volney Hurd to describe the critical function. (It was he who hired Leslie Allen for the Christian Science Monitor in 1929.)

> Using a pyramid as typifying the human expression of mankind, we find the median line pretty near the bottom. The only way we can get that line up is to count on the small area at the top to carry on with unflagging faith and energy. . . I looked over the medium for its promise, and then tried to carry out within my powers the high level treatment that it deserved to keep the median line above the bottom.[52]

In a similar, though stronger moralistic vein, Saul Carson expressed his view of the need for the critic to uphold standards: "The unforgiveable sin for a critic is to cater to the lowest common denominator."[53] Paul Cotton of the Register and Tribune (Des Moines) believes the critic should "always keep in the back of his head the idea of doing what he can to raise broadcasting standards."[54] And, finally, the same concept of function (even to the familiar metaphor of the fly) is repeated by Marya Mannes of the Reporter:

> One function of the critic is to give people a better standard of judgment so that in time they will demand better programing and reject the inferior. The critic must advocate standards and explain why there should be public protest. The critic must be a gadfly since people are lazy and will continue to take poor stuff.[55]

Having completed a general review of the critics' opinions about one of their major functions, it is now appropriate to touch upon specific ways in which they feel their columns can help maintain standards. First, critical writing reflects a skill in dissection. The critic isolates the factors which contribute to or detract from the quality of a program and then explains his total judgment about that program to his readers. This is, of course, nothing more than the analytical process already described. (see p. 111 and p. 113.) It requires a "discernment" which Miss Mannes believes to be the result of the critic's exposure to life, to art, and to the wide world of books.[56] In theory, at least, the public who reads these analyses will utilize its newfound artistic education to demand higher quality programs from the loud speaker and the screen.

In addition to declaring whether a show is good or bad and why, standards can be upheld by what Jack Cluett refers to as direct "editorializing for improvements in broadcasting." For example, he has repeatedly urged the television industry to appoint a czar to distribute the top ten programs and keep dramatic fare like "Studio One" and "Robert Montgomery Presents" from overlapping.[57]

Mr. Cluett also believes that critics improve standards by discovering and "boosting" new talent. He is proud of the fact that his monthly articles recognized such television performers as Wally Cox, Dave Garroway and George Gobel before the daily-paper critics mentioned them.[58] A similar contribution was made in the youthful days of radio when Ring Lardner withheld his usual acid judgments to praise the initial efforts of entertainers like Fred Allen and Jack Benny.[59] The real need for published critical applause of this sort is underscored by the fact that broadcast performances generally occur in audienceless studios. Artists and producers are encouraged by printed responses to their efforts.

Finally, John Crosby sees in the boundless areas of unexplored programing one more way in which the critic can elevate the quality of radio and television: "It's easy enough to criticize what's on the air, but I think one of the critic's main functions is to stimulate a demand for what isn't."[60]

In summary, whether critical standards are flexible or rigid is not as important as the simple fact that critics are genuinely and unanimously concerned about them. They do care for "what isn't" and hope to see it become "what is." In their various ways, they exert a cultural leadership which creates a constant demand for programs of quality.

Interpreting the Industry to Itself and to the Public

The reader of professional criticism is frequently aware that he is getting more than discussions of aesthetic standards or artistic techniques, important as these are. According to Robert Lewis Shayon, this is a logical state of affairs, since, in the final analysis, broadcasting is a unique "social phenomenon which cannot be appraised as one would an art with certain standards."[61] Actually, Mr. Shayon does concern himself with program standards, but he is undeniably more concerned with the second and broader critical function: that of exploring matters peculiar to a mass medium of entertainment, of communication, and of advertising. Mr. Shayon, along with many other critics, feels that broadcasters and their audiences must be made aware of the power and of the effects of programs produced for instantaneous reception by millions of people. Marya Mannes states the problem more specifically when she says that "television is of enormous importance in the lives of Americans, and because of this it must be rigorously examined not only for its content but for its end effects on American thought amd mores."[62]

The sociologists, the philosophers, the commentators on the American scene, the critics themselves emphasize that the broadcast media act as an often vague, but nonetheless pervasive, social force. Unlike literature, the theater, and even the movies, broadcasting can commandeer the attention (and then the attitudes and the thoughts) of large segments of the population with such rapidity and to such a degree that for a critic to deal solely with program aesthetics would be shortsighted indeed. The American ether is a vast market place where objects d'arte are displayed, where information and ideas are peddled, and where every sort of commercial product is hawked. It is the function of the critic to advise the public, who, after all, controls the franchises of the market place. The critic not only helps the public select worthwhile programs of entertainment, but he warns it about questionable propaganda. He not only guides his readers through the market place, but he tries to show them why they go to market at all, and what effects too many trips will have upon them. His praises and warnings and analyses reach not only the consumers of programs, but also the peddlers of programs and the federal policemen (F.C.C. officials) who patrol the market place.

Perhaps because of his long association with other popular arts (movies, cartoons, comics, vaudeville) as well as with radio and television, Gilbert Seldes insists that the complex function of interpreting broadcasting to society requires a kind of critic who, at the very least, would be a social scientist and at the very most a statesman:

> I am proposing a reevaluation of the popular arts in terms of . . . social effect rather than private pleasure. The ethical principles we apply to radio and movies were developed in days of theater and newspaper. . . . The number of people who accept the entertainments, where they are at the time, how much they absorb, what power they have to resist, how much time is left for cultivation of other interests are vital questions.
>
> The judgment on the place of the popular arts cannot

> be left to the moral philosopher, or the aesthete--the third judge must be the statesman. We move beyond the aesthetic question of the quality of a movie. We move beyond the moral question of whether movies are good for people. We inquire what kind of society do the popular arts tend to create? And whether in the present state of the world we can afford to give virtually absolute freedom to irresponsible individuals letting them create by their whim, the temper of the citizen's mind--his moral and intellectual climate.[63]

Taken in such a context, critical inquiry performs an urgent public service differentiated from its aesthetic activity. This second function of criticism is founded upon the realization that the mass media have a mass impact which can determine the very actions of society. Both the awesome challenge and the immense dangers of instruments like radio and television have prompted Mr. Seldes to declare that "the moment we see that a transformation is taking place, the right and the duty to direct that change becomes self-evident."[64]

Just as professional critics vary in their allegiance to absolute standards of program quality, so too, do they vary in the degree to which they accept this corollary function of "social critic." However, most of them, at one time or another, help the public direct its own destiny with regard to broadcasting by pointing out implications of legal decisions, results of research into the impact of the media, and other trends of societal concern. The column of program commentary often gives way to a column Charles Siepmann calls the "critique of policy."[65] Here, for example, are examined the motives and principles by which sponsors determine broadcast programs; and here are offered suggestions to those interested in preserving the public's stake in broadcasting.

To discharge the second function of criticism, a critic must combine an ability to teach with the ability to exhort. He must analyze with the impartiality of the scientist and propound courses of action with humanitarian enthusiasm. His most difficult task may well be the integration of an aesthetic approach to art as private experience with a social approach to a mass medium as public experience. He will undoubtedly have to develop for himself some understanding of the way in which the patterns of our popular culture are allied to what Lyman Bryson has called, "the centrality of machine technology in the American way."[66] The successful coordination of the two major functions of broadcast criticism is difficult but possible, as evidenced by the writing of the leading critics. Their awareness of the fact that they are dealing with a public art permits them to establish relevant guides for the industry and for society to follow.

Particular Concepts of Significance to the Critic of Broadcasting

Thus far, this discussion of fundamental critical concepts has included a general delineation of the purposes and professional qualities of all critics and a consideration of two specific functions of the broadcast critic. It is obvious that as the commentator about radio and television strives to uphold standards and interpret the media, his role can still be identified with that of critics in other fields; the critics of literature, of music, of the theater assume similar responsibilities for their media. However, while struggling to bring the points of view from which they write into sharper focus, some critics of broadcasting have perceived differences between the new media and the old which they feel partially differentiates their functions from those of the rest of the critical fraternity. The differences have already been alluded to as deriving from a <u>mass</u> medium which has established conditions for the preparation and reception of programs quite unlike older forms of artistic endeavor. The purpose of the present section, then, is to round out the discussion of critical concepts by concentrating in greater detail on the unique nature of radio and television and its significance for critics steeped by background and temperament in the traditional approaches to artistic activity.

The concept of broadcasting as one more art related to art in general has undergone a revision coincidental with increased study into the nature of broadcasting. Irwin Edman's contemporary definition of art is standard enough to serve as the base from which this revision can be observed. He tells us that art is the intensification, clarification and interpretation of experience.[67] This generally accepted view point was given greater specificity by Gilbert Seldes who, in his first book in 1924, recognized two subdivisions: the great arts exemplified by the work of persons like Aeschylus, Aristophanes, Moliere and Mozart, and the minor arts of which the comedia dell 'arte, the music of Irving Berlin, and the comedy of Chaplin are representative. The great arts, Mr. Seldes believes, are characterized by "high seriousness" and the minor arts by "high levity;" both are important, although the minor arts, except in unusual periods of history, "are likely to be the most intelligent phenomena of their day."[68] So far there would seem to be no conflict between the practice of art in general terms and the practice of minor arts or lively arts as Seldes preferred to call them.

Early radio and television were, at first, easily categorized by Seldes and other critics as types of lively or popular art. They, along with the films, vaudeville, and musical comedy shared characteristics common to all folk arts: within their framework of romantic, patriotic, moral conventions they could communicate to everyone.[69] All that remained was for the critics to treat broadcasting as an extension of show business and to write about it from the viewpoint of the critics of popular theater. As a matter of fact, many qualified, current critics continue to use this approach.

Over the years there arose, however, a conviction that the output of radio and television (and to an extent, film) was different from popular theater. To some critics, Seldes included, it now appeared that these media scarcely resembled even the minor arts, let alone the arts in general. Major dissimilarities were apparent in their basic aims and in their method of production and distribution. Mr. Seldes, in 1950, proffered some new tentative conclusions about broadcasting and its closest relative the film:

> In the traditional sense . . .they are uncreative. They are machine-made products, they repeat themselves endlessly, using a handful of contrived formulas for plot and stereotyped figures for characters; they are seldom the product of a single powerful imagination but are put together by groups of people who are virtually forbidden to express their own profoundest feelings about the meaning of life. . . .Our mass entertainments are compelled by their own nature to create works that can be promptly forgotten; the work of art as an imperishable object is totally foreign to them.[70]

Mr. Seldes' analysis of broadcasting is further amplified by the observations of Sydney Head, a university expert on the mass media. Mr. Head takes issue with those who criticize broadcasting "because it fails to live up to the rules pertaining to books, literary drama, paintings, or concert-hall programs."[71] He explains that such rules are largely irrelevant because broadcasting is a medium requiring financial investments so great that the only way to justify the expenditures is for broadcasting to market its products on a mass basis. The resulting syndication, supported by advertisers, is a situation where content "tends to be determined by . . . economic interests rather than by artistic or intellectual considerations."[72] Mr. Head agrees with Mr. Seldes that individual creativity is almost an impossibility in broadcasting. The individual frequently compromises as his material is assayed by producers, actors, technicians, agency and client representatives, and network continuity acceptance personnel. Consequently, "the sharp individualistic edges of the creative product are dulled with much handling. A characteristic blandness and slickness results. . . . The mass media uses artists instead of artists using the mass media."[73]

Under conditions like these, the gradual separation of broadcasting from the minor arts is understandable. Although the minor or popular arts tend to make diversion their major aim, at their best they are still skillful, though not profound, interpretations of experience; they still have their roots in reality. Insofar as broadcast programs are genuinely allied to life they can be reviewed within the familiar framework of universal artistic concepts. In proportion to their lack of relevance to any aspects of life, they create a frustration in the aesthetically trained critic which cannot be compared even to the despair of the drama critic during a bleak season. Confronted by mediocre or even wretched plays, a Broadway critic is still appraising drama. Confronted by the carefully contrived lethargy of a daytime radio or television serial, the broadcasting critic is apt to be uncertain as to what he is appraising.

More often than not, critics schooled in the standard arts have disapproved the broadcast product. Even Gilbert Seldes, who has tried to approach the mass media with sympathy and understanding, admits that:

> These particular popular arts not only convey a flat and limited picture of life, they actually encourage people to limit the

> range of their emotions and interests.
> . . . If they present a false view of life and prevent the community from raising mature and responsible citizens, their function as entertainment is not fulfilled.[74]

Mr. Seldes submits the following description of film writing as an example of a machine process, which, like the construction of a radio script, may meet the economic requirements dictated by a mass medium, but would scarcely meet the requirements of art:

> The imposed necessity to cut characters down to size, the constant preoccupation with possible objections, the awareness of authority looking over his shoulder as he writes all combine to bring the writer into using bright tricks; substituting violence for passion, activity for strength of character, invention of twists at the expense of logic.[75]

The prevailing pattern of dramatic broadcasts built upon the very techniques herein outlined has convinced many traditional critics that the channels of sound and sight transmit very little which resembles art.

Marya Mannes expresses her agreement with this point of view by focusing attention on the dissatisfaction of minority audiences responsive to art as contrasted with the enthusiastic response of most television viewers:

> We are ranging ourselves behind that segment of the television audience which is critical and demanding: the snobs, if you will, the sophisticated eggheads. . . .Through no virtues of our own, books and music and theater and art have one or all kept us company in our lives. Thanks to them and that infinite capacity for discussion which mark the egghead, we have usually been able to entertain ourselves. Our lives are often too full for television.
>
> But the people who depend most on television are apt to be those who previously found their release from reality in the narcosis of radio, comics, or Mickey Spillane.
>
> . . . Television is distraction and solace for millions on whom this civilization has imposed the crushing weight of emptiness. . .
>
> For the mass millions that infinitely repeated intrusion of commercials is a small price to pay for this release. If anything, it feeds--as it is designed to do--the enormous appetite for things that is an accepted American diversion as much as it is the basis of our economy.[76]

What would Miss Mannes require of America's supreme divertissement and most powerful medium of advertising? Her answer implies that she would appreciate some recognizable relation between television and the basic purposes of art as defined in Irwin Edman's statement. She wants television to enhance human experience whether real or imaginary:

> [Eggheads want] either the immediacy of reality . . . intimate observation of people and places and situations, or the stimulation of real imagination. . . . We want our stuff straight, the lines clear, and the areas separate. We want television that can be adult for ourselves and childlike for our children--but at different times . . . .[Most shows are family shows that] can never be either adult or childlike. They arrest adults at an adolescent level and endow children with a precocious sophistication.[77]

The words seem to echo a yearning for a return to the muses. However, most critics of broadcasting (including Miss Mannes) would probably acknowledge that the mass media will never find the road back but will, instead, carve another trail through a jungle of economic and artistic hazards to a new destination.

Critics feel it is their duty to help guide the expedition. They will never discard the old compass which points to their "true north" of artistic endeavor, but they will be on the alert to recognize other markers along the route. Two such signposts will serve as examples at the moment. One could lead in a promising direction.

Mr. Seldes reminds critics that they have been misled by radio's resemblance to drama and by television's resemblance to the movies and the theater. A more appropriate comparison can be made by recalling the attributes of the parlor game. This medium, almost a stranger to the public stage, is entirely right for the living room. It obviously accounts for the success of the quiz and panel shows, but Mr. Seldes also sees its influence in television drama:

> No matter how much machinery works in the background, the unpredictable instant stands out. . . "Marty" and "A Man Is Ten Feet Tall". . . were in the grain of television. . . .They were built out of moments, not out of acts. . . .They had in short something of the broken and improptu feel of the non-dramatic TV program.[78]

Here, indeed, is a new concept to guide the broadcasting critic in evaluating television drama.

The second signpost would seem to point toward a more disturbing future--disturbing, at least, to those who rely on the stimulation of the great arts. It is the opinion of T. W. Adorno that our present popular culture "has seized all media of artistic expression":

> The more the system of merchandizing culture is expanded, the more it tends to assimilate the serious art of the past by adapting it to the system's own requirements. The control is so extensive that any infraction of its rules is a priori stigmatized as "high-brow" and has but little chance to reach the population at large.
>
> . . . .
>
> The repetitiveness, the self-sameness, the ubiquity of modern mass culture tends to make for automatized reactions and to weaken the forces of individual resistance.[79]

Surely this concept of the new culture is one which should stir critics to a thorough reappraisal of their old functions and of the effectiveness of their traditional weapons. Perhaps critical insistance on Mr. Seldes' "unpredictable instant" in programing rather than on standards valid for other arts would prevent Mr. Adorno's "automatized reaction" from ever gaining complete sway. Insights like these emphasize that broadcasting with its unpredictable, hybrid forms, and its mass distribution of standard forms has become a strong force in mediating and creating contemporary culture.

The leading critics have accepted the obvious challenge to investigate the dimensions of this force and to help guide its future direction. They probably would nod agreement with Joseph Wood Krutch that our popular arts "formulate and transmit the pattern of opinions, habits and emotions which constitute the 'culture' and thus determine the character of a civilization"; that, "at this moment our own arts, good and bad, exercise a stronger influence upon our citizens than either the schools or churches."[80] Regardless of the critics' opinions about the exact relationship between broadcasting and the arts, and regardless of their difficulties in organizing an approach to media of information and advertising as well as entertainment, they are aware that radio and television are the most potent of the mass media and consequently the most potent determiners of our present culture. They realize that treating broadcasting with contempt or indifference would be (and has been) a serious mistake.

Instead, these critics set for themselves the difficult task of utilizing traditional critical practices when appropriate and of creating new approaches when the old seem irrelevant. At times they are more like sociologists than esthetes, more like philosophers than writers wise in the ways of show business. As broadcasting critics, they risk being bored by its repetitiveness and irritated by its commercials. On the other hand, they share in interpreting the exciting revelations of new forms, and the sober implications of new forces.

Finally, during those periods when radio and television critics are most acutely aware of their isolation from critics of the other media, it is no small intellectual consolation to realize that they still may be following complementary critical procedures established by the ancient Greeks. The application of standards to form and content is basically an Aristotelian approach to art. And when a critic also emphasizes the relationship between broadcasting and societal values, he is adopting the tradition of Plato.[81]

Strengthened by purposes from the past and challenged by the slowly developing purposes of the future, the critic of broadcasting has been a prolific, perceptive commentator on the vast array of programs emanating from the éther. It is time to turn to his specific comments about the products of radio and television.

Notes

[1]DeWitt H. Parker, The Principles of Aesthetics (2d ed.; New York: F. S. Crofts and Company, 1947), p. 2.

[2]Joseph Wood Krutch, Experience and Art (New York: Harrison Smith and Robert Haas, 1932), p. 165.

[3]Brooks Atkinson, "Credo of a Critic," Saturday Review, August 6, 1949, p. 136.

[4]Lyman Bryson, "Broadcasting and the Cultivated Minority," American Scholar, XX (Autumn, 1951), 171-72.

[5]Robert J. Landry, "The Improbability of Radio Criticism," Hollywood Quarterly, II (1946-47), 70.

[6]Gilbert Seldes, The Public Arts (New York: Simon and Schuster, 1956), p. 211.

[7]Gertrude Buck, quoted in Lester Thonssen and A. Craig Baird, Speech Criticism (New York: Ronald Press Company, 1948), p. 19.

[8]Robert J. Landry, "Wanted: Radio Critics," Public Opinion Quarterly, IV (December, 1940), p. 629.

[9]Interview with Mr. Robert J. Landry, managing editor, Variety, April 3, 1956.

[10]Henry Seidel Canby, "Good and Bad Reviewing," Saturday Review of Literature, August 2, 1924, p. 1.

[11]Craig La Driere, quoted in Robert W. Stallman, The Critic's Notebook (Minneapolis: University of Minnesota Press, 1950), p. 13.

[12]Letter from Miss Harriet Van Horne, critic, World-Telegram, (New York), May 7, 1956.

[13]Interview with Mr. Saul Carson, former critic, New Republic, April 4, 1956.

[14]Interview with Mr. Jack Gould, critic, New York Times, April 2, 1956.

[15]Interview with Miss Marya Mannes, critic, Reporter, April 3, 1956.

[16]Interview with Mr. Gilbert Seldes, critic, Saturday Review, April 5, 1956.

[17]Giraud Chester and Garnet R. Garrison, Radio and Television (1st ed.; New York: Appleton-Century-Crofts, Inc., 1950), p. 515.

[18]Interview with Mr. Jay Nelson Tuck, critic, New York Post, April 6, 1956.

[19]Gould, *loc. cit.*

[20]Interview with Mr. Gilbert Seldes, *loc. cit.*

[21]S. Stephenson Smith, *The Craft of the Critic* (New York: Thomas Y. Crowell Company, 1931), pp. 15-20.

[22]Paul F. Lazarsfeld, "The Role of Criticism in the Management of Mass Media," *Journalism Quarterly*, XV (June, 1948), p. 123.

[23]Gilbert Seldes, *Saturday Review*, September 11, 1954, p. 46.

[24]Letter from Mr. Donald Kirkley, critic, *Baltimore Sun*, April 16, 1956.

[25]Tuck, *loc. cit.*

[26]Jack Gould, *New York Times*, January 25, 1948.

[27]Interview with Mr. Robert J. Landry, *loc. cit.*

[28]Canby, *loc. cit.*

[29]Alistair Cooke, "The Critic in Film History," *Footnotes to the Films*, ed., Charles Davy (London: Lovat Dickson, Ltd., 1937), p. 263.

[30]Jack Gould, *New York Times*, May 26, 1957.

[31]Interview with Mr. Robert Lewis Shayon, critic, *Saturday Review*, April 4, 1956.

[32]Carson, *loc. cit.*

[33]Tuck, *loc. cit.*

[34]Gilbert Seldes, *Saturday Review*, November 8, 1952, p. 34.

[35]Robert Saudek, panel member discussing radio criticism, *Education on the Air*, 18th yrbk., ed., O. Joe Olson (Columbus: Ohio State University Press, 1948), p. 116.

[36]Interview with Mr. Gilbert Seldes, *loc. cit.*

[37]Gilbert Seldes, *The Great Audience* (New York: Viking Press, 1950), p. 213.

[38]*Ibid.*, p. 214.

[39]Seldes, *The Public Arts*, p. 293.

[40]Gilbert Seldes, *Saturday Review*, July 25, 1953, pp. 29-30.

[41]Seldes, *The Public Arts*, p. 161.

[42]Interview with Mr. Gilbert Seldes, loc. cit.

[43]Gilbert Seldes, Saturday Review, June 6, 1953, p. 29.

[44]Gilbert Seldes, Saturday Review, June 6, 1953, p. 29.

[45]Interview with Mr. Jay Nelson Tuck, loc. cit.

[46]Interview with Mr. Gilbert Seldes, loc. cit.

[47]Gilbert Seldes, Saturday Review, January 15, 1955, p. 33.

[48]Interview with Mr. Jack Gould, loc. cit.

[49]Jack Gould, New York Times, January 31, 1955.

[50]John Wallace, Radio Broadcast, XII (November, 1927), 37-38.

[51]Donald Elder, Ring Lardner (New York: Doubleday and Company, Inc., 1956), p. 350.

[52]Letter from Mr. Volney D. Hurd, Chief of the Paris Bureau, Christian Science Monitor, May 29, 1956.

[53]Interview with Mr. Saul Carson, loc. cit.

[54]Letter from Mr. Paul Cotten, critic, Register Tribune (Des Moines), September 6, 1956.

[55]Interview with Miss Marya Mannes, loc. cit.

[56]Ibid.

[57]Interview with Mr. Jack Cluett, critic, Woman's Day, April 4, 1956.

[58]Ibid.

[59]Elder, op. cit., p. 350.

[60]"Out of the Blue," Time, August 20, 1956, p. 72.

[61]Interview with Mr. Robert Lewis Shayon, loc. cit.

[62]Mannes, loc. cit.

[63]Seldes, The Great Audience, p. 293.

[64]Seldes, The Public Arts, p. 301.

[65]Charles Siepmann, "Further Thoughts on Radio Criticism," Public Opinion Quarterly, V (June 1941), 308.

[66]Lyman Bryson quoted in Sydney W. Head, Broadcasting in America (New York: Houghton Mifflin Co., 1956), p. 437.

[67]Irwin Edman, Arts and the Man (New York: W. W. Norton and Co., Inc., 1939), p. 34.

[68]Gilbert Seldes, The Seven Lively Arts (New York: Harper and Brothers, 1924), pp. 348-49.

[69]Seldes, The Great Audience, p. 258.

[70]Ibid., p. 3.

[71]Sydney W. Head, op. cit., p. 436.

[72]Ibid., p. 433.

[73]Ibid., p. 435.

[74]Seldes, The Great Audience, pp. 250-56.

[75]Ibid., p. 56.

[76]Marya Mannes, Reporter, May 2, 1957, p. 20.

[77]Ibid.

[78]Gilbert Seldes, "Television," The Nation, May 26, 1956, p. 457.

[79]T. W. Adorno, "How To Look at Television," Quarterly of Film, Radio and Television, VIII (Spring, 1954), 215-16.

[80]Joseph Wood Krutch, "Theater . . . Cultural Common Denominator," Theater Arts, XL (February, 1956), 24-25.

[81]Austin Warren, quoted in Robert W. Stallman, The Critic's Notebook, op. cit., pp. 16-17.

CHAPTER IV

THE CRITICS' OPINIONS ABOUT BROADCAST DRAMA

Having just suggested that radio and television critics are confreres of no lesser personages than Aristotle and Plato, one conceivably could expect that their opinions on electronic theater would comprise a minor Poetics or, at least, some tightly organized Dialogues. Such is not the case, however. When radio drama was at its height there was a dearth of critics; and television drama is still too young to have elicited any stabilized aesthetic. Moreover, the drama in both media advances toward and recedes from recognizable artistic form in a manner analogous to the wavering signal strength of a receiving set beseiged by electrical interference. The critics have had to content themselves with snippets of ideas in response to bits of theater. This handicap, coupled with the critics' journalistic limitation of writing for the immediate moment, has made it difficult to group their comments around clearly established major principles. In the sections on radio drama and television drama an attempt has been made, however, to single out certain points which appear to have received greater critical emphasis. Clarification of these points has been attempted by citing some self-contained plays which received specific mention by the critics. Separate treatment in both sections has been given to the standardized format plays which generally employ the same characters in varied situations for an extended series of programs. The chapter as a whole tries to discover what critics think of broadcast drama from the stand point of its content and production, its social significance, its most needed improvements.

Radio Drama

The professional criticism of radio drama had its beginning in the fumbling attention paid to the new form by critics whose major concern was the enormous quantity of music being broadcast. Unfortunately, as the proportion of dramatic programs increased to the point where in 1939 they included twenty percent of the broadcast menu,[1] their content and form had become so unimaginatively standardized that even the few conscientious critics were unable to construct any elaborate theories of radio theater. To be sure, the critics had brief contacts with fresh theatrical experiences emanating from their loudspeakers, and these were duly noted. But on the whole, they confined themselves to vague musings about what radio theater could be and frustrated denunciations for what it was. In 1956, with television riding high, Gilbert Seldes delivered a general epitaph for radio which could stand as a particularly pertinent summary of critical feeling about radio drama: "In top lofty terms, radio was an entertainment with hardly any aesthetic interest. To speak of 'the art of radio' always seemed grossly pretentious--unless it seemed merely funny."[2] With unintentional irony, a 1927 fan contributed the preface to Mr. Seldes' comment when he wrote to John Wallace, "As for radio plays, there are still theaters where we can see the actors act . . . radio plays will have to wait until television is a success."[3]

The satisfaction in being able to "see the actors act" had been taken for granted by theater-goers. It was not until the arrival of "sightless drama,"[4] to use John Wallace's phrase, that people began to realize the difficulties involved in presenting a play which was to be enjoyed through the aural sense alone. Early critics were obviously insistent that all the elements of the play be identifiable. A production was praised if there were no doubt as to who was speaking, or if care had been taken to provide a synopsis of the story before the action commenced.[5] Raymond Francis Yates felt that for the sake of clarity the plots of radio plays should be kept simple and the casts small (perhaps five at the most). He also emphasized the importance of including a thorough narrative description of the locale.[6] The technique of having a character introduce himself by speaking a few lines in character at the beginning of the play was considered an interesting and helpful innovation.[7] As unsophisticated as comments like these may seem a generation later, they do reveal a groping but sincere desire to help get successful radio theater underway.

Certainly these critics did not foresee that the small cast, the explicit narration, and the character introduction, if carried to an extreme, would result in a kind of anti-theater. Jack Gould, in a column marking the twenty-fifth anniversary of radio, recognized the difficulty: "The radio-drama seemed to be getting further and further away from the dramatic form itself, with narrative monologues, often excessively pretentious, being offered as a hardly satisfactory substitute."[8]

Actually, in the opinion of most critics, the one major element of radio theater for which there is no substitute is the quality of dramatic writing. This is a recurrent critical theme. Quality is deemed more important than either the simplicity of a script or its technical adaptability to radio's limitations. Quality does not neglect clarity; it presumes it. John Wallace was one of the earliest critics to emphasize the point. He wrote, in 1927, to the readers of <u>Radio Broadcast</u>

agazine:

> The simple possession of a fountain pen does not qualify a man for "writing" script . . . Each word must have the vividness of poetry. It must be chosen for its ability to assist in building up a rapid and forceful picture in the listener's mind. . . It must not only look descriptive in type, it must sound descriptive--a job for a Washington Irving.[9]

t a time when the novel possibilities of sound effects were receiving uch attention, Mr. Wallace urged aspiring radio playwrights to concenrate on "words, words, words." He felt they "should be required to ead and assimilate everyone of Shakespeare's dramas"; only then would hey begin to understand how information which performs the functions of cenery and lights is put into actors' lines.[10]

Although later critics were cheered by the few important dramatists adio produced, they would have admitted that Mr. Wallace was a more ccurate prophet than he realized when he said, "It is highly improbable at a genius at writing this sort of stuff will ever appear; the ether ave is yet too ephemeral a medium to attract great writers."[11] ifteen years is a disappointingly long period to wait for the appearance even one major writer. The reason radio lacks leadership, complained bert Williams in 1942, is only because of its neglect by men of letrs. "They forget that a paint pot is artless until an artist takes up e brush."[12]

If the course of painting depends on an artist's brush and the urse of playwriting on a writer's pen, then the course of a completed dio drama depends on an actor's voice. Vocal interpretation is, after l, the major means of communicating dramatic ideas over the radio. re again the critics have spoken out. Mr. Wallace preferred to make e distinction between the vocal skill of stage and radio actors a matter of degree: "A radio actor has to have better command of his voice and inflection than a legitimate actor."[13] On the other hand, Albert Williams sees the matter as a difference in kind.

> It all boils down to the fact that while radio is a challenge for actors, it actually demands very little acting in the Broadway sense of the word. It demands careful and studied interpretation of the words of the script in order that the meaning of the work may be etched on the listener's mind. It demands personality rather than physical vituosity.[14]

Leslie Allen summarized the matter rather succinctly when he said that "for every play that comes out of a loudspeaker as drama, several come out as mere dialogue. It is a rare radio actor who projects character and not himself."[15] In a Christian Science Monitor review for August 23, 1930, Mr. Allen complimented William Rainey for his portrayal of Hamlet on NBC's "Sunday Night Hour With Shakespeare." " He projected a reading, vigorous yet sympathetic, vibrant with emotion that built an image in the imagination of the listener."

These last few words identify the goal of all radio dramas: to arouse audience participation in the play by stirring its imagination. It is an admittedly difficult task, and Mr. Allen was one of the first critics to warn about the fact that radio drama would never be appreciated by the listener, if he merely tolerated it as background noise during living room conversation.[16] Radio drama must receive the sustained attention of an audience. Only then can the sensitive production of a worthwhile script result in the joyous experience associated with genuine theater.

Never having known an ideal radio play, John Wallace conjectured what the new form to be called "Sound Drama" might be like:

> A little like stage drama . . . a little like the opera . .
> . a little like the symphony . . . a little like literature

> . . . a little like oratorio. . . . The artist who does it will have to be playwright, composer, and poet all at once . . . or he must direct the efforts of collaborators to a unified end. . . . This imagined program will open with the vague rumble of distant voices . . . [growing clearer] to suggest the mood of the entire piece. . . . They will melt into music [and again] into human voice . . . perhaps we will hear a chorus of voices. . . . All of these various sound sources will be shunted about until the comedy, melodrama, tragedy or fantasy, whatever it is, has come to a close.
>
> If it is properly composed, it will not be tricky or hi-brow. It will be a gripping emotional thing that will completely carry us away.[17]

With an eye for the practical as well as theoretical, Mr. Allen proposed that a station or group of stations sponsor a five thousand dollar prize contest for the best sixty minute program.[18] As far as is known, no sponsor accepted the proposal and the critic's Wagnerian dream never materialized. A decade later, however, John Allen would have discerned fragments of his imaginative idea in some of the productions of Archibald MacLeish, Norman Corwin, and Arch Oboler.

Even before that brief "golden age" of radio drama, however, the critics were able to point to a few performances which contained some of the qualities for which they were searching. More than one critic, but particularly Mr. Allen, was impressed by the work of C. L. Menser of NBC who directed, in 1930, a series of short one-act plays adapted by Julian Street, Jr. from the Penrod stories of Booth Tarkington. According to the critic, the scripts were not reproductions but complete revisions to meet radio's requirements. Mr. Menser's direction was such that "small town youth lives rather than merely talks into the mike."[19] Instead of utilizing meaningless theme and incidental music, "Penrod" used music "importantly to bridge breaks with a smile. Its satirical comment on the action was a valuable contribution to the humorous effect of the whole sketch."[20]

During the same period, NBC experimented with a completely new method of production by bringing Cecil Lewis to New York to demonstrate what could be done with the multiple studio system used by the British Broadcasting Corporation. Although Mr. Allen does not elaborate on the performance of Beggar on Horseback, one catches a glimpse of John Wallace's imaginary director in Mr. Lewis who blended into a harmonious whole the output of actors, music and sound effects isolated from each other in three separate studios. The British director employed a narrator only sparingly, used sound effects symbolically and omitted music unless it served an emotional or dramatic purpose.[21] As a wistful postscript to Mr. Allen's discussion, his readers were informed that the new system demanded more rehearsal time and facilities than commercial radio could afford.[22]

A brief review by Darwin Teilhet in a 1933 issue of Forum magazine provides one more example of the infrequent type of production which would seem to meet the tenuous, but potentially artistic, standards proffered by the serious critics. Mr. Teilhet refers to Ferrin Fraser and Marion Parsonet with their "Theater of Today" series as "original geniuses."[23] Their technique of eliminating all verbal stage settings without prohibiting the action winging from scene to scene is responsible for "the first true radio drama."[24]

It should be evident from the few examples described, that most of the experimentation and most of the innovations lauded by early critics were matters of directorial, acting, and technical refinement brought to fruition in dramas not originally written for radio. Since established playwrights and poets persisted in ignoring the medium, what should have become an entirely new way of creating drama became instead the semi-creative process of treating adaptations. As unsatisfactory as this was for critics interested in a new form, the situation did provide some grist for their mills for three reasons: (1) Frustrated by the dearth of challenging drama, adaptations were usually something critics could probe with a feeling of accomplishment. (2) The fact that critics were likely to be acquainted with the original version gave them a firmer base for their comments. (3) Anytime a work prepared for one medium is adapted to another, charges of distortion can be entered by critics. The following examples of critical disappointment were selected because they represent quite accurately the misgivings most critics are apt to have about radio adaptations.

The major problem recognized by the adapter and despaired of by the critics is the constant need to condense an original work into the rigid time pattern of our broadcasting system. In reviewing a performance by Helen Hayes of "Victoria Regina," Saul Carson of the New Republic quipped that it provided "as much haste as Hayes." He continued:

> When any full bodied play or story is compressed into a half-hour . . . the emphasis on speed produces a hasty, nervous, often brutally irreverent skipping from climax to climax. . . . The finer tracings that had gone into building the big moments [are missing].[25]

Mr. Carson did feel, however, that the performance had value since Miss Hayes' respect for microphone acting managed to project, if not a thoroughly regal Victoria at least a warmer one than originally.[26]

Some critics, of course, would take issue on this point, feeling that the distortion of regality would be only one more illustration of the kind of infidelity to original artistic values which they most vigorously deplore. Robert Lewis Shayon would in all probability be counted among this group. An adaptation by NBC of E. M. Forster's Passage to India was his occasion for a thorough denunciation of the practice.

> To make everything fit neatly into the radio package unwarranted liberties were taken with time and place. Gross damage, too, was done to important values.
> . . . .
> This is how radio and TV dramatizations of almost all superior novels invariably come out. A cavalier, expedient pushing around of the unities, deletion, write-in, cut back, torn-down, point-up make quick and ship-shape for delivery and on to the next assignment.
> . . . Fundamentally the fault lies in the assumption that radio can do any novel in an hour's time . . .
> Another trouble is that programs do not pay script writers enough to warrant their taking ample time to think about an adaptation, to achieve creatively a fresh insight into it, and to search for a unique radio form in which to recast it.[27]

Is there any solution to this problem, other than to discontinue adaptations? Mr. Shayon says, "I would rather be briefed on a novel's outline, told something about its untransferable qualities, and have one scene accurately and fully done."[28]

Another solution would be to attempt adaptations only when a large enough block of time is available. Mr. Carson believes that a thorough adaptation of a literary classic can not only reproduce the literary flavor of the author but also project dramatic excitement. Whatever tampering occurs such as "the insertion of transitional narration, the articulate setting of scenes, the provision of music as background or 'bridge,' the use of sound, the employment of other devices is needed in fairness to the mass audience robbed of the sight, movement, color, costuming, lighting and other paraphanalia for a limited audience in a theater."[29] Mr. Carson cited the CBS and NBC treatments of "Madame Bovary" and "An American Tragedy," respectively, as worthwhile radio adaptations.[30]

The critics' adverse opinions of adaptations are partially balanced by compliments they have paid to the "Lux Radio Theater," which, during the forties, produced former screen plays each week over the Columbia Broadcasting System. Jack Gould felt it was "almost a model of pure radio craftsmanship, an example of unfaltering professionalism."[31] Mr. Gould noted that some of the series' success rested in the well-developed format which provided a secure framework in which the director, writer, and musical director fused their talents. But he felt the most significant fact was that the "Lux Radio Theater" had as much as three or four days rehearsal. This permitted skillful pacing unusual in radio drama. An additional factor influencing public acceptance of the "Lux Radio Theater" lay in the strong identification it could make with the locale and the characters in the plays based, as they were, on screen versions.[32]

Occasionally the "Lux Radio Theater" would elicit a critic's eager intellectual response to the content of one of its plays rather than his more frequent commendations for a fine technical production. Such pieces, as exemplified by the following excerpt from a John Crosby review of Lillian Hellman's "Watch on the Rhine," could be compared with the more profound analyses of the leading stage critics:

> I'm also grateful to Miss Hellman for giving me indirectly the chance to say something nice for a change about Lux Theater, whose meticulous and brilliant productions are generally wasted on the most frivolous material.
>
> . . . .
>
> Her characters are to my mind totalitarian individuals whose unrelenting passions clash headlong and, I'm frank to admit, make for perfectly stunning theater.
>
> Miss Hellman professes to loathe totalitarianism . . . but she nevertheless understands the totalitarian individual better than she understands the human or malleable individual. . . . She comprehends--I won't go so far as to say she sympathizes with--the undeviating man as opposed to the rational man. And since the world seems now to be divided into two camps, the one implacable, the other rational, Miss Hellman, whom I consider the first literate exponent of the future totalitarian man, occupies a position of distinctive though unenviable importance in contemporary letters.[33]

Critics were given one other opportunity in the forties to compliment the radio industry for a significant series of adaptations. Saul Carson summarizes very nicely the contribution made by the "Theater Guild on the Air":

> Before the first season [1945] was half over, plays became more flexible, the best radio writers were hired for adaptations and given greater freedom to work their own trade; time, space, and mood were permitted to move about with that fluidity which is radio's chief advantage over the legitimate stage.
> . . . Because of its "prestige" [the Guild] has found it possible to come extremely close to violating some of radio's most cherished taboos, the strict observance of which sometimes reduces sophisticated literature to hopscotch. It has done great plays and good ones.[34]

The final critical opinions of a truly great piece of dramatic literature will never be written. New editions, revivals, adaptations from stage to cinema to broadcasting will always lead to new verbal responses from the articulate members of society. And yet, for criticism to really flourish as a corollary to dramatic art, it needs the stimulus of original plays created specifically for a particular medium. Fresh ideas about a new form are derived when a critic is denied the security given him by adaptations and instead must reconstruct a different pattern in order to interpret a different experience.

It was a misfortune, therefore, to broadcasting, to the public, to the critics themselves, that they were not writing at a time when the experiments of radio's finest literary and production artists were pulsating from the transmitters. The central laboratory for creative activity in radio drama was known as the Columbia Workshop. From 1936 to 1942, the Columbia Broadcasting System presented a series of plays and documentary programs which generated excitement about radio theater comparable to the Abbey theater's stimulus to Irish drama at the turn of the century.

The Workshop provided an outlet for two kinds of artists: those in whom successful but routine service to commercial programing had developed a restlessness for experimentation which would, nevertheless, be soundly based, and those who came to radio unhampered by any prior associations, ready to follow the new muse as far as it would lead. Arch Obler, Norman Corwin, Orson Welles, Archibald MacLeish, Stephen Vincent Benet, Irving Reiss, Joseph Liss were writers and directors who would have been grateful for the assistance of the critics in developing an aesthetic for radio drama. They did receive a little critical recognition in the quality journals and in a few academic publications,[35] but in the main their work was carried on without any thorough treatment by full-time professional critics. As Robert Landry wryly puts it:

> [The original series] borrowed from British, French and German avant garde influences and was the darling of the depression progressives and the campus critics who were then discovering the popular arts including the syndicated comic strips.[36]

Mr. Landry, himself, attempted to re-establish the workshop, after its personnel had concluded highly meritorious service in patriotic programing for wartime agencies. His emphasis, in 1946, was less on the gadgetry of the early experiments and more on literary and musical quality,[37] but the new series was short lived. The Workshop idea was not successful in 1952 when it was transferred to television; nor has it had any conspicuous acclaim for its most recent [1956] broadcasts to a greatly decreased radio audience.

Meager as have been the comments of the professional critics about Columbia's extended experiment, a few examples will suffice to show that they were sincerely interested in its results. Albert Williams took the occasion of the 1940 publication of a collection of plays by Arch Oboler to announce that radio, after twenty years, had now come of age:

> Oboler, mind you, is no famous poet, novelist, or playwright who has merely turned to radio--he has written only for broadcast. . . . With this publication radio is at last formally, and deservingly recognized as a branch of letters. Radio writers like Oboler . . . work simply with the word--the bare, naked word and its meaning.[38]

Mr. Williams, again in 1942, praised the efforts of Norman Corwin: "[He] has steadily worked at infusing radio with the ideas, the lofty prose, the illumined dialogue, the fine verse of the sturdier dramatists of brave days."[39]

The rarity of worthwhile, original radio plays like those by Corwin was no guarantee that they would receive nothing but critical praise when they did come along. At least, however, they were scrutinized and not ignored. Jack Gould was somewhat disappointed in both the writing and the acting in Corwin's tribute to World War II's D-Day entitled "On a Note of Triumph":

> For all that [it] did boast on the air it was woefully lacking in one element--heart. The impression was inescapable that here was Mr. Corwin putting all the pieces together with neat precision yet not overcoming the laboratory technician's traditional sense of detachment. Every mood was projected with high efficiency, but without warmth, enthusiasm or a suggestion of participation.
>
> . . . .
>
> [Martin Gabel, narrator] gave a reading but only in rare instances did he convey the meaning . . . or project that indefinable quality which Brooks Atkinson had so aptly described as being "illuminated from within."[40]

One might apply Mr. Atkinson's phrase to all radio drama. It developed audio techniques capable of creating a thrilling, theatrical experience based on dimensions in sound; it challenged actors to a rigorous kind of ensemble performance demanding absolute precision in cues and unusual flexibility in elements of voice; it produced a few original drama series which had artistic, literary and social validity (especially those inspired by the cataclysmic events of World War II); it captured and transmitted to a mass audience the essence of a few masterpieces from other forms. But the frustrating fact remains that radio theater was never illuminated from within for more than a few brief hours during the thousands of programs which were broadcast.

The Formula Play

American radio audiences were, in the main, unaware that the bright, shiny, slick productions to which they had become addicted were low wattage affairs compared to the intense glare of true theater. They responded exactly as network and advertising executives had hoped they would to the output of a system of program construction devised to supply prodigious amounts of dramatic material regularly and efficiently. The critics, however, were not so enthusiastic. They followed the fortunes of the strictly patterned formula plays with mild interest and occasionally with unabashed disgust.

To anyone who understands and sympathizes with the creative process (and this would particularly include the critics) the rapid, calculated operations of a radio show factory would be disillusioning, indeed.

The process of standardization originates with the preparation of the script. Before discussing the critics' reactions to three different categories of assembly-line drama, it will be helpful to become acquainted with their attitude toward radio dramatists' methods. Albert Williams' sarcastic account is typical:

> The average advertiser and agency executive have a vast regard for an idea. They will indulge in long conferences to decide whether to present a comedy show, a romance program, or a murder mystery. But once that decision is reached, the creative process is, for all intents and purposes, turned off, and the mechanical process begins. . . The result is a ghost

> writing task or a collaboration between the writer who is to spin the dialogue and create the character and the advertising executives who were stirred by the original idea. In most cases, the collaboration is reasonably successful for there are definite patterns to radio programs, and any writer who knows when the chase should start, what sort of device should be used for the denouement or what sort of understatements the hero should use to endear him to the audience, can manufacture a reasonable facsimile of excitement, suspense, or humor. . . [Radio writers] are craftsmen who have learned how to stir up so plausible an hour's entertainment that if you don't follow it too carefully or think about it after you've heard it, it seems almost real.[41]

The steady succession of mystery, adventure, and crime series during the thirties and forties was radio's slightly more sophisticated but equally popular version of the dime novels and nickelodeon thrillers of an earlier day. Critical comment about these capsule dramas falls into a chronological progression from mention of specific series to generalizations about the genre.

In 1932, Darwin Teilhet analyzed briefly but aptly some of the reasons for the tremendous success of "Myrt and Marge," which was broadcast twice a day over CBS to accommodate audiences separated by extreme time zones. He praised the crisp, authentic writing of Myrtle Vail, which lent credulity to the exciting adventures of a vaudeville team on tour. He felt that the fine cast maintained an energetic tempo skillfully relieved by a technique of short dramatic pauses during speeches. The daily fifteen-minute serial, which Mr. Teilhet described as the "most advanced program of its type on the air,"[42] continued to be outstandingly popular for an entire decade.

Another series to be commended by Mr. Teilhet was a weekly thirty-minute diversion entitled "The First Nighter." This NBC dramatic potpurri employed the same leading actor and actress in a variety of sketches ranging from drawing room comedy, to farce, to melodrama and back again. Mr. Teilhet felt that consistently good writing, good ensemble acting, and a particularly realistic use of sound resulted in a thoroughly satisfying theater experience. He was impressed as much, if not more, by the evocation of place in the framework of the show as he was by the stories themselves: "A succession of illusions make the program what it is--a trip in a taxi to a theater off Times Square, the rustling of the audience, . . . the newsboys, a swift patter of sound--clear and sharp."[43]

This critic of radio drama in the early thirties was not so generous with those mystery and adventure series which had undergone metamorphoses from print to screen to air. Mr. Teilhet disliked "Fu Manchu." He was "sick unto death . . . of outrageous hokum [and could not] understand why the sponsors of such an original dramatic form as 'The First Nighter' could also countenance a pot boiler resuscitated out of a past decade."[44] The Oriental doctor's compatriot, Charlie Chan, was also denounced, although for a different reason. "The primary requisite of a radio mystery play is action. Long stretches of static conversation and water-logged soliloquies hold the brakes down on this play."[45] And Mr. Teilhet dismissed "The Foreign Legion" as a "Museum piece" of "pedestrian hokum."[46]

Intrigued by realistic effects, as early critics were likely to be, Darwin Teilhet predicted that the NBC-Lucky Strike 1932 series of police dramatizations would soon be at the top of radio mystery plays. He felt that squad cars with their sirens and crackling radio receiving sets were tremendously effective devices.[47] And so they were. Over the years it seemed as if every last police blotter and file drawer had been searched for facts which could be woven into the dramatic fabric of life outside the law, of victim and perpetrator, of pursuer and pursued. The authenticity of detail which could excite the admiration of a critic fifteen years earlier had not lost its savor by 1947, but, according to John Crosby, it had, in some instances, become downright dishonest. For real crimes to serve as the stimulus for dramatic fiction is one thing. For dramatic fiction to utilize its realistic format in order to masquerade as a public service instead of as entertainment is quite another. Crosby's review of "Mr. District Attorney" exemplifies the maturing of radio criticism:

> Its crimes are indescribably sordid . . . more importantly, they are presented with consummate hypocrisy as a sort of public service. At any rate, there are a lot of virtuous noises at the opening of the show indicating that the purpose here is the exposure of rackets. The rackets come out of the newspapers and in that respect the show touches the fringe of reality, but the details are almost incredibly preposterous . . . [the series] lacks wit, taste and imagination.[48]

As might be expected, the crime plays which had some literary merit were favorably received by critics whether they were broadcast in radio theater's youthful period or in its middle-age. The indefatigable Sherlock Holmes was complimented by both Mr. Teilhet[49] and Mr. Crosby for his appearances in separate series produced fifteen years apart. John Crosby, in particular, appreciated Holmes' and Watson's "sonorous prose decorated with precise and crusty verbs, each as carefully turned as the gingerbread on a Victorian chair . . . It gives homicide a degree of dignity notably lacking in the American production."[50]

What the home-grown, streamlined, 1950 crime series entitled "The Spade Caper" lacked in dignity, it made up for in freshness of style and tightness of plot, if we are to believe John Crosby. This "shrewd mixture of sex and violence . . . contains narration which is about as brisk and laconic as it can get."[51] The critics have a deep seated belief that even an admittedly routine dramatic diversion is worthwhile only to the degree that its script exhibits some compositional artistry. When they hear the results of imaginative writing, critics are quick to commend, just as Jack Gould did with reference to "Mystery Playhouse," a 1947 radio series from the British Broadcasting Corporation: "There is a place in radio drama for a script in addition to sound effects, music bridges, [etc.] . . . And the idea of having a writer rather than a mechanic tell a story on the air has proved eminently successful."[52]

In summary, it is obvious that skillful writing and skillful production in themselves are not enough to evoke the highest critical acclaim from professionals. The periodic tale of adventure, of mystery, of violence not only has a limited entertainment objective, but it is also confined by a rigidity of pattern serving only to emphasize the dullness and mediocrity which would be natural hazards for any program as repetitiously popular as this type has been. John Hutchens offers a plausible explanation for the attraction such shows have for an audience. They combine escape from the humdrum with vicarious pleasures which often include a stimulation of curiosity and a matching of wits with the detective who is usually an interesting character in his own right.[53] Although most of the critics would agree with John Crosby that radio-drama of this type is "short on creative ability" and "long on technical excellence,"[54] they would also recognize that this very technical finesse is the essence of such drama. If a radio adventure play has well paced action heightened by logically and psychologically effective sound, it has fulfilled its theatrical obligation. It will continue to attract audiences in spite of many script implausibilities, which Jack Gould attributes to the difficulty "of trying to start a narrative, maintain uncertainty, and reach a climax all in the allotted thirty minutes [or less]."[55] It will remain unscathed, if not as art, at least as craft, even in the face of such sarcastic downgrading as this concluding comment by Harriet Van Horne:

> All you need to put on a radio mystery is a script costing $250, half-a-dozen actors costing $1,000, a sound man (provided by the network) to fire the blank pistols . . . plus an organist who knows just which chord to strike when the script directions say, "Sting!" . . . And this to millions of people in hammocks, hot little apartments, and cool mountain greeneries, is standard summer entertainment. They expect it, along with sudden squall, flies and mosquitoes.[56]

The blood and thunder formula of night time drama was diluted with the tears of wronged heroines in radio theater's most successful, original dramatic form, the daytime serial. These fifteen-minute stories, broadcast from Monday to Friday, represented the zenith in machine-tooled drama, just as the package soaps to which their fortunes were allied represented triumphs of factory production. Statistics alone will not indicate audience fascination for this type of theater, but they will help. Since the appearance of the first few "soap-operas" in the early thirties, the form grew in popularity until, by 1940, it was responsible for some eighty-four percent of all daytime broadcasting and claimed the attention of forty million listeners.[57] It was reported that in 1939, Frank and Anne Hummert, with the assistance of some five hundred writers, spun the plots and dialogue for no fewer than eighteen serials.[58]

The general policy of a critic who could no longer ignore this theatrical phenomenon was to condemn it with either acidity or humor sometimes supported by semi-scientific polls of audience reaction. Raymond Knight, for example, elicited judgments from his Woman's Day readers in 1940. He reported that ninety percent of the ladies disliked daytime serials because they were too depressing.[59] John Hutchens furthered this view by vigorously supporting a New York psychiatrists' 1942 report that these little dramas broadcast in such large quantity were partially both the symptom and the cause of emotional frustration in women.[60]

Pot-shots in the popular press and a few clinical reports in academic journals comprised the meager body of comment about daytime serials until James Thurber (in no sense a regular critic) published a humorously devastating analysis of "Soapland," as he chose to call his 1948 series of five articles in the New Yorker. The tone for the entire study is set by the following famous prescription:

> A soap opera is a kind of sandwich, whose recipe is simple enough, although it took years to compound. Between thick slices of advertising, spread twelve minutes of dialogue, add predicament, villainy, and female suffering in equal measure, throw in a dash of nobility, sprinkle with tears, season with organ music, cover with a rich announcer sauce and serve five times a week.[61]

Despite the air of sophisticated amusement with which Mr. Thurber regarded radio's domestic drama, his study provided a thorough description of the history and production of "soap operas." It stimulated other critics to appraise the form, and from their deliberations have come at least two general concepts. The first is a kind of grudging admiration for a new style of slow-motion dramaturgy, a retardation of plot and character development skillfully contrived within a matrix of dialogue resembling sentimental, middle-class gossip. The housewives, for whom these "infinite extensions of plot in which the sum of action is inaction"[62] were produced, quite unconsciously helped to dictate the serials' compositional style. To speak of neighborly, gossipy dialogue merely confirms the fact that the cast had to seem like the people next door who had lived there for years and were going to stay for years more. Daytime audience loyalties might be meager and slow to mature but once nurtured they were remarkably long lived. Female identification with "Pepper

Young's Family" was so complete that a periodic visit with them was as much a necessity as a telephone chat with a dear friend. A fifteen year life span was not unusual for programs like "Just Plain Bill," "Ma Perkins," or "The Road of Life." Consequently, the story-line of such dramas had to amble rather than rush along.

Long term audience loyalty was not the only reason for stretching the action in these aural equivalents of the comic strip. The housewife, no matter how loyal, is also a busy woman subject to distractions and emergencies with which most script writers would not want to vie. The solution to this problem in audience concentration was what Gilbert Seldes has called "the master stroke."[63] The daytime serials are written to be heard perhaps three days out of five -- a situation which necessitates frequent summaries and the constant Penelope-like raveling and unraveling of an event. Mr. Seldes says that "the techniques of the serial are founded on an assumption of immortality. We will know [the characters] forever, hence the slow pace of development, the absence of dramatic solutions . . . We do not expect old friends to be dramatic or amusing every time we see them -- we merely like to be in their company."[64]

The truism that misery loves company emphasizes the kind of old friends whom we are apt to meet in the daytime serial. And this in turn emphasizes the second major principle by which the critics would characterize these programs: Soap operas are distinguished from other types of radio drama in the fact that the stories revolve almost entirely around strong, noble ladies of perpetual sorrow. It is Gilbert Seldes' theory that the content of these plays is specifically determined by their tactical style of delay. Happiness is an emotion which demands a swift tempo and yet soap operas can never end. It is inevitable, therefore, that the stylized hesitancies both in the writing and in the vocal delivery concern themselves with the more naturally sustained mood of grief.[65] Impose this mood upon a character designed for a female audience and the long suffering heroine is the result.

Even she, of course, cannot deny the heroine's traditional dramatic function of taking some action. By contrast, then, the male characters must remain weak and indecisive, manipulated by the leading lady who controls the tempo of the story. And so the stories go, bathed in what John Crosby calls that "mood of sustained anxiety [rather than suspense] which is both the curse and stock in trade of radio soap opera." He continues:

> Soap opera heroines are perpetually on the brink of losing something valuable--their careers, their husbands, their homes, their virtues--to list them more-or-less in the order of their soap opera importance.[66]

Lest the male critics be accused of reacting partially to the degraded state of men in the American daytime serial, the following comment by Marya Mannes is included: "This 'thing' is a bundle of inane contrivances, false motivations, and emotional rampages. . . .The process of reason is wholly absent in these daytime serials."[67]

Although the professional critics had little respect for the content of most soap operas, some of them felt that the form would lend itself admirably to a treatment of ethical concepts such as those pertaining to religion and race -- ideas which can best be developed slowly and thoroughly. Apparently they were not hopeless idealists because there was one daytime serial which received encomiums as important as the Peabody Award. "Against the Storm" was conceived originally as an anti-fascist story by its author, Sandra Michael. Not destined for the long term popularity of many of its competitors, it nevertheless, played across the board at NBC from 1939 to 1942, and for a brief time in 1944. The serial moved to the Mutual Broadcasting System in 1949 and continued to concern itself with the experiences of a post-war progressive on a college campus. It was soon off the air again but had one more brief revival on the American Broadcasting Company network in 1951.

"Against the Storm" was praised at various times by critics like Jack Cluett, who told his readers that it was "not filled with maudlin sentiment, facile philosophy, or incredible plots,"[68] or by John Hutchens who complimented Miss Michael's characters for being "recognizable human beings instead of figures carved out of the sponsor's product. . . They can think. They have been around."[69] Saul Carson was highly impressed with the author's "skill in combining a serious understanding of humor, tolerance and adult dramatic values," and with "an integrity that can balance poetic tenderness with a deep anger at injustice."[70]

Once again it is evident that the professional critics do not condemn formula radio plays when they contain vigorous, adult writing which interprets the contemporary world with sympathetic understanding rather than with sentimental wistfulness. Even the snail-like pace of daytime serials might be acceptable to the critics if they at least treated ideas which were dynamic. Mr. Seldes described the serial as "the only art form in which nothing happens between the acts."[71] Most critics would go one step further to say that nothing happens during the acts either.

There was brief hope that the static quality of soap operas might undergo a refreshing change when they were adapted to television. The visual image would have to move, if it were to justify its existence as television drama. But let no one underestimate the strength of a highly popular form to resist change. John Crosby, who early in 1951 had heralded with mock solemnity the advent of television's first daytime serial, concluded a later analysis of seven such programs by stating that their major props were the telephone and the cup of coffee — obvious devices permitting characters to transfer their radio gossip to the screen. Another popular device, he reminds us, is to have a picture of the heroine day-dreaming while a pre-recorded tape makes her thoughts audible. Mr. Crosby ruefully states that "all the girls -- Elaine Carrington, Irna Phillips [serial authors] -- to whom we owe so many years of dramatized agony on radio are invading television, bringing their curious norms along."[72]

Television soap operas have not achieved anything like the popularity they had on radio, and it may be that the form is destined to die out. Certainly, for most of the critics, this would be in no way regrettable. They cannot agree with Professor Marshall McLuhan that these little playlets are very close to actual domestic experience and that they are valuable for their embodiment of the great American tradition of the hometown.[73] Professional critics demand that even this type of drama deal more realistically with the variety of life's experiences and with the men and women who are involved in those experiences.

The term "situation comedy" describes the final genre of radio theater with which this section will deal. Allied in format and structure to both the weekly adventure program and the daytime serial, these comedies, nevertheless, seemed to elicit more respect and even genuine interest from professional critics. Historically, part of this respect may be traced to the unprecedented popularity and valid creativity of "Amos 'n' Andy." When the National Broadcasting Company brought Messrs. Gosden and Correll from Chicago to New York in 1929, they erected the foundation of what was to become a national listening habit every week night at seven o'clock. The old vaudeville routines which depended on sight gags were useless for radio, and, furthermore, straight joke material was devoured too rapidly. One solution to the problem of radio humor was admirably conceived by this Negro-dialect team. As Darwin Teilhet described it in 1932, they developed a story line with a sustained climax like the old movie serials, created (with unusual vocal flexibility) a number of stock character types, and perfected a system of vowel change malapropisms upon which most of their humor depended.[74] The fresh simplicity of the program initially attracted a large audience, and then the accident of a depression which kept people at home assured it continued popularity. Eighteen years later, in 1947, Jack Gould honored Amos 'n' Andy for their ability to shift to a half-hour per week tape-recorded program.[75]

When the program made another shift to television in 1951, however, Saul Carson pointed up a long standing but not widespread adverse criticism of the show. He concurred with the National Association for the Advancement of Colored People which objected to stereotyped characterizations: "My feeling is that Amos 'n' Andy has long outlived its day. . . . In this social context I see nothing 'cute' about shiftlessness and little that's 'amusing' in groups of characters who live on the legal edge of chicanery."[76] Perhaps because of protests like these the video adaptation of "Amos 'n' Andy" was only mildly successful. Broadcasting still provides a living for this thirty-year old team, however. The adroit, black-faced comics are now disc jockeys who reminisce about the good old days of show business.

The glowing success of this early serial comedy seemed to generate a number of other dialect plays which received favorable mention by the critics. Obviously, the dependence of such programs upon aural effects, upon incongruities in intonation and pronunciation patterns not only made them easily adaptable to a sightless medium but actually heightened their comic base.

Gertrude Berg, the author of "The Goldbergs," which became a network favorite in 1928, had the unusual distinction of receiving praise not only from radio critics but from theater critics as well when a play based on the radio series opened on Broadway in 1948. The applause she received then for her "simplicity, honesty, and warm belief in common humanity"[77] was an accurate summary of previous critical affection for the sentimental American-Jewish family comedy which had entertained a vast radio audience for years.

Other situation comedies which depended, at least partly, on dialectal flavor for their audience appeal were the rural or small-town bits of Americana. Leslie Allen told his Christian Science Monitor readers in 1930 that "radiocasting" had undergone an improvement in quality with the arrival of the Tarkington series "Penrod." "In content and manner the program speaks to the listener in a language he knows because he has lived it. That is radio entertainment at its highest level."[78] Another Tarkington inspired series, "Maud and Cousin Beth," was less acceptable to Darwin Teilhet who complained that it was mediocre. Mr. Teilhet did feel however that "Vic and Sade" gave Arthur Van Harvey the opportunity to breathe life into the characterization of a small town family man with an adolescent son.[79]

A shift of dramatic locale to the big city made it possible for audiences to enjoy the dialectal humor of New York. In 1942 John Hutchens recommended frequent visits to "Duffy's Tavern" where Archie, the bar-tender, and his friends assaulted the language thereby amusing "all right-thinking citizens."[80] And Saul Carson was quick to praise "My Friend Irma," which had started as a 1947 summer replacement on one of the net works. He felt this comedy about a working girl was highly amusing, even though he took exception to Irma's landlady -- a drunken Irishwoman. As was the case with Amos 'n Andy, Mr. Carson thought it was "possible to be funny without that kind of harmful nonsense."[81]

This brief list of situation comedies receiving favorable critical attention would not be complete without mentioning "The Halls of Ivy," which interestingly enough achieved success at the very beginning of night time radio's decline. Jack Gould's comment brings us full circle from Amos 'n Andy's broad dialect comedy to the Ronald Colemans' highly educated entertainment. His appraisal stands as a summary of general critical feeling about this story of campus life.

> [This is] one situation comedy where the people talk as they might in your own home and not as radio seems to think they should . . . .[Their] lives are thoroughly adult and literate . . . Hear the English language beautifully spoken.[82]

Whether formula comedies were tailored to fit the requirements of a daily serial or a complete weekly escapade, the cast of characters remained the same. Actors playing these roles were generally not included in any adverse criticism which professional commentators cared to make. As a matter of fact, many of the regular formula dramas could boast alumni who later rose to fame in the theater and movie worlds. "The Goldbergs" alone employed, at various times, Van Heflin, Joseph Cotton, Marjorie Main, and Garson Kanin.[83]

But if the skill of the script writer did not involve creating new characters for each program, it was still sorely tried to fashion plots about which seemingly fresh jokes could be written. The common criticism, of course, emphasized the staleness of situations, of jokes, and eventually of the characters themselves, who, even if they had not been conceived as stock types (and many of them were) became stock types after several seasons and after the arrival of competing programs constructed along identical lines. On the other hand, the critics generally complimented these plays for their polished comic production techniques -- the brisk pacing, precision timing of laugh lines, inventive sound and music effects.

As a matter of fact, the professional critics' opinion of all radio drama, self-contained as well as series plays, can be stated simply as disappointment over the contrast between the sterility of dramatic content and the richness of technical production. The critics were less inclined to be harsh with comedies, which at least had the virtue of not taking themselves too seriously, or with adventure plays, which made no attempt to masquerade as anything but light entertainment. Their severest form of condemnation was to ignore them. It was the pretentiousness of the groaning soap operas as they attempted to solve "real life" problems, or the timid, truncated versions of great stories, or the self-consciously arty, original dramas for which the critics reserved their greatest scorn. Gilbert Seldes felt that radio could have moved in the direction of a kind of expressionist technique since attempts had been made in that direction by Corwin and MacLeish. However, the time and place were not ripe for the development of artistic radio theater.[84] Certainly the professional critics arrived too late upon the scene to give strong encouragement to genuine artists who were bold and imaginative enough to create a powerful new form of drama. Perhaps the frustration of hearing just enough exciting theater to convince them of radio's potential is responsible for the critics' oft reiterated complaint that the dreary state of radio drama evolved from the attitude held not only by sponsors, but by actors, playwrights, and other artists of the theater that radio was a third rate medium.

Television Drama

For the first period of its life (1948-1955), television drama, particularly "live" drama, generated an aura of excitement and of artistic pioneering which nurtured the talents of many new writers, actors, and producers. Professional broadcasting critics shook off the lethargy into which radio had lulled them and from the very start began to appraise the fascinating theatrical toddler. They were joined by a growing group of amateur critics, whose equally advantageous "seats on the aisle" led them to compare notes with the professionals. Stimulated by the response of articulate viewers and by the vast, silent, but intensely interested general audience, (Sixty million people viewed a single performance of "Peter Pan" in 1955.), television drama became the cultural leader of the new industry.

Such preeminence, actually, would have been difficult not to attain. The very idea of visual drama combined with aural drama, of living theater in one's home, is grand to contemplate. A sponsor's elation at having a large audience with eyes riveted to the screen would make him amenable to underwriting the high costs of production. Caught up then in the glamour and tension of continual "first nights," performers and audiences alike are exhilarated by the immediacy and spontaneity of live television theater. This is, as John Crosby reminds us, "a medium that can grab the whole country by the scruff of the neck in a single evening. By the next morning the whole country is talking."[85]

Certainly the critics were talking. As early as 1941, Gilbert Seldes, after experimenting with television programing at CBS, anticipated the reaction of thoughtful audiences who might be inclined to demand too quickly an uncontaminated new art form of the highest quality. He admitted that original material would perhaps be more significant as a creative force; but he reminded his readers that material adapted to television can also be a valid example of creativity and that the arts live by cross fertilization. Mr. Seldes also warned that practical production measures would undoubtedly provide more mediocre than great entertainment.[86]

These early comments suggest a structure for examining critical responses to television drama. Of initial interest will be a discussion of concepts about self-contained plays written originally for television. Then the critics' reactions to adaptations will be considered. Although it will not be entirely possible to delete comments about production techniques from comments about dramatic content, the tools of television drama (particularly the camera) will receive separate attention. Again, a separate division has been reserved for the critics' opinions about the standardized series plays. Throughout this entire section on television drama, it will be evident that Mr. Seldes' reasonable expectations of program quality did not prevent some strong expressions of disappointment. But disappointment is not the same as disillusion, and instead of the hopelessness with which many critics viewed the radio scene, their remarks about television drama can be interpreted as statements of encouraging concern.

The Original Play

There was at the outset the usual plea for the medium to acquire the services of fine dramatists. Harriet Van Horne, for example, felt that one way to up-grade the twenty-five drama shows per week scheduled over the networks in 1951 would be to search out new stories and give writers every opportunity for work.[87] She was joined by Jack Gould who felt that television had a responsibility not only to utilize the craftsmanship of established playwrights but to realize that the theater needed the stimulation of new minds and new ideas. Mr. Gould apologized for not giving the conscientious efforts of the 1952 "Gulf Playhouse" a critical boost. He realized that even though a particular drama might be mediocre, the young playwrights employed by this program reflected, as a whole, a genuine theater artistry.[88]

For all of the television dramas which Philip Hamburger complained had not "a human being in the crowd,"[89] or which Marya Mannes condemned for being "formless" or "cliche-ridden,"[90] there nevertheless emerged, during the early fifties, a core of dramatic literature by maturing playwrights which commanded the reserved respect of the critics. It redounds to the credit of sponsors whose names are now landmarks in the history of television theater ("Kraft TV Playhouse," "Westinghouse Studio One," "Philco-Goodyear Playhouse") that they subsidized for several seasons the energetic, often thoroughly rewarding, hour long productions of talented newcomers to the theater. Dramatists like Paddy Chayefsky, Horton Foote, Robert Alan Arthur, Tad Mosel, Reginald Rose, Rod Serling, and David Shaw were frequently praised by the critics, as were producers Worthington Minor and Fred Coe who supervised the performances of their scripts.

Essentially the critics were pleased with the playwrights' realization that great theater for television did not mean theater in the grand manner nor even in the moderately heightened manner of the legitimate stage. In theme and writing style these dramatists were primarily concerned with making the small, realistic slice of life dramatic or with depicting the small person's reaction to large issues. Since Paddy Chayevsky's plays received more critical attention than those by other authors, they will serve as a prime example of the kind of original dramaturgy elicited by television. John Crosby has neatly summarized Mr. Chayevsky's contribution:

> It is Chayevsky's great gift to be able to write as if he were viewing these people through a keyhole, a style absolutely suited to the intimacy of the television medium.[91]

"These people" refers, of course, to the earthy, sincere, well-meaning but bewildered inhabitants of a technological society who are manipulated by forces only dimly perceived. The leading character of the play "Marty" symbolizes the kind of protagonist to whom critics and audiences responded -- a homely bachelor enmeshed in an almost unbearably poignant love affair. Jack Gould praised the play for its "austere and tender artistry which caught the poetic element that can exist in even the most unglamorous and drab individuals . . . a disciplined appreciation of reality in every day life."[92]

Again it was the artistic reality of a plain family in turmoil over the kind of wedding demanded by the daughter which gave Mr. Chayevsky's "The Catered Affair" a universal appeal. "His people are human," wrote John Crosby, "and even if you have never set foot in the Bronx, much like the people next door."[93]

The critics had some differences of opinion about the degree of control over dramatic elements exercised by a writer like Chayevsky. For example, Gould thought his transitions in "Marty" were "overly sharp" and that he had a "tendency to telegraph in advance his climactic scenes,"[94] while Crosby praised him for an "unerring"[95] sense of theater. But in the main, the leading critics were convinced that Chayevsky and seven or eight other new playwrights were making a remarkably vigorous and affective contribution toward a fresh form of theater.

It mattered little whether the dramatist was concerned with the stress of jury duty on an average man (Reginald Rose's "Twelve Angry Men") or with adolescent bewilderment (Horton Foote's "A Young Lady of Property") or with the clash of ideals in the career of a rising young executive ("Patterns" by Rod Serling). What did matter, as far as the critics were concerned, was that these fifty-minute dramas had believability and high emotional impact. They were the creations of writers who knew how, as Gilbert Seldes phrased it, to make "the sense of life which only art can deliver to us . . . come off."[96] Though their locales varied from city flats to suburban homes and from crowded offices to more tasteful private suites, these plays generally dealt with middle-class people facing the kind of middle-class problems posed by social outcasts in a respectable neighborhood, relentless purges at the office, or by the paradoxically devastating loneliness of our complex, interdependent civilization. The outstanding qualities of these plays were, in the critics' opinion, their concentration on character instead of action, on restricted episodes rather than on lengthy, broad scenes, and on the nuances of genuine dialogue.

As a measure of the critics' recognition of the high standards set by leading television writers, it is interesting to read their reactions to a successful Broadway dramatist's initial piece for the new medium. Robert Sherwood's "The Backbone of America," which should have been a major event in the 1953-54 television drama season, was, instead, a major disappointment. Mr. Gould called the play "trite, disorganized and surprisingly uninspired."[97] He charged that the story of an American family which resists selling its soul to an advertising agency for a publicity stunt had the "short comings of which [Robert Sherwood] has been wont to accuse TV. He equivocated and turned wishy washy. . . . He wavered between a satire and a drama of protest and finished with neither."[98] Robert Lewis Shayon suggested one reason for the play's weakness. He felt that the playwright was unknowingly condescending, that he was not sure whether an audience unfamiliar with the legitimate theater would understand him if he wrote as he usually did for the theater.[99]

The production so aroused Marya Mannes that after dismissing Mr. Sherwood's play as an ironic failure, she went on to analyze the elements which go into the writing of good television plays. She is convinced that "intimacy with faces, with emotions, and with words" are the great moments in television drama. Since the distractions of the legitimate theater are eliminated there is action enough in the dialogue and facial expressions of people. Television is a highly efficient medium for drama. It is as if:

> the power of impact is in direct ratio to the exigency of space. . . . Space means diffusion, contraction strength.
> . . . .
> Television is a place for the poet--the master of mood and of word. The place for implication, for simplicity, even for silence.
> . . . .
> The writer for television should watch ordinary men and women telling stories on programs of appalling crassness and bathos. He will discover how triumphant is the human being --how powerful is the word of truth. This is why millions look at TV--they are seeing themselves. This communication so direct and so limitless is open to the thinkers, dreamers, creators of this country if they want it.[100]

A small but prolific group of playwrights continued to meet such standards season after season. The time was ripe for sterner demands from the critics.

The initial interest with which the critics approached original television drama in the late forties had shifted to a cautious pleasure in the early fifties. By 1954, however, there was evidence of a growing disaffection for the continual melancholia of the new writers. Apparently stories of the quiet anguish of ordinary people stunned by life ceased to move the critics.[101] To be sure, the serious hour-long plays were far superior to, and a great relief from, the noisy mayhem of standardized crime; but a drama can be almost anything but drab, if it is to continue to excite an audience. It must contain at least a hint of exultation, a measure of optimism about mankind's ability to act with understanding, a modicum of spiritual triumph, if it is to justify its stature as an art.

As early as January, 1954, a play about some school children who called a meeting of their negligent parents to teach them a lesson in ethics, elicited a grumble from Philip Hamburger of the New Yorker. He labelled Reginald Rose, the author of "The Remarkable Incident at Carson Corners," a member of "the modern, beat-the-audience-over-the-ears school of playwriting, the practitioners of which . . . imply that every evil deed in a naughty world is the result of the collective guilt of mankind in general and 'the system' in particular. . . .There is not one parent in the crowd who stands up, spanks the children, and packs them off to bed."[102] John Crosby broadened the complaint in May when he charged that there existed "a literary neuroticism that is all over the place" as evidenced by "so many TV plays in which hopelessness is the basic plot element."[103] But it remained for Jack Gould to deliver the major diatribe a year later in August, 1955. He introduced his polemic by stating that the medium was "spawning a bunch of psycho-neurotics who have found it more profitable to work off their frustrations on a typewriter than on a couch. . . .There's only one dominant theme on TV: Life is hell."[104]

Mr. Gould felt that preoccupation with the problems of the little man doomed to failure and loneliness might very well represent a conscious desire on the part of the dramatist to escape creative responsibility. Since the lonely hero is logically inarticulate, "there is no need for a dramatist to sweat out a scene that involves some reasoning, some resolution of a dilemma, some conflict or as an extreme measure some interesting dialogue."[105] Tension and suspense can be captured by the close-up lens. "In the electronic age the writer does not have to see into his character: the image orthicon attends to that."[106]

None of the critics seemed inclined to excuse the plethora of dismal themes on the grounds that the theater should, after all, reflect life and that it was only doing its duty to portray, so truthfully, our confused and fearful society. On the other hand, the critics were not necessarily yearning for sweetness and light, although John Crosby did look forward to the return of the comedians when he could send his "handkerchiefs to the laundry."[107] They would have been interested in characters who had not only strength of character, but the ability to express that strength in clear, firm, poetic dialogue. Robert Lewis Shayon expressed the critics' position when, after seeing a television adaptation of Thornton Wilder's "Our Town," he disagreed with Paddy Chayevsky's contention that the new medium was displaying the best playwriting in the nation:

> The video craftsmen have yet a deal of growing to do . . . . [They] have yet to achieve this kind of theatrical poetry. Their levels of conflict and thesis, their insights are far too cluttered with the immediate debris of life around them.[108]

By the mid-fifties enough original dramas had passed their brief hours on home screens to elicit a second unfavorable response from the critics. Actually, it is partially related to the hopeless motifs discussed above. Although television writers can skillfully create protagonists involved in experiences with which most audiences are only too familiar, many of them seem unable to construct an aesthetically satisfying conclusion for their dramas. Jack Gould describes the difficulty very well:

> Dramas often move swiftly and convincingly, developing character conflict and building to a climax, and then suddenly they collapse. Instead of a denouement, there is a closing commercial.[109]

The effect of these unresolved plays on John Crosby and Marya Mannes was far from pleasant. "You are left emotionally," says Mr. Crosby, "just about where you were in the first fifteen minutes. It's a frustrating experience."[110] Miss Mannes deplores the fact that she has frequently "been excited by the potentialities of a given hour-long drama only to be left empty and cheated of memory or meaning."[111]

One reason for this state of affairs lies, as has been shown, in the type of ineffectual people portrayed in these plays. They cannot work their way out of their difficulties, so the plays have no end; they just stop. Another reason might be found in the time restrictions presented to the television playwright who must see that his piece is spoken in the fifty minutes alloted to him out of broadcasting's valuable and carefully chiseled blocks. However, some of the professional critics are not prepared to accept these reasons as completely valid; nor are they willing to accept a more respectable literary reason which would hold that since the forte of television drama lies in plays of character rather than action, then the vignette and the character study are synonymous with drama.

Jack Gould feels that the more basic explanation is a reluctance on the part of playwrights, producers, and sponsors to take the kind of definite stand on a thesis which would effect a specific conclusion: "Significantly, unresolved endings seem especially peculiar to dramas dealing with contempory issues. Fear rather obviously still stalks the air waves."[112] Mr. Gould refers, of course, to the fear of offending not just an audience seeking entertainment, but an audience which will eventually be seeking a sponsor's product.

Although this commercial spectre which has haunted the artistic side of broadcasting through the years will be further discussed in the chapter on advertising, it is still appropriate in this section on drama to examine the evidence for Mr. Gould's opinion. It is a point of view which needs to be briefly clarified by the reminder that the interests of television theater are intertwined with the economically, politically, and socially conservative interests of the owners and advertising clients of the industry. Mr. Gould supports his position by referring primarily to plays dealing with the business and political spheres. For example, he cites the heart attack of the father in Robert Shaw's "Paper Town" as an unsatisfactory resolution of the ideological conflict between the power hungry father and his more humane son.[113] A play called "Thunder in Washington" by David Davidson sidestepped, in Gould's opinion, the inescapable duel between a Congressman and a businessman toward which it had been building.[114]

Robert Lewis Shayon also contributes evidence to support the theory that weak endings may be purposefully related to business pressures. He lauds the medium for presenting Rod Serling's frank, powerful drama of life in the business jungle. But he is, nevertheless, stunned at the way

"Patterns" damns the viciousness of competition at the executive level and then, in the last few moments, has the high-minded hero of the struggle agree with the villain that rugged competition alone is the way to self-fulfillment:

> It is shocking to think that the moral climate of our time is so committed or befogged that a drama of such seriousness should fail to penetrate into the utter issue raised by the situation and to stand up and be counted on the side of decency.[115]

This failure "to penetrate into the utter issue," whether it is reflected in a drama about the little man whose will is dissipated by confusion, or the play about a big man whose will is dissipated by fear of change, is allied to a broader phenomenon discerned in television drama by Gilbert Seldes. He applies to the phenomenon a phrase first used by Ring Lardner, Jr., the "Caine Mutiny effect":

> Bringing into play a vast amount of sympathy for liberal or unconventional ideas and people and then slapping the audience in the face for being sentimental idiots. . . Wherever the individual rebels, succeeds and seems to triumph, the last word goes to the established order--or all words are drowned in soft music and everybody in tears.[116]

It is as if the playwright, realizing the power he had with words, with emotions, with visual images, deliberately sought to divert that power from paths which his own convictions had established earlier in his stories. The result was a weakening of what might have been dramas of social protest and a diffusion of the catharitic effect an audience has come to expect from deep personal involvement with a dramatic character.

These, then, have been the major complaints about the major original plays for television. The critics demand that leading dramatists broaden the experimental courage they have shown in writing about controversial themes; that they continue to write with feeling (perhaps with more optimism) about the capability of the average person to deal with life: and that they, as well as their sponsors, continue to realize that the promising start of drama on television has produced a country of astute critics thoroughly capable of appreciating highly provocative, artistically stimulating plays. As a mass medium, television, of course, will always transmit an avalanche of shallow potboilers. If, however, it can keep its core of talented writers from completely deserting broadcasting for Hollywood and the stage, (as they are showing a disturbing tendency to do), there are exciting new directions for original drama to take. Jack Gould pointed this out very clearly when he stated that "the need is for more drawing room comedy, satire, and bravura theater. Television drama is top heavy with social discussion conducted in a cubbyhole."[117]

Adaptations

Adaptations not only provided television studios with material until original plays were forthcoming, but they also continued, consciously or unconsciously, to force television drama both from its routine trivia and from the cubbyhole confines described above. The comparatively broad dimensions of the stage play, the vast scope of the novel, even the variety of the short story form, provide a second area for creativity and for criticism in television drama.

Although there has often been little unanimity in the critics' appraisals of individual adaptations, they tend to reiterate one common point which it is appropriate to mention at the outset. Mr. Shayon could be speaking for all of the critics as he addresses himself to this problem, just as he did in the case of radio adaptations (see p. 149):

> An inevitable thinning out process seems to take place in adapting full length plays to television—even one hour

television. Robust characters emaciate into walking shadows. Having no opportunity to know these telescoped individuals in their nuance, we find it difficult to care about them . . . .[Those programs] which do not limit themselves to stage plays [or novels?] often achieve better results. They take the essence of a story and attempt a reasonable television treatment instead of slavishly, and sometimes gruesomely, cutting an original play script.[118]

Keeping in mind, then, that compression seems to be a major factor of adaptations with which critics reluctantly compromise, let us turn to their more specific comments about Shakespearian and other theatrical classics, as well as novels and short stories, produced for the home viewer.

The plays of the Bard generally received less than an enthusiastic reception from television critics. They were inclined to applaud the effort but not the result. Often they were expressing their disappointment in the compression factor referred to above -- a compression not only of time but of space and, more seriously, of complex meanings. After viewing a Maurice Evans' production of "MacBeth" for the "Hallmark Hall of Fame" on NBC (1954), Mr. Shayon felt that the "scaling down for general taste and comprehension [left] the play's nerve ends . . . tied in neat surgical curlers, so the vital fluid of it is lost."[119] Mr. Gould was even more specific about the same performance:

The compelling sweep of the unified whole appeared sacrificed to the demanding technical gods of TV.

. . . .

A protracted series of capsule scenes and close-ups made the play . . . seem necessarily episodic. The tricky camera angles, the overly studied visual perspectives and superimpositions and the confusion of entrances and exits gave too much emphasis to the players and not enough to the dominance of the play. . . .On the home screen MacBeth was too much the story of man against man rather than man against fate.[120]

Remarks like these are not to imply that all tampering with Shakespeare was deplored. Some cuttings of his texts were highly complimented. Philip Hamburger called the Maurice Evans' "Hamlet" (1953), another "Hallmark Hall of Fame" production, "poetic editing of the highest sort."[121] And even Mr. Shayon admitted, after viewing a unique CBS production of "MacBeth" set in the distant future, that Shakespeare could actually profit "from the competent, uninhibited cutting of passages."[122] In fact, he felt that imaginative cutting complemented other aspects of the production resulting in a performance which was a refreshing creative challenge to tradition. For example, Judith Evelyn as Lady MacBeth performed the famous sleep-walking scene while lying in bed.[123] Worthington Minor's unusual modern dress version of "Julius Caesar" for "Studio One" in 1949 was another production requiring innovations in editing and style of presentation which received favorable notice from the critics. Harriet Van Horne, for one, labelled the experiment an "outstanding success."[124]

Although the text and general production techniques might be accepted, the vocal competence of the actors was sometimes questioned. The following comment by Philip Hamburger concerning a "Kraft Television Theater" production of "MacBeth" (1950) is probably a recognition of a disadvantage in television drama which will be more thoroughly discussed a little later -- the disadvantage that comes from actors not being able to live long enough with their roles to feel comfortable during a performance. Mr. Hamburger said that these particular actors:

> sounded for the most part as though they felt a profound resentment against Shakespeare and all his work. They read their lines with a mock solemnity that was, all in all, pretty funny, and they maintained a curious sing-song rhythm.[125]

There were also vocal failings in Orson Welles' "King Lear" for "Omnibus" (1953), according to Mr. Hamburger. He called the performance "gibberish" and went on to say that it was really "a colloquy between an actor and his colleagues with little or no regard for the audience."[126] John Crosby, on the other hand, commented that:

> Welles, who suffers from gigantism of manner and mind . . . was every inch a king . . . and his voice, a redoubtable organ, was superb in declaiming some of the most sweeping poetry in all of Shakespeare.[127]

These last contradictory remarks illustrate another fact about critics and television drama. In general, critical opinions about specific adaptations, especially of the classics, are apt to be less unanimous than they would be for new plays. The influence of theater tradition, of individual familiarity and prejudices with respect to great plays and with respect to a mass medium are factors which account for diametrically opposed views. No better way to conclude this brief discussion of televised Shakespeare could be found than to quote in detail from two reviews of the Maurice Evans' "Hamlet" referred to a moment ago.

> I must confess that a certain sense of astonishment and disorientation came over me a week ago Sunday . . . Maurice Evans' "Hamlet" . . . was so splendid, mobile, imaginative and graceful that it has left me speechless with admiration. Under Albert McCleery, [the play had] excellent fluid camera work . . . an intense, mercury like quality . . . [Evans'] performance was a triumph of intelligence and talent.[128]
>
> (Philip Hamburger)

> Evans' televised "Hamlet" struck me as a terribly monotonous performance. Evans' voice is one of the great organs of our stage but it seems to have got stuck in one key. No matter how great or how trivial the message, Evans gave it full power.
>
> . . . There was an incessant chatter of magnificent poetry mingled with some rather routine stuff, neither one nor the other getting change of pace or significance.
>
> . . . [Re costumes] King Claudius (Joseph Schildkraut) looked as if he had wandered in from "The Student Prince." . . . Ophelia looked as if she had just wandered in from a cocktail party next door.
>
> [Sarah Churchill] was a poignant and sweet Ophelia. [and Albert McCleery did improve on Shakespeare's mad scene by having her] forcibly restrained by a doctor and a nurse.

. . . .
While McCleery's pacing was pretty bad, camera handling was excellent, and there were some memorable pictures. Also the Hallmark Company, which sponsored the play, deserves great credit for undertaking such an ambitious project.[129]

(John Crosby)

Mr. Crosby's last sentence pretty well sums up critical reaction to these cultural experiments. To be sure, the critics have made additional specific comments about problems of television technique when producing Shakespeare and these shall be examined shortly, but in the main, critics are willing to compliment ambitious attempts while still perceiving faults in execution.

Because of their limited appeal, Shakespearian productions have been few on television. But other segments of the literary world, particularly modern stage plays, have provided a welcome source of materials. Like their Broadway parents these video children must run the risk of critical praise or scorn, particularly with respect to quality of acting. Unlike their elders, however, they must justify their skeletonized dimensions and their adaptability to camera requirements. It is interesting to contrast the somewhat eager and naive reviews of the first radio plays, twenty years earlier, with Jack Gould's devastatingly perceptive criticism of an old Broadway play brought before the cameras in 1947. (It must be remembered, however, that critics for the new medium could draw, to some extent, on cinematic traditions.)

The Theater Guild . . . ventured into the strange new world of television last Sunday night and promptly fell on its art. . . . It offered a pretentious truncation of St. John Ervine's "John Ferguson" which left no emotion or electron unused.

. . . The Guild staff seemingly stood out on the apron of the stage and went to work as if holding a Brownie. The consequence was that the audience saw little more than a succession of slides.

. . . The effect [of the cutting] was to squeeze together one emotional peak right after the other. . . .The players had a fine and frenzied time.

. . . Nobody in television, not even the Theater Guild, is ready to ride no hands.[130]

A year later some production companies, at least, had matters under control. Saul Carson thought that one of Philco's contributions to the 1948-49 season was a fine presentation of "Dinner at Eight."

> From compact sets to tight condensation, meticulous care was given to every detail required of television drama. . . . The acting was angled to the television camera rather than to the older theater's larger stage.[131]

Mr. Gould's condemnation of a play for being photographed from the apron and Mr. Carson's praise for one which was acted more closely into the cameras does not mean, however, that the entire impact of an admittedly well-written stage play is directly proportional to the proximity of the pickup. In fact, Robert Lewis Shayon, after watching "Hedda Gabbler" on NBC in the summer of 1950, seemed to feel that the actors (including Jessica Tandy) were unable to free themselves:

> from the narrow confines of the close-ups and close medium shots of the TV cameras. . . .Their performance lacked bite, passion, eloquence, and purpose. Is TV doing the cause of classic drama a service by pressing the old plays so tight that they have neither time nor room in which to breathe the breath of life?[132]

His question points up a factor which critics must take into account whenever they watch an adaptation of a stage play. Even though more ideas on this matter will be introduced in the discussion of technical problems, it is obvious that there is no single answer, since each play and each scene in each play requires an individual decision.

Notwithstanding the importance of such things as camera positions and textual condensations, one of the more interesting aspects of adaptations, as far as the critic is concerned, lies in the fact that his freedom from the responsibility of interpreting a new script often permits him to concentrate on the quality of the acting. An interesting example of unanimity in critical opinion occurred when Tallulah Bankhead appeared in the title role of "Hedda Gabbler" on the U. S. Steel program early in 1954. John Crosby felt that the characterization of Hedda was distorted because Tallulah had become so strong a comic character, as the result of jokes about her on other programs, that she was not truly convincing in a tragic role.[133] Philip Hamburger was not so gracious in permitting her an excuse. He simply felt that this version of the play was "distinguished by a lack of integrity and by a persistant attempt to turn Ibsen's thoughts topsy-turvy . . . a messy, shrill, and meaningless hour."[134] But it was Mr. Gould who prepared a more thoughtful, detailed analysis of her performance. After complaining that she could not be understood because of a tendency to turn away from the microphone, he went on to say:

> But in the large sense Miss Bankhead seemed overly concerned with her performance for its own sake, and the forcefulness of her personality tended to obscure the evil woman she was portraying. The cowardice, deceitfulness and malevolence of Hedda never seemed to come into a gripping focus.
>
> Where there should have been a sense of forbidding tragedy there was flamboyance, the grand gesture and the toss of the hair. Miss Bankhead's pirouette in the climactic death scene was especially disconcerting. Under the circumstances, it was difficult to care about Hedda's plight one way or another.[135]

Although Mr. Gould may have been disappointed in this particular adaptation, he has explained several times why he believes stage plays translated into television's terms will always comprise an exciting and highly effective portion of the broadcasting schedule. A stage production which has survived the trials of pre-Broadway revisions and which has undergone the perfected polishing of arduous rehearsals foreign to the haste of television, or a production which calls before the cameras actors who have made previous stage roles a part of themselves, cannot help but contribute an artistry and a conviction unique to television drama. Mary Martin, who, with her Broadway company, performed the complete musical version of Barrie's "Peter Pan" twice over NBC, demonstrated, in Mr. Gould's opinion, the accuracy of his theory.

> "Peter Pan" was glorious because it had spontaneity and yet was so professionally perfect and assured. . . ..Each jewel was brought to its own distinctive sparkle by patience, imagination, and fantastic hard work.[136]

As the productive labors of the legitimate stage have had their failures and successes on television, so too have the adaptations of novels and short stories. These are, perhaps, even more hazardous projects, since the dramatic values in such literary forms may be too unconventional, too complex, or simply too resistant to the shape of dramatic dialogue for a worthwhile television treatment. Nevertheless, the industry's demands for dramatic entertainment must be met. So out of the mill tended by timid censors and courageous producers, by literary hacks and creative authors, have come both damned and inspired performances. And no one is more righteous in his indignation than the critic who has seen objects of literary art misshapenly transformed for another medium. The following are examples of critical condemnation for the calculated misuse (usually, but not always, with a view toward expurgating it for the masses) of a great man's art.

Somerset Maugham has been both patted and slapped. Although Philip Hamburger felt embarrassed by at least one show in a dramatic series of Maugham's short stories,[137] John Crosby took the series as an occasion to say some kind things about him in an essay entitled "Grand Old Man of English Letters." He was particularly grateful for the fact that Maugham knew how to resolve a story without employing violence. For an example,

Mr. Crosby selected a production of "Winter Cruise" in which "no one marries anyone; no one gets shot; no permanent alterations are made anywhere except in the characters of the people." And he concluded by saying, "On television in 1950, Maugham's stories strike me chiefly as wise, as knowing and -- this would surprise the old man when he first wrote them -- as curiously gentle."[138]

Certainly Robert Lewis Shayon was not in the least gentle in his condemnation of a television adaptation of Mr. Maugham's "Of Human Bondage" in 1951. After describing how Philip Carey's touching search for maturity was diluted to an insipid version of his infatuation for Mildred and his eventual marriage to the pure young daughter of a friend, Mr. Shayon asks:

> How was Maugham's tale honored or the entertainment of the television audience enhanced by this fatuous distortion of the values of a fine novel to suit the hit-and-run hypocrisy of expedient mass media assumptions.[139]

He goes on to scold Mr. Maugham and other great writers for relinquishing their material "to the potential abuses of video mercenaries."[140]

Jack Gould was, at one point, less inclined to blame authors for this state of affairs. In his opinion, "it is the supercilious busybodies of agencies and sponsors who are willing to sacrifice literary integrity for assorted and bizarre reasons of commercial expediency."[141] The particular program which angered Mr. Gould was the 1952, "Schlitz Playhouse" version of Ernest Hemingway's "Fifty Grand," the story of a boxer who bets on his opponent, is double crossed and strikes a successful foul blow to win the money after all. Since the basic credo of television is never to present crime as attractive, the adaptation had the fighter bet on himself, lose the money, but still retain the love of his family. Such tampering, of course, not only does a disservice to the audience by giving them a false account of a brilliant short story, but it also insults them by presuming that they are too "bereft of education and moral values to withstand even momentary exposure to the seamier side of life."[142]

As a matter of fact, the critics hold the view that literary hypocrisy is, itself, a seamy side of television life. They simply cannot see anything honorable in the practice of attracting viewers by publicizing a forthcoming production by a famous author and then drastically revising his material for actual presentation. When William Faulkner prepared his own hygienic television dramatization of "The Brooch" in 1953 (sans weak-willed boy, wife who is a tramp, and suicide finale), Jack Gould decided it was time to include the author in his denunciation of this practice:

> He only betrays a new and promising medium, if he accepts the theory that he will reserve his meaty stuff for other media and condone any literary trash for video. Many famous writers tend to belittle TV as an artistic freak and continue to feed it their less valuable properties. The networks often encourage this double standard.[143]

Brief mention should be made here of the fact that the industry sometimes adds to an adaptation, a tarnished worldliness which the original never had. Mr. Gould used the phrase "cultural obscenity" to describe a "Kraft Television Theater" production of "Alice in Wonderland" in 1954. He deplored the brash gags of Charlie McCarthy, who was only one of the sophisticated gimmicks employed in the program. He felt that a classic of this sort had won its laurels by being itself and that any retelling needed "to be approached with awe, understanding and devotion."[144]

The critics are usually less harsh in condemning an adaptation for being a scaled down version of the original, than they are for the fact that its ethical base has been shifted. They still express their disappointment, however. Jack Gould complained that the entire production of "Treasure Island" in 1952 needed broadening. The initial exposition was too long, leaving little time for shipboard and island scenes; and the action was restricted to cramped sets and cramped closeups. He felt that the medium must make more of an effort to meet the requirements of a classic.[145] And John Crosby simply dismissed an "Omnibus" presentation of "The Iliad" in 1955 as being "a little epic, which is a contradiction in terms."[146] If a more complete production is impossible from the standpoint of time and techniques, some critics would prefer, as they did in the case of radio adaptations, to settle for one skillfully presented episode which would motivate the viewer to read the original work.

Adaptations are not necessarily anathema to the critics as a brief sampling of favorable comments will indicate:

> "Kitty Foyle" (1950): achieved considerable charm and poignancy.[147] (Philip Hamburger)

> "The Last Tycoon" (1951): a first rate television production.[148] (Robert Lewis Shayon)

> "Great Expectations" (1954): The greatness of Dickens . . .lies (at least partly) in the violence of his extremes -- the extremes of poverty contrasted with elegance, cruelty and tenderness, happiness and misery . . . Doria Folbiat, who did the adaptation, preserved the spirit of Dickens wonderfully well. . . .Dickens, it seems to me, could provide a perfect treasure trove of drama for television.[149] (John Crosby)

> "The Caine Mutiny Court Martial" (1955): Superb . . . [Wouk showed] consummate skill in unfolding yards of exposition so compellingly that it became intensely dramatic. . . . After a weekend of this, of NBC-Evans' "Devil's Disciple," . . . of Omnibus' "She Stoops to Conquer," who can say there's nothing worth watching on television?[150] (John Crosby)

Occasionally a drama will appear on the television screen which startles the entire critical fraternity into wide-eyed admiration for the rarely tapped artistic power of the new medium. Such an event occurred in September, 1953, with "Studio One's" adaptation of George Orwell's "1984." It will stand as the concluding exhibit in this discussion of adaptations. The fact that the play concerned an idealogical debate as well as an emotional conflict increased the audience's debt to a medium which has not been noted for its presentation of plays of ideas. Since much of the television dialogue was not in this novel of a terrifying world dictatorship, and since no previous performances were any clue to settings or costumes, the broadcast version represented a genuinely creative production from start to finish. Jack Gould rhapsodized that "the new television season has come alive. . . .Word, picture, movement were integrated to achieve a poetic whole that was truly indigenous video . . . a triumph of the ensemble -- director, adapter, scenic designers and an inspired cast."[151] Even Philip Hamburger who was inclined to be dryly cynical about most television plays said: "The results were stunning, and off hand I cannot recall seeing any other television drama quite so imaginatively and effectively presented as this one."[152] John Crosby, too, was enthusiastic in his praise. He complimented Studio One for maintaining standards which kept it out of "the easy mire of mediocrity," and permitted only one bitter note to creep into his review when he reminded his readers that even though CBS permitted this protest against the totalitarian future "every actor in the show had to be checked by the network's casting office to make sure they had never had a politically incorrect thought."[153] Such acclaim demonstrates the heights to which the new drama can rise. The account would not be complete, however, without the following comment from Robert Lewis Shayon which demonstrates how economic realities insure the rarity of performances like this: "A leading player on the show told me that the client 'hated' the story, found it 'depressing' and decreed that nothing like it should ever be done again."[154]

A brief summary of critical opinion about the content of self-contained dramatic programs on television reveals that the early strength of this theatrical form lay in the diversity of its adaptations. Later honors came as original plays tailored to the peculiar intimacy and time restrictions of the medium achieved a power of their own. Interestingly, comedies were not the major successes of television theater. Adaptations and original plays about serious personal themes and occasional social and controversial themes were more apt to achieve the theatrical power which critics appreciated. As the period of this survey (1948-1955) drew to a close, it appeared that more lavish ninety-minute productions on a bi-monthly or monthly basis rather than the common sixty-minute formats would begin to receive a major share of critical attention and that on these longer programs the adaptation might come into its own. During this seven year period the critics have constantly urged the world of commerce to join hands on an equal basis with the world of art so that faithful adaptations and courageous original pieces can be presented. From such a collaborative effort television theater will, indeed, contribute to the vitality of our culture.

Production Techniques

Live drama on television, regardless of the source of the script, is a hydra-headed art. Its utilization of cameras, obviously, gives it some of the scenic freedom of the cinema, while its dependence on microphones and the time structure of broadcasting ties it to the practices and traditions of radio; but the simultaneousness of its production and reception gives it the reality, the presence of the stage. The complexities of this technical trinity of the theater arts have intrigued the critics, and their technical comments, although chiefly concerned with camera usage, represent notes toward what, as time goes on, may become an aesthetic for television drama. The following statement written by Robert Lewis Shayon, in 1950, sets the tentative tone for all these observations and reminds us again how young the new medium is:

> The unit of drama on the radio as on the stage is the moving line. The unit of films is the shot. . . .As everyone knows television drama borrows the units of films, radio, and stage and scrambles them all together in a crazy quilt pattern. . . . When TV finds its true, functional unit I suspect all the present limitations won't matter. . . .[Until then] you have to admit that the radio versions [of drama] are slicker, smoother, and swifter. They have more pace, excitement, and tension. . . . Until television solves its problem of tempo and rhythm, radio gets my vote for drama.[155]

There seems to be little question that the essence of the television unit to which Mr. Shayon refers will derive from the perceiving eye of the camera, guided by, but not subservient to, the dialogue (spoken and silent) of a drama. Perhaps because of his long interest in the movies, as well as his experience in television, Gilbert Seldes is the critic whose ideas about the artistic importance of the camera are most helpful here. To him, the camera is an extension of the mind of the spectator. It reveals the story in conformity with the way he thinks.

> It is the mind, not the eye, that creates long shots and medium shots and closeups; and the well handled camera satisfies us by being true to our thoughts and, when it acts for the heart, to our desires.[156]

Mr. Seldes uses the illustration of a person seeing everyone in a room [long shot] and then focusing on the one he loves or wishes to avoid. "The closeup here measures the concentration of our emotions."[157] He goes on to describe how the rapidity with which images change as one camera and then another is called into play can transmit exciting action, and conversely, how holding a camera on a scene for longer than thirty seconds helps to transmit qualities which portray characters in depth. Mr. Seldes develops the interesting thesis that the two camera shows of early television, unable to engage in rapid cutting, helped create a style of writing and production which made plays of character development the unique contribution of television drama. It is his belief that as more cameras are utilized the style of video will become the style of Hollywood with a resultant downgrading of quality.[158]

No matter how many cameras are employed, the critics agree that the basic image of television drama is the closeup or at least the highly restricted view. The small receiving screen limits the breadth of intelligence which can be transmitted at one time. It becomes the responsibility of the television artist to so manipulate this limitation and to so fuse it with other aspects of the play -- the dialogue, the lighting, the movement, the sound -- that it transcends itself in communicating its moments of truth. Evidence of this kind of artistry is alluded to by Jack Gould who says that Worthington Miner in "Julius Caesar":

> fused movement, word and lighting into creative imagery . . ..He used depth of field to overcome the camera's awkwardness in encompassing a wide stage. . . .He focused on the legs and feet of the crowd rushing off to Anthony's speech rather than trying to show a large panorama. . . .The play had the fluidity of the films and the actuality of the stage which made it pure television.[159]

On occasion, the closeup medium can even enrich the qualities of a play prepared for another medium. Mr. Gould felt that this happened in the television production of "The Caine Mutiny Court Martial" which had been a stage production. Speaking of Lloyd Nolan's characterization of Captain Queeg, Mr. Gould said: "In television closeup his portrayal acquired even added heart-rending dimension and detail, a gripping and poignant study of an individual's disintegration."[160]

As often as the critics have been impressed by the emotional impact of the closeup technique, they have been disturbed by the fragmentation which the same technique imposes on a play. Although their concern can be dismissed as originating in the natural, nostalgic bias of the regular theater goer (since specific complaints generally refer to stage plays adapted to television), nevertheless, the criticism is worth examining.

An early expression of the difficulty came in 1947 when Jack Gould discovered that the confinement of actors to a small screen tended to interfere with a "play's fluidity and continuity."[161] He was joined by Philip Hamburger, who commented on a 1949 performance of "Kind Lady" that if television was to achieve some of the illusion of the theater, it would have to back its cameras away from its actors and compromise between closeups and distance shots.[162]

With the passage of several seasons and many plays upon which to reflect, critical discernment became sharpened to the point where Mr. Gould, for one, felt compelled to write an entire essay on the matter. There is a dependence and an interplay between characters in many dramas which will become apparent only if the audience is permitted to stand off and watch these reactions. He cites the Atlantic City scene from "The Skin of Our Teeth" (1955). A specific instance in the scene occurred when Florence Reed's shout of "Bingo!" as Sabrina and Mr. Antrobus go to the cabana, should have told in Brooks Atkinson's phrase "the whole story of female cunning and masculine weakness." Instead, reflects Mr. Gould, because one image followed another, the scene "had the impact of a damp fire-cracker."[163] Another play which suffered from the closeup technique was "The Petrified Forest," which, in Gould's opinion, lacked the sustained tension generated by the constant awareness of the presence of Duke Mantee in the room.

> It was a little as if a theater goer did not sit in his seat but instead went up on the stage and ran around to peer directly at whichever actor was speaking at the

> moment. . . . It's not the proper way to comprehend a play's true dimension.[164]

John Crosby's comments about the same play are remarkably similar:

> On the stage . . . you are always acutely aware of all the other characters and their conflicting drives. . . .Television has great depth but hardly any width at all. The camera must dart from one character to another. . . .This particular kind of stage craft in which many different kinds of emotion are boiling in different parts of the room is always going to lose a lot when transferred to TV.[165]

Critical opinion, then, seems to feel that as necessary as closeups are to the building of tension in crucial scenes or to revealing important qualities of a particular character they can, in Mr. Gould's words, "be a crude and destructive tool, destructive of a play's larger mood and meaning, its subtleties, its humor or its suspense."[166]

Certain other elements in television theater have proved to be, if not destructive of a play's meaning, at least a distraction from it. Brief mention will be made of them as a negative contribution to an aesthetic for television drama. Allied to the misuse of the closeup, would be simply a preoccupation on the part of a production staff with jarringly unusual visual compositions. Jack Gould complained that a "Studio One" production of "Macbeth" was disappointing because of its "labored pursuit of distinctive camera shots which tended to take precedence over the words of the bard."[167] Another distraction, according to Gilbert Seldes, is the temptation of actors to play to the camera rather than to each other. In fact, directors often tell them which camera to play to.[168] Both he and Mr. Gould feel that distractions of this sort are permitted because of the mistaken tendency of television drama never to tolerate a visually static moment, as if the unfolding of an idea, or the trembling of an emotion were not dynamic enough. A final and perhaps more overwhelming distraction, since it dictates against audience imagination, is the frequent reliance of producers on scenic effects rather than on the playwright and the actor to create high moments of the theater. Mr. Gould roundly denounced the practice after watching "King Richard II" on NBC (1954). He felt that the immense realistic settings required an accommodation by the cameras which made the actors difficult to identify thus obscuring the play. Even the recital of a famous soliloquy was blurred not by the camera distance but by having to compete with flames from a fireplace in the foreground of the picture. He concludes:

> Are we so numb from so much television that the beauty of the picture drawn only in words must be denied us? . . . Part of TV's great advantage in dealing with Shakespeare is its independence of the proscenium arch and its ability to bring its audience face to face with the players.[169]

As an optimistic postscript to these complaints, let it be remembered that there was at least one impressive experiment with simplified staging during this period. Albert McCleery's "Cameo Theater," in the early fifties, utilized space staging against drapes and cycloramas. His concentration on actors and lines was favorably received by the critics.

In summary, what may seem like unnecessary carping about production techniques was in many instances the kind of suggestion that follows a sincere compliment. The critics were novices in evaluating these first seven years of dramatic production on television. They were trying to relate the known in traditional theater to the unknown of electronic theater. They appreciated experiments even as they felt them to be failures. To a man they have pleaded that the one hope for television is to continue experimenting under "live" conditions in order to avoid the narrow channels into which commercial radio settled and, particularly, in order to avoid abdicating all responsibilities in favor of film production.

The critics are predisposed against Hollywood becoming the chief manufacturer of television dramas. Without attempting to justify their attitude, all that is necessary here is to report that they feel the vigor of the New York stage lends the new medium a little of the creativity of traditional theater and an esprit de corps, a dedication which broadcasting desperately needs. The critics feel that there is a sincerity of approach to the drama emanating from New York studios which would simply cease to exist, if operations were transferred to Hollywood. Critics say that, throughout its history, the movie capitol has underestimated public taste. To couple the timidity of broadcasting with Hollywood's lack of vision would be disastrous for the unstable creativity of television theater. John Crosby sums it up by reminding his readers that "Hollywood's general effect has been toward the mediocritization of everything it has got its hands on."[170] And Jack Gould bluntly states:

> What's lacking most vividly in Hollywood is a compelling incentive to be good. The business of making films is just that -- a business.
>
> . . . .
>
> [Hollywood] fails to realize that television has made this a country of critics. . . .Discrimination and judgment in evaluating shows are being developed on a national scale.[171]

Even if the film industry were to mend its ways, many of the critics place a high premium on qualities inherent to a live production. Their major reference is to the quality and impact of the acting. Harriet Van Horne, who feels that insincerity is immediately apparent on television, mentions its effect on famous movie actors:

> The camera has a way of peering right to the depths of the personality. . . . It's axiomatic that Hollywood's great stars drift through space on borrowed radiance. It's not surprising that many of the cinema beauties have gone home hating the new medium.[172]

It may be appropriate to point out here that New York actors, many of whom have been trained in the psychological subtleties of "the method," are well suited to the intense realism of television's close-up style, although, according to Mr. Shayon, the variability of their "emotion of the moment" technique is apt to be a hazard in the precise chaos of a studio.[173]

Again, it is the acting which, in John Crosby's opinion, creates the stark contrast between the "deadness of filmed shows" and the "vitality and an air of intelligence" of live shows:

> The cast is "acting," in the true sense of the word, a coherent story in front of what it well knows is a large audience. Live television has (for lack of a better word) immediacy which communicates itself to the cast and to those of us at home.[174]

For this first period of televised drama, the announcement, "Live from New York," had been, in the minds of the critics, a true slogan of quality and of theatrical integrity. By 1955, an undeniable shift to film was accomplished, at least in the series plays. The hour long live drama still maintained a place of honor in telecasting, but the transference of an occasional program of this type to live broadcast from the west coast was watched with trepidation by the critics. From New York to Hollywood to film seemed an inevitable progression in their minds. If they proved to be correct, the "miracle of the instantaneous,"[175] as Gilbert Seldes phrased it, was doomed to become history.

The Televised Formula Play

If the half-hour stories of crime, adventure and fun, of gun, horse, and blonde could somehow or other be kept from adding up to generations of entertainment in one brief television season, the critics might be more enthusiastic about them. Although Jack Cluett is referring to crime plays alone, his bored comment symbolizes the general attitude of the critics toward comedy and adventure programs as well. After reading that there were seventy-four crime programs per week on radio and television, Mr. Cluett wrote, "Ninety percent are cut from the same cloth. They are spasmodically good, bad, indifferent, and if you've heard one you've heard all."[176] Notwithstanding the finality of such a summary, this section will point out a few programs which received serious appreciation and analysis from the critics, and it will attempt to record some of the major conclusions the critics reached about these forms.

A crime has shock value, and a play about a crime tends to operate on the level of broad melodrama. When "Dragnet" first made its appearance in the fall of 1951, the critics were agreeably shocked, not by the melodrama, but by its deliberate absence. They praised this series of authentic cases from the files of the Los Angeles Police Department for its lack of frenzy, its understatement, its calculated realism. John Crosby's review is typical:

> Crime shows aren't automatically baleful and we should stop thinking of them that way. . . . Frequently [Dragnet] is a little classic of realism. The emphasis is on crime detection rather than crime commission. . . .To [Jack Webb] belongs the credit for the show's quiet honesty, its meticulous attention to detail, its absence of theatricality.
>
> . . . There is a little too much narration, and too little drama. An occasional spark of humor wouldn't do any harm either.[177]

Just as "Dragnet" added stature to a form which had seemingly worn itself out by repetition first in radio then in television, so did the CBS program "Suspense." What began as a series of skillfully produced terror shows with no significant relevance to the contemporary world, slowly broadened its scope under producer Martin Manulis. He realized that there was taut drama in the classics, in historical fact, and in the true escape stories of our present divided world. Mr. Crosby mourned the demise of this program in 1954, because he felt it such such a successful attempt to raise the cultural level within a particular genre.[178]

Essentially, what the critics seem to appreciate in the higher quality formula dramas is the effort to deliver a kind of realism which will in turn permit the communication of some genuine insights about our human condition. This is the goal Robert Lewis Shayon is seeking when he expresses the "hope that the mass media will stop using the criminal as a rich whipping boy some day and . . . [instead] disseminate some humane and socially useful insights into crime."[179] It is the kind of dramatic function Marya Mannes is encouraging, at least by implication, when she condemns plays of foreign intrigue for distorting the picture of our relations with other nationals, for showing "honest Americans 'taken in' by those cultured, dangerous, morally rotten Europeans."[180] The same critical appreciation is reflected in John Crosby's praise of "Gunsmoke" (a radio western later transferred to television) for the refreshing, mature realism of a sheriff "cast in something less than the heroic mold."[181] The critics are not asking for a revolution in this dramatic field; they are merely urging that these forms raise their sights without becoming highbrow.

Occasionally, the critics are frustrated in their desire to improve standards in this area of entertainment, because they are confronted with the task of evaluating a fascinating program superior both in writing and in production, and yet suspect as to integrity of concept. The 1954 television season saw the arrival at NBC of a series as expertly fashioned as "Dragnet" but concocted from medical cases in hospital files rather than from criminal cases in police files. "Medic" replaced the shock value of crime with the pathos of illness, with the tension of life and death hanging in the balance. Most critics recognized the strength of its writing and the skill of its production. Marya Mannes' report is a good example:

> ["Medic"] is actually more absorbing than gruesome, more suspenseful than morbid, more touching than nauseating. . . because James Moser is a creative writer who is able to build character and enlist compassion so that the realism of the operating room is preceded and given meaning by imagination.[182]

However, as the series prospered, even to the winning of a Sylvania ward for its high purpose, many critics felt that there was indeed a confusion of values present. Most of them still did not agree with Philip Hamburger's complaint that the program was "a gross amalgam of scientific lingo and third rate soap opera,"[183] but, on the other hand, neither could hey accept Jack Cluett's commendation of the show as "a bold venture into he field of truth and realism . . . [whose] honest, forthright purpose annot be compared with highly questionable scenes of murder."[184] Miss annes felt that the very power of the program contributed to "making us nation of hypochondriacs . . . obsessed by our weaknesses to the exclu- ion of our strengths . . . looking constantly not so much for the 'father mage' as the 'doctor image'."[185] She suggested (again in line with the dea of urging maturity in programing) that "what we need is a television now showing us that doctors are as human, as fallible, often as unpro- ressive and profit-minded as the citizens they treat. For a change some- ody should tell us how to stand without leaning."[186] John Crosby was in- ensed that anyone would intimate that "Medic," as good a show as it was, d any true dignity of purpose:

> The chief purpose of "Medic" is to cut down the ratings of its husky competitor on CBS, "I Love Lucy." . . . It has a punch like Rocky Graziano's, but I don't know that this entitles it to any grand awards. . . "Medic" is as phony as a three dollar bill.[187]

To praise the genuine and damn the counterfeit, while peering with red eyes at a ceaseless flow of mediocre theater pieces, is the unenviable duty of the critics who attempt to assess the standardized half-hour shows. It may be that they obtain some relief from the concern with which they approach crime and adventure stories when they turn to observations about situation comedy. Certainly the critics seem to write more voluminously and in a more carefree manner about this segment of television drama. This is not to say that they are not serious about comedy. It is merely that they are more relaxed and less irritated by their critical task, even though, as Gilbert Seldes reminds them, they are treading on dangerous ground. He feels that readers of criticism are more apt to be miffed about slurs as to their tastes in comedy than they are about their other cultural choices:

> We become hypersensitive . . . when we laugh and are told, in effect, that we are braying. We may try to believe that the person is merely trying to be superior, but there is always the uneasy feeling that perhaps he is superior.[188]

Nevertheless, the critics have gone right ahead to express their opinions about situation comedy and so shall this section proceed to examine those opinions.

Obviously, a silent stare (not even a smile let alone laughter or a bray) was the considered response of some critics to this genre. To be sure, Mr. Hamburger did narrow his definition of situation comedy to mean domestic situation comedy, but he was perfectly aware that that category alone would include almost all of the comic trifles produced by the medium. The definition speaks for itself:

> Perhaps one of television's greatest contributions is its creation of a type of program we shall call, for lack of a better term, the Half-Hour-Domestic-Comedy-Situation--Farce-Husband-and-Wife-Playlet-Plotlet-Aberation-Fhawpp.[189]

He goes on to describe these playlets as being peopled by comic strip characters whose low mental ages involve them in predicaments leading to minor climaxes every five or six minutes. They generally communicate by gestures punctuated with "Zowie!" "Wham!" "Kersplash!"[190] which is the extent of the dialogue. It is possible to abstract from the extreme cynicism of this judgment the familiar plaint of professional critics that incredible plots, immature characters, and shoddy writing do not make good comedies.

When the butt of all this feeble inventiveness is the male head of the household, the critics counter even more sharply. John Crosby observed bluntly, "It's a tough rap we Pappas have to take--a single man can show signs of intelligence but the minute he spawns children he reverts to idiocy."[191] A finger of scorn was pointed specifically at Ezio Pinza who appeared in 1954, as a widower with a large brood in "Bonino" on NBC. Robert Lewis Shayon recalled the handsome, confident figure Mr. Pinza had cut in "South Pacific" and said resignedly, "Now there is only the stereotype of pater Americanus, well meaning, terribly stupid, and utterly inadequate in every department of life except his profession. Weep for Adonais!"[192] Perhaps the most cruel bludgeoning was reserved for William Bendix in "The Life of Riley," who, Mr. Crosby charged, was the "stupidest of a whole array of stupid husbands . . . [with a] fairly dopey wife and a mornnic teen-age daughter."[193]

The critics do not sense in these distortions of domesticity any viciously calculated displays of maladjusted society. They are simply reacting vigorously to appalling excuses for comedy. They are only too grateful to commend plain believability as the highest criterion for this kind of theater. Jack Gould wrote about Robert Young in "Father Knows Best":

> Father, in this show, is a human being who goofs sometimes but never becomes a low-comedy dimwit. Mother conducts

> herself with appropriate dignity. . . .[The children's] diabolical tendencies are nicely balanced by appealing qualities. . . .[They are] interesting and amusing people, not comic book psychopaths.[194]

The basis of believability is to be found first and foremost in the script, although the winsomeness, casualness, and naturalness of the acting enhances the written word. Peg Lynch, the author of "Ethel and Albert" received a great deal of praise from many critics for her ability to dissect and then accurately and artistically reconstruct the husband-wife relationship in terms of light comedy. Gilbert Seldes felt it rose out of and reflected "the natural rubbing-along-together, exasperated and indulgent relationship between the characters."[195] And John Crosby felt the roles were played by Miss Lynch and Alan Bunce "with such reticence and understatement that it was not only charming but very, very funny."[196] "Ozzie and Harriet" was another domestic comedy which met the critical criterion of credibility. Mr. Crosby liked it because the dialogue reflected genuine human understanding and the children were "not so all fired full of fresh air and wholesomeness that you'd like to kick them."[197] And Gilbert Seldes felt that the play was so written that Ozzie and Harriet conveyed:

> a special matrimonial feeling which does more for the institution of marriage than all the open propaganda for it in "One Man's Family." These people . . . are pleased with one another, interested, often surprised and come out of their irritations with understanding--not standard in the popular arts where it usually runs to a kind of nagging between strangers that ends in an artificially contrived reconciliation.[198]

This brief survey of acceptable family-life comedies would not be complete without mention of "The Honeymooners," a series somewhat hard to categorize since its situations were so carefully tailored to the buffoonery of Jackie Gleason, and since its surface atmosphere, at least is so devoid of any sentimentality. Nevertheless, it, too, had plausible plots laid in the almost dismally realistic surroundings of a lower middle class neighborhood. Mr. Seldes felt this video marriage was unique but genuine:

> One gets the distinct conviction that no marriage ever existed between [Gleason] and Audrey Meadows until the end when projecting and hamming and plain bad acting falls away and he is a simple, disappointed man, plain spoken and not over the edge of right pathos. [His wife sympathizes] and in that single moment the characters come together in marriage.[199]

The critics, then, are asking that wherever the comic family on television has its home, be it suburbia or walk-up flat, its talk sound like home and its actions look like home (consistent, of course, with the permissible exaggeration of the comic tradition.) Mr. Seldes, who has made the most thoughtful survey of these fictitious families, states the touchstone for five domestic comedies:

> The commonplace materials and the flat language of these sketches are in themselves positive virtues; they are counterweights to the heavy but shallow drama of the more pretentious hours, and they keep alive in television the precious sense of the reality of people, the accent of simple truth.[200]

Although many of the critics seem confident that insights about human relationships will come as an indirect concomitant of any script which is composed with wisdom and sincerity, Mr. Shayon speaks out for the most overtly didactic play as well:

> Within their proper sphere of entertainment the family situation comedies on the air could make a painless contribution if they would occasionally use their devices not as the end but the springboard for tender, true moralizing, the kind we get from "Mama."[201]

His reference here is to Peggy Wood's warm, sane portrayal of Mama in "I Remember Mama," which enjoyed immense popularity for several seasons on television. This was a comedy of sentiment to be sure, but it treated authentic problems with humor, and more, with true understanding.

Mr. Shayon maintains that there is a consciously planned, sponsor motivated, hard and soft rhythm to format plays; that the hard show "accents the primitive, the naturalistic, the irrational, the violent, the horrible . . . [while the soft story may be] sentimental, cerebral, nostalgic, patriotic, informative, even educational."[202] Consequently, within a particular series, a certain situation will be scripted and produced with one or the other treatments in mind. As mild a show as the juvenile series "Lassie" can, for example, emphasize the active excitement of physical adventure one week and stress a lesson in human relations the next. Obviously, he would urge that the formula of nine hard shows versus four soft in every thirteen-week cycle be reworked in the direction of a more equitable balance.[203]

Domestic comedy does not quite describe the swift, brittle farce which enthralled audiences almost throughout this entire period of television drama under the title "I Love Lucy." It had themes, settings and characters common to domestic comedy. But more than these, it had in Lucille Ball a brilliant comedienne whose flamboyant precision could somehow transform the carefully plotted exaggerations of the script into a hilarious but genuine commentary on marriage. Jack Gould charted her qualities as an actress:

> Her gifts are those of the born trouper rather than the dramatic school student. . . .Maybe it is the roll of her big eyes. Maybe it is the sublime shrug which housewives the world over well understand. Maybe it is the superb hollow laugh. Maybe it is the masterly doubletake that tops the gag line. Whatever it is, it comes out the split-second instant that spells the difference between a guffaw and a laugh.[204]

It is interesting to note that even from this type of broad farce the critics demand a basic plausibility in the script. Jack Gould says:

> Every installment begins with a plausible and logical premise. Casually the groundwork is laid for the essential motivation: Lucy vs. Ricky. . . .It is in the smooth transition from sense to nonsense that "I Love Lucy" imparts both a warmth and a reality to the slapstick romp which comes as the climax. The viewer has the sense of being a co-conspirator rather than a spectator in completely unimportant yet amusing high jinks.[205]

Although home and mother is the most popular matrix for the creation of situation comedy (perhaps because television is naturally thought of as family theater), there are other locales and lives which lend themselves to comedy treatment. Both "My Friend Irma" and "The Halls of Ivy" made the transition from audio to video with critical approval. John Crosby eferred to the bachelor girl comedy as evidence that the aside, as a ramatic device, was returning to the theater. He felt that Kathy Lewis' arration directly to the audience not only helped save desperately needed ime in a thirty minute show, but that it conveyed the personal touch of he story teller, a technique so well suited to television.[206] And Philip amburger complimented the cast of "Irma" for its "abandoned, extra-imension gaiety, almost as though they were standing off looking at the haracters they portray and laughing at them."[207] "The Halls of Ivy" ontinued to delight audiences with its quietly civilized wit. It may even ave helped assure the reception of another quiet comedy set in an academic nvironment. Wally Cox created an immediate favorable response with the incerity of his characterization of Robinson Peepers, a modest but warm nd receptive high school science teacher. Mr. Hamburger said he had "never eard him say anything or watched him do anything on television that I elt was alien to him."[208] John Crosby also reacted to Mr. Peeper's onesty. "He's a very real person, not a caricature, as are so many omedy characters."[209] These were all pleasant comedies, brightly writ-n, brightly acted — a credit to the steady talent of their creators.

It was Mr. Crosby's opinion that such modest entertainments filled an admirable niche in the broadcasting schedule. He said of one of them:

> It is an intimate operation, reasonably priced, and largely dependent on slick writing, excellent casting and . . . knowledgeable direction. . . . [Its personnel are] appealing enough to be welcome once a week without being so over-poweringly possessed of personality that you tire of them.[210]

To start this discussion with Mr. Hamburger's revulsion at situation comedy, and to end it with Mr. Crosby's compliment to the genre, would be to deemphasize two important general conclusions and one minor one. Several years before television became a significant part of the entertainment world, Gilbert Seldes wondered whether comedy in the new medium would have to decrease its verbal emphasis.[211] Thousands of programs later, the critics report that in their opinion it is the dialogue which will indeed make or break even a television show. The programs they have chosen to commend are those which are well written. When a series is ranked as being of poor quality, or when a previously praised series begins to slip, its dependence on too much visual humor or at least on tiresome repetition of verbal humor is apt to be cited as the main cause. In either case, the antidote is better writing. Mr. Gould attempted to analyze the reason for the low estate of the "sight gag" which he complained was the dominant motif of the 1953 television comedy season:

> The sight laugh is basically a complementary embellishment [in comedy] not a way of life. There is no substitute for a well-constructed plot in a half-hour play or a sketch, no substitute for the spoken line with the point of view that provides the laugh.
>
> . . . .
>
> ["Lucy," "Ozzie and Harriet," and "Mr. Peepers" have a] basic and recognizable validity to both the setting and situation of each show, and this endows them with the stamp of genuine farce as opposed to crude slapstick dressed up with puns and other pretenses to dialogue.[212]

Just one year later, Mr. Gould reluctantly pointed out that "Lucy," too, was utilizing the method of comic expediency in its extreme reliance on the sight gag. The program had become the victim of Gresham's law operating in the field of all standardized format shows, not just the comedies: As a series continues, runs out of fresh ideas, and begins to feel the pinch of competition, it searches for things to do and is final-y reduced to the level of its competitors.[213]

The critics' conclusion that situation comedy invariably suffers from oor writing and poorer visual slapstick, leads to a second, less well efined, but even more important conclusion. And that is, that the ntire form tends to reflect an anti-cultural bias which ignores impor-ant societal virtues. Gilbert Seldes, utilizing a specific program as a ouchstone, summarizes this general critical viewpoint. He had just seen ne of the "You'll Never Get Rich" series in which Phil Silvers burlesqued ne self-improvement, leisure time program imposed upon an army unit:

> The glee of everyone at kicking art around was excessive, and there was a pervasive and unfunny vulgarity about the whole thing.
>
> . . . There are hundreds of hours [on television] at this level of entertainment and intelligence. . .
>
> . . . In this case the anti-attitude--against art and education and history and intelligence and gentleness--was in high relief.
>
> The acceptable, merely acceptable, second rate pours out like lava covering everything in its path. No one can prove that more intelligent programs--this side of highbrow--wouldn't do well. And no one needs to prove that the exceptional program justifies its place, even when it doesn't pay off. That is social value.[214]

To end this section on a note of neutrality instead of strong dis-pointment, it is interesting to discover that the critics generally have me to accept the fact that regular series plays are not bad just because ey are on film produced by a television branch of some major Hollywood udio or by one of the large independent film companies. Over the years e picture and sound quality of the filmed program have been improved, l directors have begun to combine the best techniques of both media.

It is now possible for the critics to concentrate on the story rather than on the mechanics of transmission. It is this concentration, of course, which still leads them to equate the standardized play with the assembly line production system of Hollywood and to hope that television drama will always maintain a balance between live and filmed plays.

Recapitulation of Broadcast Drama

When the critics' attention shifts from the immediate dramatic stimulus presented to him by the vibrating speaker or the glowing screen, when he leaves the intimate theater to contemplate its broader significance, what are his thoughts? This final summary can be organized as a logical progression starting with the critics' opinions about the attitude of the workers in broadcast drama, the result of those attitudes on the theatrical product, then the effects of this product on the audience, concluding with some suggestions for the improvement of this area of broadcasting.

The artistic appreciation and sensitivity of the critics invariably has been jarred into disapproval at the haste and almost calculated indifference with which broadcast dramas are produced. Ben Gross reports the casual manner in which early radio artists either disregarded appointments completely or strolled into studios late.[215] They, of course, were contributing their services free; but even later, when sponsors became employers and the observable atmosphere of the studio was brisk and businesslike, there was still lacking an inner discipline on the part of production companies. Perhaps it was the business point of view, with its primary emphasis on skillfully produced commercials and secondary emphasis on the drama itself, as well as the prodigious schedules which demoralized the artists. At any rate, had they been writing at the time, the major professional critics would undoubtedly have agreed with Merrill Denison's judgment of radio acting during the thirties:

> No coherent philosophy [of radio acting] exists . . . . The sincere actor accustomed to the artistic discipline of the theater . . . is soon made aware in the radio studio of a cynical and callow indifference toward any sustained efforts leading to perfection.[216]

Mr. Denison listed type casting and doubling in parts as vices, and he felt that in the hands of inexperienced directors there were no rehearsal sessions, merely practice sessions, "no standards of excellence just a happy pragmatism satisfied with 'good enough' . . . Those in radio view the audience with contempt."[217]

This general disenchantment with the methods of radio theater has tended to carry over into television criticism. Twenty-two years after Mr. Denison's article appeared, Marya Mannes attended a rehearsal of an "Omnibus" drama and recorded her impressions:

> The core of all television weakness . . . [is] the diffusion of waste--waste of time, waste of people, waste of money . . . . In the theater certainly, and in the best movie making, there is a ritual and a discipline that I found absent here. There was an aggressive slackness throughout the company (and I believe this is typical) that bordered on indifference, and very little of the cohesive tension that characterized a unified project.[218]

The critics realize, of course, that the development of cohesiveness takes time. They also realize that the one reaction of an artist to a medium which will not give him time to perfect his art, will be the assumption of an indifferent attitude calculated to disguise his nervousness. Again and again in their articles, the critics inveigh against the tyranny of time which does so much to destroy quality in broadcast drama. Goodman Ace compared the production schedule of a movie with the schedule of a television play and left the conclusion to his readers:

In Hollywood, after months of preparing a script, rehearsing it, shooting the picture, editing, and cutting, a movie is ready for a sneak preview. Then there follow the retakes, some re-editing and recutting, and even then the end product is only occasionally an A picture.

What chance has a television show to compete with a movie when it's written, rehearsed, edited and cut in a week? Or even a filmed television show turned out every week or two?[219]

And Mr. Shayon similarly contrasted the legitimate stage with television:

Time, valuable time in which to create drama, to develop character, time and time alone can do these things — and time in its contracted rather than its extended form is present master of TV.[220]

Time is the master which necessitates employing the same writers and the same actors over and over again. The tried and true is expedient, while experiments are time consuming. Jack Gould warns the industry that television "cannot afford the luxury of type casting," because the number of appearances an actor will make before a viewer, will proportionately decrease his ability to create for the viewer the kind of illusion upon which any theater depends.[221] A comparable fate awaits the author whose well of plots may very likely run dry, leaving the disillusionment of repetition to destroy dramatic excitement. The critics believe that this tradition of indifference compounded by haste followed by deeper indifference is a viscious circle tending to inhibit the release of creativity necessary for great theater.

The impatient pressure to fill the daily program log and the exhausted creativity of those who undertake the job are two factors which result in what the critics call the repetitive mediocrity of broadcast drama. Gilbert Seldes describes the process and the product in most discouraging terms:

To present the same thing day after day and still to hold an audience . . . [takes great] ingenuity . . . making the old seem new, by adding small portions of actually new

> elements from time to time . . . making each individual program as easy to forget as possible . . . [writing] in order to be forgotten. . . .This pumping out of never-ending waters of oblivion may be the most serious count against radio as a public service. It reduces the created entertainment to the level of a commodity . . . [like] a paper plate.[222]

Although this dismal metaphor must be accepted as the critics' over-all judgment of radio drama, there remains still the tentatively optimistic view that television theater has not yet lost its complete identity as drama. Mr. Gould feels that the medium is still young and fresh, and less limited in its possibilities than radio. Consequently, it is continuing to attract more talented entertainment specialists. They bring with them standards and procedures of the other arts which will tend to prevent a complete retreat into the rigid mold of radio.[223] "Television," he says, "is being forced to hew to the values of show business and less and less to the criteria of the advertising world."[224] Certainly, it is safe to say, that the critics have seen positive values, even thrilling creativity in many live, hour-long performances. They have eagerly contributed to maintaining the deserved prestige of this new theater. On the other hand, they have already tended to consign the situation comedy and the tale of adventure to the same wastebasket with the paper plates of radio. As the first seven years of television broadcasting drew to a close, the critics hailed the networks' growing number of full length (or almost full length) adaptations of famous plays and musical comedies. These shows, lavishly dressed, and carefully rehearsed, added sparkle and excitement to each season. And because they were special events, irregularly scheduled, the critics took hope that this was a deliberate attempt on the part of television to avoid broadcasting's deadly trap of the routine.

These countless segments of theater move out of the studios into the homes, thereby raising another major question, the answers to which are less unanimous than others the critics must provide: What effect, if any, do these histrionics have on their audiences? First, let it be stated that the critics are aware of the lack of scientifically valid evidence for their opinions in this area. Their pronouncements derive from deduction, from limited observation, from a sense for the tenor of the times, from a shifting of the burden of the proof to those who would deny that these mass media have direct, though intangible effects. Let it also be stated that the critics' opinions on this matter are generally less extreme and less virulently expressed than detractors would admit.

The common charge that broadcasting (of course not drama alone) debases taste, generally brings an industry refutation that they are merely giving the public what it wants. Mr. Seldes takes the offensive immediately by stating for his critic colleagues their premise that broadcasters do in fact <u>create</u> audiences for particular programs. He reminds the industry that it has frequently pointed with justifiable pride to the audience it built for classical music. This premise granted, it is but a step to define audience building as an effect and to conclude, therefore, that broadcasting <u>can</u> have an effect upon an audience. Gilbert Seldes realizes the industry is less interested in claiming the audiences it has built for the "neurotic daytime serials and sadistic murder playlets," but this too is part of their responsibility, and it is part of the critics' responsibility to remind them of it.[225] Mr. Seldes will go further and state that "ideals of excellence and of ways of living" are influenced by what audiences receive from broadcasting.[226] This is no more nor less than a major principle undergirding professional criticism, even though certainty of effect with reference to a particular area such as drama is difficult to ascertain.

A persistent topic for critical discussion in this area is crime programs and children. Although the critics are unwilling to commit themselves to supporting any specific listing of deleterious effects, they tend to agree that the producers of broadcast drama err in two ways: they schedule programs of violence during children's viewing and listening hours, and worse, they make very little effort to create outstanding dramatic programs specifically for children. The critics have frequently called broadcasters' attention to improper scheduling. Jack Gould's column entitled "Murder Will Out" is typical. He submitted a scathing review of a radio program produced by NBC at ten o'clock on a Saturday morning. He charged that in spite of the network's own policy against such content during children's hours the "Adventures of Frank Merriwell" was actually a "saga of assault, arson, larceny and horror."[227] Mr. Gould even printed a sequence from the script to drive home his point. Most critics have deplored the fact that many early evening shows deal with adult crime and adventure themes, and that the late afternoon and supper programs also treat of violence either from gun toting cowboys or space ship gangsters.

Educators' television surveys drawn up in statistical terms of violent acts per week, per show, per minute have been reported by the critics with the general comment that time devoted to this kind of programing prohibits time being devoted to other dramatic themes which might be more constructive for the children to watch. John Crosby expressed the following opinion:

The worst indictment of the picture business is not what it is

> doing for children's TV but what it isn't doing. . . . There will always be a certain amount of Roy Rogers around; the broadcaster's duty--and the parents ought to insist on it--is to counterbalance Mr. Rogers with some imaginative and reasonably instructive program. The main sin is one of omission.[228]

Marya Mannes contrasted the American pattern of children's programing with the British pattern which omits "the violent, the vulgar, and the sordid -- injurious, they unequivocably believe, to the young."[229] She went on to suggest that a censorship as simple as that of deleting the shot and the knockout blow would compel writers to create "people who can live dangerously without gun or fist, who solve problems and conquer foes without resort to force. . . The weapons of primitive man are what our children are now accepting as legitimate (if used by the hero) even laudable means."[230] The same idea was underscored by Mr. Crosby who thinks that the mass media drama of excitement, whether prepared for adult or children's viewing, uses violence directly for the machinations of its plot, not, as did Twain or Dickens, as a natural outgrowth of moral indignation.[231] What is needed, the critics agree, are more dramatic programs which will pleasantly stimulate a child's imagination and broaden his vision of the real world. This could be done, says John Crosby, if the networks would produce their own children's programs and not permit any other agencies to do it for them.[232] Gilbert Seldes' point of view is eminently sensible even though it may seem to be lacking in idealism: "Variety is even more important than excellence, and this must be particularly true in regard to children who are forming their interests."[233]

Just as the critics believe broadcasting should widen the interests of children, so also do they believe it should offer adults a varying texture of dramatic themes. The repetitiveness described above is probably not evil in itself, nor are critics necessarily eager to sensationalize the alleged effects of any particular kind of drama program. If there is any observable consequence, it may lie in the vague realm of conditioning an audience toward a certain attitude or frame of mind. Here again, the thinking of Mr. Seldes can be utilized, since he has examined the process carefully and, in a sense, has crystallized the viewpoints of other critics. Specifically, Mr. Seldes believes that radio and television drama (operating as they do almost solely in the field of comedy or, at least, non-cerebral action) have taught audiences to despise, not only the intellectual, but even the average person who thinks rather than stumbles his way through life. School teachers, scientists, artists, bookworms have been portrayed as silly inept dreamers whose problems are finally solved by the good-natured guy of common sense, who has never had a profound thought in his life. There is involved in this style of dramaturgy (which, incidentally, easily lends itself to a variety of plot devices) a subtle ego gratification for the audience who enjoys it. Thus pleased with themselves, the audience is more inclined to listen uncritically to the commercial message. Everyone concerned with the process, from audience to sponsor to network is pleased, except the critics, who doggedly believe that entertainment can be based upon reason as well as slapstick, upon brain as well as upon brawn. They believe that standard dramatic fare tends to lead audiences down paths of comedy for comedy's sake and violence for violence's sake and leave them with a desire for nothing but more of the same wasted hours. The final outcome of such a state of affairs is that audiences conditioned not to want to think during an entertainment, will also not want to tune in on the media's serious explorations of our human condition.[234] Drama, then, which should open new insights to an audience, actually shuts them out.

Throughout this entire section, many suggestions for the improvement of dramatic fare have either been implied or stated. It remains to summarize a few of the major critical suggestions, as well as to point up one or two not previously mentioned. Since drama starts with the written word, it is obvious that the literary composition is one of the critic's chief sources of concern. To all that has been said about permitting free range in time and theme for dramatists' ideas, Jack Gould produces one more small suggestion from the scholar-critic, Gilbert Highet, which addresses itself specifically to those who labor on the daily or weekly format of the bulk of broadcast theater:

> The way to meet repetition is not to find new adventures, but to invent new facets to the personality and the situation will take care of itself.[235]

And because this next problem will be a constant one for television, Goodman Ace's stern command can stand constant repetition:

> I urge [broadcasters] to place as high a value on adult, intelligent, witty dialogue for TV as they do now on violence, or slapstick or often witless action.[236]

For the writer and producer who are seeking new forms, as well as for audiences who might enjoy seeing them, the critics have a number of suggestions. Not that change will come easily, says Robert Lewis Shayon, especially if contradictory network policies like the following, which can do nothing but frustrate a writer, must be circumvented:

> We present . . . a family show--which all may view without offense to any age group. . . .We usually want a happy ending either accomplished or implied. . . .We want serious plays with great impact presenting personal problems of a universal nature.[237]

But assuming that fear will some day leave the studios, there are at least three areas for dramatic literature which have never really been touched. Most important is the inventive field of satire. Jack Gould lamented that there was "hardly a wisp of satire on the contemporary scene, nor any sardonic and subtle commentary based on personal experience or viewpoint."[238] Surely this could provide fresh material for dramatists. John Crosby challenges another group of playwrights to specialize in superior television plays for the half-hour format, an area which has been notoriously lacking in talent.[239] Finally, almost all of the critics at one time or another have praised the all-star, special event dramas for injecting badly needed vitality into monotonous seasons. Mr. Gould even ventured the thought that "the special evening, with a whole night's programing integrated into a new and perhaps grander design "might be forthcoming."[240] Although the BBC Third Programme utilizes this concept on radio, it would be a daring break from present American television scheduling, which is, of course, a direct heritage from radio's iron-bound pattern of regular, recurrent blocks of identical programs. For the networks to accept new types of drama would be a great stimulus, indeed.

Another department in which they could exert leadership, according to Mr. Crosby, would be in the recruitment and training of actors. Instead of bidding against each other for Hollywood talent at exorbitant salaries, they could divert the money to hastening the development of a superb group of television actors as well as to bringing prestige to themselves:

> For the $50,000 that was paid Ginger Rogers for a one shot appearance on NBC, the network could run a school training a score of talented youngsters for a couple of years.[241]

When a splendid script is brought to life by a splendid cast, critics often bemoan the fact that it is for one performance only. Their demands for repeat showings have occasionally been honored, although the industry has not put into regular effect any of the plans suggested by the critics. It was an excellent television production of Barrie's "The Little Minister" in 1950 which prompted Philip Hamburger to suggest that the authorities consider repeating it on successive evenings.[242] Perhaps this idea was responsible for the short lived attempt on the part of WOR-TV, an independent station in New York, to produce full-length adaptations of famous plays and have them run five nights in a row.[243] Jack Cluett suggested a special program to be entitled "Best of the Week" which would repeat plays the critics thought particularly worthwhile.[244]

Perhaps the most optimistic trend which the critics have observed in the new medium of television has been its reliance on and contribution to the other theatrical arts of stage and cinema. Writers, directors and actors are beginning to move from one medium to another with a more whole hearted devotion to all facets of theatrical art. Jack Gould described three events in 1955 which he felt emphasized the developing liason between the various forms of theater: CBS contributed ten thousand dollars to the American Shakespeare Festival Theater at Stratford, NBC purchased the rights for the first showing of a new British movie on television, and Gore Vidal's television satire, "Visit to a Small Planet," was to be produced on Broadway. Such interdependence would not only help television find materials, it would also permit television to give the other branches of theater a magnificent avenue for promotion. The greatest benefit of all would come from the fact that writers would no longer save their best ideas for other branches, if they felt that adaptations from television were likely.[245]

The flow of cross currents from various arts brings in its wake ideas for new scripts and new productions which necessitates focusing attention on a final suggestion from the critics: there should be continual experimentation in the art of broadcast drama. In 1944, when radio seemed to be at a standstill, John Hutchens proposed that the summer would be an excellent time for studios to give new writers, actors, ideas, and techniques an opportunity.[246] His procedure has been followed to some extent, but as a rule, at least with television, the pattern has been to curtail drastically all live programing, including experimentation, and to devote summer schedules to kinescopes of winter programs. No matter when experiments are conducted, they are an absolute necessity in the opinion of Mr. Seldes:

> [Programs] all tend to perpetuate themselves. And, as they also propagate imitators, they constantly reduce the area of experimentation. This is the only serious charge to be made against them--the idea that Shakespeare or Noel Coward "ought" to rate higher than Red Skelton brings in totally irrelevant considerations, moral or political in nature. But the need for experimentation lies in the nature of our broadcasting system. It cannot fulfill its own commercial function of bringing entertainment to all kinds of people unless it breaks its own formula at times.[247]

he power and the responsibility for experimentation lies first with the roadcaster and then with the public, which must be receptive to the idea change, if not to any particular new form. Dramatic art is, after all, ommunal in its nature. Given the serious dedication of the industry and e artists, it can bring performer and audience together in a thrilling perience which is the mark of great theater. The critics could think no better future for broadcast drama than to wish it frequent comments ke the following which appeared after a modest summer production by Stuo One called "The Storm." Robert Lewis Shayon admitted it was a thrill- with a very thin plot, but it did have one "transcending element--rror."[248] The element was not in the script but "it came into being-- extra dimension, a creative commentary--in every nuance of the writing, casting, acting, lighting, camera work."[249] This one performance, amid the highly publicized programs and the mediocre stock-in-trade of just one television week, exemplified that to which any art form aspires: a rising above the confines of its particular category. Mr. Shayon's challenge to television is the challenge implicit in all criticism of broadcast drama:

> If TV creators would seek to define and exploit particular opportunities for transcendence there would certainly be more peak moments on TV screens.[250]

Notes

[1]Kenneth G. Bartlett, "Trends in Radio Programs," Annals of the American Academy of Political and Social Science, CCXIII (January, 1941), 16-17.

[2]Gilbert Seldes, The Public Arts (New York: Simon and Schuster, 1956), p. 69.

[3]John Wallace, Radio Broadcast, X (April, 1927), 567.

[4]John Wallace, ibid., VIII (March, 1926), 577.

[5]Jennie Irene Mix, Radio Broadcast, VI (January, 1925), 462.

[6]Raymond Yates, Popular Radio, X (September, 1926), 480.

[7]Leslie Allen, Christian Science Monitor, March 1, 1930.

[8]Jack Gould, New York Times, December 30, 1948.

[9]John Wallace, Radio Broadcast, XII (December, 1927), 141.

[10]John Wallace, ibid., VIII (March, 1926), 577.

[11]John Wallace, ibid., XII (December, 1927), 141.

[12]Albert Williams, "Radio and the Writer," Saturday Review of Literature, XXV (October 24, 1942), 44.

[13]John Wallace, Radio Broadcast, VIII (March, 1926), 578.

[14]Albert Williams, Listening (Denver: University of Denver Press, 1948), p. 63.

[15]Leslie Allen, Christian Science Monitor, November 15, 1930.

[16]Leslie Allen, ibid., February 15, 1930.

[17]John Wallace, Radio Broadcast, XIII (May, 1928), 32.

[18]Ibid.

[19]Leslie Allen, Christian Science Monitor, March 1, 1930.

[20]Ibid.

[21]Ibid.

[22]Leslie Allen, ibid., March 15, 1930.

[23]Cyrus Fisher [Darwin Teilhet], Forum, XC (October, 1933), 256.

[24]Ibid.

[25]Saul Carson, New Republic, November 29, 1948, pp. 27-28.

[26]Ibid.

[27]Robert Lewis Shayon, Saturday Review, September 8, 1951, pp. 46-47.

[28]Ibid., p. 47.

[29]Saul Carson, New Republic, October 25, 1948, pp. 26-27.

[30]Ibid., p. 26.

[31]Jack Gould, New York Times, September 12, 1948.

[32]Ibid.

[33]John Crosby, Out of the Blue (New York: Simon and Schuster, 1952), pp. 79-80.

[34]Saul Carson, New Republic, October 10, 1949, pp. 22-23.

[35]An excellent analysis of the work of Corwin, Oboler, and MacLeish appears in William Matthews, "Radio Plays As Literature", Hollywood Quarterly, I (October, 1945), 40-50.

[36]Robert J. Landry, "Memo to Young Scholars, Critics," Variety, February 1, 1956, p. 30.

[37]Ibid., p. 34.

[38]Williams, Listening, pp. 149-50.

[39]Ibid., pp. 146-47.

[40]Jack Gould, New York Times, May 20, 1945.

[41]Williams, Listening, pp. 49-50.

[42]Darwin Teilhet, "What America Listens To," Forum, LXXXVII (May, 1932), 278.

[43]Darwin Teilhet, "On the Summer Air," ibid., LXXXVII (June, 1932), 383.

[44]Cyrus Fisher [Darwin Teilhet], ibid., LXXXVIII (December, 1932), 384.

[45]Cyrus Fisher [Darwin Teilhet], ibid., LXXXIX (April, 1933), 256.

[46]Cyrus Fisher [Darwin Teilhet], ibid., LXXXIX (May, 1933), 319.

[47]Cyrus Fisher [Darwin Teilhet], *ibid.*, LXXXVIII (October, 1932), 255.

[48]Crosby, *op. cit.*, pp. 235-36.

[49]Darwin Teilhet, "What America Listens To," *Forum*, LXXXVII (May, 1932), 278-79.

[50]Crosby, *op. cit.*, pp. 230-31.

[51]Crosby, *op. cit.*, pp. 232-34.

[52]Jack Gould, *New York Times*, August 3, 1947.

[53]John K. Hutchens, "Crime Pays - On the Radio," *New York Times Magazine*, March 19, 1944, pp. 16-17.

[54]John Crosby, "Radio and Who Makes It," *Atlantic Monthly*, CLXXXI (January, 1948), 27.

[55]Jack Gould, *New York Times*, May 30, 1948.

[56]Harriet Van Horne, "The Replacement Season," *Theater Arts*, XXXV (June, 1951), 55, 100.

[57]Katherine Best, "'Literature' of the Air, Radio's Perpetual Emotion," *Saturday Review of Literature*, April 20, 1940, p. 11.

[58]Francis Chase, Jr., *Sound and Fury* (New York: Harper and Brothers, 1942), pp. 189-90.

[59]Raymond Knight, *Woman's Day*, III (August, 1940), 4-5.

[60]John K. Hutchens, *New York Times*, November 30, 1942.

[61]James Thurber, "Onward and Upward with the Arts," *New Yorker*, May 15, 1948, p. 34.

[62]Marya Mannes, *Reporter*, September, 23, 1954, p. 48.

[63]Gilbert Seldes, *The Great Audience* (New York: Viking Press, 1950), p. 113.

[64]*Ibid.*, p. 114.

[65]*Ibid.*, p. 116.

[66]Crosby, *op. cit.*, p. 77.

[67]Mannes, *loc. cit.*

[68]Jack Cluett, *Woman's Day*, XIII (January, 1952), 88.

[69]John K. Hutchens, *New York Times*, October 19, 1941.

[70] Saul Carson, New Republic, October 15, 1951, p. 22.

[71] Seldes, The Great Audience, p. 115.

[72] John Crosby, Herald Tribune (New York), August 31, 1953.

[73] Marshall McLuhan, The Mechanical Bride (New York: Vanguard Press, 1951), p. 157.

[74] Darwin Teilhet, "What America Listens To," Forum, LXXXVII (May, 1932), 276-77.

[75] Jack Gould, New York Times, December 21, 1947.

[76] Saul Carson, New Republic, July 23, 1951, p. 22.

[77] Thurber, loc. cit., p. 35.

[78] Leslie Allen, Christian Science Monitor, January 25, 1930.

[79] Cyrus Fisher [Darwin Teilhet], Forum, LXXXIX (May, 1933), 318.

[80] John K. Hutchens, New York Times, December 6, 1942.

[81] Saul Carson, New Republic, May 5, 1947, p. 40.

[82] Jack Gould, New York Times, January 1, 1950.

[83] James Thurber, "Onward and Upward with the Arts," New Yorker, July 3, 1948, p. 45.

[84] Seldes, The Public Arts, p. 69.

[85] John Crosby, Wisconsin State Journal, (Madison), April 13, 1955.

[86] Gilbert Seldes, "The Nature of Television Programs," Annals of the American Academy of Political and Social Science, CCXIII (January, 1941), 138-44.

[87] Harriet Van Horne, "The Living Theater on Television," Theater Arts, XXXV (September, 1951), 53.

[88] Jack Gould, New York Times, December 21, 1952.

[89] Philip Hamburger, New Yorker, July 1, 1950, p. 53.

[90] Marya Mannes, Reporter, February 2, 1954, p. 39.

[91] John Crosby, Wisconsin State Journal (Madison), December 17, 1954.

[92] Jack Gould, New York Times, May 27, 1953.

[93] John Crosby, Wisconsin State Journal (Madison), May 25, 1955.

[94] Gould, loc. cit.

[95] Crosby, loc. cit.

[96] Gilbert Seldes, Saturday Review, October 18, 1952, p. 32.

[97] Jack Gould, New York Times, January 3, 1954.

[98] Ibid.

[99] Robert Lewis Shayon, Saturday Review, January 16, 1954, p. 34.

[100] Mannes, loc. cit.

[101] Except for Gilbert Seldes. See The Public Arts, p. 183.

[102] Philip Hamburger, New Yorker, January 23, 1954, pp. 73-74.

[103] John Crosby, Wisconsin State Journal (Madison), May 24, 1954.

[104] Jack Gould, New York Times, August 7, 1955.

[105] Ibid.

[106] Ibid.

[107] John Crosby, Wisconsin State Journal (Madison), September 12, 1954.

[108] Robert Lewis Shayon, Saturday Review, October 22, 1955, p. 29.

[109] Jack Gould, New York Times, December 11, 1955.

[110] John Crosby, Wisconsin State Journal (Madison), January 27, 1955.

[111] Marya Mannes, Reporter, November 3, 1955, p. 39.

[112] Gould, loc. cit.

[113] Ibid.

[114] Ibid.

[115] Robert Lewis Shayon, Saturday Review, February 26, 1955, p. 24.

[116] Seldes, The Public Arts, p. 193.

[117] Jack Gould, "Television Today--A Critic's Appraisal," New York Times Magazine, April 8, 1956, pp. 12-13.

[118] Robert Lewis Shayon, Saturday Review, October 28, 1950, p. 47.

[119] Robert Lewis Shayon, ibid., December 18, 1954, p. 28.

120 Jack Gould, New York Times, November 29, 1954.

121 Philip Hamburger, New Yorker, May 9, 1953, p. 68.

122 Robert Lewis Shayon, Christian Science Monitor, January 23, 1951.

123 Ibid.

124 Harriet Van Horne, "The Living Theater on Television," Theater Arts, XXXV (September, 1951), 53.

125 Philip Hamburger, New Yorker, May 27, 1950, p. 94.

126 Philip Hamburger, ibid., October 31, 1953, p. 104.

127 John Crosby, Herald Tribune (New York), October 23, 1953.

128 Philip Hamburger, New Yorker, May 9, 1953, pp. 68-69.

129 John Crosby, Herald Tribune (New York), May 24, 1953.

130 Jack Gould, New York Times, November 16, 1947.

131 Saul Carson, New Republic, October 8, 1948, p. 28.

132 Robert Lewis Shayon, Christian Science Monitor, June 24, 1950.

133 John Crosby, Herald Tribune (New York), January 11, 1954.

134 Philip Hamburger, New Yorker, January 23, 1954, p. 73.

135 Jack Gould, New York Times, January 10, 1954.

136 Jack Gould, ibid., March 13, 1955.

137 Philip Hamburger, New Yorker, November 11, 1950, p. 99.

138 Crosby, Out of the Blue, pp. 82-83.

139 Robert Lewis Shayon, Saturday Review, April 21, 1951, p. 31.

140 Ibid.

141 Jack Gould, New York Times, February 24, 1952.

142 Jack Gould, ibid., January 27, 1952.

143 Jack Gould, ibid., April 12, 1953.

144 Jack Gould, ibid., May 16, 1954.

145 Jack Gould, ibid., May 11, 1952.

146 John Crosby, Wisconsin State Journal (Madison), April 8, 1955.

[147]Philip Hamburger, New Yorker, February 25, 1950, p. 95.

[148]Robert Lewis Shayon, Saturday Review, March 24, 1951, p. 29.

[149]John Crosby, Wisconsin State Journal (Madison), June 20, 1954.

[150]John Crosby, ibid., November 25, 1955.

[151]Jack Gould, New York Times, September 23, 1953.

[152]Philip Hamburger, New Yorker, October 3, 1953, p. 86.

[153]John Crosby, Herald Tribune (New York), September 27, 1953.

[154]Robert Lewis Shayon, Saturday Review, February 13, 1954, p. 33.

[155]Robert Lewis Shayon, ibid., November 4, 1950, p. 28.

[156]Seldes, The Public Arts, p. 12.

[157]Gilbert Seldes, Saturday Review, October 17, 1953, p. 39.

[158]Ibid., pp. 39-40.

[159]Jack Gould, New York Times, March 13, 1949.

[160]Jack Gould, ibid., March 21, 1955.

[161]Jack Gould, ibid., March 30, 1947.

[162]Philip Hamburger, New Yorker, November 26, 1949, p. 79.

[163]Jack Gould, New York Times, September 18, 1955.

[164]Ibid.

[165]John Crosby, Wisconsin State Journal (Madison), June 4, 1955.

[166]Gould, loc. cit.

[167]Jack Gould, New York Times, November 11, 1951.

[168]Seldes, The Public Arts, p. 186.

[169]Jack Gould, New York Times, January 31, 1954.

[170]John Crosby, Herald Tribune (New York), March 19, 1952.

[171]Jack Gould, New York Times, July 10, 1955.

[172]Harriet Van Horne, "Coaxial Cable," Theater Arts, XXXV (August, 1951), 103.

[173]Robert Lewis Shayon, Saturday Review, February 18, 1956, p. 26.

[174]John Crosby, Herald Tribune (New York), March 19, 1952.

[175]Seldes, The Public Arts, p. 15.

[176]Jack Cluett, Woman's Day, XV (February, 1952), 202.

[177]John Crosby, Herald Tribune (New York), February 6, 1952.

[178]John Crosby, ibid., January 18, 1954.

[179]Robert Lewis Shayon, Saturday Review, May 5, 1951, p. 25.

[180]Marya Mannes, Reporter, January 6, 1953, p. 35.

[181]John Crosby, Wisconsin State Journal (Madison), August 27, 1954.

[182]Marya Mannes, Reporter, October 21, 1954, p. 42.

[183]Philip Hamburger, New Yorker, September 25, 1954, p. 89.

[184]Jack Cluett, Woman's Day, XVIII (December, 1954), 12.

[185]Mannes, loc. cit., p. 43.

[186]Ibid.

[187]John Crosby, Wisconsin State Journal (Madison), December 4, 1954.

[188]Seldes, The Public Arts, p. 159.

[189]Philip Hamburger, New Yorker, January 24, 1953, p. 69.

[190]Ibid.

[191]John Crosby, Wisconsin State Journal (Madison), June 9, 1954.

[192]Robert Lewis Shayon, Saturday Review, November 27, 1953, p. 54.

[193]John Crosby, Herald Tribune (New York), June 21, 1953.

[194]Jack Gould, New York Times, March 25, 1955.

[195]Gilbert Seldes, Saturday Review, August 22, 1953, p. 28.

[196]John Crosby, Wisconsin State Journal (Madison), December 17, 1954.

[197]John Crosby, Herald-Tribune (New York), June 21, 1953.

[198]Seldes, loc. cit., pp. 28-29.

[199]Seldes, loc. cit., p. 29.

[200] *Ibid.*

[201] Robert Lewis Shayon, *Saturday Review*, October 13, 1951, p. 44.

[202] Robert Lewis Shayon, *ibid.*, March 3, 1956, p. 24.

[203] *Ibid.*

[204] Jack Gould, "Why Millions Love Lucy," *New York Times Magazine*, March 1, 1953, p. 16.

[205] *Ibid.*

[206] John Crosby, *Herald Tribune* (New York), February 1, 1952.

[207] Philip Hamburger, *New Yorker*, March 8, 1952, p. 55.

[208] Philip Hamburger, *ibid.*, April 18, 1953, p. 110.

[209] John Crosby, *Wisconsin State Journal* (Madison), November 19, 1954.

[210] John Crosby, *Herald Tribune* (New York), February 1, 1952.

[211] Gilbert Seldes, "The Nature of Television Programs," *Annals of the American Academy of Political and Social Science*, CCXIII (January, 1941), 141.

[212] Jack Gould, *New York Times*, February 22, 1953.

[213] Jack Gould, *ibid.*, March 21, 1954.

[214] Gilbert Seldes, *Saturday Review*, December 31, 1955, p. 27.

[215] Ben Gross, *I Looked and I Listened* (New York: Random House, 1954), p. 70.

[216] Merrill Denison, "The Actor and Radio," *Theater Arts Monthly*, XVII (November, 1933), 852.

[217] *Ibid.*, p. 855.

[218] Marya Mannes, *Reporter*, November 3, 1955, p. 38.

[219] Goodman Ace, *The Book of Little Knowledge* (New York: Simon and Schuster, 1955), p. 21.

[220] Robert Lewis Shayon, *Saturday Review*, May 17, 1952, p. 29.

[221] Jack Gould, *New York Times*, March 9, 1952.

[222] Seldes, *The Great Audience*, p. 110.

[223] Jack Gould, "TV At the Crossroads: A Critic's Survey," *New York Times Magazine*, March 9, 1952, p. 50.

224 Jack Gould, New York Times, April 24, 1955.

225 Gilbert Seldes, "Radio, TV and the Common Man," Saturday Review, August 29, 1953, p. 39.

226 Seldes, The Public Arts, p. 3.

227 Jack Gould, New York Times, September 19, 1948.

228 John Crosby, Herald Tribune (New York), July 31, 1953.

229 Marya Mannes, Reporter, October 27, 1953, p. 38.

230 Ibid.

231 John Crosby, Herald Tribune (New York), March 1, 1953.

232 John Crosby, Wisconsin State Journal (Madison), July 26, 1954.

233 Seldes, The Public Arts, p. 243.

234 Mr. Seldes' ideas about this matter can be found in The Great Audience, pp. 266-67, and The Public Arts, pp. v-viii, pp. 176-77.

235 Jack Gould, New York Times, November 23, 1952.

236 Goodman Ace, Saturday Review, October 28, 1950, p. 46.

237 Robert Lewis Shayon, Saturday Review, February 13, 1954, p. 32.

238 Jack Gould, New York Times, February 22, 1953.

239 John Crosby, Wisconsin State Journal (Madison), July 12, 1955.

240 Jack Gould, New York Times, November 6, 1955.

241 John Crosby, Wisconsin State Journal (Madison), February 20, 1955.

242 Philip Hamburger, New Yorker, April 29, 1950, p. 58.

243 Robert Lewis Shayon, Saturday Review, May 17, 1952, p. 29.

244 Jack Cluett, Woman's Day, XVIII (April, 1955), 151.

245 Jack Gould, New York Times, June 5, 1955.

246 John K. Hutchens, New York Times, June 18, 1944.

247 Gilbert Seldes, Saturday Review, November 26, 1955, p. 29.

248 Robert Lewis Shayon, Saturday Review, October 3, 1953, p. 45.

249 Ibid.

[250] *Ibid.*

CHAPTER V

THE CRITICS' OPINIONS OF LAUGHTER, GAMES, AND MUSIC ON THE AIR

Drama may be the most complicated of the broadcast arts representing, as it does, a synthesis of many other arts, but it has never been the most popular form on either radio or television. The dial twisters of these mass media tend to pause more frequently for the punch lines of the comic, the tears or tinsel of the party game, and the rhythm of the latest tune. The critics have paused with them to evaluate (generally in briefer form) what they have found. These areas of programing have transferred their traditions, their stars and, in some cases, even their formats from radio to television. Consequently, the sharp demarcation between the media will not be followed in this chapter. There will be, instead, chronologically arranged sections devoted to comics and the variety program (both adult and juvenile), to quiz and audience participation shows, to popular music, and to serious music respectively. The purpose in each section will be to discover what important perceptions trained critics have had about artistic performance and social value in this spectrum of entertainment.

Laughter

Philosophical and aesthetic niceties aside, people tend to define the entertainment of show business as that which gives them pleasure, and that which gives them pleasure as that which makes them laugh.

Nothing could be more natural than for the common medium of broadcasting to recognize this common definition of entertainment by selecting as its chief pillars of support the great comedians of the vaudeville stage, supplemented by studio trained performers. From the inception of the networks in the late twenties, which made the employment of famous comedians feasible, until the arrival of television, the jesters demonstrated a constant drawing power. Audiences numbering in the millions laughed with them week after week, parroting phrases like "Vas you dere, Charlie?" or "Yuh wanna buy a duck?" until they became national currency.

With the arrival of video, the maintenance of such popularity became more difficult. The sight joke, besides being less adaptable to topical comedy (a mainstay of weekly radio humor), required tedious hours of rehearsal. Even comics born to television struggled to keep routines polished yet seemingly fresh. A partial solution to the problem of revitalizing an inevitably mechanized humor lay in the staggering of performances by any one star. Although the comedians' position in the new medium is less exalted than it was, they still retain a favored place in broadcasting; and if this discussion of critical opinion is to be complete, it will be necessary to examine what the critics have had to say about general patterns for this form of comedy and specific skills in its presentation.

Stripped of the careful and, in some cases, complex story lines of situation comedy or full length comedy, the humorous platform routine, as Robert Lewis Shayon reminds us, is "a chain of gags . . . and the idea is to have the gags follow each other in quick succession . . . [with] this precipitate rush from punch line to yak [making] for pace and tempo."[1] The process has been for the writer who composes the gag to collaborate with the comedian who brings to the gag his polished sense of vocal delivery (particularly timing) and in the case of television an equally polished pattern of gestures and facial expressions. The collaboration usually results in the creation of a character who transforms each new situation into humor, with his own personality remaining unchanged.

Although the number of comedians in broadcasting has given us a variety of characterizations ranging from the malapropistic Gracie Allen to the haltingly frustrated George Gobel, the basic scheme of their routines has been the comedy of insult. This, according to Jack Gould, is "the adult manifestation in humor of the youngster's urge to unseat a top hat with a well directed snowball."[2] Sometimes the insults spill over into a rising crescendo of weekly jousts between opposing comedians, as it did with Fred Allen and Jack Benny in the forties. At other times, it takes the form of self-disparagement. Often the comedy of insult provides an excellent opportunity for a secondary character to hurl the sharpest barb. Mr. Gould points to Jack Benny's Rochester, Bob Hope's Colonna, Fred Allen's Claghorn:

> [The stooge] enables his listener to share in mankind's most ennobling experience--to tell somebody off.
>
> . . . .
>
> The dramatic device is to present . . . a gag [for the star] which appears unlikely to be topped. It is then that the stooge leaps to the kill, cutting down Mr. Big with a better line which is all the more humorous because it comes from the unexpected quarter.[3]

Cutting Mr. Big down to size need not only concern letting Jack Benny or Bob Hope know what cheap skates they are. In a world of grave issues and graver men, the technique of comic insult can be used with equal effectiveness to reduce our worry or anger to laughter. The topical joke, carried to satiric perfection by Fred Allen, is an admirable device for writers who must meet a weekly deadline. It might be called the comedy of social rather than personal insult.

Notwithstanding the remarkable stamina of this theme with variations, Mr. Crosby and Mr. Seldes feel that its mechanized operation in broadcasting tends to dilute the true personality either of the comedian or the character he has created. John Crosby is convinced "that the essence of comedy, the best of it, was the imminence of tragedy." He recalls audience sympathy for the poignant Charlie Chaplin or Buster Keaton and goes on to say:

> The present crop of millionaire comedians--the Milton Berles, Bob Hopes, Bing Crosbys, Jack Bennys--are a different breed. You feel that nothing untoward can happen to these wealthy folk. Chaplin was richer than all of them but he kept his private personality entirely separate from his public one. The contemporary comic, with his jokes about his racehorses, his ball clubs, and his bank account, doesn't.[4]

Mr. Crosby implies that this personal topicality which helps supply the comic with desparately needed material also tends to destroy him in our affections.

Gilbert Seldes reaches a somewhat similar conclusion, although by a more devious route. It is his opinion that broadcast comedy utilizes two different elements: "the human being making the comedy [eg., Jimmy Durante] . . . and the character created by this human being [eg., the parsimonious Jack Benny] ." When, in the frantic search for material, "writers and producers begin to perfect situations and gags, they multiply the activity of the created character and proportionately diminish the strength of the personality"[5] which can be a serious detriment in broadcasting. In any event, the master comic depends for his success not only upon evoking laughter but upon establishing a genuine bond between himself (or the character he has created) and the audience.

Having briefly established the basic framework within which comedy is constructed and realizing a little of the subtle hazards of the art, let us review the critics' records to see what adaptations and techniques important comedians have developed to keep America laughing in its living rooms. It did not take long for comics to realize that a radio studio was not a stage, and that gags delivered over the air often fell flat unaccompanied by the visual slapstick with which they had always been integrated. Aural slapstick through cleverly manipulated sound effects was an alternative successfully developed by "Stoopnagle and Bud" in the early thirties. Darwin Teilhet complimented them highly but recognized a limitation to their contrived humor:

> They shed no inward comic light upon their material . . . [Their props] are deliberately manufactured and presented for their own separate and unrelated interest instead of being employed to build up comic force.[6]

This early experiment in placing major emphasis on the comic possibilities of sound effects reached its zenith in the frenzied but wearing clatter of the Spike Jones "orchestra." It became, of course, a necessary although not major device in most comedy routines, with the outstanding example being the resounding din emanating from the hall closet of the McGee's whenever the door was opened.

Radio necessitated the development of other techniques to compensate for the lack of sight. Leslie Allen reported in the <u>Christian Science Monitor</u> for April 5, 1930, that Mr. Raymond Knight, producer of the "Cuckoo Hour" for NBC, trained his casts to "emphasize, reiterate, punch" the humor home; and to assist them, he cued in comic music to supply the "black out punch" typical of the climax of laughter attended by cutting the stage lights in a theater performance. It is interesting to note that in the same article Mr. Allen called upon critics to be charitable in evaluating radio humor since performers were in the unique situation of having to proceed without the guidance of immediate audience response.

As radio comedy faltered its way through these early seasons, it became apparent that dialogue with some revelation of character in its gags was basic. In contrast to the serialized ventures of "Amos 'n' Andy" and their many imitators, a type of relaxed, plotless but specifically verbal humor of character began to achieve success in regular quarter-hour sketches during the thirties. Darwin Teilhet's negative view of these programs is understandable. In their quiet, somewhat indifferent, stream-of-consciousness style, they reflected little of the hardened, polished routines of comic tradition. He accused "Clara, Lu 'n' Em" of being "unable to decide whether they have a burlesque, a satire, or a realistic version of the lives of their wretchedly tiresome smalltown gossips."[7] And he dismissed Mr. and Mrs. Goodman Ace by saying that although they "may be bridge experts, they would not qualify as expert actors."[8]

On the other hand, there was an intimacy and an absence of force in these wisps of comedy which made their short but periodic visits welcome season after season. The characters in these programs were not acting in a theatrical sense; they were visiting, like the neighbors next door. Audiences chuckled at their eccentricities and looked forward to the next call. It may be that Leslie Allen tuned in on the mid-west trio while their humor was still fresh, but his review of "Clara, Lu 'n' Em," written two years before Mr. Teilhet's, represents an opposite reaction:

> Clare, Lu and Em roam carelessly from one subject to another and back again, if an idea oozes out from a subject

> that seemed to be squeezed dry already. For radio humor that expresses character and for that reason appeals to adult intelligence, Clara, Lu, and Em have no superiors.[9]

If seniority is any indication of comic talent, the Ace's were remarkably talented. Although their sketches had made them network favorites for over fifteen years (see p. 70), they might easily have been ignored after a two year vacation. Nevertheless, they were again warmly received by the critics in 1948, and the following excerpts from John Crosby's welcome analyzes their comic skills:

> Jane Ace is another Dulcy, another Irma, another Gracie Allen, another Mrs. Malaprop, though in her defense it ought to be added she got there ahead of most of them. She is a woman of sunny amiability who takes an extremely literal and subjective view of everything around her. This makes life extremely easy for her and extremely difficult for everyone else.
>
> . . . .
>
> Goodman Ace, the brains of this team, tags along behind his wife acting as narrator for her mishaps in a dry, resigned voice (one of the few intelligent voices on the air) and interjecting witty comment. The couple's conversations are usually masterpieces of cross purpose.
>
> . . . .
>
> While most of the action revolves around the scrapes Jane gets into, Ace, who writes the scripts, uses his program to take a few pokes at radio, the newspapers and the world in general.[10]

The indigenous comedy of sound effect and of informal rambling was highly successful in radio, but so also were the refurbished routines of long-established stage comedians who began to focus their formidable talents exclusively on verbal fireworks. So well known did the varied formats of these comedy programs become, that the professional critics seldom took time to describe them, choosing, instead, to present capsule judgments of each star. Occasionally the shift of a program to television motivated a fresh appraisal of a comic's skill. The ensuing discussion will briefly trace the critical fortunes of leading comedians as they trod the difficult boards from microphone to camera.

Burns and Allen, Bob Hope, and Eddie Cantor were famous for the energetic speed of their comic delivery. The long suffering husband and the nit-wit wife were both complimented by Darwin Teilhet and Ring Lardner for the delightful humor they brought to the 1932-33 radio season. Gracie Allen was, in Mr. Teilhet's opinion, the "cleverest comedienne on the air,"[11] while Mr. Lardner appreciated being able to point to Gracie as "the best evidence I know of that a real comic can make you laugh without making you blush."[12] Gilbert Seldes evaluated their contribution twenty years later when George and Gracie were achieving success on television:

> They still use a lot of verbal comedy . . . and it is very, very good. . . . In the creation of instant merriment, Gracie easily comes first; in the creation of the atmosphere of comedy, of which the quick laugh-getter is only a part, and not the best part at that, George is the prime mover.[13]

A sassier, more brittle speed characterizes the style of Bob Hope who has always depended upon the verbal wisecrack even in his television appearances. John Hutchens, at a time [1941] when comedy programs were the most popular on the air, admired Mr. Hope's "lively material, good delivery, and air of spontaneity"[14] more than he did the talent of any other comedian. However, Hope has also been criticized for lacking adult material.[15] In Mr. Seldes' estimation, Bob Hope has managed to fuse both his personality and his technique into the delivery of a constant theme: "'a funny thing happened to me on the way to the studio' routine."[16]

The last example of the speed comics is Eddie Cantor who somewhat incongruously manages to combine immense vitality with immense sentimentality. Ben Gross describes him as "lacking subtlety" but being "rich in sentimental corn [and] broad strokes of comedy."[17] In a younger period of his life, Mr. Cantor could have made the transition from audio to video even more easily than Gracie Allen or Bob Hope, because his famous rolling eyes and expressive body would have met the new medium's visual demands. However, Mr. Cantor is an aging man whose appearances on television are moments of appreciative respect, if we are to believe Jack Cluett, rather than periods of scintillating comedy. The following comment by Mr. Cluett reveals the high regard our nation reserves for its top jesters, who are noted almost as much for community service as they are for their comic spirit. He is justifying the applause given to a man who no longer has a voice or dancing ability:

> [Cantor] receives it for a lifetime of service, family devotion, spunk and clean living and not for a corny Weber and Fields skit. . . . The cheers are for a sixty year old man who lost everything in the '29 crash and then began all over again at the bottom . . . for his unselfish work in War Bond drives . . . for the good old days.[18]

Satire has always stood in sharp contrast to sentiment and bears almost no relation to nonsense. Broadcasting which can devote countless hours to comedy in the first two forms and can even countenance some topical jokes at the expense of serious national issues, has almost no sense of humor about itself. This is related, of course, to its orientation toward the business world. Consequently, the few comedians whose specialty is satire and who feel the need to sling their barbs in all directions are a rare but important province for the professional critic. In the early thirties, Raymond Knight burlesqued radio programing to the delight of Gilbert Seldes.[19] After minor skirmishes between sponsors and Arthur Godfrey and Henry Morgan who satirized commercials in the forties, Bob Elliot and Ray Goulding established themselves as partial heirs to this minor kingdom of comedy. Jack Cluett felt theirs was the most amusing comedy since the days of Stoopnagle and Bud, and he urged NBC to restrict their appearances so they would not run out of material.[20] Their comedy, however, seemed too labored on television, and they quickly returned to radio.

But the most famous satirist ever permitted to broadcast on a continuing basis was Fred Allen. As early as March, 1933, Ring Lardner commended his own caution for postponing criticism of Mr. Allen until his first two programs. Finally convinced that Fred's "originality" and "good comedy sense" were operating, Lardner predicted, "He's up there to stay."[21] In October of that same year, Darwin Teilhet approved of his "uneasily dry witticisms."[22] A decade later, John Hutchens noted with admiration how Mr. Allen's "flat, nasal voice fits the oblique satire in his material,"[23] and in 1948, John Crosby singled him out for praise because he had a mind of his own which drew its jokes from "newspapers not a joke file."[24] It was this last element in Mr. Allen's comic genius which the critics most appreciated. Each week for years, Fred Allen wrote the scripts for his 'casts, building sketches around current news events, regional foibles, and broadcasting's eccentricities. He frequently complained about the studios' censorship of his material because the barbs were entirely too sharp.[25] And in the end, it was this kind of employer tampering which prevented his successful transition to television. The disgust of the critics was general. Philip Hamburger could only express bewilderment that:

> A man with the great comic resources of Fred Allen should have such a hard time finding an outlet for his abilities on television. . . . Fred's "Judge For Yourself" is a program, the details of which defy rational explanation. . . . If someone would just let him alone people might be laughing from one end of the country to another.[26]

Jack Gould interpreted his difficulty as being "cast as a performer which he is not rather than a humorist which he is . . . Fred doesn't need the seltzer bottle; he has a mind which TV has not yet discovered."[27] Gilbert Seldes summed up the tragedy of a free comic spirit which, though it was steadily (not spectacularly) popular for twenty years, was continually at odds with the cautiously regulated medium broadcasting had become:

> The great failure has been with Fred Allen, for whom everything was done and overdone, always on the presumption that to let him do what came naturally would not work.[28]

Although the industry may have failed to tap fully the comic energy of Mr. Allen, it, of course, engaged many other comedians who developed techniques for television with varying degrees of success. As radio comedy necessitated the sloughing off of slapstick, television comedy, at least in its earliest seasons after World War II, motivated slapstick's return chiefly in the person of Milton Berle. This comedian's television career (He was never an outstanding success in radio.) has interested the critics very much because of its shifting pattern. In the late forties, his wild gyrations before the cameras made him the most popular performer in the country. Even the critics, who were somewhat pained by Berle's antics, felt that he was at least testing the medium's sight possibilities to an unusual degree.

A careful inspection of his comic mannerisms by Philip Hamburger resulted in this detailed, rather repelling description: (1) "He puts his hands in somebody's mouth." (2) "He crooks his elbow and simultaneously bends his fingers in a claw-like gesture that gives him the air of a singularly distressed primate." (3) "He twists his mouth and reveals his teeth in an exertion that, at least to me, signifies nothing."[29]

John Crosby said that these early programs were successful only because Mr. Berle gave the audience twice as many frayed jokes as anyone else.[30] And Gilbert Seldes referred to the comedian as "the triumph of the hotfoot," a man whose "vulgarity flowed like the Mississippi, muddy but powerful," who "spent his strength in knocking out the audience."[31] Even though Mr. Seldes was little amused by Berle, he concluded that his success was based on television's remarkable ability to transmit the reality of a person. Because the mannerisms and the vitality were the "natural" Berle, the audience saw a "genuine man" and were pleased.[32]

The natural man could not, however, save himself from an even more natural waning of popularity as television programing increased in scope and grandeur. But, with the amazed approval of the critics, Milton Berle opened the 1952 season not only with a successful new format, but with an almost entirely new personality. Instead of small units of slapstick interspersed with music, the show became a well-plotted hour-long musical comedy. Instead of a bawdy ego-centric who had to dominate an entire routine, Berle retained all of his old energy but channeled it into a more likable character who had learned to play with others. Chief credit for this transformation (startlingly unusual in broadcasting's rigid world) was given to Goodman Ace, who supervised the writing of what John Crosby described as a comedy of character cleverly constructed around a few basic, humorous traits upon which variations could be played and into which guests could be integrated week after week.[33] Jack Gould praised Mr. Berle for learning how to lower his voice, how to throw away a line, how to approach humor with the light rather than the heavy touch.[34] And Mr. Hamburger, whose jaundiced observations introduced this discussion about "Uncle Miltie," now concludes it by stating that "Berle is now in my book a funny, funny man--one of the last of the clowns who employs a technique that doesn't depend entirely on a file of gags."[35]

Again and again, the critics express their admiration for comedy which, despite its reliance on carefully linked jokes, is, nevertheless, imaginatively but soundly derived from honest human desires. Although by predisposition and by long contact with radio's verbal humor they may seem to frown upon visual slapstick, they still appreciate the values which Gilbert Seldes discerned many years before in the comedy of the Keystone Cops:

> It is one of the few places where the genteel tradition does not operate, where fantasy is liberated, where imagination is still riotous and healthy. In its economy and precision are two qualities of artistic presentation; it was still everything common and simplest and nearest to hand. . . . It could become happily sophisticated without being cultured.[36]

This last phrase is a clue to the comedy of Sid Caesar and Imogene Coca. Theirs was a more subtle slapstick, involving finer perception of the different characters in life's human comedy. They were new to broadcasting, having entered television in 1950 from the night club circuit. Robert Lewis Shayon observed that "a sense of play is the pre-requisite of enjoying a joke,"[37] and certainly this sense of play communicated itself in the performances of Caesar and Coca. Gilbert Seldes said, "What made them . . . so different from the dominant sub-Berle type was that both of them used all their skills to put over--to put across--not themselves, but the series of characters they were creating."[38] Mr. Caesar is a masterful pantomimist and dialectition whose success, Jack Gould thought, lay in his "appreciation of the ordinary, commonplace situations in life rather than the extreme absurdities to which so many comedians are addicted."[39] And his perfect partner was Miss Coca, also a fine pantomimist, who knew how to infuse the small gesture with "gaiety," "intelligence" and "humor."[40] Mr. Seldes compared both of them to Charlie Chaplin: Miss Coca for her ability to portray three or four emotions at one time without exaggeration and sentimentality, and Mr. Caesar for being able to demonstrate how a person behaves and why he behaves that way "leaving us unaware of the moment or place where the two manifestations are joined."[41] When this creative partnership was dissolved, having fallen victim to the ravenous appetite of television, Gilbert Seldes took the occasion to emphasize once again what he feels is the uniqueness of the medium to impress upon an audience the personality of the artist rather than the topics, or characters with which he deals:

> When they parted company, the event was an important item on the television page; when Godfrey parted company with a third-rate and almost unknown singer, it was front page news. . . . Godfrey, like Berle and Gleason, had become eight feet tall . . . like each of them, he had put across a priceless commodity, himself. Caesar and Coca had brought into the American living room a variety of people.[42]

One aspect of television comedy with which the critics slowly became disappointed was the camera's revelation of the strain and hard labor exerted by comedians whose prime appeal lay in the sight gag. Critical approval tended to rise as evidences of sheer physical projection decreased. This partly accounted for the ease with which Jack Benny, a top trouper from radio, slid into television. Over the years he had developed a smoothly functioning team of writers and actors, who knew how to create splendid verbal humor. In 1933, Darwin Teilhet urged his readers not to miss Jack Benny and Mary Livingstone's "unwatered frivolity."[43] And in 1951, Goodman Ace wrote the following:

> A year ago the critics cried that action was the main requisite for a good television show. . . .
>
> Now along comes a new star, stands in front of a curtain just as he stood in front of a microphone . . . and the critics,

fed up with the frantic frenzies of the comics who have made a shambles of our parlors, discovered Jack Benny.[44]

In addition to welcoming the reappearance of Mr. Benny, the critics were very gracious in their praise of a new television star who also emphasized verbal rather than physical wit. George Gobel seemed to fulfill Mr. Ace's dictum to the letter:

> The best way to keep [comedians] fresh and welcome is to keep them from becoming overbearing. Quiet conversation and intelligent writing along with a minimum of camera angles, production, and frenzy might do it.[45]

Mr. Gobel's quietness was the great success of the 1954-55 season. His droll observations and youthful, innocent face drew from the critics such comments as the following:

> Gobel's monologue is the most amusing I've ever been privileged to hear on TV.[46]
>
> (Jack Cluett)

> [Mr. Gobel's] is a sly, impish humor and it sneaks up on you in unexpected ways. . . . The monologues start slowly but Mr. Gobel is masterful at building them and building them until presently you're falling off your chair.[47]
>
> (John Crosby)

> His low pressure and off beat humor is often good fun . . . . He knows the art of relaxation and ambles all over the studio casually dropping his dry quips as he goes.[48]
>
> (Jack Gould)

Difficult to classify but impossible to omit in this discussion are two final comics, who have practiced their art in all three media (stage, radio, television): Ed Wynn and Jimmy Durante. Ben Gross reminds us that it was in April, 1932, that Mr. Wynn first donned his Texaco Fire Chief's helmet and made history by letting the radio audience hear the laughter of a live studio audience.[49] It was a merriment which lasted several seasons built upon what John Crosby has called the comedian's "infinite fantasy and imagination."[50] In Philip Hamburger's opinion,

Wynn's appearances on television were even more rewarding:

> We see the man's implausible face, his fluttery hands, his tight-fitting jacket, bumpkin pants, and outrageous shoes, and we see, too, his glorious grab-bag of tricks. . . . Anyone who doesn't enjoy Wynn is an enemy of the human race.[51]

Apparently Mr. Wynn's technique on television was composed of two qualities which are rare in the realm of sight comedy: swiftness and quietness. Mr. Gould describes what he saw in a 1949 performance:

> He is all over the stage, yet to an astonishing degree preserves that element of intimacy which is so vital to video. . . . He adjures the machine gun ad libs . . . and he is not addicted to beating you over the head until you laugh. . . . Ed is content to settle for the smile, which is remembered longer.[52]

Jimmy Durante's style is explosive, calculated to evoke broad laughter. Although Mr. Teilhet, in 1933, felt that his routine was too long,[53] Durante received the highest praise from Philip Hamburger in 1951:

> He seems to have an uncanny instinct for this new and baffling medium. He knows, for example, that the TV camera picks up the slightest gesture and the faintest expression, and gives each gesture and expression a strange special emphasis by reducing it on the tiny screen to something bigger than life. . . . Through some magic each motion is kept within range of the camera, and no motion is out of proportion to any other. As a result, Durante's personality emerges in all its barbarous and frenzied glory.[54]

Mr. Seldes may stand alone in reserving this exalted position for Jimmy Durante, but his opinion is worth reading:

> If I call Durante, rather than Chaplin, the great comic spirit of our age, it is because the particular roaring laughter, the uncontrollable, almost unbearable laughter Durante can bring out, may be an inheritance from Chaplin, but it is now his, and the tone of that laughter, which is the tone of pure joy, no one else can evoke.[55]

With respect to television comedy, the critics have had to be as flexible as the medium. Their own laughter has told them that the small screen can transmit humor for the ear as well as the eye, cerebral comedy as well as physical comedy. What they ask from all comedy is what Mr. Gould felt was lacking in a performance by Martha Raye in 1955: "Of style and wit there was virtually none, only the obvious, laden with the indelicate."[56]

The last word in the previous sentence points up two specific improvements which some critics have long felt were needed in broadcast comedy. One concerns off-color material. It is obvious that most of America's great clowns use the night club and the mass media as platforms. It is equally obvious that the club atmosphere and the home atmosphere present problems in the adaptation of material. At least one critic of radio and one of television has cautioned broadcasters in these matters. Ring Lardner, from whom more shall be heard in the section on popular music, urged censorship in no uncertain terms:

> Somewhere in the books there must be a rule against rough cracks. The good comic don't [sic] use them. The bad . . . average three per broadcast. . . . I say these things at the risk of being considered queasy and a prude. At the risk and in the hope. . . . The censors, if they are not in the coma for which I have given them credit, run no such risk and share no such hope.[57]

In television's initial days, Jack Gould took it upon himself to remind the industry of a similar responsibility. He felt that suggestive routines would be more difficult to control in video where gestures generally cannot become part of a script which has been checked in advance. He insisted that the individual conscience of both the broadcaster and the performer needed to operate in denying "license, which can be uproarious in a cabaret [but is] often deadly in the parlor."[58]

Particularly offensive to many critics are the humorous routines between a comic and some serious artist which, they feel, inevitably vulgarizes the latter and by so doing indicates a contempt for culture.

Gilbert Seldes remarked about the way radio personalities often flatter studio audiences and degrade guests. They present operatic stars who pretend ignorance of music or speakers who apologize for erudite vocabularies,[59] and a downgrading occurs similar to that in situation comedy. In Mr. Crosby's opinion the program in which Jimmy Durante was teamed with Helen Traubel, in which the clown was "set up against a person of towering dignity" was a tiresome attempt at comedy.[60] The pattern was even more thoroughly denounced by Marya Mannes. She said of opera stars participating in comedy acts on popular television shows:

> Probably quite unconsciously, they make a laughing stock not only of themselves but of the standards they used to uphold. They are successful now because they have come down to our level, not --as before--because they have raised us to theirs.[61]

Realizing, perhaps, that any coup would be useless, the critics have amiably accepted the fact that comedy has long been king of broadcasting. Having enjoyed the reign of the jesters, themselves, their disappointments are few. Jack Gould feels that any comic will eventually lose his glitter in the unceasing buffeting of the broadcast schedule; that no human being can develop more than a few beautifully polished talents and routines in a lifetime. It is regretful but inevitable that standards for television comedy become lower with the assistance of audiences who are willing to trade quality for convenience.[62] Gilbert Seldes, on the other hand, accepts the situation with optimism. He sees a positive good, a sense of well-being deriving from an audience's frequent, regular visits with a comedy star:

> We expect to be amused when Jack Benny appears, amused in a specific and limited number of ways. When this happens, we experience a great sense of satisfaction, not only because Benny has been amusing, but because a whole psychological system of desire-and-fulfillment has been in action.[63]

It may very well be that the audience experiences fulfillment, but

Goodman Ace is sure that comedy writers, to whom he offers advice, do not. He places the blame for their frustration on the vicious competition for high viewer ratings:

> The writing that goes into a comedy show is reflected in the rating that show gets in the surveys. That is true only if the rating is low. If the rating is high it reflects the talent of the comedian. When a show is in rating trouble a conference of the writers is called and, little by little, young, fresh comedy writer, your lofty ideas will be whittled down to accommodate what is erroneously considered the level of mass consumption. Cryptic comments are rewritten into broad boffolas and scathing satire into euphemistic yaks.
>
> If your show is filmed for residuals--to be reshown some years later--you will have to forgo your desire to write the finest comedy, that which says something about the current way of life, because sponsors might find it untenable a year or so hence.[64]

Here again is an expression of disappointment similar to the feeling critics had about situation comedy. They seem to be happiest when the laughs are relevant to life, when wit is allied with wisdom, when gags can be used as guides. To be sure, the critics are amused by wild slapstick and the comedy of personal insult, but there is a yearning for something else in the field of laughter. Jack Gould mused about the fun of having Fred Allen and George Jessel simply comment five minutes a week about items in the morning paper. He concluded his reverie by asking:

> Where are the joyous delights of the impish fantasy that spoofs our contemporary customs or mores? Heaven help us if the existing television sense of humor is accepted as the national standard.[65]

Audiences who conceive of entertainment in terms of laughter frequently recall not only the comedian, but the panoply of song, dance, and specialty number of which he is often the focal point or at least the master of ceremonies. It would be a mistake, therefore, to omit discussion of the variety or revue type program. Although most critics have seldom envisioned the broadcast review in terms like those used by Gilbert Seldes to describe Broadway's famous stage revues, his ideal does bear some relation to the broadcast product:

> The good review pleases the eye, the ear and the pulse; the very good revue does this so well that it pleases the mind. It operates in that equivocal zone where a thing does not have to be funny--it need only sound funny; nor be beautiful if it can for a fleeting moment appear beautiful. It does not have to send them away laughing or even whistling; all it needs to do is to keep the perceptions of the audience fully-engaged all the time, and the evaporation of its pleasures will bring the audience back again and again.[66]

Even though the aural stimulus was the only avenue open to the producers of the "Eveready Hour," their revue format must have been popular for it did keep audiences coming back again and again from December 4, 1923, when it was first aired, clear through the period of the twenties. A sampling of comments about the program indicates the quality of its leadership in developing radio techniques. James Young, in a 1925 issue of Radio Broadcast magazine, reported with interest that an Armistice Day program was set in an army camp. The entire entertainment evolved from this setting and obviated the need for the "boresome announcer."[67] And John Wallace complimented the program a couple of years later for its "novelty" in using the "Show Boat" idea with a narrator and separate characters "much the same as a radio play."[68] Ben Gross summed up the contributions of this first variety program by reporting that it offered "drama, music, comedy, poetry, and factual material [which] appealed not only to the mass desire for easy entertainment, but also to the adult intelligence."[69]

During the next decade, the sixty-minute variety hours were the leading programs on radio. Ring Lardner vigorously commended them "for good showmanship in assembling a troupe that will perform once a week and hold the interest of even as dumb a drove of oxen as the great invisible audience (and the dumber drove that frequents NBC)."[70] He was particularly fond of the "Maxwell House Show Boat" but was a little dubious about the Rudy Vallee program, which would be "good if Rudy confines himself to sing a couple of U. S. Nasal Academy numbers and if guest stars will not feel everything they say panics an audience."[71] Artificial joviality also irritated Darwin Teilhet. He felt that "Showboat" had "all the confusion incidental to a tenth rate musical comedy" and that it was presided over by one Captain Henry, "the most offensive combination of that folksy pandering so successfully marketed by Philip Lord and Tony Wons."[72] Mr. Teilhet's greatest scorn was reserved for Al Jolson who appeared in 1933 on the "Chevrolet Program:"

> Like an old billy goat, he has a fondness for bleating. The audience of free passes explodes with terrific applause after each quip and bleat. He makes the mistake of playing to the people in the live audience. He is a showman suffering from sentimental dry-rot and laziness.[73]

In spite of critical insults like these, variety programs were so continuously popular, that in radio's crucial hour (suffering as it was from the 1950 inroads of television) an NBC production entitled "The Big Show" starring Tallulah Bankhead with Goodman Ace as chief writer, actually did revive interest in night-time radio. The resuscitation was only temporary, of course, as video became the logical home of broadcast variety programs. The most famous of these has been the "Ed Sullivan Show" which, despite the following sneer by Saul Carson during its first season, has enjoyed success throughout the entire 1948-1955 period of television:

> Ed Sullivan is clumsy, tongue-tied and pitiful as a master of ceremonies. . . . Most of Sullivan's features are tasteless. . . . In short, Sullivan's show threatens not only to stop television in its tracks but to push vaudeville back into the tomb.[74]

As this program progressed, however, it became apparent that Mr. Sullivan was merely pushing vaudeville in a different direction rather than back into the tomb. John Crosby credited him with breaking the barrier of sameness, which had plagued the broadcasting of two decades. Instead of revolving solely around popular music, the comedian, the guest star, Mr. Sullivan's variety programs assayed the entire field of entertainment. Indeed, a listing of his offerings (ballet, a bit of opera, biography, a scene from a play, a salute to a film) is somewhat reminiscent of the old "Eveready" programs.[75] For example, Mr. Crosby was grateful for an entire hour of the dancing of Marge and Gower Champion, who, in his words, were "light as bubbles, wildly imaginative in choreography, and infinitely meticulous in execution."[76]

It may have been audience delight with this kind of variety programing which encouraged the Ford Motor Company and later the General Electric Company to attempt vastly expensive productions of single jubilee programs over all networks. In the critics' opinions, the Ford show (1953) was superior. It was a fifty year review of the nation's life done in a "tuneful," "zestful," even "lovable" manner to quote Mr. Shayon and Mr. Crosby.[77] Unfortunately, the grand design of the "Light" program (1954) was not well received, primarily because it failed to elude the hazard of all variety: top-heaviness. Philip Hamburger complained that Mr. Selznick, the producer, had ideas about the wonder and glory of America which were "composed of cliches larger than Superman."[78] And John Crosby took the occasion to remark:

> Television, it seems to me, is in about the phase the talkies were in back around 1929 when they were producing things like "Show of Shows" which contained everything from Rin Tin Tin to John Barrymore declaiming bits of Richard III, the idea being to overpower you with sheer quantity.[79]

It is sheer quantity of time, of course, which has always threatened to overpower the broadcaster, and his devices to meet the emergency have been unique indeed. To entice early morning and late evening audiences, a kind of informal variety program was created by the networks, containing chit-chat, informative interviews, capsules of news, popular tunes, and frequent commercial announcements. Interestingly enough, "Cheerio," one of the earliest and most popular of these programs, elicited the appearance of Mr. Aylesworth, president of NBC, who informed listeners that the show would remain unsponsored.[80] Leslie Allen sympathetically described the program and its performers [Cheerio, Gil, the Sweet Lady, Jerry, Pat, Didie and Blue Boy] but refrained from any negative judgment on the grounds that the program "should remain unfettered by unimaginative criticism."[81] Darwin Teilhet did not share his enthusiasm: "For a week I got up early enough to tune in 'Cheerio' and his canaries. Henceforth I won't be deluded into sacrificing sleep for doses of optimism."[82]

Twenty years later the critics were rising early and turning in late to report on television's equivalents of "Cheerio." Time had added communications gadgetry, big city sophistication, and America's basic preoccupation with things. Of NBC's "Today," an early morning variety program, Saul Carson said:

> With studied nonchalance, Garroway presides over the whole shebang, kingpin of the animated supermarket which NBC's publicity writers call modestly "the nerve center of the planet."
>
> . . . .
>
> With all the time [two hours] given to this show, it should be able to get beneath the surface . . . beat the backwoods . . . reflect America and the world.[83]

"Today" was followed by a program for women. Jack Gould thought "Home" was a good idea but that the amount of straight talk caused the pace to drag. He also disliked the constant emphasis on the female audience:

> The program is so determinedly pro-housewife and pro-mother in its approach that a little more material of general interest might not be amiss. There may be someone in the audience who would not be averse to being respected for her brain rather than her sex or pocketbook.[84]

Robert Lewis Shayon called "Home" a "heavenly department store, a valhalla of gadgets and gimmicks, a cloud of electronic dust returning to dust. It frightens one again and again to accept that programs such as these mirror the mind and heart and the interests of the American wife and mother."[85] An opposing view of the show was contributed by John Crosby, who thought that the program was "well thought out and thoroughly planned . . . to utilize television's great potentialities rather than simply to make some money out of them."[86]

Mr. Crosby's voice in this matter was definitely a minority one. Appreciative as the critics were for the light humor and broad range of material, they seemed genuinely appalled by the amount of advertising in these magazines of the air. Jack Gould complimented Steve Allen whose comedy in "Tonight" was "rooted in an amusing appreciation of the immaterial, irrelevant and unimportant;" but he condemned the program's rampant commercialism: "Guests, who often appear to singularly good advantage on Steve's show, have been left stranded in mid-sentence while a spot commercial was put on."[87] Mr. Hamburger summarized the disappointment of the critics very well: "The word 'variety' has lost its former meaning. The so-called acts are merely casual, haphazard, almost impromptu fillers separating one commercial from another."[88]

This last remark, however, illustrates what Mr. Seldes believes is the major critical fallacy with regard to standards for broadcast variety programs. Mr. Hamburger's concern about commercials may be entirely valid, but his disgust at the casualness of the fillers could be entirely irrelevant. The bright but informal presentation of personality rather than the performance of a polished routine is, perhaps, the only criterion by which to evaluate these segments of broadcasting. Mr. Seldes is ostensibly discussing Garry Moore, but he could be talking about Arlene Francis or Jack Paar or even Arthur Godfrey in the following exposition of his theory about the variety format:

> [Garry Moore's] program is one of half a dozen that seem to have no form. It breaks itself up at times, it varies in quality as the conversation of any group of people might vary with changes in their frame of mind or even in their rate of metabolism, but it is never stupid. You feel yourself in the presence of a man who has clearly set out to please you--but not at the expense of his own integrity (or yours). . .
>
> Gary Moore and his program are examples of a kind of creative adaptation in which commercial broadcasting has been notably successful. . . . They stand as a warning to critics not to judge the popular arts by standards drawn from older entertainments--even from older popular entertainments. . . . Vaudeville tried to entertain a small, self-selected, paying audience gathered once a week, at most, in a particular place and prepared to give all its attention to a variety of acts . . . perfected over a long period of years.[89]

Flattered and warmed in the company of these performers and their friends, who are never annoyed when home duties momentarily distract, the viewer or listener truly feels that he has been entertained, though the critic may disagree.

No matter what critics generally thought of the variety program, most of them were captivated by the fresh and easy charm of a late night show which had its inception in Chicago. The "Garroway at Large" melange deliberately substituted quietness for raucousness and developed a fluid technique of lighting and camera work which enhanced its varied moods. At a time in the late forties and early fifties when many cameramen were still learning just to keep out of each other's way, the Garroway crews were, in Harriet Van Horne's words, using "a television camera the way an artist uses a brush . . . with . . . awareness of the beauty that lurks in shadows as well as the beauty that dances in light . . . They roam at will . . . they glide, they spring, they swoop."[90] The beauty of the photography was allowed full sway by the unobtrusive mannerisms of Mr. Garroway and his cast. Philip Hamburger, in searching for phrases to describe what he called the Garroway idea, came up with, "a strangely boneless half-hour" and "a tiny oasis of peace and quiet." He was eager to applaud a program in "conscious rebellion against the Whoop-de-do type of revue."[91] John Crosby appreciated the style but was more reserved about the universality of its appeal:

> One must never get excited about anything. One must be terribly, terribly, terribly casual about everything and relaxed almost to the point of stupor.
>
> . . . .
>
> For this reason, I have small doubts that Garroway will ever win the popular acceptance of, say Arthur Godfrey, which, it appears, is NBC's aim. He is a special taste, possibly a little fey for wide esteem.[92]

In the early fifties, the Chicago School, as it came to be called, developed a creative cooperation and dedication in its staff which was unusual in the larger show factories of New York and Hollywood. And for a time (until network headquarters summoned them) their originality and ingenuity, which substituted for lavish budgets, resulted in critical acclaim for programs other than the Garroway show. One of these will serve as an admirable introduction to the critics' opinions of juvenile variety programs, since they saw in "Kukla, Fran and Ollie" proof that broadcasting could serve children with artistry. Deft imagination was the catalyst producing the delightful, if implausible camaraderie of several puppets, a live actress, and a musician. Their whimsical activities were the result of the creative ideas and organization of puppeteer, Burt Tillstrom. Jack Gould said, in 1949, that this program was:

> The most charming and heart-warming excursion into pure make-believe

> that is to be found in television today.
>
> . . . Mr. Tillstrom employs a form of presentation which is thoroughly comprehensible to even the very young members of his audience, but he never makes the mistake of being condescending. . . . He directs his satirical glance at all manner of subjects. . . . He gets over a host of educational values by the simple expedient of being amusing and never once getting near the word "educational."[93]

Philip Hamburger did not concur; he slurringly referred to "avant garde puppets--obscure like The Cocktail Party."[94] But Gilbert Seldes rhapsodized:

> They accomplished that most desirable miracle of reconciling the fastidious to the average taste, of being admired by one and all. . . . Aesthetes could point out that it was pure television, and the enthusiasts for the Chicago school of TV originals could note that it was also spontaneous. Before television had lived three postwar years, it had created a masterpiece. At the same age the movies were barely more than a peepshow and radio was still transmitting the heartbeats of a butterfly caught in a submarine.[95]

That this masterpiece should derive from the area of children's programing is almost more amazing than the fact that it came so early in television history. Certainly radio's contributions to the children's hour had developed few noteworthy traditions. For an occasional program like "Skippy" recommended by Darwin Teilhet,[96] there were hundreds of audio comic strips and children's amateur hours through the years which went unmentioned by the critics. But the almost frightening fascination which the glowing screen had for children led the critics to evaluate many juvenile television programs.

Keeping in mind the qualities appreciated in "Kukla, Fran and Ollie," it is not difficult to understand why "Mr. I. Magination" should have been favorably received. The title was not a misnomer in the light of Philip Hamburger's account of this show which told stories as if they were perceived through a child's eyes:

> Everything about the program . . . has an air of integrity.

> . . . The humor is modest and restful. The music is as friendly as Mr. I. Magination himself. The boy actors avoid that poisonous precocity. . . . The program captures the quality of a child's imagination--an unfettered and quite lovely thing.[97]

Again, with reference to this program, Jack Gould emphasized that the performer who has a sensitivity for the child's point of view, must not equate that with acting like a child; and he complimented Mr. I. Magination for avoiding cuteness and condescension.[98]

In addition to imagination, and a healthy, youthful orientation, the critics believe that simplicity is a characteristic of a superior children's program. Mr. Gould felt that one of the assets of "Danny Dee," a local New York presentation, lay in the fact that Roy Doty, the cartoonist-story teller of the s ow, was the only person to be seen and heard on the screen.

> Herein may lie one of the key answers to a perennial problem of children's programing. By not giving each of his characters an individual voice he avoids the pitfall of excessive and overly vivid dramatization which so often can lead to abuse in video. . . . The young viewer is always aware that the adventures of Danny Dee are a make-believe story. . . . Mr. Doty achieves credibility without suggesting actuality.[99]

Simplicity suggests quietness, or at least the absence of confusion. In children's variety shows, as well as adult's, the critics almost invariably condemned pointless explosions of activity. Perhaps the strongest scolding came from Mr. Gould after viewing Pinky Lee's old vaudeville acts and silly games on NBC in 1954:

> . . . a tasteless, witless, and crude half hour that calculatedly exploits behavior in children that sensible mothers and fathers do their best to curb. . . . [Five P. M.] is a logical period for a child to unwind and slow down.
>
> Mr. Lee's program is dedicated to precisely the contrary objective. . . . The whole operation is a sort of organized frenzy designed to whip children into a high emotional pitch.[100]

Similar, although milder judgments were expressed about "Howdy Doody's" three ring circus for the youngsters. And it was with an almost audible sigh of relief that John Crosby welcomed "Captain Kangaroo," a fugitive from Howdy's mad escapades, to a new CBS variety program:

> Coming from one of the noisiest shows on the air, he has created one of the quietest. He also recognizes what so many people don't--that children are eager to learn. . . . It's all very gentle, relaxing, and above all, successful.[101]

Periodically, critics revive the entire problem of the broadcast program for children. They tend to agree, as was indicated in the last chapter (see pp. 217-18), that juvenile preoccupation with adult crime dramas is unfortunate; and that the high concentration of violence in programs designed for children is also unsatisfactory. They feel that inane and frenzied slapstick can never be a substitute for creative, imaginative adventure. The critics are also in basic agreement that the motivation for such programing is economic. John Crosby is humorously realistic about this fact: "No cereal company is going to pay for intellectual stimulation when his sole interest is salivary stimulation."[102] But, significantly, the critics are not in agreement about remedies for the situation. Robert Lewis Shayon believes that impetus for change will come only after a massive study-in-depth on the effects of television on children--a study which could, perhaps, be carried on by some foundation.[103] John Crosby feels the situation could be remedied more easily by simply having the broadcaster treat children's programs as a public service to be paid for from other broadcast revenues.[104] He is not so sure, as a matter of fact, that previous studies by well-meaning groups have not resulted in a censorship by code and a dilution of creativity to the point of ridiculousness.[105] Gilbert Seldes urges broadcasters to revise their indifferent stand which maintains the status quo as long as no definite proof of bad effects is forthcoming. The least they can do, he feels, is to leave some room in their scheduling for braver experiments than they have yet attempted.[106] However, even the least broadcasting can do may be extremely difficult, for what it has done seems to have satisfied its audience so well. To children and adults alike, the big laugh symbolizes radio and television. If comedy and variety are in top place as favorites, what can be wrong with broadcasting? To the critics, the big laugh may sound a little hollow or badly timed, but then, they are expected to be glum.

Games

Despite the adaptations music halls had to make for radio and television, they were still recognizable as forms of show business and were thus familiar to the critics. When all aesthetic distance was shattered and the audience got into the act, the critics realized that a new form of entertainment had arrived. Audience participation shows and panel shows (which employ, if not members of the audience, at least persons who admit to a wide variety of other occupations) are more closely allied to comedy than to any other broadcast form. Gilbert Seldes has dubbed them "parlor games" and sees their function as one of diversionary amusement. He suggests they be considered a type of spectator sport or an entertainment in the nature of a card game or high-school commencement exercises.[107] Lacking reliable traditional guides, the critics have attempted a tentative analysis of the appeals such programs make, of any disturbing consequences they may have for their audiences, and of their personal response to them. Although these light diversions have their roots in radio, most of the critics' comments concern television, where, faithful to the following prediction of Albert Williams, they have been extremely popular:

> Audience participation programs, the bane of evening radio, will possibly blossom in television. It has been bad enough listening to people laughing at something we could not see. The only thing worse will be to find out what it is they are laughing at.[108]

Mr. Williams was, of course, not speaking derogatorily of a quiz show which was not only the grand-daddy of the type, but was to give the form the most prestige it would ever have. "Information Please," according to Gilbert Seldes, never had as its true objective the function implied in the title. It was, instead, a kind of experiment in pure "amiability," "a device for getting some merry conversation from people without the danger of getting too much of it, since the master of ceremonies changed the subject every three or four minutes."[109] When the panel, which had had great success during the forties on radio, moved in front of the cameras, opinion was divided. John Crosby described it as "intellectual mugging, a man showing off the content of his brain as diffidently and charmingly as he knows how."[110] But Jack Cluett advised it to return to radio: "Closeups of brains aren't necessarily pretty. The cameras weren't on the right people at the right time."[111] The program did not take Jack Cluett's advice; it went off the air entirely, leaving the field to a score of other panel shows, and eliciting this fond farewell from Mr. Seldes:

> No commercial panel show in television aspires to one tenth of the general air of civilized men and women in pleasant converse that "Information Please" had at its best.[112]

To enjoy the privilege of pleasant, albeit trivial, converse in our living rooms with a literary critic, a pianist, a columnist, an actress on vacation is one thing; but to employ professional wits for an amateur amusement is quite another, in Jack Gould's opinion. He said of the entertainer like Fred Allen, or George Kaufman, or Ogden Nash, all of whom moderated such programs:

> He has been publicly seduced and reduced to the role of a spear carrier, a helpless soul who is expected to provide silly little sallies for the exhibitionists who wander on in television's panel shows. . . . What madness drives television to such waste of intelligence? Consider the limitations upon the wit: no controversial quips, politics is out, sex is out except for planted suggestive questions, any ad lib that might ruffle any organized group is out. Conformity in wit too, soon will mean full denial of wit.[113]

Mr. Gould's passing reference to planted questions raises the whole issue of "planned" spontaneity. Just what responsibility does a broadcaster have to insure that an impromptu program meets the definition of the word? John Crosby views his responsibility simply as an aesthetic one: "The studied ad lib, . . . the off-the-cuff wisecrack which was authored by six gag writers . . . are all getting a little labored."[114] Mr. Seldes, however, sees the broadcaster's responsibility as a moral imperative:

> A program presented as unrehearsed must be unrehearsed. The importance of being honest about these matters is a double one: if the audience is being deceived, it may resent the imposture; and if the imposture continues, the use of television for downright falsification will become that much more common.[115]

If television quiz shows lack the urbanity of their progenitor, if they waste the time of skilled artists, if they are hypocritical in presentation, how do critics explain their continuing importance in the broadcast schedule? Very easily. The programs cost little to produce and draw a tremendous number of viewers. Audiences enjoy matching wits with experts, but more significantly than that, they enjoy, in Jack Gould's words, "watching the reaction of a human being to the unexpected."[116] Is not this last point a clue to the relationship between these living room contests and the comedy and drama of more traditional theatrical forms? The parlor games combine the excitement of theatrical conflict with the ego-satisfying, intimate association of average people either with their fellows or with glamorous personalities.

This brief general view has dealt primarily with the historically (at least) respectable quiz game. A closer examination of specific programs reveals, however, that the basic idea of having members of audiences or panels guess secrets, interpret pantomimes, or answer questions, is only the starting point for diverse enterprises whose natures have caused critical consternation.

Tears are traditionally supposed to be a step away from laughter. So it is conceivable that the cheerful quiz could by a slight change of format become the misery quiz. "Strike It Rich," a CBS program on radio and television in the late forties and early fifties, probably elicited more critical abuse than any other presentation. Only contestants in dire need were permitted to compete for funds which would help them solve the problems they described to an anxious, nation-wide audience. Failure to win the quiz game frequently resulted in offers of help from sympathetic listeners. The emotional pull of the program was powerful, since the winnings were so high and the real-life crises so imminent. Philip Hamburger expressed his opinion in terms of light sarcasm:

> Any time I feel particularly gloomy, I look in on "Strike It Rich" since I can be reasonably certain of finding people on the program who feel more miserable than I do. This tends to cheer me up.[117]

But Jack Cluett wrote, "I can scarcely describe my loathing for this morbid presentation of human suffering . . .[with its] handouts of merchandise, all aptly tagged with manufacturer's names . . . its feeble pretense of being a quiz program [and with] the shocking admission that it's designed 'for top entertainment value.'"[118]

When the New York City Welfare Department complained that families failing to get on the program remained in town to become public charges, Jack Gould wrote the following denunciation:

> This type of program represents advertising gone absolutely stark, raving mad. . . . Grown men in their right minds don't try to make a buck from a fellow citizen's suffering. . . . What is important is that men of such public stature and leadership [executives of the industry] should want to be responsible for putting such unspeakable bathos on the airwaves.[119]

Gilbert Seldes agreed with the others that if this was entertainment its only parallel lay "in the distant past when the polite world went visiting in the prisons, and not on errands of mercy, and the gallants of the town took their ladies to see poor Tom in Bedlam."[120] He did not attempt to excuse the program, which, of course, had its imitators, but he did offer this additional explanation of the genre's appeal:

> It may be appalling to watch someone sobbing over the merciless blows of fate, but it is appalling only because what one sees is true, not false. And in a world where the false is virtually standard currency [Consider the preponderance of recorded, edited programs on the air.], the sudden breaking out of a true emotion purges us, for a moment, of a second rate one. This is not the catharsis of Aristotle; it is, in a sense, television's medicine for its own illnesses; the low concept, the weakened will to create, the intellect betrayed; and it comes to us in the course of the most flagrant exploitation of misery for profit. But in its dreadful way it reaffirms one of the greatnesses of television, its capacity to transmit truth. It reaffirms also the too-often-doubted human capacity for facing the truth and finding exhilaration in it.[121]

Participants in these programs earned such fabulous prizes for so little skill that the shows were called giveaways. It was an apt nickname, for sponsors gave away money and products in return for advertising, participants gave away their privacy about their inmost thoughts and problems in return for goods, and audiences gave away their time in return for emotional titillation and escape from loneliness. The programs appeared in the habiliments of show business (bright lights, a stage, units of scenery, an orchestra) under the coordination of a talented master of ceremonies, who introduced each "act" and rushed it through to its climax. And yet, the whole did not add up to theatrical entertainment; it was reality in the guise of unreality rather than the other way around. Critics could not approach their evaluations by the book. All they could do was to draw occasional analogies to the theater and give vent to their private feelings.

Having sampled the worst the critics have thought, it is now in order to accord passing reference to minor evils in the games department. "This Is Your Life" is a living diary outlined before the eyes of the startled guest of honor from whom all preparations have been kept secret. During the program's initial season on NBC radio in 1948, Saul Carson had misgivings about its "hocum," but he was willing to concede it did enable an audience to see "close at hand . . . the small things that make up the sum total of an ordinary American's life."[122] When the program moved to television and the critics writhed in embarrassment at the strained efforts of guests struggling to maintain composure during the sudden appearances of loved ones, their disgust was general. John Crosby reflects their attitude:

> No one has yet spit in [Ralph Edwards'] eye, told him to mind his own business and walked off the stage, but I live in hope that some day somebody will. The show is in monstrously bad taste.[123]

Although audiences, and even most of the participants, may feel that the gifts heaped upon them are fair compensation for their emotional ordeal, the critics refuse to applaud such affronts to human dignity. Marya Mannes reported "the intrinsic horror" of "Bride and Groom," a program in which a couple is interviewed, married, showered with gifts, and packed off on a thrilling honeymoon all in full view of the television audience:

> In spite of the camera's pitiless eye, they manage to seem moved and be moving--a triumph indeed of human innocence over commercial exploitation.[124]

By the time the childhood game of "Truth and Consequences" had been subjected to the creativity of the broadcasters, it had become, according to John Crosby, "a monstrosity of vulgarity":

> The quality of this [studio audience] laughter--if that's the word for it--is quite different from that at even the dizziest comedy show. You'll find traces in it of embarrassment, of sadism, and of drooling idiocy. It's a frightening noise, and to be sure you can see it as well as hear it, the cameras are frequently turned on the audience while they are in labor.
>
> . . . The participants are indescribable except to someone with the gifts and the space of Charles Dickens. Their appearances are not helped much by the fact that this horrible operation is on kinescope, which is murky enough to malign them and not quite dark enough to obscure them entirely.[125]

The horrified reaction of the critics to many of these entertainments can be partially balanced by noting their more favorable opinion of "You Bet Your Life" and their less vitriolic opinion, at least, of "The $64,000 Question." Guiding contestants through a simple quiz while exposing them to his witticisms has become a full time job for former cinema clown, Groucho Marx. Participants do indeed risk their lives when they place them in the quietly mad hands of the leering, cigar-chewing comic. In 1948, Saul Carson thought "You Bet Your Life" was a radio program which completely wasted Mr. Marx's talents.[126] But Jack Gould felt the program was a remarkable showcase for Groucho:

> His whole credo is to put his contestants through the third degree with a running stream of wisecracks that in themselves often add up to a subtle commentary on contemporary life. . . . His specialty is to sustain the non-sequitur longer than probably any other wag in show business. . . . If he leans rather heavily on the comedy of insult, he prefaces his derogatory whimsy with considerable common sense.[127]

Transferred almost unrevised to television, the program was still a critical success, proving once again to Goodman Ace that the only video action necessary is that of moving lips emitting "bright, adult sounds."[128]

Another quiz show, having the virtue of presenting contestants with superior knowledge, made its appearance during the summer of 1955. The excitement which boosted this program into prominence evolved not only from the fact that a participant's earnings could multiply to a top of $64,000 and be lost with one misstatement, but also from the fact that the contestants worked at one job while possessing amateur expertise in another area. After gruelling weeks in front of the cameras, those who reached the pinnacle were the nation's darlings. Jack Gould had this to say about Gino Prato, the cobbler who was an expert on opera:

> What made Prato an entrancing figure over night was his own personal modesty, pluck and intelligence. A nobody, in short, turned out to be a warm and intriguing guy.[129]

The critics also admired the clever dramatic format of the show. As the prize money mounted, contestants moved into an isolation booth, musical tension increased, and questions were drawn from sealed envelopes in the care of a banker flanked by two policemen. Even as he credited the genuine drama in this program, however, Robert Lewis Shayon was disturbed by its symbolism which he compared to Greek tragedy:

> Regard the agonizing loneliness of the spotlighted figure in the sound-proofed booth. He is face to face with the very meaning of his life, with the most desperate crisis of his aspiration. And the community, the audience, the fifty million who pity and fear, who echo the unutterable prayer of a mammon culture--observe . . . how they are dismembered by the trial, the suspense, the unendurable torment of the hero who is expiating publicly their private, unacknowledged sin of greed.[130]

Here, said John Crosby, was a show "glorifying avarice,"[131] and Gilbert Seldes pricked America's conscience by reminding it that the glittering goal of even this program was the philosophic opposite of our historic, rugged, do-it-yourself way of life.[132]

This section on games began with the mild observation that they were a transplant of harmless parlor amusements directly to broadcasting. And now the section concludes with the suspicion that they may not be completely harmless and that they are frequently unamusing. The critics' concern seems a little ridiculous on the surface, as if they were equating tiddley winks with a subversive activity. Yet, when hour upon hour is spent at games, the critics believe that they are right to ask that these occasions be also a time for close contact with brilliant conversationalists or for simple fun with ordinary friends. They believe that the broadcast games' massive exploitation of emotion degrades participants and cheapens audiences, and that its incessant obeisance to materialism warps a fundamental part of our national philosophy. Mr. Seldes would, to some extent, support his fellow critics in their beliefs, even though he is less convinced of the harm of these programs. More important, however, he would remind them to make sure their condemnation does not derive from frustration at not being able to apply to the games, the criteria they have always applied to theatricals. He, himself, is not yet sure just what these games are, but he offers some ideas which may assist future critics. He is referring especially to "The $64,000 Question," but he could be speaking of all broadcast games:

> The program brings into high relief the essential dual nature of radio-television, a nature at war with itself being partly entertainment as we knew it in the past (drama, variety, etc.) and partly a lower-keyed effort to engage (not necessarily to absorb) the attention of masses of people by having something going on--chatter, exhibition of personalities, games and the like.
>
> . . . A kind of sub-attention is all we give them. . . . Critics, being professionals, consider these programs "empty" and in this they are not far wrong, because the programs are full of excitement about nearly nothing. But judgment cannot be rendered against them by the precedents of the past. A new thing has come into the world and for lack of a new word we still call it "entertainment."

. . . The question for statesmen (and the answer is worth more than $64,000) is whether the best use of the air would be made if the mass of programs offered to us merely satisfied the negative quality of being innocuous, when so few are bold enough to be disturbing, to challenge the mind and uplift the heart of the audience.[133]

The plea for cautious concern contrasts with the general critical tone of disparagement evident in professional discussions about this program area. It reflects the understandable contradictions which will occur until critics come to terms with a new hybrid unit of entertainment.

Popular Music

A major portion of programing (particularly in radio) remains relatively unscrutinized by the professional broadcast critic. It is not so much that he is completely ignorant of popular music; it is just that the variety and depth of material in other areas provides a more fruitful source of ideas for his columns. After all, when a critic has written that a certain musical program has "finished orchestrations, richness of coloring, incomparable program balance,"[134] and when he has given some detailed illustrations to prove his points, what more can he say about it which would be of continuing interest to the lay reader next week and the week after that? Nevertheless, there were important personalities and important program planners in the musical world whose efforts reached the ears of the critics, and they responded, however briefly.

Although famous singers, who appeared on the prestige variety shows or on shorter programs of their own, may have accounted for a small portion of the sixty percent of radio time devoted to music,[135] during the medium's heydey, their audience popularity was so enormous that the critics could not ignore them. Of Rudy Vallee, Darwin Teilhet wrote in 1932:

He is a minstrel with a Yankee background in a mechanical

> age. He has the flexible voice and tonal range of a balladist without volume. . . . He has abstained from some of those nasal tonal effects [see p. 256] he was formerly so proud of.[136]

Poor Morton Downey did not warrant even such mild praise from either Mr. Teilhet or Mr. Lardner. The popular tenor was dubbed "a cream puff" in one review,[137] and Ring Lardner said he was just getting to the point where he could "distinguish Morton Downey from Kate Smith without looking at my watch, when the depression [1932] hit the tobacco business [Camel Quarter Hour] and schedules were shuffled."[138] When Downey appeared on the Woodbury program several months later, Mr. Lardner, calling him "the male Lily Pons," wrote:

> On a half-hour program glutted with an orchestra, an announcer, and cheer leaders for the merchandise, there was only one singer of one sort; from ten to fifteen minutes in which to offset the purifying effects of the soap plug with suggestive or merely snappy songs, and only one falsetto to sing them.[139]

In addition to providing specific criticisms of singers, Mr. Teilhet was one of the few critics to explain some of the aesthetic differences in format of these early popular music programs. In the May, 1932 issue of Forum he wrote the following comments about three cigarette musical programs:

> The "Camel Hour" blasted away prejudice against fifteen minute broadcasts by developing elaborate musical signatures and closings, building up spots for personalities, and sugar-coating sales messages. Eric Barnouw and Charles Gannon, the D. W. Griffiths of radio, designed Camel to be the opposite of Lucky Strike's blaring orchestra reminiscent of tent shows and circus barkers. They have given it a soothing and soporific blend.
>
> Whereas Morton Downey and Tony Wans [whose sentimental readings neither Mr. Teilhet nor Mr. Lardner could endure] share attention with the orchestra, the Chesterfield Program welds Alex Gray and [Nathaniel Shilkret's] orchestra into one coordinated unit. Advertising talk is slipped in before the program starts to move. . . . [The Chesterfield] fadeout is . . . improved by a teaser medley of the following night's music.[140]

Bing Crosby, whose voice, according to the Decca record company, has been heard by more people than any other voice in the history of the world,[141] was criticized by Ring Lardner for his crooning:

> Both [Russ Columbo was also included.] are extremely proficient in the art of not hitting a tone on the nose. They sneak up on it or slide down to it or miss it entirely. . . . They usually start from two to six or seven beats behind the orchestra.[142]

Despite Mr. Lardner's objections, this relaxed vocal style seemed consistent with the idea of singing to small living rooms from a small studio. Some fourteen years later, Jack Gould complimented Frank Sinatra for capturing the extraordinary informality and sense of relaxation projected by Bing Crosby.[143]

Though Mr. Crosby may have trailed the orchestra, he went on to become a leader in the entertainment world. And one of his innovations, according to Gilbert Seldes, has tremendously affected the future of broadcasting. Bing Crosby persuaded the networks that mistake-proof shows, pre-recorded at the artist's convenience, would be accepted by the public. Small stations had, of course, existed on this basis. But with the adoption of the idea by the networks, it was Mr. Seldes' opinion that the final compromise of "live" excellence had been accomplished; from that time forward the beneficial interplay between performer and audience (even though unseen), the helpful tension toward genuine communication would give way to an intangible slickness and artificiality that was a denial of broadcasting's true essence.[144]

Kate Smith may not have been responsible for a revolution in the Crosby sense, but she became, nevertheless, almost as powerful a personality. From her early appearances on the LaPalina Cigar program, she climbed steadily in popularity. John K. Hutchens said, at the beginning of her twelfth season in 1942, that she was the "most artful of popular singers. . . with the common touch and the virtue of obvious sincerity."[145]

She was a singer who exemplified the mass media's tendency to magnify characteristics quite unrelated to the original talent of a performer. Somehow she was transformed from just a pleasant voice into an institution--a process which irritated John Crosby, who observed a television performance in 1951 in which Miss Smith presided over a talent show besides contributing songs of her own:

> She is presented as a sort of American institution, like Thanksgiving, something that doesn't require explanation. . . . The confounded show even opens with a shot of waves breaking on our rock encrusted shores, pans next to a shot of the American flag, concentrates briefly on the star-studded section of the flag and dwells finally on a single star--symbolizing, as I gather it, Miss Smith, America, motherhood, and the National Broadcasting Company.
>
> . . . .
>
> None of this was very bad but nothing was very good either. In any case, it didn't add up to anything that resembled a television show and I can't quite figure out what Miss Smith is doing there. They're trying, I speculated, to make a female Arthur Godfrey out of her. But is there any great need for a female Arthur Godfrey, or for that matter, a male Arthur Godfrey?[146]

Generally, if a popular musician was able to project an intimate sincerity (over radio or television) rather than a pretentiousness larger than life, he received critical approval. Mr. Hamburger's negative amazement at the florid style, dress, and mannerisms of a television pianist was typical of other critics' reactions: "I guess Liberace has to be seen to be believed. He has the curliest black hair imaginable, and it is Simonized like a new Buick Roadmaster."[147] The critics were so distracted by the trappings of the show that they seldom mentioned the quality of the music. On the other hand, John Crosby's review of Dinah Shore's television program was typical of critical reactions in the opposite direction:

> Miss Shore as usual drenches us with charm, good taste, and high spirits and, incidentally, sings as if she liked the job rather than as is the custom--as if someone were roasting her over a slow fire.[148]

The reference to Miss Shore's good taste focuses attention on Ring Lardner's lone crusade in the early thirties to restore sense and virtue to popular songs. The inanities of lyrics elicited some of Lardner's most delightful columns. As one example, he offered evidence that his whole family tried to improve on the words to "Night and Day." Their reconstruction of one verse went like this:

> Night and day, under the bark of me
> There's an Oh, such a mob of microbes
> Making a park of me.[149]

But the good humor in Mr. Lardner's column disappeared when he heard a radio song which he thought was too suggestive. In an article entitled, "Off-Color," he listed several reasons for his campaign against smut: (1) "Sex appeal employed for financial gain makes me madder than anything except fruit salad." (2) "A large percentage of the invisible audience is composed of old people who retain the faculty of being shocked and of children between the ages of nine and sixteen who . . . can't help wondering what the heck when they hear songs that glorify defiance of the seventh amendment to Moses constitution." (3) " I am curious as to whether there is such a thing as radio censorship." (4) " I am curious as to whether the sponsors and their advertising agencies are just plain dumb or as broad as the ocean and as lewd as the sky."[150] This was a rather pathetic critical episode since the reaction of the industry, of fellow critics, of the general reader to Mr. Lardner's indignation was one of amused indifference. The columnist's biographer records, however, that at least one song, "As You Desire Me," was revised as a result of Mr. Lardner's objections.[151]

Most of the professional critics were not too concerned and therefore not too detailed in their comments about popular music, or else their observations were part of longer reviews of comedy and variety programs. However, a few scattered production notes appeared from time to time which help complete this discussion of broadcasting's juke box. In 1927, Gilbert Seldes noted that jazz music seemed to be more faithfully reproduced by the loudspeaker. This, he mused, could be attributed to the fact that low base notes were not so important to jazz, whereas, symphonic music required a most delicate adjustment of the receiver to capture an entire range of sound.[152] And in 1934, Darwin Teilhet suggested reasons for the success of Glen Gray's Casa Loma band, which could have served as criteria for other dance orchestras: "Mr. Gray has a first class honky tonk orchestra. . . . The outfit is expert through the entire instrumental range. . . . They push the lyric meter, even the word accent into the beat and measure of the tune."[153]

Programs of gentler music were occasionally evaluated by the critics. John Wallace was not too happy about a 1927 Thomas Cook and Son "Travelogue" series with melodies supposed to call up geographical connotations. The "Song of the Volga Boatman" reminded him of garlic. "But," he wrote amicably, "somebody must like the things or they wouldn't still be going on, so we will cease quarreling with them and merely refrain from listening to them."[154] Jack Gould not only listened to all of Frank Hummert's light musicales produced for various networks, but wrote a pleasant piece about them in 1948. Of the "American Album of Familiar Music," "Manhattan Merry-Go-Round," "The American Melody Hour," "Your Song and Mine," and "Waltz Time," he said:

> The ballad or waltz tempo is employed exclusively. This is "corn" done with expert professionalism. . . . The five programs have a common appeal--ease of listening. The straight melody is adhered to with almost a religious fervor, and the lyrics are pronounced with uncommon clarity.
>
> The net result is that the habit of listening to Mr. Hummert's

> programs can be acquired almost as painlessly as middle-age spread. . . . Week in, week out the pace is leisurely, subdued.[155]

And finally, as if to prove how broad the interests of critics are, Saul Carson actually attended the twenty-second radio anniversary of the "Grand Ole Opry" in 1947, in the kingdom of hill-billy music, Nashville, Tennessee. He particularly complimented Bradley Kincaid for digging "into forsaken mountain hollows for old ballads--a real contribution to culture."[156]

No group of critics could be expected to evaluate the ceaseless din of the "platter" shows, but periodically they would listen with care to many of the major musical programs--jazz, popular ballad, and country music. These, after all, presented the tunes of Broadway and the tunes of Main Street. If broadcasting were to be fully interpreted, their melodies could not be completely ignored.

Serious Music

In the vast spectrum of programing, one small segment has been the occasion for some of broadcasting's greatest critical triumphs and the scene of its severest critical disappointments, although in most cases the judgments have been those of professional music critics. Radio held thrilling promise indeed for serious music in all its forms. John Wallace's columns in the twenties were filled with suggestions for creating a stable framework for the transmission of great music. It was his belief that "instrumental music should be the backbone of the radio program," and that "plays, comedies and speeches are the mere sauce to the roast beef because you can't see the people."[157] If anyone questioned the available audience for this type of music, Mr. Wallace confidently predicted that radio would raise the "incontrovertibly low" taste of the average American, since it was already "exposing the nation nightly to better things in music than it is accustomed to hear."[158] As for those who were presently educated to fine music, radio would increase their joy, since they could concentrate on the sound alone and not be distracted by the sight of the orchestra.[159] Stations had only to put into effect recommendations like Mr. Wallace's for program unity, and serious music would be well on its way:

> If the "Valse Triste" and the "Itchy Foot Rag" are put on the same program, one or the other or both are going to suffer. . . . The bigger and better stations have in response to the nowise concealed wishes of the listeners largely gotten away from the kaleidoscopic type of program. . . Mixing in a lot of fundamentally different things . . . means that the edge is going to be taken off all of them. . . . The ideal state of affairs will have arrived when each station adheres to one type of offering for at least sixty minutes on end.[160]

Mr. Wallace hoped, of course, that there would be many sixty-minute units of classical music. Unfortunately, however, station programing moved in the opposite direction, and the critics were unreservedly bitter about the preponderance of "jazz" on the air. After hearing a jazzed version of "Silent Night," Miss Mix, the first critic for Radio Broadcast magazine, exclaimed, "To what base depths the mind of man can sink!"[161] She urged listeners, particularly parents who spent money for musical training for their children, to complain to program managers.[162] A fellow critic, Raymond Yates of the Herald Tribune (New York), conducted a vigorous propaganda campaign during the middle twenties for more serious music, publishing in his daily column letters which supported his stand.[163] By the late twenties and early thirties, vigorous pleas had given way to wistful expressions of disappointment. "If radio had progressed in its proper channel," said John Wallace, "we would have some ten or twenty symphony orchestras bearing the names of stations which organized them."[164] And Leslie Allen could only wonder at how the rendition of a "single symphony . . . blankets the tremulous memory of a hundred crooners."[165]

Even though the critics were disappointed that a feast of musical riches was not forth coming, they were still grateful for crumbs. Mr. Allen penned an open letter to Walter Damrosch whose musical appreciation programs were the cultural pride of NBC in the early thirties:

> Amidst the strident welter of commercialization that rides the ether waves, your voice and the strains of your orchestra sound like the limpid notes of a flute played courageously beneath an elevated railway structure.[166]

Under the nurturing competition of the networks, classical music programs did increase during the middle thirties. CBS presented the Philadelphia Symphony Orchestra with Leopold Stokowski and the New York Philharmonic under Arturo Toscanini in separate series. Darwin Teilhet complimented Mr. Stokowski for his experiments in microphone placement which resulted in "tonally clear" reception; and he appreciated Mr. Toscanini's choice of selections--"often dramatic, never too abstract or difficult to hold the amateur of good music."[167] A year later he reviewed the Cadillac Concert series and exclaimed, "The prodigious flow of superb sponsored music makes March a month to go down in the annals for your grandchildren."[168] Although sponsored serious music programs were seldom as common as Mr. Teilhet implies, CBS and NBC presented weekly full-dress concerts for over two decades. Reviews for these events, however, were usually written by the music critics of a publication's staff.

Even so, when programs of this nature were first transferred to television, the broadcast critics were interested in the concerts' visual aspects. The search for some general rule of camera movement during a concert has not yet been concluded, though the majority of critics would seem to prefer relatively static picture transmission. Jack Gould said of a Toscanini concert in 1951:

> Trick camera angles and unique production effects . . . often serve to clutter up good programs. . . . [This was] a priceless music lesson . . . [but] the travels of the camera made it difficult for the viewer to pay attention to the score.[169]

Both he and Robert Lewis Shayon felt that the camera could rest on the conductor's face for extended periods:

> Mr. Toscanini, seen giving free expression to his imagination, becomes a universal fugue. The experience is communicated to the listener-viewer, and he, too, is caught up and enriched.[170]

Goodman Ace asserted that cameramen should simply stop trying to devise new angles from which to shoot their pictures, a procedure which he was sure would be welcomed by the musician:

> I doubt that Horowitz will ever play a television piano until he is assured that the cameramen will lock their cameras on one shot at a genius at the piano and let the movement be in the beauty of the music itself.[171]

This would be too restricting a regulation as far as Mr. Shayon is concerned, and he suggested that the guide for camera movement should, in the final analysis, rest, as it does in all the arts, upon whether "emotion--genuine, great, and good" is the result.[172] He recalled, as an example, the effectiveness of slow dollying and panning which seemed to be synchronized with a singer's phrasing in an NBC "Recital Hall" program.[173]

Just as the task of reviewing concert music was frequently assumed by a specialized critic, so too were the evaluations of broadcast opera. The critics of broadcasting generally accorded performances grateful acknowledgment, leaving detailed comments to those more musically proficient. Darwin Teilhet, for example, praised the new ribbon microphones installed at the Metropolitan in 1933 for their "well-nigh perfect" reproduction qualities, but he said very little about specific operas.[174] The famous Saturday afternoon broadcasts from the Metropolitan Opera House were, of course, practically the only productions of their kind on radio. With the arrival of television and NBC's "Opera Theater" presentations of the standard repertoire as well as of works written specifically for the cameras, the critics were moved to fresh appraisal. Mr. Shayon saw in television opera an exciting new area for artistic experimentation:

> Technically, television opera permits a wider use of the medium's optical bag of tricks. Fantasy is not, but could be, a forte of television. Drama story editors shy away from it. The assumption is that the mass mind is not a fantasy mind. Opera offers unexplored vistas for stylization on television and the producers should plunge in more boldly.[175]

Jack Gould was quite satisfied with the progress the new musical theater was making. He felt that "NBC Opera Theater has tried to widen sights for all of opera . . . [in] a cultural contribution that transcends mere media."[176] Surely, it was such transcendence which led John Crosby to devote an entire column to the beauty of Gian Carlo Menotti's "Amahl and the Visitors," commissioned by NBC in 1951. He discussed the performance, but more than that, he tried to analyze the secret of Menotti's power:

> Menotti's great virtue . . . is a simplicity and integrity of purpose which leads him straight to the heart of the matter.
>
> . . . .
>
> Because he is unabashed by the outer trappings of sentiment, he writes directly about mother love, about poverty, about crutches, about miracles, somehow purifies them and transforms them into genuine and profound emotion. This is a very great gift indeed, the quality of candor, and one which Menotti, almost alone, seems to possess these days.
>
> He can hardly write a line of music which doesn't seem exactly suited to the particular moment of the drama, inflaming the mind and the heart simultaneously and intensifying

the dramatic effect to an almost unbearable degree.

. . . .

As for Mr. Menotti, I can think of no higher praise than to say that everyone who saw it was a little better as a person and as a Christian than he was an hour earlier.[177]

It is, perhaps unfortunate, but quite understandable, that professional critics of broadcasting tend to relegate the appraisal of serious music to majors in the area and to deem the appraisal of popular music scarcely worth their attention. Ideas in the serious field seem to elude verbal discussion by laymen, and the repetitious froth in the popular field seems barren of any ideas whatsoever. Nevertheless, the steady reader of broadcast criticism comes to realize that the critics have a sympathy for and even an awe of great music which compels them to urge more of it in the schedule. They also sense a relaxed acceptance on the part of the critics for light music, which, if it were only less prevalent, would be more entertaining.

Recapitulation of the Critics' Opinions About Broadcast Entertainment

Critics have two qualities in particular which inform their thinking and vitalize their emotions: imagination and a moral viewpoint. In their imagination, they are never alone at their receiving sets. Huddled about them are five million other souls listening to identical sounds from loudspeakers, or twenty million watching identical pictures flash upon luminescent screens. It is then that their disgust at banality or their exaltation in excellence becomes a moral force infusing their comments. Given the fact that, primarily as the result of their broadcasting system, the American people are the most entertained individuals in history, to the point of being deafened by day and blinded by night, the critics' imagination and moral sense operate to produce certain conclusions about this realm of entertainment.

Casting its shadow over every critical discussion about broadcast entertainment, be it drama, variety, quiz or music, stands the sin of sameness; but it is particularly evident in the area of light entertainment. There are several specific ways in which these programs are the same. They are noisy rather than quiet. They are built upon the fanfare and the guffaw, the strident, staccato voice and frenzied applause, with laughter and clapping dubbed in when studio audiences are not used. They magnify the foolish rather than the intelligent, or at least the ridiculously clever, rather than the remarkably bright. They place a premium upon the personality who has, in Mr. Seldes' phrase, "high visibility" (a gay but genuine projection of the self) rather than upon the skilled artist. Audiences grow to love these performers for their friendliness rather than to admire them for their talent. And finally, these programs succeed because of an amiable dependability quite unrelated to the creativity traditionally expected in the entertainment arts. Their basic formats may have required an initial creativity, but their week to week presentation demands glibness from the performers and mild interest from the audience. Their power derives from excellence at forming audience habits rather than from ability to entertain through artistic excellence.

Although the critics have come to realize that the economic base of broadcasting and the psychology of show business in the living room have necessitated new approaches to entertainment, they are, nevertheless, unrelenting in their demand for relief from sameness. Willingness on the part of the industry to accept the "off beat" would, according to Mr. Seldes, have meant the continued nurturing of "Kukla, Fran and Ollie's" quiet humor and the recognition that the wit, taste, and audience pull of

Sid Caesar and Imogene Coca were indicative of some new directions for television drama.[178] The critics encouraged the experimentation of Sylvester Weaver, an NBC executive, who was acutely conscious of the need for television to avoid radio's ruts. It was he who initiated the concept of irregularly scheduled major events, which jolted regular programs off the air and momentarily shocked the industry and the audience with a new appreciation of the medium. Though critics may have cringed at the condescension in Mr. Weaver's "Operation Frontal Lobe," which was a plan to effect the insertion of cultural tidbits into standard entertainment programs, critical commendation for the idea was general.[179]

Conscious of the need for other positive ideas to counteract sameness, the critics did their best to keep the suggestion box full. Jack Gould, for example, feels that program planners should realize the "housewife owns a mind in addition to a kitchen"; that they should give the children puppets and Westerns, but also give them programs about our cultural heritage; and that in the evenings, adults should be offered not only clowns, but courses in art and literature, and even in the study of the social effects of television itself.[180] "Be it Bach, botany, ballet, or boogie-woogie," says Mr. Gould, "television must make use of every facet of our culture which it can command. A mass audience . . . [does not] inevitably require a drift into mediocrity."[181]

The virtues of variety can be ours to some extent, say the critics, if, as adults, we conscientiously use the station selector switch to achieve balance in our listening and viewing schedules and in the schedules of our children. But of even greater importance, the broadcasters must exercise, after consultation with the public if they wish, the creative leadership they theoretically assume with the granting of their licenses. Mere toying with change, however, will not satisfy the critics, although it may provide a climate for what they feel is broadcast entertainment's raison d'etre: the presentation of units of activity which frequently transcend the limits of the media and satisfy the attending audience with the revelation of emotional, intellectual and spiritual truth whether through laughter or tears, drama or music.

Notes

[1]Robert Lewis Shayon, Saturday Review, November 4, 1950, p. 28.

[2]Jack Gould, "How Comic Is Radio Comedy," New York Times Magazine, November 21, 1948, p. 67.

[3]Jack Gould, "They Say the Right Things at the Wrong Time," ibid., March 24, 1946, p. 22.

[4]John Crosby, Out of the Blue (New York: Simon and Schuster, 1952), p. 56.

[5]Gilbert Seldes, Saturday Review, January 10, 1953, p. 32.

[6]Cyrus Fisher [Darwin Teilhet], Forum, LXXXVIII (December, 1932), 384.

[7]Cyrus Fisher [Darwin Teilhet], ibid., LXXXIX (June, 1933), 382.

[8]Cyrus Fisher [Darwin Teilhet], ibid., LXXXVIII (December, 1932), 382.

[9]Leslie Allen, Christian Science Monitor, May 2, 1931.

[10]Crosby, op. cit., pp. 50-51.

[11]Cyrus Fisher [Darwin Teilhet], Forum, LXXXIX (March, 1933), 192.

[12]Ring Lardner, New Yorker, March 18, 1933, p. 57.

[13]Gilbert Seldes, Saturday Review, May 2, 1953, p. 37.

[14]John K. Hutchens, New York Times, September 28, 1941.

[15]Jack Gould, New York Times, September 29, 1946.

[16]Gilbert Seldes, Saturday Review, June 27, 1953, p. 32.

[17]Ben Gross, I Looked and I Listened (New York: Random House, 1954), p. 134.

[18]Jack Cluett, Woman's Day, XV (January, 1952), 6-7.

[19]Gilbert Seldes, New Republic, May 20, 1931, p. 20.

[20]Jack Cluett, Woman's Day, XV (October, 1951), 180.

[21]Lardner, loc. cit., pp. 56-57.

[22]Cyrus Fisher [Darwin Teilhet], Forum, LXXXVIII (October, 1933), 256.

[23]John K. Hutchens, "The Secret of a Good Radio Voice," New York Times Magazine, December 6, 1942, p. 27.

[24]John Crosby, "Radio and Who Makes It," Atlantic Monthly, CLXXXI (January, 1948), 26.

[25]For a humorous account of Fred Allen's encounters see his Treadmill to Oblivion (Boston: Little, Brown and Co., 1954).

[26]Philip Hamburger, New Yorker, September 5, 1953, p. 74.

[27]Jack Gould, "A Primer of TV Comics," New York Times Magazine, May 3, 1953, p. 12.

[28]Gilbert Seldes, The Public Arts (New York: Simon and Schuster, 1956), p. 75.

[29]Philip Hamburger, New Yorker, October 29, 1949, p. 91.

[30]John Crosby, Wisconsin State Journal (Madison), September 24, 1954.

[31]Seldes, The Public Arts, pp. 143-44.

[32]Ibid., p. 145.

[33]John Crosby, Wisconsin State Journal (Madison), January 20, 1954.

[34]Jack Gould, New York Times, October 11, 1953.

[35]Philip Hamburger, New Yorker, October 4, 1952, p. 118.

[36]Gilbert Seldes, The Seven Lively Arts (New York: Harper and Brothers, 1924), p. 24.

[37]Robert Lewis Shayon, Christian Science Monitor, October 7, 1950.

[38]Seldes, The Public Arts, p. 148.

[39]Jack Gould, New York Times, August 6, 1950.

[40]Philip Hamburger, New Yorker, May 27, 1950, p. 92.

[41]Seldes, loc. cit.

[42]Ibid., p. 149.

[43]Cyrus Fisher [Darwin Teilhet], Forum, LXXXIX (June, 1933), 383.

[44]Goodman Ace, The Book of Little Knowledge (New York: Simon and Schuster, 1955), p. 114.

[45]Ibid., p. 116.

[46]Jack Cluett, Woman's Day, XVIII (January, 1955), 10.

[47]John Crosby, Wisconsin State Journal (Madison), November 7, 1954.

[48]Jack Gould, New York Times, October 3, 1954.

[49]Gross, op. cit., p. 124.

[50]John Crosby, Wisconsin State Journal (Madison), November 23, 1954.

[51]Philip Hamburger, New Yorker, November 26, 1949, p. 113.

[52]Jack Gould, New York Times, October 16, 1949.

[53]Cyrus Fisher [Darwin Teilhet], Forum, XC (November, 1933), 319.

[54]Philip Hamburger, New Yorker, January 6, 1951, p. 66.

[55]Seldes, The Public Arts, p. 167.

[56]Jack Gould, New York Times, January 30, 1949.

[57]Ring Lardner, New Yorker, July 30, 1932, p. 24.

[58]Jack Gould, New York Times, January 30, 1949.

[59]Gilbert Seldes, The Great Audience (New York: Viking Press, 1950), p. 206.

[60]John Crosby, Herald Tribune (New York), May 27, 1953.

[61]Marya Mannes, Reporter, January 13, 1955, p. 37.

[62]Jack Gould, "TV at the Crossroads: A Critic's Survey," New York Times Magazine, March 9, 1952, p. 50.

[63]Seldes, The Public Arts, p. 201.

[64]Ace, op. cit., p. 29.

[65]Jack Gould, New York Times, February 22, 1953.

[66]Seldes, The Seven Lively Arts, p. 133.

[67]James C. Young, "New Fashions in Radio Programs," Radio Broadcast, VII (May, 1925), 83.

[68]John Wallace, Radio Broadcast, X (January, 1927), 273.

[69]Gross, op. cit., p. 94.

[70]Ring Lardner, New Yorker, June 17, 1933, pp. 44-45.

[71]Ibid.

[72]Cyrus Fisher [Darwin Teilhet], Forum, LXXXIX (January, 1933), 64.

[73]Cyrus Fisher [Darwin Teilhet], _ibid._, LXXXIX (February, 1933), 126.

[74]Saul Carson, _New Republic_, November 8, 1948, p. 27.

[75]John Crosby, _Wisconsin State Journal_ (Madison), November 27, 1955.

[76]John Crosby, _Herald Tribune_ (New York), May 29, 1953.

[77]Robert Lewis Shayon, _Saturday Review_, July 4, 1953, p. 33.

[78]Philip Hamburger, _New Yorker_, November 6, 1954, p. 127.

[79]John Crosby, _Wisconsin State Journal_ (Madison), October 29, 1954.

[80]Leslie Allen, _Christian Science Monitor_, January 17, 1931.

[81]_Ibid._

[82]Cyrus Fisher [Darwin Teilhet], _Forum_, LXXXIX (May, 1933), 320.

[83]Saul Carson, _New Republic_, February 4, 1952, p. 22.

[84]Jack Gould, _New York Times_, March 5, 1954.

[85]Robert Lewis Shayon, _Saturday Review_, April 10, 1954, p. 38.

[86]John Crosby, _Wisconsin State Journal_ (Madison), March 15, 1954.

[87]Jack Gould, _New York Times_, November 3, 1954.

[88]Philip Hamburger, _New Yorker_, October 9, 1954, p. 91.

[89]Seldes, _The Public Arts_, pp. 80-81.

[90]Harriet Van Horne, "The Chicago Touch," _Theater Arts_, XXXV (July, 1951), 37.

[91]Philip Hamburger, _New Yorker_, January 28, 1950, pp. 63-64.

[92]Crosby, _Out of the Blue_, p. 30.

[93]Jack Gould, _New York Times_, March 27, 1949.

[94]Philip Hamburger, _New Yorker_, March 18, 1950, p. 80.

[95]Seldes, _The Public Arts_, p. 136.

[96]Cyrus Fisher [Darwin Teilhet], _Forum_, LXXXVIII (July, 1932, 64.

[97]Philip Hamburger, _New Yorker_, March 18, 1950, p. 82.

[98]Jack Gould, _New York Times_, May 29, 1949.

[99]Jack Gould, _ibid._, December 27, 1953.

[100]Jack Gould, _ibid._, November 8, 1954.

[101]John Crosby, _Wisconsin State Journal_ (Madison), June 15, 1955.

[102]John Crosby, _ibid._, May 16, 1954.

[103]Robert Lewis Shayon, _Saturday Review_, July 31, 1954, p. 36. See also Mr. Shayon's excellent book _Television and Our Children_ (New York: Longman's Green & Co., 1950), for a more complete treatment of this problem.

[104]Crosby, _loc. cit._

[105]Crosby, _Out of the Blue_, pp. 122-124.

[106]Seldes, _The Public Arts_, p. 243.

[107]_Ibid._, p. 104.

[108]Albert Williams, _Listening_ (Denver: University of Denver Press, 1948), p. 121.

[109]Seldes, _The Public Arts_, p. 86.

[110]John Crosby, _Herald Tribune_ (New York), July 4, 1952.

[111]Jack Cluett, _Woman's Day_, XVI (October, 1952), 48.

[112]Seldes, _The Public Arts_, p. 87.

[113]Jack Gould, _New York Times_, September 11, 1953.

[114]John Crosby, _Herald Tribune_ (New York), December 5, 1952.

[115]Seldes, _The Public Arts_, p. 90.

[116]Jack Gould, _New York Times_, January 23, 1955.

[117]Philip Hamburger, _New Yorker_, April 24, 1954, p. 143.

[118]Jack Cluett, _Woman's Day_, XVI (November, 1953), 15.

[119]Jack Gould, _New York Times_, February 7, 1954.

[120]Seldes, _The Public Arts_, p. 105.

[121]_Ibid._, p. 100.

[122]Saul Carson, _New Republic_, November 29, 1948, p. 28.

[123]John Crosby, _Wisconsin State Journal_ (Madison), October 23, 1954.

[124]Marya Mannes, Reporter, January 6, 1953, p. 35.

[125]Crosby, Out of the Blue, p. 160.

[126]Saul Carson, New Republic, November 10, 1947, p. 36.

[127]Jack Gould, New York Times, December 11, 1949.

[128]Goodman Ace, Saturday Review, October 28, 1950, p. 46.

[129]Jack Gould, New York Times, August 14, 1955.

[130]Robert Lewis Shayon, Saturday Review, September 24, 1955, p. 26.

[131]John Crosby, Wisconsin State Journal (Madison), September 11, 1955.

[132]Seldes, The Public Arts, p. 120.

[133]Ibid., pp. 102-103.

[134]Darwin Teilhet, "What America Listens To," Forum, LXXXVII (May, 1932), 279.

[135]Kenneth G. Bartlett, "Trends in Radio Programs," Annals of the American Academy of Political and Social Science, CCXIII (January, 1941), 16-17.

[136]Cyrus Fisher [Darwin Teilhet], Forum, LXXXVIII (July, 1932), 64.

[137]Cyrus Fisher [Darwin Teilhet], ibid., LXXXIX (April, 1933), 256.

[138]Ring Lardner, New Yorker, June 18, 1932, p. 34.

[139]Ring Lardner, ibid., February 25, 1933, pp. 57-58.

[140]Darwin Teilhet, "What America Listens To," Forum, LXXXVIII (May 1932), 277.

[141]Seldes, The Public Arts, p. 126.

[142]Ring Lardner, New Yorker, June 25, 1932, p. 30.

[143]Jack Gould, New York Times, September 22, 1946.

[144]Seldes, The Public Arts, pp. 123-39.

[145]John K. Hutchens, New York Times, September 20, 1942.

[146]Crosby, Out of the Blue, pp. 101-02.

[147]Philip Hamburger, New Yorker, September 19, 1953, p. 105.

[148]John Crosby, Herald Tribune (New York), September 10, 1952.

149 Ring Lardner, New Yorker, May 6, 1933, p. 37.

150 Ring Lardner, The Portable Ring Lardner, ed., Gilbert Seldes (New York: Viking Press, 1946), pp. 660-61.

151 Donald Elder, Ring Lardner (Garden City: Doubleday and Company, Inc., 1956), p. 355.

152 Gilbert Seldes, New Republic, March 26, 1927, p. 140.

153 Cyrus Fisher [Darwin Teilhet], Forum, XCI (February, 1934), 127.

154 John Wallace, Radio Broadcast, X (February, 1927), 377.

155 Jack Gould, New York Times, May 30, 1948.

156 Saul Carson, New Republic, December 15, 1947, p. 32.

157 John Wallace, Radio Broadcast, XII (January, 1928), 219.

158 John Wallace, ibid., VIII (April, 1926), 668.

159 Ibid., p. 669.

160 John Wallace, ibid., VIII (February, 1926), 446-47.

161 Jennie Mix, Radio Broadcast, VI (March, 1925), 885.

162 Jennie Mix, ibid., VI (January, 1925), 454.

163 Many of his columns, particularly during the fall of 1924, printed letters from readers.

164 John Wallace, Radio Broadcast, XII (January, 1928), 220.

165 Leslie Allen, Christian Science Monitor, October 17, 1931.

166 Leslie Allen, ibid., June 13, 1931.

167 Cyrus Fisher [Darwin Teilhet], Forum, LXXXIX (January, 1933), 62.

168 Cyrus Fisher [Darwin Teilhet], ibid., XCI (March, 1934), 189-90.

169 Jack Gould, New York Times, November 11, 1951.

170 Robert Lewis Shayon, Christian Science Monitor, January 15, 1952.

171 Ace, The Book of Little Knowledge, p. 121.

172 Robert Lewis Shayon, Saturday Review, August 11, 1951, p. 32.

173 Ibid.

174 Cyrus Fisher [Darwin Teilhet], Forum, LXXXIX (April, 1933), 254.

[175]Robert Lewis Shayon, Saturday Review, March 13, 1954, p. 39.

[176]Jack Gould, New York Times, February 6, 1955.

[177]Crosby, Out of the Blue, pp. 227-29.

[178]Seldes, The Public Arts, pp. 138-39.

[179]See, for example, John Crosby, Herald Tribune (New York), February 3, 1952, and Marya Mannes, Reporter, March 24, 1955, pp. 37-39.

[180]Jack Gould, "What TV Is--And What It Might Be," New York Times Magazine, June 10, 1951, p. 24.

[181]Jack Gould, New York Times, December 17, 1950.

CHAPTER VI

THE CRITICS' APPRAISAL OF BROADCAST NEWS AND OPINION

Facts and figures, scandal and surmise, all traveling with the speed of light, have bombarded the American public in response to its desire for news and opinion. If entertainment has had its triumphs and trials recorded by the critics, so, too, has this diverse informational area which includes the broadcasting of news, commentary, discussion, and politics. Filling a small percentage of the total broadcast schedule, these programs have, nevertheless, drawn remarkably large and steady audiences; and in their coverage of special events, they have often captured the eyes and ears of the entire nation. Consequently, the critics are interested in the skills required to inform and persuade by means of radio and television, and they are concerned about the problems inherent to such programs. Since, for example, what is termed point of view in a playwright may be construed as bigotry in a commentator, and since artistic controversy in a drama may be less serious than political clashings in a public forum, the critics must consider matters divorced from the entertainment area, such as problems of editorializing and techniques for presenting the whole truth. The following sections, then, will assay critics' judgments about the quality of the four information services mentioned above, which, whether sponsored or sustaining, provide audiences with backgrounds of knowledge and conjecture.

News

As far back as 1931 when Leslie Allen protested that the reading of items from a newspaper was not a bona-fide news broadcast,[1] professional critics have encouraged attempts to achieve genuineness in such programs. They hoped that copy would be prepared in accordance with the kind of "economy of language" and compression into "significant fact" which Amy Loveman, editor of the Saturday Review of Literature, praised as characterizing the excellent news reporting during World War II.[2] In 1937 Gilbert Seldes frowned upon news broadcasts which strived for a semblance of reality by using appropriate but artificial sound effects in the background.[3] And the critics, of course, decried any style of vocal delivery which was too heavily tinged with a false-seeming emotion.

Then, when news broadcasts appeared on television, other elements interferred with the kind of sincerity critics appreciated. Marya Mannes was not only displeased with newscasters' smiles: "Facts are not meant to ingratiate."[4] but she went even further and said that reporters were "an awkward and superfluous factor" on a screen which should pictorialize the event being reported.[5] Jack Gould, on the other hand, felt that too great a concern for the visual resulted in feature material receiving more emphasis than news. He suggested, in 1949, that John Cameron Swayze read the straight news and that any feature material follow his presentation: "Keep the news and the show business each in its own place."[6] When Kenneth Banghart appeared on NBC-TV in 1954, Mr. Gould wrote that the program had:

> no intrusive visual gimmicks, no frills and no interruptions. Mr. Banghart's newscast is unusually well edited; he delivers the summary without tricky inflection. In short, he puts the news above the picture which is as it should be.[7]

Reading the news over the air will always be second best, of course, since the supremacy of radio and television lies in transmitting the actual, and since the describing or showing of a news event as it occurs is the ultimate in straight reporting. Despite the blindness of radio, talented ad-libbing at the scene of the excitement can provide a swift, powerful and accurate eye witness report. Mr. Allen came to appreciate skill at impromptu speaking when he listened to four different announcers at the time of Wiley Post's world circling flight in 1931 and decided that Paul Dumon, because of his lack of repetition, was most effective.[8] Another convincing demonstration of the value of the ad-lib report occurred during the eighteen day Munich Crisis in September, 1938, when H. V. Kaltenborn's eighty-five newscasts kept America riveted to its radio sets.[9] Such instantaneous transmission constitutes a public service which no other medium can provide. Saul Carson was extremely proud of the thorough 1948 presidential election return broadcasts by every major radio network and hundreds of small stations: "The press couldn't possibly give the people of this country the kind of exciting, minute by minute news expected from radio."[10]

Expectations from television were, of course, equally high. Before the medium had really gotten underway in the late forties, Albert Williams stated that it was "best geared for seeing things happen that actually happen, rather than heavily created unreality."[11] The critics columns reported television pickups with great interest. For example, at the laying of the United Nations Building cornerstone, in 1949, Philip Hamburger remarked, "Here was history in the most minute detail. . . . I had the feeling, as I watched it, that television was fulfilling a high function--if it wants to fulfill a high function."[12]

To most of the critics the doubt expressed in Mr. Hamburger's last phrase is justified, since on-the-scene reporting in radio as well as television has never been undertaken with the efficient devotion its importance warrants. At times the reporting of an emergency is fumbled because of the deep reluctance of broadcasters to upset their regular schedules, and at other times the coverage of a special event is executed with so much fanfare and boasting from the industry that it is difficult to separate the program from the medium carrying it.

Ignoring responsibility is obviously the more serious charge and one which has greatly disturbed Jack Gould. Two incidents in particular focused his attention on the indifferent manner in which broadcasters are apt to respond to an important news story. In 1952, President Truman, during a dinner speech announced his decision not to run for another term. CBS was the lone television network carrying the address, which actually went to only eighteen cities, since another thirty-six affiliates did not schedule this special event. The announcement came at 10:57 P. M., so that most of the eleven o'clock newscasts did not mention it. Although stations did interrupt programs with a brief special bulletin, broadcasting continued its regular course with only one station returning to the scene of the dinner and the excitement which the President's decision had created. Of this lack of responsibility, Mr. Gould said:

> Networks think not as journalists but as merchants of time. . . . But broadcasters must learn that the event as it happens is television's greatest attraction. Cost is a factor but it must be accepted as part of the hazards of a business in which every broadcaster participates by choice.[13]

He refused to excuse broadcasters for their inability to react immediately to an emergency when they constantly operate under split-second decisions. He called for putting executives in charge of news who would be given the power to delay succeeding shows, omit commercials, or do whatever "good news sense dictates."[14]

On another occasion, when the United Nations Security Council was engaging in stormy sessions eventually leading to the first emergency general assembly in the organization's history, only one television station in the country carried the proceedings extensively. Mr. Gould furiously called the networks' failure "stupid, selfish and irresponsible --an absolute mockery of the industry's obligation to serve the public interest." He continued: "If TV is to be only a parlor carnival, let it say so and stop its pompous proclamations about being in the field of communications. . . . When vital history was being made, NBC video was fascinated by 'Queen for a Day' in Hollywood."[15]

Such a denunciation is evidence of the frustration most critics feel when these potentially powerful news media are paralyzed by other interests and a "hot" story is lost forever. It might seem surprising that the ideals which a journalist-critic like Mr. Gould would urge upon his newspaper's chief competitor are so high. But he sees broadcasting and the press as complementing each other's services to the immense benefit of the public. Since broadcasting will always have the edge in speed, he feels it should develop specialized staffs who can get the story on the air immediately, leaving the press to provide evaluation, background and a permanent record. If the story can be televised so much the better; such an operation would keep newspaper men objective, accurate and alert.[16]

While bearing critical castigation for broadcasting so few actual news events, the industry has generally been permitted to bask in glory for those it has aired, at least until the critics discern particular problems at second glance. Some of the most satisfactory comments came to television for its early broadcasts (1949-50) from the United Nations.

Although Mr. Hamburger had misgivings about the wisdom of the Ford Motor Company's sponsorship (He wondered what networks did with all their money.), he felt that the "U. N. broadcasts should be of inestimable value in clearing up some of the misconceptions of the post war world."[17] He and Mr. Shayon perceived an excitement in these telecasts which made them interesting beyond their capacity to inform. Mr. Shayon called attention to "the quality of drama emanating from U. N. telecasts,"[18] and Mr. Hamburger compared a session with Mr. Malik and Mr. Warren (delegates to the Security Council) to "a game of parliamentary chess" during which the conflict was increased because cameras were focused solely on the faces of the two principal players.[19] The critics' interest in these international games availed nothing, however, since the "eyes" of the spectators were shortly capped and carried back to home studios. Four years later John Crosby ruefully reminded his readers of the wasted resources for television programing at the United Nations headquarters:

> Technically the United Nation's television facilities are as good as anything you'll find anywhere--and yet they are hardly ever used. . . . Even when debate on immensely newsworthy topics rages at white heat, no network will carry it live. The time has been sold.[20]

Though time was not available for chess on the grand scale, almost as if in answer to Jack Gould's petition, the networks did venture into televising a few smaller but perhaps nastier local games. The success of the United Nations broadcasts had prompted the New York Times critic to remark in 1950 that cameras would be invaluable to the public, if they were trained upon Congressional hearings.[21] Six months later, Senator Kefauver with his Crimes Investigating Committee flickered into focus on the receiving tubes of homes across the nation. Here was all the thrill of a genuine cat and mouse activity enhanced by the sanctions of national necessity and the democratic process. Professional critics began immediately to analyze the production elements in this legal and parliamentary contest which conceivably could have exasperated audiences into switching off their sets rather than fascinating them into switching off their irons and stoves and even factory machines to watch.

Although Mr. Hamburger dignified the proceedings by seeing in them a demonstration of the "methods by which a society questions its leaders,"[22] Jack Gould approached the hearings as a piece of theater with important implications for television producers. Audience interest was maintained basically by unusual glimpses of under-world activity and by tense clashes between witnesses and committee members. But beyond that the realism portrayed by the cameras was utterly compelling. The spontaneity of the cast was reinforced by their lack of makeup: "Faces had the naturalness of life itself. There was depth, perspective and shading whereas so often people on TV look 'washed out!'" Further, Mr. Gould felt that the producers who simply let their cameras rest on the room during recesses were wisely considerate of the audience's ability to contemplate its own conclusions. Commentators on some channels, who talked on and on to fill time, exemplified "old-fashioned, out-dated radio." In summary, a producer should let "the camera tell its own story in its own way" and the viewer should be permitted to "do his own reporting."[23]

Robert Lewis Shayon felt, however, that the viewer needed guidance, even editorializing by broadcasters, at least at the conclusion of the sessions. He suggested that the hearings be followed by well-prepared documentary programs:

> I want leadership and direction by the experts--criminologists, psychologists, sociologists, statesmen, yes, even philosophers. I want to know whether the Senate crime hearings were merely the unhappiest circus I ever saw--or whether this thing called television can really make a positive dent in our mores.[24]

Intensely interested though they were in the "show," some critics, including John Crosby and Saul Carson, wondered if millions of additional pairs of eyes peering into the committee chambers did not result in a serious new twist to traditional federal procedures. Similar doubts were, of course, raised by legislators, lawyers and civil groups throughout the country. Mr. Crosby felt that a national audience increased the underlying emotions in the hearings, modified the answers and the behavior of witnesses, and aroused the populace to a far greater degree than would otherwise have happened. Although this might be beneficial when crime legislation was under consideration, he foresaw dangers to the calm atmosphere required for committees studying such areas as foreign policy: "Then we'll have to judge the proceedings not on the physical attractions or personal problems of the witnesses but, of all things, on what they have to say."[25] Saul Carson asked:

> What if the issues were ideological, instead of political or criminal? . . . Is there a way to trust the good sense of our citizens to practice democracy on a mass scale--and at the same time protect the innocent: make it easier for the honest man to defend himself?"[26]

Mr. Seldes answers some of these criticisms abruptly: "If the existence of the audience is having an evil effect . . . I would sooner have Congress mend its manners than take away the right of the people to look upon their law makers."[27] And despite the intimation of levity in Mr. Gould's comparison of the hearings to theatrical drama, he was soberly convinced of their citizenship value. In a later article he took issue with those who feared the propriety of televising such events. He believed that much of this agitation was inspired by politicians themselves, whom he accused of wanting to use broadcasting for their purposes on their terms, but of hesitating to allow their constituents to see them at work. Mr. Gould called upon television's leaders to secure their rights in this important area of public service. He even surmised that, in addition to informing the nation, such programs might discipline government officials into more serious behavior. As for the distractions caused by the mechanics of television pickup, Mr. Gould felt they were far less serious than the traditional operations of newsreel and still photographers. He suggested that the entire system of news coverage might bring less confusion into a hearing, if newsreels were taken from the picture tubes, and if members of the press utilized video in quarters outside the hearing room for their reports.[28]

The prerogatives of a free press have taken decades to develop. So that differences of opinion with respect to the privileges and responsibilities of two additional media of information appearing in the space of thirty years are only to be expected. However, were the new media convinced (as is the press) of the <u>duty</u> to inform, more progress would have been made in establishing a philosophy and a structure of operation for broadcasting events of this nature. Public enthusiasm alone for the Crime Committee telecasts and again in 1954 for the more spectacular coverage of the Army-McCarthy hearings, should have prompted some considered decisions by the industry and the Federal Communications Commission. But the inevitable vacillation of an industry which has not yet been able to devise a communications rationale capable of balancing entertainment with information, and which has received little direction from its licensor or its audience, results in a makeshift policy dedicated to monetary expediency rather than to the welfare of society.

The professional critics generally tend to favor more complete and more regular broadcast news of this kind. Jack Gould, for example, saw that radio could recapture some of the prestige it lost to television if it would carry legislative hearings more frequently.[29] And Gilbert Seldes proposed more transmission of governmental activities for two reasons: first, the networks and the public believe "there is specific value in having full and immediate broadcasts of certain public events,"[30] and second, the present policy of expediency will seriously influence our political life, since hearings which are convenient to broadcast will acquire special value to the detriment of balance in public information.[31] In spite of the costliness of "all news or none," Mr. Seldes agrees with Mr. Gould that the public interest, which broadcasters are licensed to serve, demands implementation of thorough news coverage. Mr. Seldes suggests that expenses could be reduced by a pooling of the networks' talent, facilities and time.[32] Of course, there exists the danger of men in public life being transformed by the presence of cameras into skillful actors rather than competent statesmen, and there exists the danger of the inflammatory chance remark being heard by millions or its more likely counterpart, the innocuous remark dictated by fear of misstatement wasting the time of millions.[33] But some carefully established policies, and wisdom on the part of broadcasters, participants and audiences will, in the opinion of most critics, make these risks entirely worth the running.

Lying somewhere between the straight newscast which reports what happened and the on-the-scene broadcast which reports what is happening, is a type of edited realism which, by means of taped or filmed comments made by participants at the scene, reports what was happening. Two examples elicited opposing critical opinions and emphasized the fact that interstitial commentary determines whether such segments of recordings are to be classified as news or opinion programs similar to documentaries. Jack Gould, in 1948, commended a series produced by the Mutual Broadcasting System called "Radio Newsreel," which strictly limited narration and emphasized the stories of personalities involved in events. He considered the program an innovation which truly realized "radio's journalistic potential."[34] But Robert Lewis Shayon, writing in 1951 of similar programs--CBS's "Hear It Now" and NBC's "Voices and Events"--was unimpressed, primarily because he felt that actuality alone was of little service to the public:

> Here, I submit, is a limited use of facilities, materials, and of manpower. . . . The listener at the loud speaker suffers from a surfeit of the images of the actuality. . . . What he needs is a lot more help in putting together the parts of the puzzle. . . . Let [news producers] go ahead and apply a point of view, editorial or esthetic [to actuality tapes]--any point of view so long as it is honest, creative, responsible and courageous.[35]

Mr. Shayon's plea is not unusual. As grateful as the critics are for the efforts of stations to supply audiences quickly and (when possible) directly with reports of world-wide activities, they seem to be even more anxious that the public be apprised of the significance of those activities. After hearing of a station which was flying a man to Europe for a week-end of news gathering preparatory to assembling a "first hand report," John Crosby doubted if even "jet-propelled news coverage" was sufficient for the task of truly informing the public. He wryly commented:

> The assimilation of all this information and opinion, the presenting of it in some coherent and meaningful whole, the contribution to the Wisdom of the American people . . . will have to be worked out later. The big thing is to get there and get back fast.[36]

It is clear that Mr. Shayon and Mr. Crosby are calling, partly at least, for more commentary in addition to news. Facts are apt to be more useful if accompanied by interpretation. Although their request has validity, broadcasting, as we shall see, has not been derelict in providing programs of commentary.

Commentary

Straight news on the air is a service appreciated but largely taken for granted by the critics and the public alike, with the exception of special, on-the-scene events which will always create some degree of excitement. Commentary on the air, however, has elicited more concern, at least from critics. The reasons are obvious. The newscaster, of course, practices selectivity as he builds his program, but generally his items are objectively worded. The commentator, on the other hand, surrounds the objective fact with subjective analysis, interpretation and opinion. The newscaster reports events; the commentator attempts to explain their significance. His is a more creative function entailing risk and controversy; it therefore attracts more attention from the critics.

Commentators were not in heavy demand until the public seemed to require spokesmen who had the nerve (if not always the brilliance) to attempt to fit the cataclysmic events of the middle thirties and then of the war period into some pattern. Nevertheless, there were some before this period. H. V. Kaltenborn received a brief but complimentary notice from Leslie Allen in 1931. Mr. Allen, however, preferred William Hard whom he described as "incisive and forceful."[37] A gossip-columnist, who appeared on a Lucky Strike program in 1932 and who slowly shifted from comment on trivia to pronouncements on major issues, apparently intrigued Darwin Teilhet. He felt that Walter Winchell was a "symptom, as well as a scandalously engaging institution of our times" with a "brassily impertinent tongue,"[38] an "indomitable, brazen assurance," and a voice which had the "incredibly fascinating clatter of the newspaper press."[39] Labelling both the staid Mr. Kaltenborn and the raucous Walter Winchell as commentators is logical only if one remembers that they dealt with opinion as well as fact, unlike Lowell Thomas or Edwin C. Hill (also prominent at the time) who were straight newscasters.

With the increase of political tension and violent activity in world affairs, the networks started to build reportorial staffs and carry sponsored newsmen, who found it increasingly difficult to maintain the impersonal stands which seemed traditionally to be desired by the government and the broadcasters. Perhaps chaos demands commentary. At any rate, even the F.C.C.'s Mayflower decision of 1941 (repealed in 1949), which forebade editorializing by stations, did not prevent the rise to fame of several commentators. The more recent impact of a few of them upon the critics will now be examined.

Briefly put, professional critics prefer cold commentary to hot. This does not mean they eschew all emotion, but rather that they want it touched with the coolness of reason. They like commentators, who, in the words of Marya Mannes, "address the mind" rather than "aim at the viscera."[40] Two examples of the emotional analyst are to be found in Mr. Winchell, whose popularity continued from the early thirties into the early fifties, and in Gabriel Heatter, whose longevity is almost as great. Miss Mannes, in words which are apt and typical of other critical comment, describes Walter Winchell as a combination "Messiah, Revere, and Cassandra" and Mr. Heatter as "absurd" and "portentous."[41] And Jack Cluett says: "The risk you run in getting news from Mr. Heatter is that you completely lose all sense of proportion and relative values. Everything he says is dramatic news. . . . He's radio's number one medicine man."[42] Miss Mannes would go further and say that this inflammatory style in wording and delivery is <u>calculated</u> to make an audience lose its sense of proportion with regard to specific ideas:

> [The aim of such commentators is the] deliberate destruction of faith in government, in our allies, in the United Nations. . . . [This is] a form of disloyalty practiced openly by the very men who are most active in crying "treason!"[43]

The opposing type of commentary, say the critics, can be illustrated in the work of Elmer Davis and Eric Sevareid. Speaking of the former, Philip Hamburger said:

> He has something to say each week and says it courageously, analytically and brilliantly. . . . I know of no one who can compress so much news and so much clear and reasoned opinion into fifteen fleeting minutes.[44]

Similar qualities are attributed to Mr. Sevareid, who was one of the few commentators to have a brief run on television in addition to his regular radio assignment. Mr. Hamburger described him as "a quiet, intelligent, thoughtful man, perceptive, self-controlled, and independent,"[45] while John Crosby thought his program had "bite and intelligence and opinion galore."[46] Mr. Sevareid has also been praised for his style of writing. Jack Gould said that his evening "essays" on radio contained:

> the felicity of phrasing of one who appreciated the magic of words and knows how to use it. . . . He can go to the core of events and pluck out the meat and often the humor. . . . His observations on manners and morals are enhanced by a singularly quiet, deft, and amusing touch.[47]

If the emotional commentators tend to use their histrionic talents for propaganda in its unsavory sense, for what purpose are the contrasting talents of the second group of commentators employed? The critics assume that the fundamental purpose of all commentary is that of providing information in depth--a matter of supplying extensive background and considered judgments about an issue so that an audience will have some basis for an eminently thoughtful conclusion. Miss Mannes contributes the following operational definition of "the reasonable commentators' criticism":

> [It] emanates from established facts and careful consideration. They feel a responsibility toward the audience which would forbid any snap conclusions, distortion, or lifting of words out of context. They have integrity not to be intimidated by phobias of the moment, not to cater to popular emotions, not to suppress facts. Reason has no Hooper rating but it may prevail as long as reasonable commentators are on the air.[48]

It is significant that the newscasters and commentators most commended by the critics are those directly in the employ of networks. In fact, no single programing unit within each of the three major networks has received more critical praise than the news staff. These highly intelligent reporters and analysts were brought together in the crucial periods preceding and during World War II. They have been together long enough to establish standards and modes of operation which result in swift but thoughtful news coverage. The reason for the steady excellence of network personnel lies, so critics believe, in the greater freedom of operation permitted them. Oftentimes, they broadcast on a sustaining or unsponsored basis, or advertisers buy time on their programs under the stipulation that there will be no control of content. They are less hampered, therefore, by editorial restraints frequently imposed upon sponsored commentators, and they are at least partly relieved of the temptation toward a sensationalism which will bring aggrandizement to themselves and prosperity to their sponsors. Mr. Gould used the release of Drew Pearson in 1953 by ABC because of sponsor difficulties as an occasion to urge a complete divorce of this area of programing from advertising:

> Separation of news and advertising matter is not an academic whim; it is essential protection for the advertiser and newspaper man alike. . . . The only sensible path is to remove all commentary from direct sponsorship.[49]

His suggestion assumes that commentary has a place in the program schedule, but even the basic assumption has raised questions just as difficult to decide as the matter of sponsored commentary. Commentary quite naturally involves editorializing, and yet the role of the newsman has never been too clear. Reference has already been made (see p. 309) to the F.C.C. reversal of an earlier order. Editorializing by stations is now permitted, providing they present opposing views. Critics generally approved the new decision, feeling that, at least, the networks could be trusted to maintain an editorial balance in their staffs as well as in the commentators brought to them by sponsors. Mr. Carson, however, was alarmed primarily because he felt the government was abdicating all supervision over programing.[50] But Mr. Seldes was even more concerned over the practical difficulties broadcasters would have trying to balance opposing views.

In March, 1954 these troublesome issues were raised by a broadcast which may well go down in history as the media's most famous editorial program. Edward R. Murrow, CBS newscaster, commentator, and producer of "See It Now," undertook an analysis of the personality and techniques of the violently controversial Senator Joseph McCarthy. His was a sponsored (Alcoa), thirty-minute essay composed of commentary and sound-film clips of various events in the Senator's career—events in which the Senator could not help but damn himself. There was no question in the critics' minds that technically, aesthetically, and persuasively the program was a masterpiece. Philip Hamburger said simply, "I felt as if I had had an education,"[51] and Jack Gould commented grandly:

> Last week may be remembered as the week that broadcasting recaptured its soul. . . . For once television was a leader not a passive camp follower in the realms of public opinion.[52]

Although there is no conclusive proof as to the strength of television's leadership in swaying public opinion, it is more than coincidence that Senator McCarthy's prestige and influence seemed to go into a decline after the broadcast.[53] For Mr. Seldes, at least, television's power as an editorial instrument requires very careful examination, even though in this instance he tended to sympathize with its target. The crux of the danger, he believes, exists in broadcasting's well-nigh impossible task of fulfilling all that is implied in the term <u>equal time</u>, which has been the traditional method for presenting opposing viewpoints in an editorial controversy. Although the Senator was given a half-hour on the same series several weeks later, he did not have the same financial resources, and more important, the same talented television staff at his command. (Equal time on radio usually means one speech replying to another, but the drama in the visual elements of the new medium is obviously more difficult to counter with equal effectiveness.) Moreover, Mr. McCarthy would not have an identical audience, nor could he dispel the feeling of being an invited intruder on a program which, during two years, had built a massive reputation for honesty in the presentation of all its issues. "It is more important," said Mr. Seldes, "to use our communication systems properly than to destroy McCarthy, and every new development in the handling of controversy in television, particularly, needs to be examined to make sure that the enthusiasm of a crusading liberal hasn't placed new weapons in the hands of the demagogues."[54]

In his later thinking about this situation, Mr. Seldes proferred the idea that equal time might better be interpreted to mean half of the same program developed as rebuttal using the same resources as were available to the initiators of the period. Another way to solve the injustices in dealing with controversy would be to restrict editorializing to the realm of ideological conflicts, thereby avoiding attacks on individuals and the necessity for rebuttals. To separate the idea from the individual propounding it might require a kind of delicate diplomacy which would result in the complete evaporation of an entire program. However, until broadcasters have devised clearer rules, Mr. Seldes would not permit the expose of individuals in an editorial program, nor would he permit the commercial sponsorship of any type of editorial attack.[55]

Other critics do not see the necessity for such drastic measures. Jack Gould agreed that CBS should have made equal financial and program resources available to Senator McCarthy,[56] but he felt that editorial "balance is just as effectively achieved and clarity often far better served if one side of a controversy is presented coherently and without interruption on one program [and] the other side on a subsequent broadcast." Aware of potential dangers, he would still insist that the broadcaster go ahead, fulfilling "his difficult assignment with judgment, discernment, and care."[57] And John Crosby would simply vest his faith in the good sense of the audience:

> It seems to me that Murrow has influence simply because he doesn't misuse it and the minute he tried to, he wouldn't have it.
>
> Perhaps I am over optimistic, but I feel strongly that the American people not only cannot be gulled, but would violently resent any attempt at persuasion on matters they hold dear. They will buy the toothpaste, they will laugh at the jokes, they will tune in by the millions. But these are matters of no moment.
>
> The moment you get into areas where they feel deeply . . . skepticism mounts. In fact, it might be stated as

Crosby's Law that the more important the subject is the less influence the guy with the mike has.[58]

Certainly, it is obvious that most of the professional critics, regardless of instances of misused editorializing, encourage more commentary rather than less. The comparatively favorable record of radio in this area has predisposed them to expect integrity, courage and wisdom in a commentator. In 1950, they deplored, with Jack Gould, the fact that "TV is practically devoid of straight forward interpretive opinion."[59] Realizing that television producers were inclined to dismiss the static picture of a man talking, they were excited and encouraged by Mr. Murrow's editorial experimentation with the use of film plus commentary. This was close to the documentary form, as shall be seen in the next chapter. Robert Lewis Shayon even suggested that if commentary had to be made more visual, why not entrust it to puppets.[60] But one still feels that critics are in the end lovers of talk and that they would really prefer nothing more than a Sevareid or an Agronsky or a Davis quietly seated in front of a camera. John Crosby saw it once and liked it. He said:

> There is a certain alchemy of visual personality which means the difference between one man holding your fascinated interest . . . [and another] oring hell out of you. . . . [I particularly liked David Brinkley of NBC for his] pungent and economical style of prose, an engaging face, and a dry, sardonic tone of voice which carries great authority.[61]

Talks covers an extremely wide range and so does broadcast commentary. In order to round out this discussion, it is necessary to see what critics have had to say about radio and television personalities who comment on many areas outside the socio-politico domain reserved for news commentators.

Down through the years there has been very little discussion of the arts over commercial stations. Broadcasting has concentrated on performance rather than on cogitation. But from time to time there were short series of spoken essays on various topics. Critics have paid particular homage to Alexander Woollcott, who deserved recognition for longevity as well as quality. Starting in the late twenties and continuing for over a decade, he could be heard with fair regularity commenting on various cultural events. Leslie Allen said of Mr. Woollcott, who, in 1930, broadcast a book review program every Tuesday at the prime period of 7:45 P.M.:

> The secret of his success is his ability to pack into a single sentence or two a vast deal of youthful enthusiasm. The timbre of that enthusiasm graces the sound of his voice.[62]

Twenty years later John Crosby read some of the old scripts of this book reviewer who was then better known as the "Town Crier" and was moved to write the following:

> There isn't anyone approaching Woollcott on the air today. If there were I doubt that he'd survive. Woollcott became entrenched in the earlier days when radio was more receptive to individualists. He went his own way without fear of sponsors or Hooper. And, of course, you can't do that anymore. Even at this late date, his scripts are conspicuously individualistic, sometimes enchanting, frequently infuriating but always Woollcott.[63]

In a shift from the sublime to the ridiculous, Mr. Crosby, who seems to be particularly interested in the casual commentator, turned a scornful eye upon radio's Hollywood gossips. He quipped, in 1947, that Jimmy Fiddler's stand was "against sin and, to a somewhat lesser extent, in favor of virtue:"

> Mr. Fiddler's moral purposes are as intense as those of a small town spinster, and his methods are identical. He is, for example, strenuously opposed to Hollywood celebrities publicizing their misdeeds and he voices this disapproval (as well as a detailed account of the misdeeds) over two national networks every Sunday night.[64]

Mr. Crosby dismissed the contrived excitement of all such revelatory sessions in a 1950 column entitled, "Would They or Wouldn't They and Who Cares?" from which the following excerpt is taken:

> But at that point (9:17 P.M.E.S.T. Sunday), the issue was: Could Lex explain? Would Arlene forgive? Louella [Parsons] said they'd get married. Hedda [Hopper] said they wouldn't. Millions of us tossed in our beds that night, wondering.[65]

It is with a kind of malicious glee that some of the critics pen irreverent columns about broadcasting's popular, (and in contrast with respected personal essayists) scatterbrained commentators on trivia. Television, in particular, seems to place a premium on women whose poise, beauty and vitality comprises a photogenic charm that insures the popular success of many light programs. Philip Hamburger and John Crosby describe the species but confess they are at a loss to discover any significance in what they are doing. Mr. Hamburger portrays the new television woman as a person who is "chic, tense, commercially minded, out all night, has that high falutin manner of speech generally associated with imitators of British actors and speaks, for the most part, nonsense."[66] And John Crosby says they "are characterized by a fearful kinetic energy, a phenomenal gift of gab, an overwhelming femininity of movement . . . and that special female gift for total irrelevance."[67] The ladies generally interview one or two guests per program with whom, says Mr. Hamburger, they are "enveloped in mutual admiration."[68] The shows are mixtures "of gossip, backbiting and impudence delivered at breathless speed" which, combined with constant gestures, provide a spectacle Mr. Crosby finds "vastly more entertaining than some of the dog acts on Ed Sullivan's show."[69]

The critics appreciate the entertaining wit of a Woollcott or a John Kiernan, but they are even more grateful for the sincere yet informal intellectuality which such commentators contribute to the broadcast schedule. In contrast they tend to be repulsed by the spurious excitement of the gossip and chit-chat shows. Occasionally, even the staccato revelations of the sports commentator have been scrutinized and found wanting. John Crosby exposed the fictions which infused many of Bill Stern's famous biographical sketches of athletes:

> Even the word "hearsay" is a rather generous description, implying, as it does, that Stern's stories have reached the stature of legend and therefore are beyond the irksome confines of journalism. This is misleading. Many of the most lurid of Stern's "legends" originated in the teeming brains of his writers and started on their way to legend only after Stern put them on the air to his devoted audience which runs well into the millions.
>
> . . . .
>
> Stern's method of delivering these whoppers is in many ways even more startling than the stories. He tells them in short, declarative sentences, bristling with exclamation points. After every sentence or so, a studio organ delivers what in radio parlance is known as a "sting," a chord or series of chords which are the closest musical equivalent to an elevated eyebrow.[70]

Just as critics were looking for the genuine (even to the actual) in the presentation of news events, so too were they on the alert for sincerity and honesty in commentary about news events as well as about other aspects of life. To see the world of business and government, of art and culture, yes, of sports and glamor filtered through the sensitive and intelligent mind of a responsible commentator, results in glimpses of trends, of meanings, of possible courses of action for which confused and anxious audiences stand indebted to broadcasting. On the other hand, were audiences to see the world through the astigmatic eyes of unreasoning prejudice, or the narrow, mean eyes of slander, they would be, indeed, the victims of broadcasting. The professional critics would agree that even though programs of news and commentary are relatively meager, their quality, with some exceptions, has been good. They would like to see more such programs on television without any decrease of them in radio. A program area which needs exploration by broadcasters would be commentary by nationals of other countries beamed to the United States.[71]

In summary, the critics like good talk. Their delight would be unbounded if broadcasters would make available more commentators possessing the qualities which Mr. Shayon saw in Gerald W. Johnson on ABC-TV:

> As a biographer he sees events in life size, psychological scale; as an historian he illuminates them with the perspective of rear-projection; and as an essayist he shapes his views with humor, satire, and literary form. Harness these forces in a dry, almost a cracker-barrel delivery of plain truth . . . and you have an arresting combination. Spice it with a courageously liberal cast of mind, and you have a refreshment of the air waves which is audacious, stimulating, and vastly entertaining, not to mention useful.[72]

Discussion

The ethics and the techniques of show business comprise a basic approach to almost all broadcast programs whether their function is that of entertainment or not. The realization of this fact has made professional critics only slightly more willing to compromise the cooperative search for truth which they feel should characterize the discussion program. Consequently, they are interested but often disappointed surveyors of this genre on radio and television, since the competitive search for truth is usually more exciting and therefore more entertaining to the audience.

"America's Town Meeting of the Air," which made its debut in 1935, typifies broadcast formats which throw questions like gladiators into the arena and then permit histrionic lions (who are authorities on the topic) to tear them, and sometimes each other, apart. On the occasion of the program's fifteenth anniversary, Saul Carson said that it "often loads its questions and matches opponents chosen for their pugnaciousness and prejudices rather than for their willingness to discuss a subject fairly."[73]

That radio had established a fairly constant pattern of mixing fisticuffs with enlightenment is evident in this sigh of relief from Jack Gould who appreciated a change in a 1944 program moderated by Sumner Welles: "There is a complete absence of psuedo-excitement or 'performance' that not only is restful but is an incentive for greater attentiveness on the part of the listener."[74]

The pyrotechniques of broadcast discussion are not confined to the traditionally inflammable, political topics of programs like "Town Meeting." Literary criticism, which, at first glance, might seem to be a fairly staid area for discussion, boiled merrily into the microphone when "Author Meets the Critics" went on the air in 1947. John Crosby's review is typical of the divided mind with which most critics approach these programs:

> It's misleading to suggest that "Author Meets the Critics" is only a hair-pulling contest. Only about half of it is, which is possibly a little too much. Nevertheless, it is frequently literate, almost always entertaining, invariably informative. It helps arouse interest in books (though some of the books aren't worth the trouble) . . . . As a literary discussion it lacks the urbanity usually associated with books and the detachment that ought to accompany criticism. But if it had these qualities it probably wouldn't be such a good show.[75]

Critics find themselves in the position of having to admit that a program is a good show, while feeling in the backs of their minds that oil and water just do not mix--that the irridescent surface gleam of the oil of entertainment obscures the pure water of reasoned ideas underlying a discussion.

Entertainment seemed to receive even greater emphasis when discussion programs were televised. This is understandable, since video which is more frightened of the static program than radio continued and even heightened opportunities for injecting entertaining conflict into informative discussions. For example, "Court of Public Opinion," televised by Dumont in 1948, utilized a court room setting and legal proceedings for putting ideas dramatically on trial. In another instance, Jack Gould felt that television moderator Theodore Granick of "The American Forum of the Air" was all too skillful "at generating a maximum of heat and emotion in a debate and a minimum of light and information."[76]

As time went on, Mr. Gould viewed with actual alarm what he termed a "qualitative decline [particularly] in the discussion of current issues." In his opinion, the broadcasters' determination to pit several political spokesmen against each other results in theatrically successful but ideologically thin programs: "A participant barely has a chance to express a viewpoint before it is instantly neutralized by a contrary opinion." This kind of jockeying is "just an invitation to intellectual chaos not to education on the day's issues." In fact, the "unremitting emphasis on conflict in government may mean something over a long period of time--something for historians and sociologists to study." Mr. Gould suggests that a way out of the difficulty would be to permit exciting panel shows but to also make room for the televised address which can be a more thorough, more coherently organized piece of thinking."[77]

John Crosby, on the other hand, is less perturbed about remedying the situation, since he feels the results of these programs are beneficial:

> They [forum programs] are the closest thing to bear-baiting that remains legal in this country. And while watching bloodshed the guy at home can harbor the respectable feeling that he is being educated on public issues and public personalities--and, as a matter of fact, he is.[78]

nd speaking later of "Meet the Press," a program where leading officials submit to relentless often embarrassing interrogation by determined reporters, Mr. Crosby said: "It lures a lot of listeners into hearing matters of public concern which they might not ordinarily pay any attention to."[79]

Still a third reaction to incendiary discussion programs came from Robert Lewis Shayon. Like Mr. Gould, he accused broadcasters of devising sessions where participants could "sound-off" without necessarily having to think. Instead of scheduling straight talks to make up for deficiencies, however, he recommended utilizing a devil's advocate on these programs, whose duty it would be to "probe all the points of controversy's compass." Mr. Shayon calls this the method of dialectic rather than the method of advocacy. He feels that the typically violent, abrupt and unthinking exchanges between participants only more deeply confirms the prejudices of audience members who automatically root for their previously selected champions. With skillful prying into unanswered questions and unfollowed trains of thought, he believes ideas might begin to flow which would excite listeners or viewers into establishing new patterns of thought for themselves: "Only this is discussion in the real sense; the rest is wind-in-the-willows."[80]

Surprisingly enough, there seem to be young people who know more about discussion in this "real sense" than adults do. "Youth Wants to Know" is a television program in which teenagers ask, with refreshing candor, Senators and Cabinet members to explain their philosophies and their actions. Philip Hamburger said their questions are "generally much more penetrating and germane than a great many questions asked by trained newsmen on other programs."[81] And Marya Mannes' only regret was "that guests are not obliged to answer questions as directly and honestly as they are put. . . . Youth Wants to Know but it is Not Going to Be Told and that has come to be one meaning of politics."[82] Even with this limitation, Miss Mannes prefers such a program to many vapid youth discussions of the kind she so accurately describes in the following passage:

> The natural child is the unexpected and censorable one. . . . But when they are first screened for I. Q., presentability, and "leadership," then constricted by such subjects as "How Can We Best Further Brotherhood?" and then led by adroit and knowledgeable adults who see to it that they neither stray from the subject nor express unworthy opinions you have a mighty dull half hour.[83]

A profusion of bright sparks followed by darkness, of explosions followed by dead silence is not the only negative complaint critics have made about discussion programs. They sometimes feel that important issues receive only a surface scratching because too many authorities, in a manner reminiscent of the entertainment world's all star cast, are squeezed into a program. Even if they were gracious and unsnarling, they simply would not have time to develop their points. Such was the reaction of Jack Gould and Philip Hamburger to Mrs. Roosevelt's debut as hostess on a half-hour television discussion program in 1950. She had assembled nine guests, who were to share their thinking about atomic energy. Consequently, said Mr. Gould, the program was limited "to a mere series of platform speeches. . . . The need for simplicity and clarity was particularly urgent."[84] And Mr. Hamburger expressed the "hope that she will bring her distinguished guests back soon, under less cluttered conditions."[85]

This last phrase is particularly apt, since freedom from confusion and time to think are conditions which should prevail if the listener is to become actively involved in a discussion.[86] They were conditions which, as a matter of fact, Mrs. Roosevelt and her daughter had been able to establish a few years earlier in a series of morning chats for housewives on ABC. Saul Carson had complimented them "for giving some millions of women an opportunity to find adult conversation in daytime radio's wasteland of fatuity."[87] Another morning discussion program on NBC called, "It's a Problem," utilized a panel of experts who apparently managed to investigate delicate issues of marriage, divorce, and race prejudice with "equal intelligence and directness."[88] At least one evening program called "Conversation" also managed to achieve an air of unrushed, thoughtful amiability. It, however, did not deal with controversial issues of imminent concern. Jack Gould called "Conversation," which was more successful on radio than television, "an island of good humored intelligence amid all the Gleasonia to be found on the Saturday air waves."[89]

The same, clear atmosphere is likely to exist in an interview situation between two people. It may account, in part, for the fine critical reception given an NBC series of interviews with contemporary thinkers. For example, Bertrand Russell appeared in 1953, and Philip Hamburger, who had once declared his "unlimited respect for the potentialities of television as a public forum,"[90] felt that Mr. Russell stretched the limit even further, not only because of his wisdom, but also because of the way in which the interview was executed:

> I don't know who at NBC conceived the notion for this presentation, but he certainly deserves the whole hearted thanks of every tv-set owner who, stunned by fratricide, patricide, ordinary homicide, and quiz programs, may have begun to wonder what the set was doing around the house anyway.
>
> The program that brought Lord Russell before us was a model of intelligent simplicity. . . . The interviewer was Romney Wheeler . . . a person who believes that a television interviewer ought to be seen only fleetingly and heard hardly at all. . . . The camera did not switch back and forth between him and Lord Russell as though some sort of intellectual tennis match were underway.[91]

Speaking of the entire series of distinguished interviews, John Crosby said, "It is surprising and heartening to hear the babble of reasonably intelligent words come out of the machine that is supposed to have crushed this medieval form of entertainment."[92] Mr. Shayon, too, enjoyed the Russell interview, but he recognized it as a rarity in the discussion field, and he cautioned college television producers in particular not to be misled by a form which would seem to have been made for the campus: "The conversation piece, so ready at hand, ought to be resisted at all costs unless there is a Russell in the ivy. This imitation of the form without the combustible spirit is a shoal."[93]

The critics may condemn panel and forum discussions and even interview programs for being too violent or too rushed or too evasive; and information may be sacrificed for entertainment, but even the worst of such programs call the attention of the audience to important issues and ideas. There is, however, one type of discussion program which lacks a single redeeming feature, at least in the opinion of Mr. Cluett and Mr. Crosby. The psuedo-clinical interview on radio may have had its genesis as far back as the early thirties when Darwin Teilhet was warning his readers about a former medicine-show barker who, as "The Voice of Experience," dispersed advice on the psychological problems of those who wrote to him.[94] Answering mail, of course, would not be as emotionally interesting a program as one in which persons with problems actually appeared on the air. For many years, a former taxi driver, John J. Anthony, acted as confidante and self-educated psychiatrist to hundreds of disturbed exhibitionists. Jack Cluett described the morbidity of Mr. Anthony and sarcastically invited those who "want to hear how the other half lives, works, murders the king's English (and each other), to tune in."[95] John Crosby was not so light-hearted in his condemnation of Mr. Anthony's return to the air after an absence of several seasons:

> Years ago Anthony outraged all the recognized social agencies with his easy, unstudied and flippant solutions of the most complex problems of human relationship. Now he has escaped their jurisdiction by putting everything in the hands of the Deity where it's rather difficult to diagnose the results and sacrilegious to protest if there aren't any.
>
> . . . .
>
> Anthony, of course, is still working at the old stand of human suffering and he still can't quite prevent himself from smacking his lips with enthusiasm over an especially juicy case. He even gets this enthusiasm into the commercials which he rolls off his tongue sonorously, sanctimoniously and, at the same time, happily.[96]

Here is utter degradation in discussion programs and an example of broadcasting's short-sighted viewpoint with respect to genuine public service. Hasty, even questionable solutions are proffered to suffering souls whose troubles should be treated in private, while the thoughtful consideration of major societal problems all too frequently remains unaired, or takes the form of an undisciplined scrap. Critics welcome the deep, authoritative probing of the serious panel, and the witty, knowledgeable banter of the casual discussion. To be informed by breadth of fact and opinion is to be better prepared for solving life's problems and enjoying life's experiences. Critics urge that broadcasting's potentials in the discussion area be tapped much more fully than they have been to date.

Politicians and Political Conventions

Regardless of the disdain which Americans are supposed to hold for the politician and his turbulent activity in conducting the business of government, they express an intense spectator interest, at least, in his selection and in his public appearances. Recalling how KDKA, a Pittsburgh station, aroused tremendous interest in broadcasting when it announced the Harding-Cox presidential election returns in 1920, it is easy to understand why the airwaves continue to play a major role through the years in projecting the leaders and the operations of democracy into citizens' homes. The professional observer has made some interesting comments about the utilization of radio and television by candidates, office-holders, and party workers. His ideas are too fragmentary to comprise a politician's handbook, but they are, nevertheless, a valuable account of this type of informational program.

Having listened to the broadcast of the 1924 Democratic Convention, an editorial writer from the Saturday Evening Post predicted that radio would result in:

> the debunking of present day oratory and the selling of higher standards of public speaking . . . [and that] silver tongued orators whose fame has been won before sympathetic [visual] audiences are going to scale down to their real stature when the verdict comes from radio audiences.[97]

Although the author of this editorial may have overlooked the fact that the real stature of a radio speaker might be increased rather than reduced since he was now accessible to audiences numbering in the millions, he was correct in predicting a change in the style of public address.

Darwin Teilhet catalogued specific vocal virtues which he heard in prominent politicians of the early thirties and they could be summed up, perhaps, in two words: intimacy and sociableness. With reference to verbal style he felt that those who abjured noble statements and complex phraseology for simple even entertaining discourse, no matter how important the message, would be assured of a better reception by the radio audience. Al Smith and Senator Borah were selected as good examples of the new radio politician. He particularly complimented Governor Smith for having the courage to ad-lib, in spite of his tendency to make grammatical errors. As a matter of fact, he thought his colloquialisms stood him in good stead coupled as they were with his fearlessness in saying what he believed. On the other hand, Mr. Teilhet thought President Hoover's voice was detrimental for radio work, since it gave the "effect of an old fashioned phonograph in need of winding." Although he recognized the value of Franklin Roosevelt's clear, educated voice, he suggested that "he watch his Harvard accent since a large number of voters west of the Mississippi have strong ideas about anyone who neglects an 'R' or rests lovingly upon an 'A'."[98]

Apparently, mistrust of President Roosevelt's accent disappeared, since he received the accolade of critics and public alike for his masterful radio communicative ability. Not the least of his success lay in, what Ben Gross analyzed as, his ability to give emotional appeals "the illusion of cold logic" and to invest large issues "with a sense of intimacy."[99] Mr. Gross reports that the idea for the famous "fireside chats," through which Roosevelt made political issues a vital common concern, came from Merlin Aylesworth, the president of NBC. These talks which the president read from a loose leaf notebook were, says Mr. Gross, built word upon phrase upon sentence with "the invisible audience in mind."[100]

If the rule had been for politicians to scale down their oratorical powers when using the microphone, it was repeated even more strongly when they stood in front of television cameras. "Quiet sincerity," predicted John Crosby, "will be the characteristic of the TV politician of the future."[101] And from other critical comments, it became evident that a speaker would have greater success in achieving this characteristic if his appearance carried an air of informality. From 1948 on, then, the television techniques of various political leaders were examined for their effectiveness in conveying the image of quiet sincerity. At the 1948 convention in Philadelphia, President Truman's device of using written notes supplemented by ad-lib remarks established a spontaneity which Jack Gould felt "could become a widely copied pattern on video."[102] Those who were unskilled at the impromptu method, could learn, as Mr. Eisenhower did for the 1952 campaign, to read from large cards which, John Crosby indicated, still permitted a personal, direct-to-camera touch.[103]

In regard to cameras, it is interesting to note Mr. Gould's appreciation of the fact that Vice President Nixon, during one speech, employed a single camera only. This dispensed with the frightened look of the amateur who tries to follow more than one camera, and it contributed to closer audience contact:

> The intrusive mixture of angle shots, closeups and distant shots . . . is avoided. Rather there is a promotion of true rapport between the speaker in the studio and the audience in the home with no theatrical busybody coming between them.[104]

But it remained for Thomas Dewey in the gubernatorial campaign of 1950 to conduct the first major experiment in televised political informality. He sat on the edge of a desk and answered questions for several hours telephoned into him from all over the state. John Crosby saw two benefits in this type of program:

> First, it humanized Thomas Dewey as he had never been humanized before. . . . Secondly, and more importantly, it eliminated the normal pomposities of political rhetoric. A man thinking on his feet is likely to blurt out the truth, rather than the well-rounded, wind-filled phrase. . . .
> . . . .
> Television throws a merciless white light on phoniness. The candidate had better know what he's talking about and he had better not try to evade a question. The candidate, I'm convinced, could be ugly as a hedgehog; it is not his looks that television puts under scrutiny; it is his ability.[105]

Although handsomeness as a specific attribute is not deemed important, sociability of manner--the gestures and expressions of amicability--is. Mr. Crosby felt that General McArthur looked too austere and forbidding.

while Senator Taft seemed impatient and carried a cold grin of hostility.[106] Adlai Stevenson, on the other hand, who could not be described as having too frosty a manner, nevertheless, "chose," in the opinion of Ben Gross, "to be witty rather than humorous--and that, so the argument runs, was fatal."[107]

Actually, of course, Mr. Crosby is correct when he says, "There is no single right way for a candidate to behave on television. . . . [His task is] to display at best advantage his most conspicuous talents and to suppress at all costs his shortcomings."[108] In summary, the talents most critics believe to be helpful are those which convey to listening and viewing audiences the qualities of warmth, of sincerity, and of a knowingness devoid of flippancy and pedantry.

The new mass media may have banished the distortions and the emotional force of old fashioned oratory, but there remained the uncomfortable feeling that even the directness and quietness of television could be manipulated for a less than completely fair approach to the public. As much as he appreciated the genuine tour de force of Mr. Dewey's question and answer session, John Crosby reminded his readers that such a program had its pitfalls: "Many of the questions hurled at Dewey seemed rigged; all of them were certainly screened; the embarrassing ones were probably eliminated."[109]

Marya Mannes, writing, of course for a publication which supported Mr. Stevenson in the 1952 campaign, described in unflattering terms the television assistance his opponent received from Thomas Dewey and Claire Luce:

> Dewey seen only from waist up has stature; his clean, neat "open" face fills the screen; his eyes pin yours with a compelling show of candor. Miss Luce's fragile beauty, her look of troubled concern when serious, of feminine radiance

> when amused, dazzle the eye while deflecting it from her rabbit punches. Their smiles, as recurrent as they are mirthless, their unshatterable coolness, their plausibility, have--at the time--a deadly efficacy.
>
> It is on TV screen . . . that a certain coarseness is revealed beneath this external refinement. . . . [Dewey] read eighteen newspaper headlines about Harry Truman in a speech before the Young Republican Club on October 20. To quote from them was to quote from distorted fractions of the truth.
>
> . . . .
>
> [Miss Luce's] tactics, however, were on no higher a level than Mr. Dewey's. . . . On September 30 she "proved" by lavish use of carefully selected films, maps, and papers that "Red deals" had been made at Yalta, etc.[110]

This opinion, despite its obvious partisanship, does indicate that television need not necessarily be synonymous with truth and that all the electronic gadgets and visual aids opened wide to serve the politician, might, in the end, only narrow the view of the voters. Broadcasting may differ essentially from tent oratory only with respect to technique and the size of the affected audience. It is this last difference which bothers Gilbert Seldes. For him, slander within earshot of a handful of people is not the same as slander broadcast to the nation, even though the electorate tends to shrug off both types as mere political hazards. He felt the virulence of the 1954 Congressional Campaign on television was particularly damaging to the fairness upon which democratic elections should rest:

> The American tradition is to laugh all these things [malignancy and slander] off as campaign oratory. . . . When it is heard by millions at home . . . the tradition of magnanimity is only an encouragement to further filth in the next campaign. I propose an end to forgiveness. I base it on the dangerously magnified capacity of television to hurt.[111]

Having examined critics' reactions to individual practitioners of political speech making on the air, let us turn to their reactions to political conventions on the air. Unlike the entertainment world which conducts its auditions and rehearses its cast in private and then rings up the curtain, the political world auditions its stars, and puts on its greatest rehearsal and greatest performance simultaneously in full view of the audience. This makes a party convention a mixture of boredom and excitement, of orderliness and confusion, of pure hokum and true emotion, of serious debates and flamboyant harangues. It is a three-ring circus, but it is also a national town meeting.

Critics, on the whole, were more than pleased with the views brought to them by the television cameras. Their remarks primarily concern the 1952 conventions since these were so definitely television events. It was the first time "All sides," according to Philip Hamburger, had "sought [television] out, bargained for its favors, and generally pampered it." And, he continued, "The cameras . . . maintained a wonderful impartiality . . . direct and unbiased."[112] Robert Lewis Shayon congratulated the medium for its "magnificent reporting job, rich in distributional success and generous with consequences for our now fluid political mores."[113]

One of the consequences of televising the conventions, says Mr. Hamburger, is the way in which the cameras stimulate "one's sense of participation in matters that concern one deeply. . . . [They make] the viewer a member of a community vastly larger than his own without demanding that he sacrifice any of his individuality."[114] This feeling of fellowship is partly the result of television's almost awesome ability to familiarize the home spectator with complete strangers, "as though one were confined with them during the crossing of the Atlantic."[115] From each successive hour of intimate contact with nominees and delegates, with prominent officials and commentators, comes the powerful realization that here, for better or worse, is the collective "voice and face of our free institutions."[116]

The critics have perceived other less fortunate consequences which may be minor in comparison with the superb education and stimulation of the public, but which, nonetheless, are worthy of consideration. Any decision to televise a political event is, at least in our system of broadcasting, an important financial decision. From the time when portions of the 1924 conventions were broadcast, until the 1948 campaign, stations and networks had initiated and proudly accepted the financial burden of extremely broad, on-the-scene reporting of the politicians' most exciting show. The tradition of treating the conventions as straight public service programing was partially set aside in 1948 when NBC and *Life* magazine undertook to present the activities in Philadelphia and to advertise their own activities at the same time. Although there was some protest, it was not until 1952 when large manufacturers of consumer goods offered to underwrite the six-million dollar cost of the broadcasts that more widespread, critical misgivings were expressed. John Crosby cautioned his readers:

> It's important . . . to note that money has got its foot in the door. . . . There is, in short, a steady and perceptible lowering of the high standards which once governed the broadcast of election news--in so far as money is concerned.[117]

Gilbert Seldes analyzed in some detail the possible consequences of commercial sponsorship. Most important, he felt, was the fact that the basic principle of free time for political discussion was in jeopardy, and that conceivably a new formula could move into operation, gauging the amount of time a party was given to the amount of money a sponsor would contribute. He voiced a second fear: "It is unthinkable that a sponsor should prejudice the report of a political event, but I have often found that the 'unthinkable' is often what a lot of people are thinking." Mr. Seldes recalled John Crosby's account of an incident during the 1948 telecast when an angry splinter group of Southern Democrats was asked by a broadcast director to stage a throwing away of their convention badges for the camera. They were not shown pinning them on again. "Who," asks Mr. Seldes, "will draw the line between effective showmanship and the good little undiscoverable fake?" Add to these items of concern, the question as to whether an unpopular movement such as Henry Wallace's 1948 Third Party would receive sponsorship, and whether non-sponsor stations would be able to give their audiences effective coverage and the entire matter takes on more serious dimensions than might, at first, seem evident.[118]

Despite these troublesome points, Mr. Seldes was not displeased with the 1952 sponsorship. He felt that commercials, tedious though they were, remained admirably separated from the programs and that the networks' additional revenue permitted them to hire crews and equipment for wider, more flexible coverage than had ever been given a convention before.[119] It may be that recognition of these dangers by the public, the industry, and the political parties is all that is necessary to prevent any reportorial distortion by the media.

Another possible unsatisfactory consequence of televised conventions may be a surfeiting of the public with respect to political affairs and a subsequent lessening of interest in the election process. Although Mr. Seldes reported optimistically that the 1952 conventions were received by some thirteen million homes,[120] Mr. Gould was disturbed by the number of Americans who did not tune in. He wondered whether great sections of the public were so "addicted to entertainment that they can't do without it for a few days," and whether there wasn't a point beyond which television might "contribute unintentionally to inertia among the electorate."[121]

The parties, themselves, may have had similar fears, because no sooner had the sights and sounds of the conventions left the living rooms of the nation, than program planners went to work to make the remaining few months of the broadcast campaign as entertainingly persuasive as possible. An additional eight or nine million dollars came from party war chests to pay for network rallies replete with cinematic and stage stars, for glorified fireside chats from swank hotel suites, for skillful film documentaries, and man-on-the-street interviews, and finally, for special spot announcements prepared by leading candidates with the assistance of advertising agencies. Mr. Seldes' summary of the successful broadcasts in the campaign indicated that they "seemed not to use abstraction at all: they appeared to be dealing always with the concrete, the simple fact, surrounded by clusters of prejudice, traditions, stereotypes."[122]

It is quite possible that the simple though clever image will always be the political image transmitted by radio and television. The alliance of these media with the sponsored message and with popular entertainment is of such long standing and of such closeness that neither profundity nor complexity is ever apt to be aired. Those who yearn for a thorough presentation of issues may have to be satisfied with the few parliamentarily respectable sessions at the national conventions and a few straight speeches thereafter. Otherwise, show business and politics will combine to produce the quick slogan and the automatic vote. Robert Lewis Shayon comments with weary cynicism:

> The ultimate would be the relegation of the argument to the status of the commercial--in jingle form. . . . As for sober reasoning, that would scarcely be missed. When has it been present in politics or on television?[123]

The saving grace of the carnival atmosphere surrounding our elections, which broadcasting seems to amplify, rests in the awareness of the public that political stunts are the expected campaign orders of the day. The critics are suspicious, however, of the propaganda effects of occasional unexpected stunts employed chiefly by the party in power as it reports to the nation during its tenure. Back in 1933, Darwin Teilhet referred somewhat sarcastically to "NRA whooplaloo," which he hoped would be presented "only one night over two national networks."[124] Just twenty years later Goodman Ace reviewed a presidential cabinet telecast in these words:

> Slick is the word for the B. B. D. and O. [Batten, Barton, Durstine and Osborn Advertising Agency] job.
>
> . . . .
>
> It was like a look behind the scenes at what people liked to think was our government at work. And it was warmly comforting to contemplate a government which worked so smoothly, with such precision and with barely a miscue. It was television selling the government to the people; a new product, on the market only five months.
>
> . . . .
>
> Whether the pace can be sustained in subsequent shows is problematical. Perhaps it would be best to slow down a bit. Everything moved with such rapidity, lines were spoken so glibly and often mashed with camera shots and props, that the gist of the dialogue was sometimes lost.[125]

And in 1955, Marya Mannes wrote a bitingly satiric review of the Republican Party's "Report to the Nation" in the style of a Russian reporter sending home tips to the Kremlin on how to imitate our rulers' "techniques of government by TV."[126]

The critics have seen in broadcasting, media which can educate the citizens of this country to political maturity--a maturity which recognizes that out of ideological diversity will come cooperative answers to the problems the government must attempt to solve. So powerfully have these media been able to project political sincerity and truth, that they feel it would be indicative of serious failure, if broadcasting facilities were to be misused either by bumbling amateurism or by too commercially oriented a professionalism. It would be even more serious if a nation, ill-informed about a candidate, a party plank, or a government policy, were to remain ill-informed because of financial restrictions imposed by the broadcast media, or, worse, because of program techniques calculated to obfuscate.

It is the nature of professional critics to urge constantly that broadcasters extend themselves in these informational areas. First they compliment, then they call, not only for more responsible commentary, but for more forums structured in depth, and for more devotion to high public service concepts in political reporting. Broadcasting has almost overwhelmed us with swift, frequent briefings on world-wide events. Now, say the critics, it must take the time (Television's failure could most certainly be radio's success in this area.) to round out the briefings with background information, thorough discussions, and authoritative commentary. Broadcasting has helped to make us one world through capsule news; it must help to keep us one world through comprehensive interpretation of the news. One program form which endeavors to combine news, commentary and discussion in an aesthetically interesting dramatic setting is the documentary, whose critical analysis becomes the subject of the next chapter.

Notes

[1]Leslie Allen, Christian Science Monitor, September 12, 1931.

[2]Amy Loveman, "New Dimensions in Information," Saturday Review of Literature, May 17, 1941, p. 10.

[3]Gilbert Seldes, "Screen and Radio," Scribner's, CII (July, 1937), 58.

[4]Marya Mannes, Reporter, January 6, 1953, p. 34.

[5]Marya Mannes, ibid., July 7, 1953, p. 40.

[6]Jack Gould, New York Times, April 17, 1949.

[7]Jack Gould, ibid., January 29, 1954.

[8]Leslie Allen, Christian Science Monitor, July 11, 1931.

[9]Ben Gross, I Looked and I Listened (New York: Random House, 1954), p. 161.

[10]Saul Carson, New Republic, November 15, 1948, p. 28.

[11]Albert Williams, Listening (Denver: University of Denver Press, 1948), p. 122.

[12]Philip Hamburger, New Yorker, November 5, 1949, p. 130.

[13]Jack Gould, New York Times, April 6, 1952.

[14]Ibid.

[15]Jack Gould, quoted in Time, November 12, 1956, p. 106.

[16]Jack Gould, New York Times, June 15, 1952.

[17]Philip Hamburger, New Yorker, November 26, 1949, p. 112.

[18]Robert Lewis Shayon, Christian Science Monitor, November 11, 1950.

[19]Philip Hamburger, New Yorker, August 12, 1950, p. 56.

[20]John Crosby, Wisconsin State Journal (Madison), December 1, 1954.

[21]Jack Gould, New York Times, August 6, 1950.

[22]Philip Hamburger, New Yorker, March 3, 1951, p. 95.

[23]Jack Gould, New York Times, March 25, 1951.

[24]Robert Lewis Shayon, Saturday Review, April 7, 1951, p. 32.

[25]John Crosby, Out of the Blue (New York: Simon and Schuster, 1952), pp. 249-51.

[26]Saul Carson, New Republic, April 2, 1951, p. 23.

[27]Gilbert Seldes, Saturday Review, July 19, 1954, p. 27.

[28]Jack Gould, New York Times, April 15, 1951.

[29]Jack Gould, ibid., March 21, 1954.

[30]Gilbert Seldes, Saturday Review, May 9, 1954, p. 24.

[31]Gilbert Seldes, The Public Arts (New York: Simon and Schuster, 1956), p. 237.

[32]Gilbert Seldes, Saturday Review, May 9, 1954, p. 24.

[33]John Crosby, for example, felt that televising Presidential press conferences was a bad idea. (Herald Tribune [New York], January 17, 1954) He decided later, however, that an occasional conference could be broadcast without too much risk. (Wisconsin State Journal [Madison], January 25, 1955).

[34]Jack Gould, New York Times, February 29, 1948..

[35]Robert Lewis Shayon, Saturday Review, February 10, 1951, p. 30.

[36]Crosby, Out of the Blue, pp. 11-13.

[37]Leslie Allen, Christian Science Monitor, July 18, 1931.

[38]Cyrus Fisher [Darwin Teilhet], Forum, LXXXIX (March, 1933), 191.

[39]Cyrus Fisher [Darwin Teilhet], ibid., LXXXVIII (October, 1932), 255.

[40]Marya Mannes, Reporter, August 4, 1953, p. 32.

[41]Ibid.

[42]Jack Cluett, Woman's Day, VII (March, 1944), 72. For further critical comments about Gabriel Heatter see Philip Hamburger's witty profile entitled "The Crier," New Yorker, January 20, 1945, pp. 23-33.

[43]Mannes, loc. cit.

[44]Philip Hamburger, New Yorker, February 27, 1954, p. 87.

[45]Philip Hamburger, ibid., July 10, 1954, p. 41.

[46]John Crosby, Wisconsin State Journal (Madison), May 24, 1954.

[47]Jack Gould, New York Times, April 11, 1954.

[48]Mannes, loc. cit.

[49]Jack Gould, New York Times, March 20, 1953.

[50]Saul Carson, New Republic, February 9, 1948, p. 33.

[51]Philip Hamburger, New Yorker, March 20, 1954, p. 71.

[52]Jack Gould, New York Times, March 14, 1954.

[53]Seldes, The Public Arts, p. 218.

[54]Gilbert Seldes, Saturday Review, April 24, 1954, pp. 26-27.

[55]Seldes, The Public Arts, pp. 226-27.

[56]Jack Gould, New York Times, May 9, 1954.

[57]Jack Gould, ibid., March 14, 1954.

[58]John Crosby, Wisconsin State Journal (Madison), November 4, 1955.

[59]Jack Gould, New York Times, December 17, 1950.

[60]Robert Lewis Shayon, Saturday Review, December 19, 1953, p. 31.

[61]John Crosby, Wisconsin State Journal (Madison), June 27, 1954.

[62]Leslie Allen, Christian Science Monitor, October 11, 1930.

[63]Crosby, Out of the Blue, p. 39.

[64]Ibid., pp. 17-18.

[65]Ibid., p. 11.

[66]Philip Hamburger, New Yorker, March 18, 1950, p. 101.

[67]Crosby, Out of the Blue, p. 97.

[68]Philip Hamburger, New Yorker, March 18, 1950, p. 102.

[69]Crosby, loc. cit.

[70]Crosby, Out of the Blue, pp. 126-27.

[71]John Crosby, for example, suggested that a BBC commentator broadcast to the United States, as Clifton Utley was doing to Britain at the time. (Herald Tribune [New York], May 29, 1953).

[72]Robert Lewis Shayon, Saturday Review, July 11, 1953, p. 38.

[73]Saul Carson, New Republic, June 19, 1950, p. 23.

[74]Jack Gould, New York Times, October 29, 1944.

[75]Crosby, Out of the Blue, pp. 162-63.

[76]Jack Gould, New York Times, July 24, 1949.

[77]Jack Gould, ibid., May 10, 1953.

[78]John Crosby, Herald Tribune (New York), September 7, 1952.

[79]John Crosby, ibid., January 17, 1954.

[80]Robert Lewis Shayon, Saturday Review, August 8, 1953, p. 27.

[81]Philip Hamburger, New Yorker, June 2, 1954, p. 74.

[82]Marya Mannes, Reporter, March 30, 1954, p. 33.

[83]Ibid.

[84]Jack Gould, New York Times, February 19, 1950.

[85]Philip Hamburger, New Yorker, February 25, 1950, p. 95.

[86]The whole question of talks programs and listener involvement is examined in a study by Robert D. Hudson, and Gerhart D. Weibe, "A Case for Listener Participation," Public Opinion Quarterly, XII (Summer, 1948), pp. 201-08.

[87]Saul Carson, New Republic, November 29, 1948, p. 28.

[88]Philip Hamburger, New Yorker, June 28, 1952, p. 75.

[89]Jack Gould, New York Times, January 30, 1955.

[90]Philip Hamburger, New Yorker, February 25, 1950, p. 95.

[91]Philip Hamburger, ibid., May 31, 1952, p. 91.

[92]John Crosby, Herald Tribune (New York), February 15, 1953.

[93]Robert Lewis Shayon, Saturday Review, July 26, 1952, p. 28.

[94]Cyrus Fisher [Darwin Teilhet], Forum, XC (July, 1933), 64.

[95]Jack Cluett, Woman's Day, VII (April, 1944), 63.

[96]Crosby, Out of the Blue, pp. 26-27.

[97]"Editorial," Saturday Evening Post, August 23, 1924, p. 24.

[98]Cyrus Fisher [Darwin Teilhet], Forum, LXXXVIII (September, 1932), 189-91.

[99]Gross, op. cit., p. 226.

[100]Ibid.

[101]John Crosby, "TV and the 1952 Elections," American Magazine, CLIII (April, 1952), 110.

[102]Jack Gould, New York Times, July 18, 1948.

[103]Crosby, loc. cit.

[104]Jack Gould, New York Times, March 15, 1954.

[105]Crosby, Out of the Blue, pp. 243-44.

[106]John Crosby, "TV and the 1952 Elections," American Magazine, CLIII (April, 1952), p. 109.

[107]Gross, op. cit., p. 232.

[108]John Crosby, Herald Tribune (New York), September 5, 1952.

[109]Crosby, Out of the Blue, p. 244.

[110]Marya Mannes, "Rabbit Punches on TV: the Governor and the Lady," Reporter, November 25, 1952, pp. 12-13.

[111]Gilbert Seldes, Saturday Review, November 27, 1954, p. 29.

[112]Philip Hamburger, New Yorker, July 19, 1952, p. 57.

[113]Robert Lewis Shayon, Saturday Review, August 9, 1952, p. 38.

[114]Philip Hamburger, New Yorker, August 2, 1952, p. 38.

[115]Philip Hamburger, ibid., July 19, 1952, p. 57.

[116]Robert Lewis Shayon, Saturday Review, August 23, 1952, p. 30.

[117]John Crosby, Herald Tribune (New York), January 21, 1952.

[118]Gilbert Seldes, Saturday Review, March 15, 1952, pp. 30-31.

[119]Gilbert Seldes, "TV and the Voter," Saturday Review, December 6, 1952, p. 18.

[120]Ibid.

[121]Jack Gould, New York Times, July 27, 1952.

[122]Gilbert Seldes, "TV and the Voter," Saturday Review, December 6, 1952, p. 59.

[123]Robert Lewis Shayon, Saturday Review, October 6, 1951, p. 37.

[124] Cyrus Fisher [Darwin Teilhet], Forum, XC (November, 1933), 318.

[125] Goodman Ace, The Book of Little Knowledge (New York: Simon and Schuster, 1955), pp. 88-89.

[126] Marya Mannes, Reporter, June 16, 1955, pp. 34-35.

CHAPTER VII

THE CRITICS' OPINIONS OF THE DOCUMENTARY PROGRAM

The documentary concentrates on the analysis and interpretation of events, issues, and ideas in a way which has elicited more critical attention than any other broadcast form with the exception of drama. It is, of course, allied to drama because of the manner in which it is constructed and produced. Unlike dramatic fiction, however, the plot of the documentary is always drawn from real life and its purpose is invariably didactic:

> The radio documentary is concerned first to give us facts about the unfinished business of democracy, to report on man's conscious or unconscious inhumanity to man. It is concerned secondly to show us our responsibility for the inhumanity in our society and to prompt us to action, though not to prescribe it.[1]

One might say that as the medieval church utilized the mystery play for popular religious instruction, so broadcasting utilizes the documentary play for popular humanistic instruction. The documentary may have the sensuous and emotional appeal of drama, but it must have a foundation of fact, and a framework of rhetoric. In practice, this form, which has been called "showmanship without illusion,"[2] may depend almost entirely on recordings and films of the locale and persons involved in the subject, or it may consist of a written script produced by actors in a studio, or a mixture of the two.

The present discussion will take advantage of the documentary's diversity to include not only the history and techniques of the form from the critics' points of view, but also to include some brief comments about programs like "Omnibus" and "Person to Person," which are more related to this informational category than to any other. In addition, the chapter will consider specific problems relating to controversy in the documentary and will conclude with a brief recapitulation of the critics' major hopes and fears for the entire spectrum of broadcast entertainment and information.

The Documentary Proper

Sound alone was an exciting new dimension in the twenties. It had connotative powers that demanded all sorts of experimentation. Consequently, it was natural for early broadcasters to think of recreating historical events through a realistic use of sound. In the summer of 1926, John Wallace described "a genuinely new type of radio program" called "Old Time Prize Fights," which he had heard over WGN in Chicago. He enjoyed the crowd effects, the gong, and the announcing of the fight as if it were actually taking place. He envisioned other historical possibilities for the technique and, as an example, thought that the destruction of Pompeii would be "thrilling."[3] Mr. Wallace again commented in the fall of that year about WGN's interesting use of old recorded speeches in a series of broadcasts on American presidents.[4] Some years later, this idea of simulating life from the past was combined with scenes of life in the present by NBC's Cheerio, who had famous men and women of history comment on typical contemporary home situations. Leslie Allen appreciated the program's balance between the humorous and the serious, and the appropriateness of the music.[5]

Such experiences in non-fictional drama proved that information from the past could be presented successfully as entertainment. It remained for the "March of Time," in 1932, to prove that the dramatization of current events could be just as entertaining and at the same time more directly informative. Darwin Teilhet was lavish in his praise of a program which undertook each week to recreate in three-to six-minute segments the major news items of the previous seven days. Vocal imitations of people in the news were only one device among many meticulous verbal and sound effects used to give each scene authority and genuineness. "Intelligence sprinkled with genius," said Mr. Teilhet, "makes the 'March of Time' what it is."[6]

Looking back eighteen years later, Gilbert Seldes disagreed with Mr. Teilhet as to the brilliance of the program's continuity, criticizing it for a "preposterous tone of portent and doom;"[7] but, he, nevertheless, recognized the value of its innovations. It provided "a new sound on the air, a new tempo, and an alert feeling for the radio medium itself."[8] In point of fact, the "March of Time" represented a progression from the operation of skill in producing the sounds of actuality, to the operation of intelligence in investing such sounds with an emphatic educational function. Here indeed was the "living newspaper" of radio minus the documentary program's major contribution, the editorial page.

Motivated by the ubiquitous interest of all art in the social ills of the dictatorship-depression thirties, even broadcasting's editorial page was not long in making some appearances. Starting in the middle thirties, both CBS and NBC, as well as a few independent stations, interested themselves in problems like housing, unemployment, conservation, and refugees from fascism. They employed writers who were given enough freedom and time to succeed in welding fact and opinion into dramatic forms of powerful emotional impact and of genuine persuasive as well as informative value. In addition, these scripts were assigned to competent acting and production staffs, an unusual procedure for sustaining programs.

As our nation grew increasingly aware of its world-wide responsibilities even to participation in a second great war, the documentary became an important part of a morale and propaganda effort subsidized both by stations and by the government. The late thirties and early forties became the documentary's period of "poetic exhortation"[9] (to use Mr. Seldes' phrase) when catastrophic events compelled authors to interpret them in universal terms, and when radio's restriction to sound alone became the perfect medium for verse. This was the time when the Corwins and the Obolers and the CBS Radio Workshop (see pp. 152-54) sang of our nation's triumphs and defeats.

So valued had the prestige and the purpose of the documentary become that broadcasters continued to call on its services after the war. When William Paley and Edward Murrow of CBS returned to civilian broadcasting, they were convinced that this radio form could help prepare the people of our country to solve the problems of peace.[10] The network created a special documentary unit of writers, producers, and researchers whose sole task was to explore and then dramatize the nation's most pressing issues. Other networks followed suit, and in the late forties large audiences found themselves enrolled for hour long seminars on such subjects as the United Nations, atomic energy, communism, civil rights, and juvenile delinquency.

To the critics, it seemed as if broadcasting had matured during the war. Perhaps the reporting of a terrible conflict and the expressing of democracy's righteous indignation left the industry unafraid of actually attempting to guide listener reaction by dramatizing new problems, most of which could not help but involve controversy. Albert Williams commended the American Broadcasting Company for its stunning four-hour reading, in 1947, of John Hersey's appalling but eloquent account of our atomic destruction of Hiroshima.[11] And Saul Carson was delighted to report, in 1948, that four independent stations in New York City "have gone documentary-happy in a craze that augurs well for the listener."[12] Some of the highest praise was reserved for Robert Lewis Shayon's 1947 study of juvenile delinquency, "The Eagle's Brood," (CBS). Mr. Williams felt that his "powerful and literate script" represented "reporting at its cleanest and clearest."[13] It projected a "situation [so] as to make it vital and significant to an uninformed public."[14] Mr. Gould also complimented CBS and ABC for opening up new possibilities for the post-war documentary. He was only sorry that the richest network, NBC, had exerted such little effort in this direction.[15]

By 1950, however, all network documentary productions had decreased. Even though Norman Corwin and other artists had transferred their talents to the exciting new arena for world discussion, the United Nations, and even though Robert Lewis Shayon was now producing, with infinite attention to research, fine historical documentaries (CBS' "You Are There"), the former widespread attention to the crusading documentary was diminishing. Mr. Carson felt that radio's attention was now preoccupied with seeking straight entertainment to combat the inroads of television.[16] And it was obvious that, for a while at least, the new medium was also going to have to concentrate on entertainment in order to remain solvent until audiences purchased sets.

To be sure, the bold efforts of Edward R. Murrow's "See It Now," which was a combined news report, informational essay, and visual editorial, periodically reaffirmed the documentary's power, particularly in video form. And there were, of course, occasional informative film studies of such topics as the rise of dictatorships, the prosecution of World War II, and progress in medicine. But the reform fervor which characterized the documentary at its peak in the forties was undeniably missing in the programs of the fifties. Mr. Seldes attributed the drift of the documentary away from its traditional liberal agitation to "the changing temper of the times."[17] Society seemed to want some surcease from confrontation with the world's ills, particularly through its favorite media of entertainment. The mood was one which sponsors were willing to indulge for reasons which will be mentioned later. And the industry seemed unwilling to engage in the sizeable expense of carrying such programs on a broad, sustaining basis. Consequently, as television was beginning to hit its stride, the documentary had all but reached a standstill.

Nevertheless, the critics had heard and seen enough of broadcasting's proudest intellectual and artistic form to have evolved some worth-while ideas about the qualities and techniques necessary to the writing and presentation of successful documentaries. Mr. Carson, who had contributed documentaries of his own to a New York station, studied the form with particular care and prescribed some general requirements for its composition. He felt that the writer, who must be chosen for his competence not for his bias, must have something important to say, that his content must be accurate and clear in its sociological direction, and fair in its treatment of the basic subject, as well as artistically interesting.[18]

Other critics would agree with these points, although they might not necessarily agree with Mr. Carson that the documentary should state a course of action[19] after it had explored a topic. Actually, there is no clear indication on the part of any of the major critics as to just how energetically a writer should support either a specific analysis of a problem or a specific solution to it. Documentaries seem to tread a narrow line between emotionally toned information and forthright but general advocacy. On the whole, their function would seem to be to stir the sensibilities of an audience while supplying at the same time a background of facts from which the audience can determine its own procedures. This twofold task of stimulating while informing probably provided the kind of indirect but concerned guidance for which Jack Gould was grateful after a CBS program on the atomic era entitled "Operation Crossroads":

> For an evening, radio was of age; and listening to it was an ennobling and enriching experience. . . .
>
> Cast off was radio's own cloak of indifference and preoccupation with the money marts, and donned was the mantle of leadership and vigorous participation in the resolution of mankind's most pressing problem.[20]

Though the documentary does not require the services of a polemicist, it cannot, in the critics' opinion, escape the need for the firm hand of the artist. A superior documentary is an artistic creation. It is not the kind of program which, according to Mr. Shayon, "the conference method can produce." He was expressing his disappointment in a Time magazine documentary about the signing of the peace with Japan, and he insisted, "You do not stay outside your material and report it in Olympian manner; you get inside it and on fire with something to say."[21]

Whether he expresses himself in poetry or prose, the documentary artist controls the flames of his ideas through skill in dramaturgy, in sound, in music and, where applicable, in visual images. He may achieve his impact as Norman Corwin did, according to Mr. Seldes: "through grouping voices, neatness of attack, timing of pauses, integrating of music, and an elaborate nicety of sound effects."[22] And he will undoubtedly exhibit the kind of superb feel for his medium which Jack Gould attributed to Andrew Allan, producer in 1952 of Lister Sinclair's "A Word in Your Ear" for the Canadian Broadcasting Corporation:

> Mr. Allan's production, magnificently attuned to the ear, was genuine radio, now practically a lost art. His use of sound effects and music were creative in their own right, but even more important, always disciplined.[23]

Although the documentary can be and usually is achieved through a collaboration of artists,[24] two of the most famous practitioners in this field often developed by themselves complete programs from script to performance. Saul Carson reviewed one of Robert Lewis Shayon's projects for "CBS Is There" in 1947:

> Writer Shayon had a number of awkward bits of repetition and clumsy phrasing in his script. But producer Shayon had cast his principals well. And director Shayon blended the voices, sound and music, built his crowd scenes so expertly, and showed so much sensitiveness in the handling of the performances, that it came off almost miraculously.[25]

A few years later, Mr. Carson, in the review of a United Nations documentary produced by Norman Corwin for NBC, described those composite qualities which characterize the great documentary artist: "He combined a poet's imagination, a realist's understanding of today's world, and a craftsman's knowledge of every trick of radio production."[26]

Having cited the general requirements of the artist who has something important to say through the form of the documentary, it is time to turn to a consideration of some specific techniques. An important device alluded to at the beginning of this chapter is the recording or film from actual life. Obviously current issues can acquire unusual authority and impact when an audience encounters the very persons most closely involved. Their hesitancies of speech and genuine idiosyncracies of manner, their expressions of true concern or true happiness deliver an immediate force to a documentary, which critics have generally commended. Jack Gould said of a program on Russian communism told through the voices of refugees that it "lets the diabolic drama of the U.S.S.R. speak for itself."[27] And John Crosby saw great value in Mr. Murrow's "See It Now," which relates events through the voices and faces of people making the news. He thought that the technique "offers a deeper insight into the headlines and the people who make them--who they are and what sort of people they are."[28]

Not satisfied with simply presenting film clips to his audience, Mr. Murrow attempted to make the actual in the program even more real. He had himself seated in front of a television receiver anticipating what the home viewer was also about to see. The device suggested that he, too, was going to view this report for the first time, thereby creating, in Mr. Shayon's opinion, greater audience empathy.[29] As an aside, it is interesting to note that Mr. Seldes did not approve of this "faint deception."[30]

In addition to heightening emotional interest in a topic, the actual portrayal of the person making the news is, in Mr. Gould's opinion, an important part of thorough reporting, recognizing "that behind every problem or event there is always the human equation."[31] Of "The Search," a series on campus research projects, produced in 1954 for CBS by Irving Citlin, Mr. Gould said:

> There is no artificial attempt to re-enact either news or the case histories of individuals: members of university staffs and lay persons speak simply and directly to the camera and are just themselves. The absence of any trace of theatricalism is the best evidence of intelligent showmanship.[32]

These real-life materials, which broadcasting can place in the hands of its documentary producers, are so intriguing to manipulate that they can be mistakenly conceived as guaranteeing a powerful program. Robert Lewis Shayon, however, was not at all impressed with the use of actuality in "The People Act," a 1952, CBS radio series, in which the citizens of various localities described how they solved community problems:

> The tape recording techniques employed are ancient radio history, fundamental forms used unimaginatively. . . . Real people are used to play "real" people in dramatized recreations of scenes--an indefensible device, since the real people are simply bad amateur actors. There is no premium in actuality per se. Often it is sheer liability.
>
> Furthermore, there is an inconsistent mixing of re-created scenes in which people "play" themselves with other scenes in which they "are" themselves. Robert Trout, the narrator, is a professional voice, not at all in key with the unpolished performance of the actuality cast.[33]

The inartistic use of the actual may detract from the value of a documentary program, but that is not as heinous a fault as the embarrassing exploitation of the actual which Philip Hamburger saw in "Candid Camera." This was a 1950, CBS program using concealed cameras to document the genuine reactions of passersby to secretly contrived, irritating situations. Mr. Hamburger charged that the producer, Allen Funt:

> has succeeded, I think, in reducing the art, the purpose and the ethics of the "documentary" idea to the level of the obscene. . . . He is demonstrating . . . that most people are fundamentally decent and trusting and, sad to tell, can readily be deceived. . . . He succeeds in making them look foolish, or in forcing them to struggle against unfair odds, for some vestige of human dignity. . . . The true documentarian must respect his fellowman and feel that what he has to say is worth hearing.[34]

Actuality, then, can be employed by the artist as one device in the documentary in order to excite the emotions, and in order to get as close to the truth as possible. The latter function is more apt to be successful if the actual is carefully edited and integrated with other portions of a script, with narration or commentary, music and sound. Skillful integration, however, can only be effected if a documentary is infused with singleness of purpose and clarity of view point. This is where the artistry of the writer is most apparent, and consequently, where the attention of the critics is most frequently focused.

Speaking, perhaps, from the wealth of his own experience in the area, Mr. Shayon has more to say about the necessity for a controlling purpose than any other critic. Several specific programs were the occasion for his remarks which comprise an informal credo about the documentary's most fundamental need. After viewing a program in which President Truman took the nation on a CBS camera tour of the White House, Mr. Shayon said:

> My only regret is that television, which grows more peripatetic, I am glad to say, seems unable to organize its embrace of the actual world around some vital idea [underlining mine] to breathe, in short, a little life of art into facts. What a rare cast! What an epic setting! And what a pity to experience no measure of the deep emotions inherent in the national drama.[35]

Often the "vital idea" in a documentary is blurred because it is too complex for the time allotted to the subject, and the writer-producer must revert to hasty generalities and stock characters. Such was Mr. Shayon's major disappointment in "The People Act," which portrayed "a sort of abstract, faceless goodness generalized from an assortment of citizens," and left the listener convinced "that life is far more complex and the struggle far more bitter than these oversimplified lessons in how-to-triumph-over-evil suggest."[36] A similar comment was made by Mr. Seldes of Norman Corwin's characters who, though completely fictitious, were more symbolic than human: "His characters were stock types--well documented but more voices than people."[37]

One obvious solution for avoiding the diffuseness of the broad canvass is to produce a documentary in depth. Again with reference to "The People Act," Mr. Shayon decried the fact that "there was no portrait of a single human being identifiable in depth by individual drive, emotion, attitude . . . [nor] could one identify a human villain."[38] But he was delighted with an NBC radio treatment of the Oppenheimer case in 1954, because it was a forty-five minute news program dealing solely and in depth with a single story. Here, he felt, was the opportunity to modify or clarify not merely reinforce listener assumptions about a controversial topic.[39] This same ability to concentrate on individuals, to show, not an event, but the effect of an event on people is, in Mr. Seldes' opinion, one of the prime virtues of "See It Now."[40] In this connection, Jack Gould's praise of a documentary on housing for being specific in its charges, even to the naming of names,[41] would be another way to particularize the form.

Regardless, however, of a documentary's horizontal or vertical scope, Mr. Shayon comes back once more to its basis in the single idea. He is actually discussing an NBC news program, but his remarks are pertinent to any documentary:

> It is not enough for a program like "Background" to devote itself to a single subject. . . . For maximum effectiveness it must develop a single idea, penetrating or powerful; and this idea must be proved in terms of its material.[42]

On one occasion, for example, he criticized a Corwin script for trying to touch on too many problems and for switching from one point to another so rapidly that the listener was confused.[43] Of ABC's documentary, "The Berlin Story," he said: "It lacked any real point of view and ultimately got lost in the complexity of the subject it was reviewing."[44]

Closely related to the superior documentary's clarity of aim, is another virtue: simplicity and lack of pretentiousness in writing as well as production. Under the constant pressure to be entertaining, such a virtue is difficult to preserve. The critics, nevertheless, have been quick to condemn exaggerated mannerisms in the form. Philip Hamburger, who otherwise liked NBC's famous 1953 film documentary, "Victory at Sea," felt that the commentary had fallen into the trap of "assuming that because the events under discussion are portentous, the words used to describe them must have a deep, dark, portentous ring."[45] He also accused Edward R. Murrow's 1953 program on Berlin as pretentious in its use of "intramural jabbering" ("Come in, Ed." "Thank you, Dick," etc.), and he wearied of Mr. Murrow's "homilies on war and peace, intoned in that voice of cultivated doom."[46] John Crosby, who admitted that trying to humanize a program on the atom was difficult, complained that some of the prose was "just a little too lush for its own good."[47] And Jack Gould has talked of "Corwinesque pretension."[48]

In contrast to the above examples, the critics have been equally quick to commend restraint in documentary style. For instance, Saul Carson congratulated Lou Hazam for his script, "Living: 1949":

> [It contains] fine, straight-forward [writing] without frills or pretensions. Under Wade Arnold's supervision, the show avoids the flamboyance that so often characterizes documentaries which try to cover a lack of content with aural fireworks. Ben Grauer's narration always lends authority to the content. You may not agree with the program's viewpoint at all times, but its credibility and restraint are impressive.[49]

And Jack Gould said of Mr. Murrow's commentary on "See It Now": "He is alternately wryly humorous, understandingly sympathetic, courteously disbelieving, or suavely hardboiled. But in each case he employs the art of understatement, and if one word will do, he doesn't use two."[50] Speaking of the same series, John Crosby felt that the intelligent assumption of its producers that any subject which might interest them would interest the audience, gave "the show a simplicity and candor missing from most other news shows."[51]

Were this confidence in subject matter and audience a common possession of documentary writers and producers, they would not need to rely on artificial verbal embellishment, on frantic tempo, or fantastic tricks. They might be able to heed a suggestion such as the one Jack Gould proffered after viewing NBC's "Living: 1948": "A slightly more relaxed pace might be in order occasionally, if only to leave something in reserve productionwise for the climaxes of the script."[52] They might also be able to receive more compliments like the one Saul Carson paid to NBC for its 1950 series on atomic energy, "The Quick and the Dead": "They didn't even use background music which too often mars educational broadcasts because producers feel that a serious thought must never be stated on the air unless it is accompanied by a dozen bassoons."[53] But instead, it is Mr. Seldes' feeling that documentary programs tend to become the victims of a popularization process whose "gimmicks" actively distract an audience from serious subject matter.[54]

Concurrent with sensationalizing the writing and production of documentaries, exists the temptation to concentrate on sensational themes, or at least on the more highly charged aspects of a theme, at the expense of a provocative thoroughness. The complete and balanced perspective is, after all, a by-product of intelligent simplicity in approach. In Mr. Gould's opinion it was lacking in a 1950 presentation by ABC of "Clear and Present Danger," a review of the presidential loyalty order of 1947:

> It had both the element of suspense and the realism of setting which always are essential to a good spy drama. . . . But in its concluding "editorial," ABC glossed over the larger implications of the loyalty issue by dismissing in one masterful understatement the question of those who have capitalized politically on the loyalty issue.[55]

Although Mr. Shayon liked the dramatic fusion of showmanship with sociology in Irving Gitlin's CBS study of the evil of narcotics, he, nevertheless, discerned in it a shallowness of motive typical of the rash of crime documentaries presented in the early fifties.

> We are experiencing a periodic crest in the old cycle of public indignation over exposure of hidden sin. The sinner, as usual, is the other fellow. . . . He is not the respectable, middle-class you and I. Therefore nobody minds hitting out at him. The nets shunt with circumspection, however, the sharp probe into the underlying social matrix that seems, for one thing, to produce more Negro addiction than white. This, in the rationale of the commercial broadcasters, is called "keeping abreast of and reflecting the times," rather than leading them.[56]

Lest these evaluations of the documentary seem to contain too much carping, be it remembered that in this form professional critics have caught glimpses of true greatness both in social motive and aesthetic skill. Their correctives are offered in the hope that such programs will make an even greater contribution toward involving the mental and emotional faculties of the mass audience in major issues. The critics grant that it is difficult to shape what Lou Frankel has called the rough edges of reality[57] into a living essay which manages to abstract the essentials of a problem without oversimplifying it or dehumanizing it and which retains liveliness without loss of true import. But they have also been eager to remind their readers of certain techniques and specific programs which depict the documentary at its best.

Mr. Frankel, who served for a few months as critic for the Nation, described how a nation-wide roundup by CBS of opinion on inflation in 1946 was effected with all of the pace and flexibility normally associated only with a studio broadcast:

> Everyone worked from a skeleton script, flexible enough to allow for asides. . . . Each speaker saved his strongest fact for the end, thus giving the next speaker a logical point to enter the program [none of the usual 'and now we switch you to -- ']. After the audience had the feel of the new participant [Detroit union man, Kansas City farmer, etc.] the interviewer came in and made the identifications. . . . Full remote

> equipment was sent out for each job. . . . It was the little individual touches that made the broadcast the whopping success it was.[58]

The results of such a technically precise accomplishment became, of course, more predictable from an aesthetic viewpoint when tape recorded comments could be edited and spliced into a documentary program. To achieve the same flexible ends with film was an even greater challenge, beautifully met, according to Mr. Seldes, by Edward Murrow:

> The outstanding technical device of "See It Now" is its intercutting for editorial effects. A typical example was the report on an event in Indianapolis, where, after being refused the use of many halls, a group of people met in the basement of a Catholic church to work out plans for creating a branch of the American Civil Liberties Union and, at the same time, a few blocks away, the American Legion Post met to denounce the other meeting. The issues involved were not trivial, and the passions were intense; by selecting those speakers who seemed to answer one another, the program had the effect of an angry face to face debate. It also had the effect of almost mathematical impartiality.[59]

As a final example with which to conclude these remarks on qualities, of the critically successful documentary, the following excerpts, touching on many factors of this broadcast form, are reproduced from a column by Jack Gould, who felt that a two-part ABC program on slums was "one of the most provocative and intelligent presentations of a public issue that radio has made in recent years."

> The first part, thanks largely to the reportorial talents of George Hicks, was an exceptionally fine documentary program. With simplicity, courage and quiet dramatic intensity it delved into the disgraceful housing conditions. . . . The second part was a discussion of solutions to the problem . . . a magnificent example of radio that was both mature and unafraid.
>
> . . . [Wire recorded, personal interviews proved] that the only effective spokesman for the "common man" can be the common man himself. . . .
>
> [Mr. Hicks] is the antithesis of radio's "voice of importance." He is unhurried; he speaks quietly and naturally; he believes facts rather than superimposed emotions can tell the story.
>
> . . . .

[The second part, the discussion, was an excellent sequel due to the] humor and perception of the moderator Charles Taft.[60]

Miscellaneous Informational Forms

The documentary is the artistic free-form of broadcasting. It varies in technique, as has been seen, from planned creation in the studio to controlled reality outside the studio, and in subject matter from the entertainingly informative to the excitingly controversial. It erases the boundary line between drama and report and, consequently, becomes a program category broad enough to admit the special interview and the cultural variety program.

As early as 1928, critic John Wallace suggested that radio introduce to its audience "people whose work gives them a unique slant on humanity--policemen, clerks, bell-hops, etc." They would present their views in their own words with no editing.[61] And a few years later Leslie Allen proposed a series of broadcasts which would "have people talk to each other about themselves."[62] Interview programs came and went with little critical reaction, but it remained for Mr. Murrow at CBS to devise a type of telecast which, although it ignored the little man, did entice important people to talk about themselves, though only rarely from a unique point-of-view. "Person to Person" aroused immediate attention because its cameras invited the viewer directly into a celebrity's home, where he chatted in the living room and was then given a tour of the place.

The critics were interested but, somehow, also disappointed. John Crosby was content to label the program "off-beat" and to admire its lack of contrivance,[63] but the only important reason he could think of for watching it lay in the "absolutely deplorable curiosity all of us have to find out how the other half lives."[64] In Mr. Gould's opinion the program was too stiff and formal and, like his predecessor, John Wallace, he thought Mr. Murrow should interview an average person occasionally.[65] It may have been Gilbert Seldes who finally discerned what was lacking, and from his comments it is possible to imagine that a more profound interview program could contribute the kind of information expected from a genuine documentary. The major drawback of "Person to Person" lies, paradoxically, in its emphasis on things rather than people:

> An obsession with prizes and signed photographs becomes the standard mark of the successful American; if ideas develop, they are quickly smothered and the camera picks up another souvenir. It is as if everyone was determined to prove that, no matter what eminence a person has achieved, the great ones of this world are not only folks, they are rather dull folks.[66]

Mr. Seldes realizes that to some extent the stiff format of this interview program is necessitated by the careful camera preparations needed, if the individual is to move around in his home. But he also wonders if its superficiality could derive from its sponsored status. As it stands now, it appeals to two somewhat questionable audience motives: the desire to associate with celebrities, and the desire to have them brought down "about to our level."[67] In summary, Mr. Seldes, along with other professional critics, is sorry that "Person to Person" missed its opportunity.

A similar though less emphatic reaction occurred with respect to a unique venture in broadcasting. The fall of 1952 ushered in the first season of a weekly television program dedicated to the different. "Omnibus" was to be a kind of cultural pace setter which, because it was subsidized by a foundation, could afford a wide variety of excursions, chiefly into the humanities.

During its first three years, critical comment about individual programs ran the gamut from superb to disastrous, and in many cases there was little unanimity of opinion. This was a situation to be expected in the light of a program which at one time would spend ninety minutes studying Renaissance life, and in another would skip in short segments from a stream-of-consciousness one-act play to a nature film to a trip through a railroad yard.

There did seem to be a major critical faction, however, whose initial and even later reaction to "Omnibus" could best be described as one of cautious disdain. Mr. Shayon said of it:

> "Omnibus" is not a program; it is a device. . . . [It] has no point of view except, "Come unto me all ye that have talent." It has no attitude. It strikes no dominant chord in spirit, form, subject, or style. . . . Not that variety of itself is a poor device. . . . "Omnibus" has no idiom. It is at present a digest; it aspires to art but achieves merely pseudo-art. . . . Let the producers steer away from the shoal of mass and the rock of neutrality.[68]

Even Jack Gould, who at the outset had hailed the series' "fresh state of mind toward TV" and its "venturesome and adult spirit in the realm of the arts,"[69] had to admit by its third season that commercial programs devoted to culture were frequently far superior. Like Mr. Shayon, he felt that the program lacked a decisive aim and that it was trying to satisfy too many people simultaneously.[70] Mr. Hamburg's expression of bewilderment fairly well sums up the critics' disappointment:

> I find "Omnibus" a perplexing program. . . . It is in the hands of literate and intelligent people who are trying their darndest to produce a literate and intelligent program. Sometimes I think they're trying too hard. The proceedings have a self-conscious air, as though all hands were saying with a certain monotony, "This is it friends; this will _really_ elevate you."[71]

Regardless of only mild critical success in programing, "Omnibus" did achieve its financial aim, which was to interest a large enough audience so that the Ford Foundation could withdraw its experimental support, having convinced the commercial sponsors taking over that culture could succeed on the air. Jack Gould had been suspicious of this goal, sensing in it a desire on the part of broadcasters to relinquish the burden of sustaining programs by placing all of their schedules at the service of commerce.[72] His fears were not shared by Gilbert Seldes who thought that a foundation's underwriting of an entertainment program was an interesting example of healthy capitalistic compromise between sustaining and commercial support.[73] Mr. Seldes realized that "Omnibus" has had its weaknesses but he felt its special value lay "in the demonstration that the principle of the lowest common denominator is not absolute in the entertainment business."[74]

Such has been the special value not only of the "Omnibus" attempt to lend excitement and sparkle to culture or of the "Person to Person" aim of introducing us to famous people without false fanfare, but of all documentary programs. Concerned primarily with sober issues, the genre has, nevertheless, developed a philosophy and a method for fusing enlightenment and entertainment without destroying the validity or dignity of its fundamental serious purpose. The great documentaries have demonstrated that there can be a highest common denominator in broadcasting. They have shown, as Marya Mannes puts it, "that the education of the heart and mind can be enduring entertainment in which the viewer ceases to be a spectator . . . and becomes a participant."[75]

Deterrents to Controversial Documentaries

The brief historical survey at the beginning of this chapter touched upon the slow atrophy of the argumentative documentary program during the fifties. Any form which must select facts and opinions about an issue and cast them in the emotional mold of even semi-drama runs the risk of arousing sensitive broadcasters and sponsors to the possibility that portions of the public might be displeased. The resultant timidity of the industry never fails to irritate the critics who generally feel that the documentary like news commentary must be honest, free and courageous.

As far back as 1933, Darwin Teilhet criticized a program called "Legend of America" for its "carefully pasteurized" interpretation of history.[76] But by the mid-fifties, the outspoken documentary (particularly "See It Now") had earned a fine reputation. The critics had just been praising the courage of Mr. Murrow for using the resources of "See It Now" to defend an air force lieutenant faced with the loss of his commission because of the leftist associations of his family.[77] And they had again lauded his determination to proceed with an interview with Robert Oppenheimer, even though he had just been dismissed from government service as a security risk.[78] Little wonder, then, that they rushed to the controversial documentary's defense when it seemed threatened by certain events.

Two examples of their concern will suffice. When "See It Now" was shifted to an irregular time slot for the 1955 season, and when "Background," an NBC news program, was moved at the same time to a less desirable Sunday position, Robert Lewis Shayon spoke out against "Schizoids in the TV Station:"

> [TV producers] are uniformly well-educated, interested in cerebral action, and aware of manifold things in the world of today. . . . Periodically, however, their faith in their professional world is sharply contradicted by the works of that world--indicating either a lack of candor, . . . or an unawareness . . . to that which is actually going on about them.
>
> . . . .
>
> [The shifting of these programs] spells an end to what the fourth estate hoped would be an era of televised "news in

depth." All the networks say they are filled with an awareness of current events and an interest in them. "Dr. Jekyll--meet Mr. Hyde."[79]

As Marya Mannes, again in 1955, watched sponsors dropping their associations with "See It Now" and "Project 20" (an NBC documentary series) and relegating Eric Severeid's commentary to a sustaining status, she rang the alarm to prevent what seemed to her cowardly desertion:

> The observation of reality, a deterrent to the enjoyment of illusion, has been considered dull. . . . Now it has been discovered that the observation of reality can be dangerous.
>
> . . . .
>
> The reaction [to visual essays like Murrow's on McCarthy] is twofold and conflicting. One is the belief among people of intelligence and vision in the mass media that the observation and interpretation of the real world can be valuable as knowledge and powerful as entertainment. The other is the suspicion of the sponsor that the impulse to think is not necessarily compatible with the impulse to buy. . . . The tragedy is that this abstention of business from controversy leads in the end to a kind of censorship through omission that no intelligent society can afford.
>
> . . . .
>
> Who will see to it that this growing and infinitely useful new form of art--the documentary in depth--becomes a part of the American diet, still so deficient in the vitamins of thought.[80]

Unfortunately, the problem of stimulating America's mind and conscience, thus inciting her to take positive steps on important issues, is not to be solved simply by insuring the sponsorship of controversial documentaries or even by convincing the networks to provide them at a good time on a sustaining basis. (Marya Mannes called upon the great foundations to assume this responsibility.[81]) The form has both an external and internal limitation which tends to hamper its usefulness as a guide to reasoned action.

Gilbert Seldes reminds his readers that whenever they consider the effectiveness of programs of this nature they must not forget "that fact is delivered in connection or in competition with fiction."[82] Audience attention flows from a light program to a serious one, from a comedian to a commentator, from a dance band to a documentary. It is his theory that the critical faculties necessary to interpret an informational or persuasive broadcast may have been lulled into inactivity by a preceding program.[83] Passive acceptance or gay indifference are not attitudes with which an audience should approach a documentary. Perhaps Mr. Carson's feeling that the documentary should be part of a broad educational campaign[84] comes from the realization that it needs psychological space in which to make its impact felt. Thus, the surrounding broadcast schedule may dampen reaction to this form.

Paradoxically, of course, the kind of impact which a documentary can deliver may be a second factor dictating against an intelligent approach to its theme. Audience thought can be dissolved by audience emotion. Such action arising from within the form itself may negate the documentary's ideal function. Jack Gould, for example, felt that the hysterical sobbing of actors in a 1947 documentary about an atom bomb attack was simply a surrender of "all pretense at discipline in the drama and concurrently in its propaganda value."[85]

The important question of the extent to which emotional elements deriving from the dramatic format detract from a thoughtful treatment of an issue has never finally been answered by the critics. Very likely no general pronouncement will ever be forthcoming since the subject of each program arises from a new social context. Nevertheless, it might be inferred from their views on problem drama (see pp. 178-181) and on commentators (see p. 315) that many of the professional critics would urge the adoption of a laissez faire attitude toward the controversial documentary, relying on broadcasting's traditional caution and the critics' sharp eyes with regard to sensationalism and irresponsibility in the news area to curb any serious abuse of the form.

As an example of critical scrutiny, consider Mr. Carson's sharp reaction to two, rousing, ABC, anti-communist documentaries of the late forties, keeping in mind, of course, the strong liberal cast of the New Republic. He disliked the vigorous editorial freewheeling of writer Morton Wishengrad's "Communism--U. S. Brand" and stormed:

> The opponent never got a break. He was propped up, pummeled from the first gong, torn apart by every technique known to radio and then pointed to as a miserable weakling.[86]

And of a program extolling the success of our famous 1948 Berlin airlift, he warned:

> It is not in the "public interest, convenience or necessity" to smear warpaint over our kilocycles and to discredit the radio documentary through awkward egotism.[87]

Mr. Carson's continual urging of documentary writers to present "a temperate evaluation of . . . clashing viewpoints"[88] places a difficult hurdle in the path of this vibrant form. But in summary, it must be admitted that the critics see an even greater hurdle to the documentary's progress in the general reluctance of the industry to become deeply involved in anything controversial.

Recapitulation of Broadcast Entertainment and Information

Discussion in these last four chapters has revolved about professional critics' views of various forms of entertainment and information on the air. This has resulted in a fragmentation of opinion about radio and television which is not totally accurate. The fact that the amazing program variety of these media emanates as a continuous output of sound and image stimulating the American audience's habit of continuous reception represents an experience in amalgamation whose interpretation by the critics remains to be examined. In addition, generalizations resulting from the critics' occasional long range perspectives of broadcasting must also receive some emphasis. It will be noted that the concepts of

Mr. Seldes are particularly pertinent to this section.

At the outset, let it be stated that some critics, at least, assume an air of optimism, believing that broadcasting, after all, follows the norms of show business in general. Radio and television, like the other entertainment media, have their good seasons and their bad, their successes and their failures, and a fair proportion of programs which are simply in between. John K. Hutchens cautioned his New York Times readers to temper their demands on radio by remembering that "Pending the advent of Utopia, it would be remarkable if there were more excellent newspapers and magazines than mediocre ones, more films that were significant than otherwise, more hits than flops in a Broadway season."[89] And his successor summed up television's entertainment offerings a few years later in these words, "Its smash hits are few and far between; passable programs are reasonably plentiful; mediocre productions are always available."[90] Broadcasting, in addition, is in the unique position, says Mr. Gould, of producing so many programs received by so many people that "both its achievements and shortcomings stand out with special vividness,"[91] implying that the medium's quality must be placed in proper perspective before condemning it too hastily.

Such eminently reasonable summations would be reassuring indeed to the public and the industry, if that were all to be said on the matter. Unfortunately, however, as previous chapters have shown, all of the critics (including Mr. Hutchens and Mr. Gould) seem to be deeply impressed by the shortcomings of broadcasting. Their specific fears for entertainment and for information have been duly noted. However, some of them feel that further shortcomings are at least vaguely reflected in the system of juxtaposition and hybridization which characterizes broadcasting's presentation of both types of programs. Mr. Seldes describes the phenomenon of entertainment and information arising from a common context:

> News and ideas were considered as separate elements at the beginning. Presently we discovered that the manipulation of symbols and the use of entertainment itself to create the atmosphere in which our ideas are formed were among the vast potentialities of the new medium.[92]

It is quite clear, at least in this early stage of critical deliberation, that the "vast potentialities" referred to by Mr. Seldes are, or could be, undesirable forces. Three have been observed in operation. One such unknown quantity concerns the degree to which tremendous emphasis on popular entertainment destroys public interest in serious informative programs or even in serious entertainment events. Realizing that their assumptions have not been validated in any scientific sense, a few critics, nevertheless, point to an interplay of possible factors which they think act to inhibit audience appreciation of serious programing. For example, radio and television in their choice of puerile dramatic themes, in their major emphasis on comedy, games, and trivial music foster a retardation of maturity in their audiences. Mr. Seldes feels that the popular arts (particularly broadcasting and films) have actually "made a determined effort to perpetuate the adolescent mind," and he cites the powerful theme of the glorification of youth in these media.[93] And Marya Mannes sees this same immaturity in our society's deparate need for entertainment:

> Few people of spiritual or mental substance . . . turn on television or radio more than a few hours a week. When they do, it is to see reality not to escape from it. . . . To turn on a crooner, a comic, a panel, a band, a quiz show or a play during the day is unthinkable. . . . Even troubling thoughts are more constructive than the avoidance of them by this means.[94]

Another factor related to broadcasting's cultivation of immaturity, is its destruction of an audience's ability to concentrate or to engage in critical thinking. So many programs are organized around a framework of foolish slapstick, or gay chatter, or other bits of innocuous trivia, that it almost seems as if their aim is one of calculated diversion or distraction of an audience's attentive powers, rather than a utilization or focusing of them. The real tragedy is that this kind of production style inevitably creeps over into serious programs which feel compelled to use similar diversionary techniques under the assumption that audiences will accept difficult material without even knowing it. Again Mr. Seldes describes his view of this situation:

> The whole entertainment side of broadcasting which surrounds its communication of ideas tends to create a mood of consent and acceptance; it cannot afford to stir and agitate the mind. We have the complex situation in which entertainment creates the audience for communication and then--to an extent --destroys our capacity to think about the facts and ideas communicated.[95]

The result of creating immature, uncritical programs for an immature, uncritical audience is obvious. There will never be much of a demand for an interest in serious programing. And there follows a more frightening, although purely hypothetical corollary: if the few serious programs which are produced, utilize the glittering methods of entertainment to distort the truth, where will be found a critically trained audience which can detect such deception?

As a matter of fact, the ticklish problem of deception cuts across many areas of broadcasting and could stand as the second undesirable force some critics have discerned in this medium which fluctuates between presenting entertainment and information and a combination of the two. There exists a kind of ethical confusion in the broadcasting world. Radio and television theater is illusory and exerts much effort to perfect deception. How much effort, then, should a broadcast parlor game, which, like a theater piece, must be rehearsed for timing and smoothness and sparkle, make in the opposite direction of attempting to be utterly honest in springing its stock of tricks upon participants? Mr. Crosby has inveighed against coaching people ahead of time on an ostensibly unrehearsed show. (see p. 267) And Mr. Seldes is even more forthright in explaining his objections to the practice:

> The morals of a quiz show are not, in the days of atomic energy, the citizen's primary concern. But if the citizen is not concerned, the statesmen might be. . . . He might begin by asking whether it is a good thing for the citizens of a country to have their senses blunted so that they cannot tell fact from falsehood. He might go further and ask whether this is not exactly what a demagogue would desire. And he might speculate on the possibility that those who fake small things may eventually fake large ones--all in the name of showmanship.[96]

Similar critical objections, as we have seen, have been raised over that distortion of the truth which comes from trying to inject irresponsible bombast into a controversial discussion or undisciplined emotion into a controversial documentary--again in the name of entertainment. These critics feel that broadcasters and audiences must be brought to realize that all of the values of their entertainment world simply may not be applicable to the entire range of programs.

Still a third discouraging force which critics have sensed in broadcasting's embrace of entertainment, while only nodding toward information, is that the misbalance or even the confusion between the two interferes with attempts at worthwhile, overall program design by a network or a station. Saul Carson believes the documentary, for all its promise, has remained ineffective because, at the whim of its economic masters, it must only engage in a "sporadic, grab-bag reaching for subject matter" and it has always lacked a "regular time" and a "definite cycle" which could be employed for building audience interest.[97] Mr. Shayon's disappointment with a 1952 NBC series of documentaries on the crisis in the nation's schools drew a similar criticism:

> Such operations cannot be thrown together hurriedly in the enthusiasm of public service spiced with promotional possibilities. They must be created by new constellations of educators, producers, audience-developers, and researchers. . . . Public service via TV needs resources commensurate with those of commercial TV. And this is still to come.[98]

Again, at the time of the Korean War, Mr. Shayon asked, with evident cynicism, three questions of broadcasters, which focused attention on the inability of the industry to organize truly purposeful schedules:

> What is the all-out capacity of radio and TV for an emergency situation? Is it "business-as-usual" with a more generous portion of newscasts, a garnishing of bond drives and camp shows, a peppering of documentaries and national unity sermons and slogans? Or is it something more, arising out of a grand plan designed in the grand manner to marshall the full mental, and emotional resources of a people?[99]

One can only conclude after analyzing their major and minor opinions about all entertainment and information on the air, that the professional critics never cease encouraging broadcasting to adopt some plan, almost any plan of programing which will leave audiences more appreciative of art, more aware of their world, more sensitive as individuals than they were before tuning in. If critics see, as they claim they do, easy, shallow entertainment displacing richer forms of entertainment and polluting informational programs, as well, little wonder that there is so frequently a tone of pessimism in their columns. Their high hopes for broadcasting make its realities seem even lower by contrast. In their depression, the critics have, as we shall see in succeeding chapters, despaired of education on the air and damned advertising.

But they have their optimistic moments, too. They are quick to praise the rare, magnificent programs, and they search conscientiously for good things to say about the vast number of acceptable ones. They are no strangers at proposing reasonable plans of their own. Their optimism may be as well founded as their pessimism, for critics do see some hopeful factors for changing the media in directions they deem favorable.

Although the public seems to have silently approved of the broadcast schedule down through the years, Mr. Seldes examined a CBS poll on audience interest in pay-television conducted in 1950 by Elmo Roper and proffered these interesting conclusions:

> This thumping vote of confidence in the present broadcasting system . . . turns out to be an almost scientific demonstration of the thesis . . . that only a fragment of the total audience cares much for what the broadcasters transmit. It is true that the audience would rather have what it now gets than have no programs at all; it is probably true that most of the audience cannot think up programs preferable to the current ones; it is also true that sponsors are satisfied with audiences indifferent to the programs. . . . But all of these put together do not constitute proof that our programs satisfy public demand, and the refinement of the Roper figures supplied in the Columbus study indicates that actual satisfaction is limited to a tiny fraction of the audience.
>
> For the Roper office was not satisfied with the mere statement (made by six out of every ten set-owners) that they would not be interested in pay-TV, no matter how attractive it was. The next question was why. And to that question only two out of every ten people instinctively said: "Because we are satisfied with the present system and the present programs."[100]

Add to this public attitude of only mild satisfaction two more facts: that television is still flexible in its aims and patterns, and that radio has had to search out new materials in order to attract minority groups of listeners, and the future of these mass media could be intellectually and artistically bright. What irony it would be if radio, as Ben Gross ventured, "in the days of its decline . . . [were to] become cultured as De Forest, Hoover and Sarnoff envisioned thirty or more years ago."[101] This may be the irony but it is also the hope inherent in change. It was in 1926, that H. V. Kaltenborn sadly shook his head and complained, "The great trouble with radio stations' directors has been their unwillingness to strike out into new paths."[102] Perhaps Gilbert Seldes should not have waited until thirty years later to comfort Mr. Kaltenborn and other frustrated critics with this triumphant credo:

> I have now returned to my first discovery about all the popular arts--that nothing is final about them. Competition for public favor [may] lead to degradation, but it [must] lead to change, and as long as change occurs we need never be without hope.[103]

Notes

[1]Charles A. Siepmann, "Radio Starts to Grow Up," Nation, December 27, 1947, p. 697.

[2]Rudy Bretz, "TV As An Art Form," Hollywood Quarterly, V (Winter, 1950-51), 154.

[3]John Wallace, Radio Broadcast, IX (July, 1926), 237.

[4]John Wallace, ibid., IX (October, 1926), 491.

[5]Leslie Allen, Christian Science Monitor, January 25, 1930.

[6]Cyrus Fisher [Darwin Teilhet], Forum, LXXXVIII (November, 1932), 319.

[7]Gilbert Seldes, The Public Arts (New York: Simon and Schuster, 1956), p. 72.

[8]Gilbert Seldes, The Great Audience (New York: Viking Press, 1950), p. 119.

[9]Ibid.

[10]Lou Frankel, Nation, March 15, 1947, p. 304.

[11]Albert Williams, Listening (Denver: University of Denver Press, 1948), p. 8.

[12]Saul Carson, New Republic, February 23, 1948, p. 26.

[13]Albert Williams, "Listening," Saturday Review of Literature, April 12, 1947, p. 63.

[14]Ibid., p. 62.

[15]Jack Gould, New York Times, August 10, 1947.

[16]Saul Carson, New Republic, June 6, 1949, p. 27.

[17]Seldes, The Public Arts, p. 72.

[18]Saul Carson, "Notes Toward An Examination Of The Radio Documentary," Hollywood Quarterly, IV (Autumn, 1949), 69-74.

[19]Ibid.

[20]Jack Gould, New York Times, June 2, 1946.

[21]Robert Lewis Shayon, Saturday Review, September 29, 1951, p. 33.

[22]Seldes, The Great Audience, p. 120.

[23]Jack Gould, New York Times, December 15, 1952.

[24]See Bernard De Voto's thorough analysis of NBC-TV's collaborative film documentary "Victory At Sea" ("The Easy Chair," Harper's, CCVIII [June, 1954], 8-13).

[25]Saul Carson, New Republic, July 21, 1947, p. 33.

[26]Saul Carson, ibid., October 10, 1949, p. 23.

[27]Jack Gould, New York Times, March 30, 1952.

[28]John Crosby, Out of the Blue (New York: Simon and Schuster, 1952), p. 248.

[29]Robert Lewis Shayon, Saturday Review, December 15, 1951, p. 38.

[30]Seldes, The Public Arts, p. 217.

[31]Jack Gould, New York Times, October 31, 1954.

[32]Ibid.

[33]Robert Lewis Shayon, Saturday Review, February 16, 1952, p. 37.

[34]Philip Hamburger, New Yorker, January 7, 1950, pp. 72-73.

[35]Robert Lewis Shayon, Saturday Review, May 31, 1952, p. 28.

[36]Robert Lewis Shayon, ibid., February 16, 1952, pp. 37-38.

[37]Seldes, The Great Audience, p. 121.

[38]Robert Lewis Shayon, Saturday Review, February 16, 1952, p. 37.

[39]Robert Lewis Shayon, ibid., May 8, 1954, p. 28.

[40]Seldes, The Public Arts, p. 216.

[41]Jack Gould, New York Times, October 5, 1947.

[42]Robert Lewis Shayon, Saturday Review, September 25, 1954, p. 28.

[43]Jack Gould, New York Times, July 17, 1949.

[44]Jack Gould, ibid., January 16, 1949.

[45]Philip Hamburger, New Yorker, April 4, 1953, p. 99.

[46]Philip Hamburger, ibid., October 3, 1953, p. 89.

[47]John Crosby, Wisconsin State Journal (Madison), September 22, 1954.

[48]Jack Gould, New York Times, January 16, 1949. For additional, lucid comments on Mr. Corwin's false rhetoric, see Bernard De Voto's review of "On a Note of Triumph" in ("The Easy Chair," Harper's, CXCI [July,

1945], 33-36).

[49]Saul Carson, New Republic, February 14, 1949, p. 26.

[50]Jack Gould, New York Times, November 25, 1951.

[51]John Crosby, Herald Tribune (New York), October 6, 1952.

[52]Jack Gould, New York Times, March 14, 1948.

[53]Saul Carson, New Republic, August 28, 1950, p. 22.

[54]Seldes, The Great Audience, p. 122.

[55]Jack Gould, New York Times, June 11, 1950.

[56]Robert Lewis Shayon, Saturday Review, August 11, 1951, p. 33.

[57]Lou Frankel, Nation, February 15, 1947, p. 187.

[58]Lou Frankel, ibid., January 18, 1947, p. 73.

[59]Seldes, The Public Arts, p. 217.

[60]Jack Gould, New York Times, May 25, 1947.

[61]John Wallace, Radio Broadcast, XII (February, 1928), 307.

[62]Leslie Allen, Christian Science Monitor, May 17, 1930.

[63]John Crosby, Wisconsin State Journal (Madison), March 15, 1954.

[64]John Crosby, ibid., September 8, 1954.

[65]Jack Gould, New York Times, October 7, 1953.

[66]Seldes, The Public Arts, p. 120.

[67]Ibid., p. 121.

[68]Robert Lewis Shayon, Saturday Review, November 29, 1952, p. 32.

[69]Jack Gould, New York Times, November 16, 1952.

[70]Jack Gould, ibid., November 28, 1954.

[71]Philip Hamburger, New Yorker, November 20, 1954, p. 193.

[72]Jack Gould, New York Times, August 19, 1951.

[73]Gilbert Seldes, Saturday Review, January 3, 1953, p. 56.

[74]Seldes, The Public Arts, p. 274.

[75]Marya Mannes, Reporter, December 2, 1954, p. 41.

[76]Cyrus Fisher [Darwin Teilhet], Forum, XC (December, 1933), 383.

[77]Seldes, The Public Arts, p. 217
John Crosby, Herald Tribune (New York), November 30, 1953.

[78]Jack Gould, New York Times, January 3, 1955.
Philip Hamburger, New Yorker, January 15, 1955, pp. 85-87.

[79]Robert Lewis Shayon, Saturday Review, August 20, 1955, pp. 23-24.

[80]Marya Mannes, Reporter, November 17, 1955, pp. 37-39.

[81]Ibid., p. 39.

[82]Seldes, The Great Audience, p. 147.

[83]Ibid.

[84]Saul Carson, "Notes Toward an Examination of the Radio Documentary," Hollywood Quarterly, IV (Autumn, 1949), 71.

[85]Jack Gould, New York Times, January 19, 1947.

[86]Saul Carson, New Republic, August 16, 1948, pp. 27-28.

[87]Saul Carson, ibid., January 24, 1949, p. 27.

[88]Saul Carson, ibid., August 16, 1948, p. 28.

[89]John K. Hutchens, New York Times, January 3, 1943.

[90]Jack Gould, "What TV Is--And What It Might Be," New York Times Magazine, June 10, 1951, p. 23.

[91]Ibid.

[92]Seldes, The Public Arts, p. 66.

[93]Seldes, The Great Audience, p. 243.

[94]Marya Mannes, Reporter, June 30, 1955, p. 42.

[95]Seldes, The Public Arts, p. 232.

[96]Ibid., p. 93.

[97]Saul Carson, "Notes Toward an Examination of the Radio Documentary," Hollywood Quarterly, IV (Autumn, 1949), 73.

[98]Robert Lewis Shayon, Saturday Review, April 19, 1952, p. 48.

[99]Robert Lewis Shayon, ibid., December 30, 1950, p. 24.

[100]Seldes, _The Public Arts_, p. 205.

[101]Ben Gross, _I Looked and I Listened_ (New York: Random House, 1954), p. 287.

[102]H. V. Kaltenborn, "On the Air," _Century_, CXII (October, 1926), 674.

[103]Seldes, _The Public Arts_, p. vii.

CHAPTER VIII

THE CRITICS' OPINIONS OF BROADCAST EDUCATION

Granting that art, entertainment, and certainly information programs may have educational value (may, in fact, have the education of the audience as a conscious function), the concern of this chapter is to examine critical opinions about radio and television as educational devices in the more formal, more specific sense. In view of the professional critics' receptivity toward affairs of the mind and toward a disciplined utilization of these media, any lack of unanimity with respect to educational broadcasting may seem strange. But they speak always from an awareness of the commercialized entertainment-voluntary audience framework within which broadcasting is carried on. It is an awareness which has resulted in expressions of disappointment, as well as relief, over the scarcity of educational programs, of the need for cooperation between the industry and educators as well as the need for separate stations, and finally, of qualities necessary for worthwhile programs. Their remarks fall logically into two brief divisions: comments about the rationale and structure for educational broadcasting and comments about techniques in educational programing.

Ideas About Educational Broadcasting

One of the earliest radio critics perceived a distinction between information and education which, whether true or not in an abstract sense, helps to explain the rough path of educational broadcasting. John Wallace declared that although radio could inform by imparting facts, it could not educate because it could not develop and discipline the intellectual and moral faculties,[1] a process depending not only on subjects inherently difficult but also depending upon systematic instruction.[2] Certainly, commercial broadcasters seemed to agree with this point of view, since they made little attempt to allocate time in their busy schedules for any systematized instruction. Such purposeful neglect on the part of the industry alienated educators and was responsible for the strong support critics were to give twenty-five years later to the plan for special television channels for education.

On the other hand, the industry did attempt to impart straight information as entertainingly as it knew how. And here it was the educators' turn to neglect a responsibility. What little broadcasting they did do could have been improved had they been less suspicious of an alliance between the instructional and informational arts and the entertainment arts. Although Leslie Allen was willing to excuse early educational programs for their "talky, bookish, lack in luster of life" quality, he called upon pedagogues to stop thinking of "radio showmanship as something unworthy of education."[3] Common as such remonstrances became, they were apparently futile, since twenty years later Mr. Seldes, despairing of the success of educational television, remarked, "educators [are] as obstinate in their suspicion of mass media as sponsors are of education."[4]

If broadcasters had allocated more regular periods at reasonable hours, and if educators had concentrated on ways to develop audience continuity, the potentials of these new media would have been more thoroughly investigated. Over the years, critics tried to help by urging the industry to make more than a gesture in the direction of cultural and educational programs and by scolding educators when they let offers of time slip through their hands.

Marya Mannes' reaction to NBC's recent policy of "enlightenment through exposure" was typical. She complimented the network for its attempt to inject bits of culture into regular programs (e.g. a ballet in a variety show, an operatic aria in a program of popular music) and sound information into news and commentary programs, but she wondered about the educational effectiveness of such an indirect approach:

> Can enlightenment come only from the outside without the active involvement of the subject? . . . To be exposed to a multitude of facts does not give us capacity to make sense out of them. Maybe . . . a great many people would prefer enlightenment straight and are worth programing for. Isn't the real goal to make the enlightenment so good in and for itself that it constitutes entertainment?[5]

This kind of enlightenment cannot be made "good," of course, except through practice on the part of educators. Mr. Carson typified other critics in his complaint that educators were not "taking enough advantage of the reservoir of excellent intentions among the money boys,"[6] and in one column he specifically criticized the director of the Metropolitan Museum of Art for refusing to cooperate with NBC because its program would have been presented at the somewhat less popular time of twelve noon on Saturday.[7]

Any broad, secure future for educational broadcasting seemed out of the question in this atmosphere of mutual suspicion and guilt until the Federal Communications Commission decided, in 1949, to entertain a proposal to reserve television channels for education, even though in the thirties a similar proposal for radio reservations had not been approved. There followed a three year tug of war between commercial and educational forces until finally, in April, 1952, some ten percent of all television channels were set aside for educational use. The professional critics played no small part in arousing educators and the public to support the proposal, though they, themselves, varied in their enthusiasm for it.

John Crosby pricked the conscience of the academic world by revealing what he thought their inner desires were with regard to this issue:

> They would, I'm convinced, be secretly relieved if these channels would go in perpetuity to commercial interests, in which case they could, in perpetuity, blame television for its commercialism, its effect on the young, its mediocrity.
>
> . . . .
>
> Television is the greatest challenge ever presented to an educator. It demands of an educator imagination, integrity, resource and plain hard work. All these things the educator has demanded of radio, lately of television. Failing to find them, he has heaped scorn on radio and now television for the lack of qualities which he has himself neglected to provide.
>
> . . . .
>
> In the meantime, though, the channels will have to be set aside while the educators educate themselves. Once these channels are lost to commercial interests they will never be recovered.[8]

While Mr. Crosby was busy rousing the educators, Mr. Gould and Mr. Carson encouraged their readers to write to Washington.[9] The critics felt that there was adequate precedent for these reservations. Like the land given to states by the federal government for education, the frequency-carrying ether was also a natural resource part of which could certainly be used for the education of all our citizens.[10]

It was in these columns that the critics set forth objectives toward which they felt educational television would strive. And it is interesting to contrast their idealism with John Wallace's debunking attitude so typical of the twenties: "We have a deep seated prejudice against that type of mind which demands of every instrument of human devising that it serve the purpose of 'uplift.'"[11] Jack Gould did not seem to mind being classed with the do-gooders when he saw that educational television could help teach our children and adults and could help disseminate the knowledge of our museums, art galleries and other cultural resources.[12]

Nor did Robert Lewis Shayon apparently mind a similar classification when he described the five goals of educational television: (1) the movement of ideas not merchandise (2) the maturation rather than the "sell" of the individual (3) the improvement of human relations (4) the exploration of new fields of subject matter (5) the preservation of Western culture.[13]

The general vigor with which most critics took up the cause of educational channels indicates their dissatisfaction with the contribution of commercial broadcasters to the area of learning. Though they were not convinced of the educators' ability or willingness to do the job, they knew that commercial broadcasters would not do it. Special channels could become an open door to future, if not to present experimentation in fields which had so much to offer our people. The critics had long complained of the lack of variety in broadcast programing and of the fact that minority tastes were so largely ignored. Some of these mistakes could now be rectified.

Interestingly enough, a few critics, though not opposed to more educational programs, were not convinced that the solution to the problem lay in special channels. Jack Cluett, for one, asked his readers to consider the advantages of a plan submitted by an advertising agency executive which would make available several blocks of excellent time for education by requiring sponsors to donate one regular period out of every four or five.[14] And Gilbert Seldes, even after the channels were reserved, proposed a solution less lax than the one just mentioned. Mr. Seldes thought that special channels might not help achieve the commendable goals of educational television, at least as far as the mass audience was concerned:

> The assignment of separate channels for cultural programs . . . removes both the commercial and the cultural broadcaster

> from the keenest pressure to compete in the market place of ideas. And it tends to indulge the educator in pedantry . . . and to encourage the commercial producer to go lower and lower in search for his common denominator, letting him be as vulgar as he likes because he is balanced by the high esthetic line on other channels. Finally, this separation prevents the cross-fertilization of culture and popularity which in my view is essential in a democratic system.[15]

He felt that the occasional seed of culture planted by a commercial program and watched by a vast audience could better come to germination, if that audience were able to look to the same station for further enlightenment. Consequently, he suggested that educators and commercial broadcasters share the same frequency with specified hours alloted to each.[16]

The issue raised by Mr. Seldes was a disturbing one for critics who, counting themselves on the side of common benefits for all, had to admit that reserved channels might result in a culturally unhealthy fragmentation of the public. Mr. Crosby, however, met the issue head on. He felt that any compromise proposals were doomed to failure. They were suggestions which, if put into practice, would "smother the educators by embracing them with open arms" leaving them in the position of being "controlled, hood-winked and eventually abandoned."[17] Mr. Crosby apparently felt that it was less advisable to risk losing specific facilities for educational programs than to risk a division of audiences into mediocre mass and cultural elite:

> My own feeling is that the educators will never in this world pry more than a token amount of time from commercial stations. I also feel strongly that education doesn't have to compete with commerce any more than Carnegie Hall has to compete with Radio City Music Hall. Each has its audience. It is, I think, an affront to the American people to say that they have to be conned into looking at educational TV by first taking a shot of Milton Berle.[18]

Despite a few misgivings, the critics generally favored encouraging whatever contribution popular commercial television could make to educational values without denying specialized stations their opportunity to extend the potential of broadcasting as far as it could go in this area.

Even though the federal government had finally decided in favor of education, state and local plans for utilization of the new channels continued to meet opposition. It was on the occasion of a New York State commission's recommendation that no public educational network be established, that Jack Gould wrote what can stand as a brief summary of critical thinking on the subject of reserved frequencies. After repeating the commission's main argument that commercial stations were able and willing to do education's job, Mr. Gould scored the short-sighted and inconsistent manner in which commercial stations usually give marginal time to education:

> Whenever heat is turned on the broadcasters for some obvious shortcomings, they rush in to make a showing. . . . Once the heat has subsided, the broadcasters return to their usual ways.

Such vacillation, he felt, could not be permitted if educational television were to fulfill its function as a "new and exciting avenue to the mind of man."[19]

The reservation of channels is, of course, only the beginning for educational broadcasting, and the professional critics have had some further suggestions to make about their operation. Mr. Shayon feels it is imperative that a new breed of men which, for want of a better name, he calls "communicators," be trained. With funds from foundations, legislatures, or some type of pay video, these staffs would, upon completion of their schooling, combine the best features of educators and showmen--half artists and half social scientists.[20] They would be equipped to achieve the high goals set for the new media of education. Nor need the benefits of such a plan stop here. "It might be," muses Mr. Shayon, "that the strongest of the educational broadcasters, plus those who would be attracted to them from the commercial field, could set up a permanent operation devoted exclusively to producing entertaining and effective social and cultural broadcasts."[21]

His suggestion has similarities to an earlier proposal of Mr. Carson's that a single station be established by a public body composed of representatives from listeners, consumers, broadcasters, laborers and others. The station would experiment with new practices and new programing, serving as a yardstick against which private stations could measure particularly their public service achievements.[22]

Although a suggestion by Jack Gould that educational staffs experiment with closed circuit television in lieu of operating on regular channels[23] seems very modest in comparison with the far-reaching proposals of Mr. Shayon and Mr. Carson, it is well to remember that all professional critics are aware of television's complexities and of a good program's qualities. However impractical their ideas may seem, educational broadcasters would do well to consider them. New stations cannot operate in an academic vacuum, since their output immediately takes its place beside the polished products of the commercial stations: "Well meaning pedagogues and students-in-training," says Robert Lewis Shayon, "cannot compete by playing at TV."[24] His final words of warning should serve to convince all educational broadcasters of the responsibility which is theirs:

> If the educators fail, educational television for all its promise will not fly; it will merely limp. If the educators succeed, then educational TV may prove to be the catalyst of an American cultural renaissance.[25]

The hopes which critics held for educational television had not yet been realized by the end of 1955. Even with the assistance of the Ford

Foundation, other philanthropic organizations, and local, civic and government funds, financial problems and the lack of public interest in converting to UHF reception remained to plague most of the potential stations. Such difficulties were not unanticipated, but the situation has prevented including any critical evaluation of America's new broadcast service. In the meantime, critics report occasionally to their readers on developments in this area, and two brief comments by Jack Gould and one by Gilbert Seldes help place the entire subject of educational broadcasting in the kind of broad context which will serve as a conclusion to this section.

Initial funds are not the only difficulty educational broadcasters face. Academic freedom may be exposed to new trials when it attempts to leave the campus for the television classroom. Mr. Gould emphasized the absurdity of an anti-political section in a proposed law to which future New York State educational stations would have had to conform:

> To avoid the inclusion of partisan material is to make impossible the art of teaching. The arts, history, commerce, literature and drama--almost every phase of human endeavor--at some time falls into the political arena.
>
> The cautious professor with tenure at stake may think it wise merely to explain on the air how to fix a leaky faucet or make lace.[26]

Or again, even political purity might not save a public station, if a legislative council could withdraw operating funds because it did not approve of the limited service education provides. When the controller threatened to cut the New York City owned radio station out of the budget because of its specialized offering to small groups such as homebound school-children and adult education classes, Jack Gould supported the station's unique function:

> For him to complain of WNYC's specialized service is to misunderstand the whole reason for the station's existence. If

> WNYC did the same thing every other station did by seeking to attract a majority audience continuously, that could be a colossal extravagance.
>
> Both non-commercial and commercial types of broadcasting are needed. They are complementary not competitive.[27]

It is this responsibility of educational channels to do what commercial broadcasters cannot do that makes it imperative for their controlling organizations to preserve every freedom in the station's limited sphere. Finally, it was Mr. Seldes' realization of the special channels' duties which made him a reluctant convert to their support:

> About them I have only a single conviction: the method of special channels should be tried and the educators should have as fair a chance as commercial broadcasters--they should be allowed to make as many mistakes, to try as many different techniques.[28]

The fair chance is as good a phrase as any to describe the general attitude of critics toward educational broadcasting. Since most of them feel radio never presented one, they insist that education must be given its opportunity to use the newest medium of communication. Experimentation is, of course, still too shallow for predicting what will evolve in broadcast education. Certainly, the shortage of teachers and classrooms at all levels will encourage broad projects in formal teaching. And it is to be hoped that the tidbits of culture on commercial channels will stimulate audiences to seek more substantial feasts on educational channels. The fair chance, as Mr. Seldes implied, also means the chance of an educational program to be right as well as wrong. Now, meager though such comments have been, let us consider what help critics can give this specialized area of broadcasting by explaining what qualities they perceive to be characteristic of successful programs.

Qualities of Educational Programs

One cannot know the subjective background of school and campus, of teacher and books from which the critics react to education on the air. One can only report common agreement among them on the need for such programs to exhibit intellectual soundness and audience understanding. And one can only suggest that educators ponder the wisdom of the critics' comments, brief and scattered though they are.

Content invariably revolves about fact, and this the educational presentation must have, if it is to rest on the kind of foundation which will give it strength and assurance amid the glittering but superficial activities of the surrounding schedule. Foundation in fact is what gave the 1953, CBS-Museum of Natural History television program, "Adventure," its appeal for Philip Hamburger. "Scholarship, science, the modesty of learning and the perspective of history were in charge of the proceedings."[29]

Only from a solid basis in fact can come a further manipulation and imposition of structure, characterizing the program which has "thought" as an even higher virtue than fact. Thought imparts to fact the dimension of truth, which, of all qualities, seems to be most highly prized by the critics. This was what Marya Mannes appreciated in the CBS documentary "The Search," which edited "the raw facts so that the shape of truth is uncluttered by 'effects,' clear and coherent,"[30] and in another CBS program "Now and Then," which presented Dr. Frank Baxter reading great words from the past. "People discovered that this was not education; this was stimulation . . . to communicate creative thought in terms that any who wish can understand."[31]

The program upon which thought has been spent and through which thought is conveyed somehow manages to reveal implications and relations which comprise a true learning experience. Mr. Shayon is particularly distressed by educational broadcasts which never go beyond the presentation of fact. He feels that such productions are still trying to fit nineteenth century educational concepts into a twentieth century device. After NBC television's first (1950) serious educational program, "Watch the World," Mr. Shayon commented:

> The emphasis is entirely on the outward, the factual, the thing done, rather than on the inward, the why, the wherefore, the human. A series of unrelated images parade across the TV screen without an accompanying attempt to provide synthesis, illumination, understanding. . . . [Impressions] must be sifted, catalogued, evaluated, fitted into some frame of reference.[32]

The superior educational program encourages an inner involvement of the audience with the material being presented. It may have to ignore departmental boundary lines and stray from the academic area, if it is to discover ways of touching as many members in the unseen student-body as possible. Certainly, one aim for education on the air is that it extend itself beyond pedagogical convention, just as it cannot help but extend itself beyond the four walls of the classroom. Mr. Shayon, commenting on a "Johns Hopkins Science Review" television program about volcanoes, put the matter this way:

> There was no poetry in it, no zest, no dash, nothing to lift the subject off the ground. . . . Educators . . . ought continually to remind themselves that "facts" alone are not enough. . . . I would like very much to have heard what the Johns Hopkins' departments of literature, history, perhaps art and music--yes, even philosophy--have to say about volcanoes.[33]

In the hands of unskilled educators, the broad view would be an invitation to chaos, and it is of equal importance that facts and their thoughtful interpretation be well organized for broadcasting. Only rarely, of course, do educators project over the air such a superior grasp of content. When it happens, a critic like Mr. Shayon is ecstatic. He once said of a series of talks by British astronomer, Fred Hoyle:

> This is one man speaking--no giant cast, no sound-effects, no cameras panning and dollying, no stagehands and technicians falling over each other. . . . This is the stuff that the science fiction boys . . . struggle so desperately to approach week after plodding earthbound week on the radio and TV schedules and fail to reach at even a shooting star's distance. This is the real thing--thought, pure, unalloyed, pellucid--and this is absorbing.[34]

In addition to exhibiting an eagerness to embrace broad implications of content, critically acceptable educational programs demonstrate other qualities. Chief among these is enthusiasm among the participants on the program. So many entertainers have enthusiasm, if nothing else, that the broadcast teacher cannot afford to appear drab and uninteresting. Enthusiasm is evident in the teacher who has vigorous curiosity in his field, coupled with an eager desire to share what he has discovered. It is a quality which, as critics remind us, can be found in kindergarten teachers as well as college professors. "Ding Dong School's" Dr. Frances Horwich had this quality in abundance. Jack Gould said: "She is clarity itself and speaks slowly but conveys a sense of excitement and conversational information that wins and holds the attention of the nursery-school generation."[35] And Mr. Shayon felt that Dr. Horwich seemed "genuinely to care about . . . [children's] intelligence, imagination, and creativity."[36]

Apparently caring about an audience and about a subject makes a difference in adult programing, too. When Dr. Baxter presented his Shakespeare course over CBS-TV in 1954, Jack Gould felt he imparted "almost immediately that most magic if elusive quality of the gifted teacher: enthusiasm." And he went on to describe it as "not the wild, almost circus-like frenzy which one Eastern professor seemed to feel was necessary sugarcoating for an understanding of the atomic era, but the deeprooted sense of continuing adventure that identifies the alert and inquiring mind."[37] This enthusiasm for ideas as well as people seems to be a special quality which, in Mr. Crosby's opinion, the professional broadcaster does not have. For example, he contrasted Charles Collingwood, the CBS moderator on "Adventure," with the scientists on a program about snakes:

> Collingwood has a tendency to smother both the herpetologists and the snakes in professional charm, verging on professional cuteness. . . . The scientists, steeped as they are in their subjects, have a non-professional charm and sincerity which is far more engaging than that of the pros.[38]

With an attitude of enthusiasm to spark and undergird a program, teaching style and production techniques can be simplicity themselves. Simplicity is, of course, a quality combining other virtues like quietness and imagination. In the presence of the enforced gaiety of commercial shows, the quiet educational program can attract attention by its very modesty. The best example was NBC's "Ding Dong School." Almost all of the critics, at one time or another during its several seasons on the air, appreciated the serenity of the program. Mr. Shayon felt that Dr. Horwich had mastered the secret of the child-world's "rhythm of thought and feeling;" that she made "of slow motion a TV art form;" and that "in a gentle, restful, evocative manner she [attempted] to draw the child viewer to push back the boundaries of his own limitations into ever-widening circles of fulfillment."[39] And Jack Cluett said that the "calm, soothing tempo of its delivery [was a] long overdue relief from the high pitched, frenzied cacaphony piped into your living room by the Howdy Doody school of raucous kid shows."[40] Mr. Crosby summed up the entire series very succinctly: "It is long on common sense, short on production."[41]

The simple program implies an intense concentration upon its subject to the exclusion of unnecessary distractions. And oftentimes the very absence of expensive paraphernalia, unavailable to the educator, permits the essence of the material to be communicated. After viewing several educational kinescopes, John Crosby praised their quality in spite of their meagre budgets. Referring specifically to "The Finder" and "Religions of Man," produced by a St. Louis educational station, and to "The Children's Corner," produced by an educational station in Pittsburgh, he said:

> The more razzle-dazzle showmanship, the less pure thought you're likely to absorb. . . . The tougher the subject, the simpler the presentation had better be. . . . You don't have to have money. You need brains, enthusiasm, and hard work.[42]

It is possible that the program which is conceived in simplicity and forged from the ingenuity and imagination of its personnel evokes closer audience involvement by paying it the compliment of expecting it to use its imagination in order to complete the presentation. Jack Gould sensed that this was happening in a spare but exciting performance of "The Telltale Heart" as part of CBS "Camera Three's" investigation of Edgar Allen Poe, which utilized actors in a simple setting with stools, a ladder, high-lights and shadow, and ominous music provided by a balladier.[43]

In summary, the program which can illuminate its content through a thoughtful, well organized interrelationship of parts, and involve its audience through an alert but simple, imaginative presentation is well on its way toward exemplifying broadcast education at its best. It is well on its way to earning the accolade once given by Philip Hamburger to CBS' "Adventure." "It treats its audience with respect, and this fact alone sets it apart from practically everything else being broadcast."[44]

The very fact that this discussion of educational broadcasting and the critics is brief, indicates the basic lack of respect which has prevailed between educators and the industry. The indifference, if not antagonism, between the two groups is not the kind of attitude which develops a flourishing camaraderie and studios humming with educational activity. The educators' contempt for commercial broadcasting is matched by the broadcasters' contempt for the bumbling teacher, with the result that audiences suffer cultural malnutrition and critics have almost nothing to report in this area. (It is also true, of course, that most of the critics write from broadcasting's hub in New York City where they have had little contact with the output of small educational stations flourishing primarily in other sections of the country.)

However, commercial television's minor but sincere and frequently fine educational programs and the slowly increasing output of new special channels may see a national change in this attitude. Certainly the professional critics live in hope that there will be cross-fertilization between the two areas. The presentation of some semblance of a united cultural front by broadcasters and educators would be much better for audiences than the continuation of a cultural schizophrenia which reduces the potential of these mass media in an important area of public service.

Mr. Seldes once wrote:

> Certainly the industry, which is so extremely proficient in other fields, has failed to find techniques to make the documentary or the cultural program widely acceptable. . . . Perhaps it can be done only by broadcasters who are not instinctively afraid of the critical intelligent mind.[45]

That some of this fear is engendered by the advertising pressure under which our system of broadcasting primarily operates will become apparent in the next chapter. Once conquered, however, what had been fear of an intelligently responsive audience could become a source of great stimulation to the broadcaster. He would experience a positive thrill in communicating to an active rather than a passive group. Regardless of unhappy experiences in the past and of financial pressures in the present, the broadcast media (both commercial and non-commercial) cannot escape the obligation to educate in the highest and most specific sense. World events move too fast and cultural contributions are too helpful to society to permit one communication tool which reaches out with the speed of light to concern itself merely with pleasant trivia.

Notes

[1]John Wallace, Radio Broadcast, IX (October, 1926), 491.

[2]John Wallace, ibid., IX (June, 1926), 134.

[3]Leslie Allen, Christian Science Monitor, August 16, 1930.

[4]Gilbert Seldes, The Great Audience (New York: Viking Press, 1950), p. 182.

[5]Marya Mannes, Reporter, March 24, 1955, p. 39.

[6]Saul Carson, New Republic, May 8, 1950, p. 22.

[7]Saul Carson, ibid., June 25, 1951, p. 30.

[8]John Crosby, Out of the Blue (New York: Simon Schuster, 1952), pp. 284-86.

[9]Jack Gould, New York Times, November 26, 1950.
Saul Carson, New Republic, December 11, 1950, pp. 30-31.

[10]Gould, loc. cit.

[11]John Wallace, Radio Broadcast, IX (October, 1926), 490.

[12]Jack Gould, New York Times, December 14, 1952.

[13]Robert Lewis Shayon, Saturday Review, December 16, 1950, p. 29.

[14]Jack Cluett, Woman's Day, XV (December, 1951), 140.

[15]Gilbert Seldes, Saturday Review, March 7, 1953, p. 37.

[16]Ibid.

[17]John Crosby, Herald Tribune (New York), December 10, 1950.

[18]John Crosby, ibid., January 23, 1952.

[19]Jack Gould, New York Times, March 1, 1953.

[20]Robert Lewis Shayon, Saturday Review, December 16, 1950, pp. 29-30.

[21]Robert Lewis Shayon, ibid., February 2, 1952, pp. 32-33.

[22]Saul Carson, New Republic, April 10, 1950, p. 22.

[23]Jack Gould, New York Times, December 20, 1955.

[24]Robert Lewis Shayon, Saturday Review, December 16, 1950, p. 30.

[25]Ibid.

[26]Jack Gould, New York Times, February 21, 1954.

[27]Jack Gould, ibid., December 14, 1952.

[28]Gilbert Seldes, The Public Arts (New York: Simon and Schuster, 1956), p. 275.

[29]Philip Hamburger, New Yorker, June 6, 1953, p. 134.

[30]Marya Mannes, Reporter, December 2, 1954, p. 40.

[31]Ibid.

[32]Robert Lewis Shayon, "Toynbee, TV, and Chicago," Christian Science Monitor, June 3, 1950.

[33]Robert Lewis Shayon, "Radio-TV," ibid., January 30, 1951.

[34]Robert Lewis Shayon, Saturday Review, February 24, 1951, pp. 27-28.

[35]Jack Gould, New York Times, January 18, 1953.

[36]Robert Lewis Shayon, Saturday Review, April 18, 1953, p. 32.

[37]Jack Gould, New York Times, June 20, 1954.

[38]John Crosby, Herald Tribune (New York), May 22, 1953.

[39]Shayon, loc. cit.

[40]Jack Cluett, Woman's Day, XVI (May, 1953), 139.

[41]John Crosby, Herald Tribune (New York), February 1, 1953.

[42]John Crosby, Wisconsin State Journal (Madison), April 17, 1955.

[43]Jack Gould, New York Times, March 2, 1955.

[44]Philip Hamburger, New Yorker, June 5, 1954, p. 79.

[45]Seldes, The Great Audience, p. 124.

CHAPTER IX

THE CRITICS AND ADVERTISING

In no other artistic, informational or educational endeavor have the marts of trade played as obvious a role in this country as they have in broadcasting. Theatrical angels hover anonymously behind the scenes; campus donors insist only upon a name modestly chiseled above an entry; even the press reserves the front page for itself and cannot demand that its readers peruse the advertisements. But broadcasting moves and breathes and has its being in an advertising milieu which is absolutely dedicated to forcing itself upon the public.

This is, at the least, a curious situation for professional critics whose first allegiance is to an excellence in entertainment and a high intelligence in the presentation of informational and cultural programs. They cannot ignore the advertising base of the industry since it helps explain so much that is on the air. And certainly they cannot ignore the commercial announcements surrounding the programs. This would be to overlook some fifteen percent of actual broadcast time, to overlook a factor relevant to a critic's response to the rest of the program, and, with no little irony, to overlook the one segment of a program its sponsor is most anxious to have a member of the audience see or hear. Thus unable to escape including evaluations of advertising with their other comments, the critics have reacted in a variety of ways. Behind all their reactions, it must be remembered, of course, that there is no reason why any critic would wholeheartedly embrace the principle of sponsorship. They might accept its financial necessity, but they would never argue that the commercial is not an intrusion.

Early Disillusionment

The mood of regretful acquiescence to the advertisers' subsidization of broadcasting, which has generally prevailed among professional critics, had its start in the middle twenties. Looking back, however, after a generation of broadcasting's forceful, direct approach to selling, some of these early critics' examples of distasteful commercials seem remarkably restrained, and their hopes that the indirect advertisement (simply mention of the advertiser's name) would become the national pattern seem remarkably naive. In a 1926 article, Raymond Francis Yates described as "crass advertising" an electric power commercial which took the form of a short narrative about Mrs. Rip Van Winkle.[1] And Leslie Allen in 1931 felt it was "rude and boorish . . . to inject a 'blurb' into the middle of a program of good music . . . [because] the sponsor makes believe he is out to entertain the listener--but he turns to exploiting the listener before the program is over."[2]

Such critical purists hoped that public disgust or even government intervention might persuade sponsors to use extreme caution in the matter of direct advertising. Zey Bouck, for example, told readers of the January 8, 1927, New York Sun:

> The mention of commercial products in broadcasting programs will necessarily continue until the public utility is supported on a basis radically different from its present status. However, it is hoped that . . . [1927 radio legislation] will provide for instances when radio advertising assumes an over-exaggerated aspect.

Even though the establishment of the Federal Radio Commission did little to hinder the strengthening of the policy of direct selling, Leslie Allen still hoped sponsors would see the error of their ways:

> Sponsors make a mistake in proclaiming themselves as "hosts" —they are guests. Guests in a home don't spend most of the time bragging about their products. Good will is of larger value than increased sales. The listener will buy your goods if he thinks well of them and of you. But if you are venal he can tune you out of the house.[3]

Despite protestations of this sort, commercial broadcasters were well aware of the fact that the public would not tune them out of the house because having to listen to direct advertisements seemed a reasonable enough price to pay for the entertainment they were receiving. And observations like those by Henry Volkening that listeners "with positive pleasure, come to think of entertainment and advertising as being practically one and the same thing,"[4] seemed to confirm the accuracy of the broadcasters' viewpoint. Consequently, even as the depression closed down their columns, the critics' sense of despair over the lost cause of minimum advertising on the air became increasingly evident. When he heard of a new college course in broadcast advertising, Mr. Allen asked sarcastically, "Would it be possible to arrange a course in good taste and make it compulsory for all commercial sponsors?"[5] And Darwin Teilhet, who had carefully clocked commercials, reported their length to his readers and campaigned vigorously for minimizing them, finally delivered a diatribe against the entire system[6] and ceased his monthly column in <u>Forum</u> magazine. Recalling his frustration some twenty years later, he wrote:

> It was a lost cause then, and still is. Personally, I dislike the principle of mountebanks . . . attracting my attention by some form of free entertainment for the purpose of persuading me to buy something.[7]

An impartial observer would, perhaps, complain about the lack of realism in these early critical opinions, especially since annual advertising billings increased from four million to more than forty million dollars at the very time the critics were writing.[8] However, the critics were simply not as impressed by the financial growth of the media as they were depressed by the poor quality and the ubiquitousness of commercial announcements. They were willing to admit the necessity for sponsorship; they were not willing to countenance the abuse of the idea. From the late twenties to the present, professional critics, as shall be seen in this next section, have expressed their complaints about the commercial in no uncertain terms.

Shortcomings of Commercial Announcements

When the critics' encouragement of indirect or institutional commercials came to naught, they turned to the defense of three virtues which they felt direct commercials should have: brevity, good taste, and freedom from any attempt at exploitation. With respect to the first virtue, they reason that if one is forced to attend a sales talk, the least the sponsor can do is to make it short and deliver it infrequently. Ring Lardner laughingly realized, of course, that the sponsor's wishes might lie in the opposite direction, and in 1933 he pictured what the perfect program would be from that person's point of view:

> Two minutes of a big name . . . just enough to prove he was really there and then fifty-eight minutes of advertising talk--talk that is always tiresome, often disgusting, and more often so childishly and manifestly untrue that large numbers of the listeners resolve not to buy the product.[9]

In equal good humor, Darwin Teilhet recommended the "Voice of Firestone" for Lawrence Tibbett's magnificent singing even though the listener had to sit through Harvey S. Firestone, Jr.'s "bedtime monologue on transportation."[10] He was not so charitable with the sponsors of "First Nighter," who, in their efforts to squeeze twelve minutes of advertising into a half-hour program, were guilty of presenting a drama "rotted away by commercials."[11]

And so specific comments ran from good humored jibes to angry oaths, although it must be emphasized that the lightly sarcastic touch seemed to be the favorite critical weapon. For example, Raymond Knight delivered a lament called "I've Got Those Commercial Blues" to his readers of Woman's Day,[12] and Goodman Ace observed that, "The cigarette campaigns now being waged on TV have become such a major portion of the clamor and ballyhoo which emanate from our screens these nights, that required dress for an evening of viewing has become a smoking jacket."[13] Presumably the critics hoped that this kind of humorous approach would help dissolve the flood of commercials to a pitiful puddle of laughable nonsense.

Their serious concern is evident, however, when the length and frequency of commercials becomes more than just a personal frustration and seems to threaten whatever aesthetic possibilities a program has. Jack Gould was particularly conscious of the deleterious effect multiple sponsorship was having on television variety shows. He reminded his readers that in the revue the lift or building of one number helps to produce a mood of anticipation for the next, thus giving the entire program a climactic tension. The constant interruption for commercials dissipates this tension. A performer, such as a comedian, who struggles to win his audience quickly, finds that after each commercial he must start all over again. "In TV the curtain is being raised and lowered altogether too often."[14]

Such breaks are also harmful to dramatic programs for similar reasons. Dramatists, of course, learn the tradition, which audiences have come to accept, of creating two climaxes in order to divide a play into three acts. But Mr. Gould again feels that the exigencies of the advertising world which call for two breaks in the middle of a show are absurd and indicate a "wanton disregard for a program's continuity."[15] And Marya Mannes points to this same problem as one which undermines (as she feels it should) the concept that advertising brings the American public "free" programs.

> The assumption that a thing is free because it is not paid for bears examining. Is not the shattering of dramatic unity by a shampoo commercial a high price for the viewer to pay for a play?[16]

Television raised an interesting problem as to the desirability of a continuous video commercial in the form of a product's name or picture placed so that it would always be on camera during a game or panel-program. The critics have said very little specifically about this matter, although Mr. Gould did comment that the industry seemed to be ignoring its own code in this respect, and that we make fools of ourselves and foreign guests on news programs performed in front of a billboard.[17]

The very phrases "billboard" or "electronic Sears-Roebuck catalogue"[18] and the critics' frequent charges of excessive commercialism indicate their basic bias against the quantity of advertising which the radio and television industry presents. It is quite likely that quantity would be less noticeable as a defect, if other factors about commercials were not irritating to the critics. These factors revolve about the lack of that elusive virtue known as good taste—a kind of gentlemanly integrity which everyone wishes could prevail in the business world.

Perhaps the most serious of the factors dictating against good taste is the actual aura of falseness which broadcast sales messages create about themselves. Gilbert Seldes states that the strongest motive in mass commodity selling is not to sell large quantities only, but to get people to switch brands. In order to achieve this reaction the purchaser must be promised something no competitor has thought of promising, and thus the energetic sell begins. "Advertising on radio," continues Mr. Seldes, "exists in an atmosphere of pressing urgency and gross exaggeration--an atmosphere of insinuated fraud."[19] As a consequence of such an environment over the years, audiences acquire, if not the harshness of the cynic, at least a suspicion and a lack of faith in advertising which is unfortunate.

With a calculated naivete which is all the more incisive for its wide-eyed wistfulness, John Crosby writes of his (and of our) disillusionment.

> I wander around the world of advertising pretty much like Alice wanders around Wonderland, neither of us quite believing any of it but not quite disbelieving it either.
>
> . . . .
>
> The unswerving faith in American advertising which I learned at my mother's knee, has--well--swerved.
>
> . . . .
>
> For years I believed these famous people smoked and ate and washed with the products they said they smoked and ate and washed with.
>
> . . . .
>
> I just don't believe these people any more. You know what I think? I think these people are paid to say these things.[20]

An aspect of the energetic or hard sell which most critics particularly dislike is the noise of beating drums and clashing cymbals, of brash staccato male voices and shrill female squeals frantically acclaiming the newest product. It may be an advertising rule that falsehoods flourish with fanfare. Certainly, says Mr. Seldes, the mark of perfection in a commercial slogan is "to say nothing emphatically, silence all questions, raise no doubts."[21] An example of extreme emphasis lay in the imposition of the choral speaking technique upon the commercial. Saul Carson in describing his reaction said:

> [Meredith Wilson] calls the device, blasphemously, a "Greek Chorus." . . . The enunciation is clear, the synchronization

> is meticulous--the Gilbert and Sullivan impact will send you out to buy earmuffs in July.[22]

Actually such a purchase might be the only way out for anyone trying to escape radio's commercial cacaphony.

It was Mr. Seldes' hope, at least in 1950, that television with its innate visual power would obviate the need for the hard sell and that full honesty might be restored to advertising.[23] But it was only two years later that Jack Cluett was disturbed by radio and television's growing use of the "spiel of the high pressure sales men,"[24] and judging from a comment by John Crosby three years later, it would take more than mere recognition by the industry of television's quiet potential. All of broadcasting was caught up in advertising's strenuous activity, and there was only one real solution:

> The noisy commercials . . . the irritating, shouting, jingling commercial will continue as long as it is successful, as long as you folks buy the stuff--so that the ultimate responsibility rests with the viewers.[25]

More directly associated with poor taste than either falseness or noise is advertising's appeal to sexual emotions and its general lack of discrimination in the presentation of commercials which children are apt to hear or see. John Crosby is not reluctant to conjure up the bogey of legal censorship when he feels the bounds of sexual good taste have been disregarded. After describing a television commercial in which a girl clad in a nightgown stood before a wind machine, he recalled the New York City police commissioner's closing of Minsky's burlesque theater and wryly asked, "Whatever happened to Commissioner Moss, anyhow?"[26] Or again, Mr. Crosby focuses disapproving though humorous attention on the cheap, often implausible connotations which ingenious advertisers draw between their products and sexual fulfillment. He had just seen a wrist-watch commercial when he wrote the following:

> The watch--if I understand this thing correctly--acts as an aphrodisiac on anyone of the opposite sex for miles around. Well, of course, it has been steadily hinted for years that various brands of toothpaste, deodorants and soaps are really love potions in disguise. But I think that ascribing these powers to a wrist watch is carrying the thing too far.[27]

Carrying everything too far has, of course, always been the chief complaint of the critic about the huckster. Commercials have been variously too long, too many, too dishonest, too noisy, too sexy and now too inappropriate for children, in the opinion of Goodman Ace. In an article entitled "Play Beer!" he inveighs against the advertising environment surrounding America's most wholesome sport:

> Drinking and smoking seem to be the stuff athletic broadcasts are made of. It makes darling viewing for the kids for whom baseball holds such fascination. . . . It's a far cry from that bygone day when baseball heroes used to tell the kids about the breakfast cereal the champions ate that made them champions. What happened to those kids? That's easy. They grew up to be big, strong, ulcerated advertising men who write the copy for the beers and cigarettes in the baseball commercials on television these days.[28]

In addition to sins committed against brevity and the dictates of good taste, there is a third shortcoming of broadcast advertising to which some critics have objected: the exploitation of a performer in order to sell a product. To speak out against the thorough intertwining of art with advertising has been one of Jack Gould's continuing crusades. In one of his earliest columns he complained about Ed Wynn having to identify himself so closely with the sponsor and felt that as a general practice the entertainers and the advertisers should confine themselves to their respective fields.[29] A few years later, Mr. Gould again stated his views on the matter:

> The source of radio's strength as an advertising force lies in its popularity as an entertainment medium. The surest way to undermine that strength is to attack the foundation of all entertainment--the integrity of the artist.[30]

And with the arrival of television, when Mr. Gould saw that star performers were coming to be evaluated solely for their records as salesmen "behind the video counter," he sounded another alarm. "In allowing the huckster to exploit directly the affection in which he is held by the public, the star is giving away, piece by piece, the very foundation of his success."[31] John Crosby was also disgusted at the extent to which theater people were delivering the commercials. In his typically sarcastic vein he commented:

> Little by little the whole acting profession is getting to be a shill for the toothpaste people. It's a great challenge to their art. Did you ever try getting emotional about a toothpaste? It's not easy.[32]

After examining these specific charges which critics over the years have directed against advertisers, the acceleration of commercialism in broadcasting stands out more clearly. Advertising moved quickly from an indirect status to a direct one and from the direct but separate sales message to the union of the message with the entertainment. Announcers became actors and actors became announcers. The fusion of entertainment and selling became complete, to the joy of sponsors and the dismay of critics. The major effects of this process will be discussed shortly, but for the moment let us consider what ideas the critics have held about controlling commercialism.

As might be expected, the critics are not agreed about how to eliminate these irritating and distasteful, if not actually immoral aspects of broadcast advertising. Mr. Crosby, as has already been mentioned (see p. 406), would turn to the public as the first and last resort. And he is supported by Albert Williams who urged his readers to turn off their sets and to carry their complaints in well organized groups directly to sponsors.[33] These critics believe that boycott, perhaps even threats of boycott, will cause advertisers to revamp commercials. As an historical aside it is interesting to note that as far back as 1930, Leslie Allen described a boycott weapon, a flashlight-like device, invented by Dr. Lee De Forest, which would blank out the advertising blurb. All that was needed now, Mr. Allen reflected, were announcers who would tell how long the commercial would last.[34]

Attempts to marshall public opinion against commercial excesses cannot be very effective according to Mr. Seldes. He believes "the sales talk is simply not pitched to the critical," and the agitation of irritated intellectuals, who might lead an assault, would be thought of as "highbrow, supersensitive and a trifle insulting" by the public they were trying to persuade.[35] Without giving any evidence for his faith in evolution, he feels that ad men will slowly come to the realization that the brief, neat, honest sales message will be more convincing in the end:

> The better the product and the more confident the sponsor is of its goodness, the more honest the commercial [will be]: So that in the long run people may come to associate quality of product with quality of presentation and feel that [the more hysterical an announcer becomes] the closer his product must be to the shoddy and the fake.[36]

The critics, of course, have not neglected to guide the ad writer by occasionally offering him examples of the kind of commercial they would like to hear or see. Mr. Lardner suggested that his model radio program would start with an honest advertisement such as, "The oil is probably as good as any other oil you can buy."[37] And Goodman Ace, twenty years later, devised what he called the honor commercial to retrieve those viewers who walked out of the room when a television announcement appeared:

> Men! Do people leave the room when your commercials appear on their television sets?
>
> . . . .
>
> What you need is the "Honor Commercial."
> The Honor Commercial is the commercial which appears

> on the television screen with the harsh, irritating hard sell faded completely out. Only the picture of the product is shown and from the speaker comes the subdued voice of an announcer almost whispering: "The sponsor has put you on your honor to buy the product which is shown here. Thank you. And now back to our program." The Honor Commercial is not like a doctor's prescription which contains several ingredients. The Honor Commercial contains just one ingredient --gratitude.[38]

In actual practice, a combination of pressures may eventually result in pleasanter commercials. To the pressure of public opinion and a natural need for change might be added the pressure to conform to a standard industry code. Even while realizing the tendency of networks and stations to disregard codes, some critics mention them as a means of curtailing poor practices. Mr. Cluett reasons as follows:

> Any network that insists on absolute adherence to its split second code usually succeeds in driving its million dollar clients on a shopping tour for more lenient commercial time limits--or a looser interpretation of what constitutes a commercial message.
>
> . . . .
>
> Until the industry sets up a single code of ethics, this competitive throat cutting will be the rule rather than the exception. An industry commissioner, as this column pointed out several years ago, is the obvious solution.[39]

While she did not suggest any particular enforcement, Miss Mannes did indicate that one of the most important regulations the industry could adopt would be "a time code universally adhered to" which would limit advertising from the current eighteen percent to eight percent.[40]

Although the professional critics have engaged in continual skirmishes with broadcasting's sponsors and have generally lost each battle, they continue to promote with vigor and often with good humor a platform of restraint, dignity, and honesty in advertising. All of them may not question, as did Mr. Gould, the sponsors' argument that irritating commercials sell goods. (He called for clear results from an impartial study.)[41] But most of them resent the hucksters' implication that audiences enjoy being gulled. They would appreciate more of Mr. Ace's "gratitude" in commercial announcements instead of lengthy, extravagant claims dinned into their consciousness.

Like Robert Lewis Shayon, most critics have never been completely happy with the image American business has projected of itself through broadcasting. He was referring, of course, to a particular television program on our industrial progress, but he might very well have been commenting on the composite picture business creates through its myriad radio and television commercials. One line in this Advertising Council presentation ran smugly, "Our expanding economy can contain a few errors." "I think," said Mr. Shayon, "that unfortunate statement epitomizes . . . a set of mind which characterizes business programs on the air. . . . In its glorification of mass satisfactions, in its praise with the lips for the individual but its doctrinaire disregard of him with the heart, it suggests the state monolith."[42] In its specifics, as we have seen, advertising contains a few errors. It glorifies the possessor of things. It promises him satisfactions it knows in its heart it cannot deliver. It talks to him brusquely, or coyly, or confidentially, but always person to person, while in the back of its mind it busily computes the mass media sales advantage in cost per thousand.

Critics are aware that these indictments of the commercial per se may appear incomprehensible to majority audiences. If such lack of understanding were simply because people have long since learned to turn a deaf ear and a glazed eye toward commercials, the system would have become self-defeating and critics might rest more easily. Obviously this has happened to some extent, but Marya Mannes still expresses a doubt which most of her colleagues would share and which represents a summation of the basic effect commercials have on the public--an effect which tends to make permanent, an unfortunate gap between the passive majority and the critical few:

> For the mass millions, the infinitely repeated intrusion of commercials . . . feeds--as it is designed to do--the enormous appetite for things that is an accepted American diversion as much as it is the basis of our economy. For the rest of us the commercial continues . . . to be . . . a profound and chronic irritant to people for whom surcease from the material world is . . . a release.[43]

Having specifically examined some of the negative critical reactions to commercial announcements, let us now turn to an analysis of broad operational defects which critics feel are the result of our sponsored system of broadcasting.

Major Program Inadequacies Deriving from Commercial Broadcasting

Of more concern to critics than the materialistic emphasis and abrasive action of commercials are defects in program structure occasioned by broadcasting's dependence on advertising. References to these defects have been made in each of the chapters on specific types of programs. It remains, however, to discuss them in closer relationship to the fundamental financial structure of the industry. The major imperfection critics attribute to commercial broadcasting, the one from which all other defects stem, is rigidity. Advertising pressures, say the critics, have imposed a constant sameness and blandness on programing and a veritable slavery on the part of the industry with regard to ratings and time patterns.

Broadcasting's inflexibility was discovered early and bemoaned at length. Only eight years after the start of audience radio, John Wallace ruefully remarked:

> We are at present thoroughly convinced that things have reached a sorry pass and that radio is standing still--

> smug, self-satisfied, and unutterably banal. . . . The sponsored program is responsible.[44]

How similar to the attitude of John Crosby, who in a 1947 radio discussion explained his dislike of the advertisers' control of radio's content:

> The advertiser's . . . point of view is automatically fixed by sales.
>
> . . . .
>
> There has been no diversity, no experiment, no change. Radio is twenty-seven years old and it was frozen fifteen years ago. There should be a constant effort to improve rather than a constant effort to conform.[45]

Again, the familiar charge was brought by Jack Gould in 1952, who only wished business would take the risks in television programing that it does in the conduct of its own affairs:

> [TV] is blindly and short-sightedly selling its ultimate greatness for a batch of synthetic popularity ratings that are boring into TV's foundations like termites. It is caught on the old radio treadmill of repetition and imitation.[46]

The cause for this state of affairs, which critics have so thoroughly deplored over the years, is not difficult to understand. For a short time, according to Mr. Seldes, the radio industry, in effect, invited sponsors to advertise on programs which audiences were enjoying. Then there came a shift in emphasis, and radio found itself acquiescing to directives from sponsors wanting programs planned for people they wished as customers. With selling in the dominant position, audiences came to be thought of as kinds of people who had to be appealed to on a mass basis.[47] Since mass tastes in entertainment and in cultural matters are assumed to be relatively narrow and slow changing, radio and advertising executives felt that programs could not be varied with financial impunity and that imitations were more likely to be financially successful than innovations. True creativity, of course, is not entirely welcome in such a situation. According to Albert Williams, the industry came to think of writers as "employees to be called in when it becomes necessary to 'build' a radio show or 'prepare' a radio script [in collaboration] not . . . with bookmen or men of letters, but with salesmen."[48]

Certainly, the concept of mechanistically produced, repetitive programs drew large enough audiences to satisfy the financial motives of broadcasters and sponsors, even if it did not please the artistic and intellectual sensibilities of the critics. They, however, have continued to argue that the policy of sameness is neither logically nor legally defensible. When Mr. Stanton of CBS talked of broadcasting as a cultural democracy giving the people what they wanted, Gilbert Seldes countered by replying that people simply took what they got. In the absence of any great variety they learned to accept and even to like the narrow zone of broadcasting's schedule. He felt that the fact that radio actually built audiences for news and classical music proved his point about other needs waiting to be served.[49] "The average man lives at many emotional and intellectual levels in the course of his day. . . . Unless his mental processes have been dulled, he looks for entertainments of many kinds."[50] Even the statistics of the industry's successes failed to impress Mr. Seldes. When the networks pointed with pride to audiences composing one-quarter of the available listeners, this indefatigable critic wondered why no one was trying to reach the other three-quarters. Their own figures, he reasoned, accused the networks of merely programing for a large minority, leaving the interests of many other groups untouched.[51]

Another assumption upon which commercial broadcasting bases its policy of "sameness" is that mass audiences will react more favorably to the familiar rather than to the strange or new. Jack Gould feels that advertisers, above all, should see the fallacy in such a premise, since their very skills have worked so well "to create a demand for a product where the demand has not existed before."[52]

Even though the logic in these refutations is unsupported by enough of the kind of financial evidence which convinces sponsors, most critics would further argue the case for variety on legal grounds. Regardless of the broadcaster's desire to satisfy the sponsor, he has still been licensed to operate in the public interest. Mr. Seldes succinctly phrases the question he and other critics eternally put to broadcasters and advertisers: "Is it in the public interest to be smothered in stale pillow feathers?"[53]

The metaphor is well chosen, since, in addition to commercial broadcasting's blight of stale repetitiveness, critics feel that financial considerations tend to promote programs which are as light and soft as feathers. Such a broadcast schedule is scathingly described, although in a shift of figures, by Marya Mannes:

> The bland, mass diet of television soothes but does not nourish. In its scrupulous avoidance of roughage--controversy, the clash of ideas, the questioning of popular attitudes--it may be having a dangerous effect on the American digestion.[54]

Her placement of the blame for mass malnutrition at the doorstep of advertisers is typical of the professional critics' viewpoint. She regrets the increasing flaccidity of video during the middle fifties and states:

> There was brave talk . . . of a time when the network, assuming more control over sponsor and agency, could balance the diet it fed the American people with more substantial nourishment. . . . [Now there are] business executives dedicated primarily to bookkeeping . . . [who at] the mention of "change" or "planning" will raise their eyebrows. The pattern is set.[55]

The critics believe there are two factors associated with the sponsors' fundamental goal of improving his business through broadcast advertising which explain the plethora of neutral shows on the air. For one thing, sponsors feel that their programs must never offend any segment of the audience. Audiences must be made, if possible, to like everything about a show, and they will thus be more receptive to taking the action recommended in the commercial. One obvious result of this sponsor attitude has been a great emphasis on programs of comedy and laughter. Mr. Seldes believes that as long as sponsors hold such a theory "comedy will continue to dominate the commercial networks, and the public appetite for non-comic programs may become so feeble that even pay-TV will not want to satisfy it."[56]

Offering comedy programs is at least a positive, even though tiresome, way to win friends and influence consumers. The negative machinations of sponsors who wish to avoid antagonizing customers have also been matters of concern for the critics. They have commented on the censorship of scripts and the diluting of climactic viewpoints in a drama's third act. So meticulous have advertisers been, particularly about subjects relating to sex and controversial social and economic themes, that they have become apt targets for critical lampoons. For example, Goodman Ace described how a typical, Madison Avenue, advertising agency executive would have handled James Barrie's "Peter Pan," if it had not been so famous a play:

> "Well this is gonna be too much for us to handle. Why don't you tell Jim whatever his name is to take it over to NBC? No use asking for trouble. First we got a girl playing a boy's part, and then we come up with this fairy business--you can imagine the letters we'll get. We got kids watching our programs!"[57]

Excessive timidity with respect to dramatic fiction may be deplorable, but sponsors' fears about the off-stage political activities of members of a cast is even worse. It was fear of letters and a dropping sales curve which prompted the sponsor of Celanese Theater in 1951 to refuse to employ actors because their names appeared in Red Channels, a book listing the purported subversive associations of entertainers. Jack Gould sharply reminded the business man of his duties in broadcasting:

> He . . . assumes the obligations that go hand in hand with the use of a medium that can influence men's minds. He is a trustee of that medium's well being and must accept his share of the responsibility that its integrity and freedom will be preserved for society as a whole.
>
> . . . .
>
> No advertiser expects a newspaper to run for cover every time a reader sends a dissenting letter to the editor. In TV the advertiser's attitude should be the same.[58]

And Saul Carson scolded audiences for not coming to the aid of the theater world during harrassment of this sort: "They are not speaking up; they are apparently willing to let Channels and its ex-G-men owners tell America whom we should hear and see on the air."[59]

Another example of the care taken by sponsored programs not to offend viewers occurred when George S. Kaufman was dropped from "This Is Show Business" for remarking during the Christmas season, "Let's make this one program on which no one sings 'Silent Night.'" His quip drew four or five hundred letters of displeasure, and although he was reinstated after a short holiday, John Crosby, for one, was incensed at CBS's servility: "How innocuous does television have to be?" he asked. "Who runs it—the letter writers or the broadcasters?"[60] Commenting later on the same incident, he said, "The idea of yielding to every small bleat of anguish from the listeners is not only morally indefensible, but practically unworkable."[61] Hedged in by many trivial taboos, writers, performers and other production personnel frequently feel utterly frustrated when their only accomplishment has been to please the sponsor and to incite no one in the audience to disagreement. This "cautious approach of the advertiser, ever anxious not to offend," says Mr. Gould, "is wholly incompatible with a vigorous, articulate and progressive medium."[62]

Not only do critics feel that the commercial system is bent almost entirely upon eliciting audience smiles, but some of them also wonder if sponsors are not happiest when the smiles are utterly blank. The second factor influencing a sponsor's choice of bland programs is the theory that a thinking audience can be distracted from concentrating on the commercial. Goodman Ace felt that audiences might have been conditioned to Shakespeare by hearing "MacBeth" for fifteen minutes Monday through Friday instead of "Portia Faces Life," but the "think" factor discouraged any such experimentation:

> I've always had the feeling that sponsors wouldn't want their audiences to start thinking. Some of them might one day begin thinking that there isn't that much difference between one cigarette and another. . . . And if they stayed tuned in to a show like "The Skin of Your Teeth" they might sit around for an hour or two after the performance discussing the meaning of the play and forget all about running down to the drugstore NOW and buying the large economy size.[63]

Mr. Gould explored the same sponsor reasoning in a column written as an interview with Mr. X, an advertising executive. The interviewee described the policy of deliberately down-grading program quality in order to exhibit the commercial to best advantage and then rationalized that this was an inherent limitation of television caused by the marriage between advertising and entertainment. Whereupon Mr. Gould abruptly concluded the interview by stating: "It isn't [a marriage]; it's a damned uncomfortable flirtation."[64] More than this, as one considers the bulk of their writings, it is apparent that critics believe the flirtation has often ended in the prostituion of broadcast programs, with the creation of audience apathy as the illegitimate goal. Gilbert Seldes summarized the whole process very clearly:

> Commercial radio [in order to sell] creates an atmosphere of acceptance; . . . to be successful a program must lower the

> threshold of doubt so that simple assertions without proof will be accepted without criticism. Of the millions who listen simultaneously to broadcasts only a negligible fraction has been trained to assess and criticize what they read or see or hear, and radio itself steadily lowers the level of healthy doubt. All the techniques of the entertainment program are used to dull critical faculties, and . . . [then] the parallel techniques of the commercial message enter.[65]

At the time (1950) of this observation, Mr. Seldes, with pessimistic concern but no direct evidence, felt that the powers of these media extended beyond any immediate program and its audience; that masses of people conditioned not to think could actually become a threat to a democratic institution such as the political elections. Notwithstanding the possible extravagance of this particular social claim, the effect of the apathetic motive on the broadcast schedule is only too accurately described by Mr. Seldes:

> If the audience need not be left in a state of mental and emotional torpor, a wider variety of entertainments, appealing to sharper mental faculties and the deep emotions, could also be offered.[66]

The critics feel, then, that commercial broadcasting is all too often mired in monotony and starved for the vitamins of thought and controversy, simply from its fear of alienating consumer-audiences.

Further, they see in the rating systems, by which program popularity is gauged, additional restraints contributing to sponsored broadcasting's rigidity. The critics do not argue with the business man's logical desire to reach as many people as possible with his sales messages. They simply feel that the broadcasting industry's frenetic preoccupation with indexes of audience size has harmed programs, entertainers, and most important, the public, and even sponsors themselves.

Primary damage occurs when the statistical nose counting of the listening or viewing audience becomes the chief criterion of program quality. Judgment is delivered by digit rather than by any sober concern with factors such as writing and production, which are basic to quality in other areas of entertainment. Goodman Ace vigorously condemns the entire system for this reason:

> The rating system alone has brought radio to the low state which it now enjoys and is rapidly bringing television to a state equally as low. Programs are judged almost solely by their ratings. Because of the ratings, a new, fresh, well-written, well produced program has little or no chance if it doesn't garner a high Neilsen.[67]

Coupled with a sponsor's almost total concern for the rating is his usual eagerness for a new program to deliver a top audience, immediately. Mr. Ace feels that in the relatively relaxed days of early radio, shows were at least given an opportunity to attract attention slowly. He mentions a famous comedy program as an example:

> One of the best comedy programs of radio, "Fibber McGee and Molly," spent several years being developed on a Chicago station before it hit the networks, because the sponsor and the advertising agency had faith in it and rating didn't matter. But sponsors these days and advertising agencies and networks are not that patient.[68]

Critics do not mistrust ratings only because intrinsic qualities are completely overlooked or hastily dismissed by audiences afraid of the new. They feel strongly that too many outside factors, totally irrelevant to a program, nevertheless influence its ratings. Jack Gould reminded his readers that the rating is a composite of factors such as the time a program is on, the network carrying the program, and the preceding and succeeding shows on the same network. "Yet none of these," he wrote, "are factors over which the art's creative forces, such as the writers, actors, producers and directors, have any control, even though they are forced to live by them."[69]

Particularly hazardous as an outside determinant of ratings is the competition between networks and stations for the largest audience at any hour of the broadcast day. Obviously groups will be split among stations. Programs of equally good quality will be seen or heard by only portions of the audience they could attract, and if the audience size falls too low a sponsor may order his program taken off the air. This amounts to death by deliberate fractionization of the audience rather than by some failing within a program. This power of ratings to seal the fate of an excellent show tends to deny the commonly accepted belief that competition is the only guarantee of fine programing.

The same power tends to create the previously deplored schedule monotony. In the race for ratings, it is easy to see why a highly successful program type breeds more of the same type often at an identical hour. But even when a competing program is in an entirely different category, a sponsor may fear experimenting with his show because he might momentarily lose a slight rating superiority. Jack Gould summarizes his view of the rating stronghold in the following excerpt:

> How creative progress is to be made or artistic integrity and variety preserved under such pressure is difficult to forsee.
>
> In short, a program is not judged for itself but rather is viewed against the whole kaleidoscopic pattern of network fare. Instead of the program making the ratings, the ratings are determining the nature of programs. . . . It is as though a Rembrandt, a Beethoven Symphony, a burlesque comic, a Tin Pan Alley ballad, a Keats sonnet, and a pulp magazine serial were to be weighed on the same scale.[70]

To be sure, the critics have occasionally utilized ratings to help focus attention on the welcome given to an outstanding cultural program. For example, Jack Gould reported the very slight audience drop off reflected in the Trendex figures on NBC's ninety-minute presentation of the Sadler's Wells Ballet in 1955. He realized the industry would be impressed by thirty million fairly constant viewers and went on to drive the point home: "The so-called 'minority' audience with a specialized taste is expanding to the proportions of a 'majority' audience that meets the qualitative business criteria of the advertising world."[71] Critics have also quoted ratings in order to stimulate small stations into activity. At one time, for example, Saul Carson felt that an independent station could successfully broadcast a British Broadcasting Corporation theater series even though it was aired opposite a network comedy show with a high rating of twenty-four. After all, he reasoned, that meant seventy-six percent of the audience was not listening to the comedy and many of them might very well be interested in a cultural program.[72] While recognizing the minor usefulness of ratings, however, the professional critics will probably continue to speak out as forcefully as they can against abuses like these briefly catalogued by Goodman Ace:

> Programs are canceled, actors are purged, a whole network is submerged--all depending on that little figure with the decimal point, which appears every couple of weeks in that little pamphlet in the advertising man's inside-Brooks Brothers coat pocket.[73]

A final operational practice of commercial broadcasting which has sometimes been frustrating to critics is the observance of rigid time patterns. As broadcasters so frequently state, "Time is money." When it has been set at different price levels depending on audience availability and sold down to the last second, a kind of monetary mummification sets in which works hardships on programs critics are apt to enjoy most. Consider what the division of all broadcasting into unalterable, even time segments does to programs that cannot by their nature meet such a standard. Scenes from plays have to be deleted, symphonic scores cut, news items trimmed, speeches left hanging because the next second has been sold to another customer. After watching a badly chopped version of "Ah

Wilderness," in 1951, Philip Hamburger groaned:

> I am still naive enough to think that some day someone in the television "industry" will have the courage to revive a play in its entirety, even if it should run one hundred and twenty-three minutes. . . . Of course there is very little hope of this taking place until the birds who currently have their claws sunk deep in broadcasting and who claim God's own air to buy and sell as they please, and at prices they have arbitrarily set, have abandoned some of their greed.[74]

As annoying as cutting can be, the critics more frequently complain about excellent sustaining programs being placed in unsold and usually inconvenient time periods. Culture seems to be reserved for very late or very early hours and Sunday afternoons. It was, however, a Saturday afternoon presentation of Dr. Frank Baxter's Shakespeare series which elicited this typical comment from Jack Gould:

> There is choice time for sponsored junk but not for a sustaining jewel. To argue the utter shortsightedness of this philosophy is a futile pastime. It is the nature of commercial TV and, like it or not, there are things which it cannot do. This is the best argument for an educational network.[75]

These brief samples of critical discontent illustrate only two of the problems created by the time policies of commercial broadcasting. In actual practice, the decision to sponsor a program takes into account many other time factors already alluded to in the discussion of ratings. Because broadcasting has been established as a continuous service from the moment the transmitter switch is thrown in the morning until the station leaves the air at night, patterns of audience flow as people tune in and out and switch from station to station (a matter quite unique in the entertainment arts) determine the time periods specific sponsors will buy. Consequently, solid blocks of mystery or quiz programs, or prestige dramas scheduled simultaneously on opposing networks become sources of constant annoyance for the critics, further examples of which would be uselessly repetitive.

Suffice it to say that the dominant sales motive, irrespective of the commercial message itself, has in the critics' opinion forced broadcasting into a mold of timidity about programs which are new or serious or both and into too rigid a respect for audience ratings and established time patterns. The critics express their dissatisfaction with this economically imposed program and schedule conformity more in the hope of cracking the mold and inducing non-conformity than in the desire to eliminate the sponsored system completely. As shall be shown in the next section, the critics are aware of advantages in sponsorship, even as they deplore its disadvantages. They would, in all probability, agree with Mr. Seldes, who feels that any critic (professional or amateur) provided he wants to retain the competitive system, can ask only "that the excesses of cut-throat competition be mitigated in favor of the public right"[76]

The Strengths and Potentials of Advertising

No critic is eternally ungrateful for the benefits which income from advertising has permitted American broadcasting to confer upon its audiences. He will admit that sponsorship has provided countless hours of superb entertainment, the profits from which have subsidized additional hours of serious cultural and informational programs. In his attempt to come to pleasant terms with the media's economic base, he has set forth what he likes about commercial messages and directions he wishes they would take. Further, he views the improvement of the alliance between advertising and broadcasting as extremely important and is only too willing to offer reasonable suggestions for its accomplishment. The critics' opinions in these matters offset, to some extent, their obvious bias against commercialism.

Next to a brief institutional announcement, which would represent almost no touch at all, professional critics prefer the light touch in broadcast advertising. It was in 1944 during radio's hey-dey, that Harriet Van Horne voiced what is still the common yearning of her colleagues with respect to commercials:

> Since commercials are a necessary evil if radio is to continue at all, we see no reason why they cannot be trimmed, sponged (or, in some cases, scrubbed), dusted lightly with humor and served up with a crisp sprig of common sense as an integral part of the program's continuity.[77]

Generally speaking, commercials which seem like entertainment and which utilize either the technique of the spoof or the technique of animation elicit more commendation from the critics than any other form. Although a sponsor might complain that submerging a commercial in satire neutralizes its effect, the critics maintain it may actually enhance audience respect for the sponsor and his product. To engender relaxed laughter in an audience is to set the product within an aura of acceptance. As early as 1930, Leslie Allen appreciated announcer Norman Brokenshire's treatment of his sponsor's credit as a shadow which pursued him, demanding recognition. "This method," said Mr. Allen, "has the grace of novelty and at least a bit of wit."[78] Again in 1933, Darwin Teilhet chuckled at Heywood Broun's comic obeisance to the commercial on his "Kaffee Klatsch" program:

> His ironically unctuous respect for the sponsor--his lack of knowledge of the product is a delight. The program receives its mellow glow entirely from the bumbling general factotum who is so little impressed by what he or anyone else has to offer.[79]

This burlesque of business had periods of recurrent popularity at the hands of commedians like Stoopnagel and Bud, Arthur Godfrey and Henry Morgan (see p. 244). When Garry Moore produced a genuine soap opera about

S.O.S. scouring pads in 1955, John Crosby nodded approvingly: "You are never quite sure when the entertainment leaves off and the selling comes on, which is the mark of a good commercial."[80]

Despite the favorable critical attention received by the spoof, it continues to be a little used form. Most sponsors are simply too serious about their products to allow them to be kidded on the air. But there is always hope that broadcasting will develop an objective maturity about its operations which will permit such commercial light-heartedness to flourish.

The arrival of television stimulated the adaptation of animation to commercials, and critics had to agree that here, indeed, was almost a new art form in itself. Robert Lewis Shayon wistfully admired the new sales technique:

> The plug is where the creative imagination, the artistry, and the cunning of the new craft have free play. I propose that a new art be added to the seven ancient ones--the art of the TV commercial. For my money, it's almost the best art the new medium has thus far demonstrated.[81]

Gilbert Seldes pointed to a commercial whose marching cigarettes were superior examples of animation:

> The vast vaudeville shows crammed into ninety seconds by Lucky Strike are far more slickly produced (and perhaps more expensive) than the often excellent [Robert] Montgomery production of plays which surround them.[82]

Even Marya Mannes, who candidly announced she could not honestly like any commercial, relented enough to admit that she could watch "without acute boredom or revulsion--the animations accompanied by jingles--brisk, cheerful, silly, ingenious, quickly over."[83] She was interested enough in the technique to devote an entire article to advertisements from the studios of United Productions of America. In her opinion, the animators in their early planning stages are "purely creative, purely imaginative

. . . [able] to translate the styles of Steig, or Thurber, or Osborn" into commercial cartoons.[84]

If sparkling satires could become as acceptable to sponsors as artistic animations, and if these two forms could occasionally be relieved by skillful documentary advertisements showing how a product is made, a major bane of the critics might even become a minor pleasure. It was Miss Mannes who specifically recommended more documentaries on the basis that straight information can be interesting even as it helps dispel the falseness of so many commercials.[85]

Obviously, the broadcasting industry cannot grant very often the kind of surcease from advertising which one station did for Christmas, 1955--twenty-four hours without a commercial! It was, exclaimed John Crosby, "Just about the nicest Christmas present we've ever had."[86] Nor does the industry seem inclined to put its faith in the selling power of the brief institutional announcement. In the absence of these alternatives, professional critics urge advertisers to adopt patterns having the virtues mentioned earlier in this chapter, and in addition, they urge them to recognize that light entertainment and unadorned information are characteristics common to critically popular commercials.

Although critics tend to couple derogatory remarks with praise, they have been so insistent about the abuses of the advertising base of broadcasting that their compliments of the system are often overlooked. For example, John Hutchens defended commercial radio in a 1942 article:

> Without stopping to check on the ratio of sponsored to unsponsored programs, you may be sure that [radio] would be doing far less than it now does were it not for the fact that one program pays for another. It is a system entailing much vulgarity, crude exploitation and downright dishonesty. But to dismiss it out of hand is the counsel of perfection. It is also to underestimate the good sense of the listening public.[87]

And even though Jack Gould frequently lashed out against commercial excesses, he could still write the following encomium:

> Preoccupied as we may be by minor irritations, it is all too easy to forget that the private radio industry has given us a service second to none. Through the process of free competition it provides us daily with the best in music, comedy, drama and discussion, all at no cost.[88]

In addition to not costing audiences anything (at least in terms of dollars and cents) this same system has managed, of course, to earn broadcasters a profit. Here again, critics generally approve. In 1954, Mr. Gould wrote, "Without the profit incentive TV would be a feeble and bureaucratic medium subject to more abuses and dangers than exist now,"[89] while Mr. Seldes stated that he had no objections "to the profits made by the managers of our entertainment industry."[90]

As a matter of fact, however iconoclastic the critics may seem in their more vitriolic outbursts against the tainted art of broadcasting, they would prefer to see private sponsorship continue, only under more positive concepts of public service. As Jack Gould has put it:

> The real, difficult and exciting challenge of running a public medium is to turn a profit and at the same time erect an institution with ever-deepening roots, with ever-growing maturity, and with an ever-expanding sense of leadership and social responsibility.[91]

It is undeniably hard to concentrate on turning a profit without turning away from social responsibilities. So hard in fact, that for Albert Williams, writing in 1947, the neglect of responsibility was precisely the history of radio's first quarter century:

> [It] is merely the history of radio operators, network managers, and independent station owners wondering not how useful to the public they can grow to be, but rather, how commercial they dare be.[92]

Critics feel, in all honesty, that the situation in the last decade of radio and television has changed very little. To be sure, they have complimented alliances such as those between United States Steel and the Theater Guild or between the Texas Company and the Metropolitan Opera for "wide latitude" in cultural programing "with a minimum of sales intrusion."[93] They have also written occasional articles such as the one Jack Gould submitted in praise of the J. Walter Thompson Company advertising agency for its 1955 support of adult theater on the Kraft and Ponds television program:

> [The company] is showing heartening respect for the importance of the play as such. . . . . Within the framework of commercial TV it seems to have found a place for the vital ingredients of creative excitement, which in the long run should prove as sound advertising as it is theater.[94]

However, add to the phrase, "the importance of the play as such," another dictum, "the importance of the public as such," and it will be seen that these are still the goals critics would urge commercial broadcasters to seek. In order for the search to be successful, some critics continue to stress that control over programing and concern for public interest can only derive from more network and station independence from sponsors. Marya Mannes is very abrupt about the matter of broadcasters rather than advertising agencies controlling the destiny of radio and television: "A public medium is a public service not a department store. Nor is it the signal corps of a commercial army of occupation whose passwords are, 'And now--a message from our sponsor.'"[95] Jack Gould, in the following excerpt, entices advertisers rather than scolds them, but his underscoring of the sharp division of responsibility between the talent and the sponsor is similar to that of Miss Mannes:

> The ability of the world of commerce to sponsor culture of vitality is potentially one of the most exciting if least noticed promises of TV. But sponsors of drama must not overlook the basic strength of that accord. It is the sponsor's right to prepare the plug; the dramatist's to prepare the play.[96]

Despite the scorn of the industry and the indifference of a large portion of the public, the critics continue to preach this concept of public service within the framework of advertising. They are by turns indignant or grateful as broadcasters and sponsors show an awareness of their responsibility to their audiences. And even though they cannot point to balance sheets for proof, most of the critics have faith, with Gilbert Seldes, that "if the broadcasters accept their social responsibility, they can continue to pile up huge profits without corrupting the taste and undermining the mental activity of the audience."[97]

In summary, it must be admitted that the critics' compliments concerning advertising are more for initial steps taken toward "the soft sell" and the courageous program than for any permanent mission accomplished. They are as insatiable for the improvement of broadcast entertainment and information as sponsors are for sales. It is their firm conviction that programing is primary and their high hope that advertising will come to recognize its necessary but secondary status.

Notes

[1]Raymond Yates, Popular Radio, IX (October, 1926), 602.

[2]Leslie Allen, Christian Science Monitor, January 17, 1931.

[3]Leslie Allen, ibid., February 1, 1930.

[4]Henry Volkening, "Abuses of Radio Broadcasting," Current History, XXXIII (December, 1930), 397.

[5]Leslie Allen, Christian Science Monitor, September 26, 1931.

[6]Cyrus Fisher [Darwin Teilhet], Forum, XCI (June, 1934), 323-37.

[7]Letter from Mr. Darwin Teilhet, former critic, Forum, May 18, 1956.

[8]Paul F. Peter, "The American Listener in 1940," Annals of the American Academy of Political and Social Science, CCXIII (January, 1941), 5.

[9]Ring Lardner, New Yorker, August 26, 1933, p. 35.

[10]Cyrus Fisher [Darwin Teilhet], Forum, XCI (February, 1934), 126.

[11]Ibid., p. 127.

[12]Raymond Knight, Woman's Day, IV (May, 1941), 12.

[13]Goodman Ace, The Book of Little Knowledge (New York: Simon and Schuster, 1955), p. 74.

[14]Jack Gould, New York Times, October 8, 1950.

[15]Jack Gould, ibid., October 18, 1953.

[16]Marya Mannes, Reporter, March 24, 1955, p. 37.

[17]Gould, loc. cit.

[18]John Crosby, Out of the Blue (New York: Simon and Schuster, 1952), p. 65.

[19]Gilbert Seldes, The Great Audience (New York: Viking Press, 1950), pp. 196, 199.

[20]Crosby, op. cit., pp. 141, 143-45.

[21]Seldes, op. cit., p. 195.

[22]Saul Carson, New Republic, January 3, 1949, p. 29.

[23]Seldes, op. cit., pp. 200-201.

[24]Jack Cluett, Woman's Day, XV (April, 1952), 151.

[25]John Crosby, Herald Tribune (New York), March 4, 1953.

[26]Crosby, Out of the Blue, pp. 140-41.

[27]*Ibid.*, p. 143.

[28]Ace, *op. cit.*, p. 63.

[29]Jack Gould, New York Times, September 17, 1944.

[30]Jack Gould, *ibid.*, October 20, 1946.

[31]Jack Gould, *ibid.*, January 8, 1954.

[32]John Crosby, Herald Tribune (New York), September 30, 1953.

[33]Albert Williams, Listening (Denver: University of Denver Press, 1948), p. 71.

[34]Leslie Allen, Christian Science Monitor, August 23, 1930.

[35]Gilbert Seldes, Saturday Review, January 30, 1954, p. 28.

[36]*Ibid.*

[37]Ring Lardner, New Yorker, August 26, 1933, p. 35.

[38]Ace, *op. cit.*, p. 79.

[39]Jack Cluett, Woman's Day, XV (November, 1951), 48.

[40]Marya Mannes, Reporter, March 2, 1954, p. 42.

[41]Jack Gould, New York Times, January 29, 1954.

[42]Robert Lewis Shayon, Saturday Review, January 29, 1955, pp. 27-28.

[43]Marya Mannes, Reporter, May 2, 1957, p. 20.

[44]John Wallace, Radio Broadcast, XII (January, 1928), 219.

[45]John Crosby, quoted in Lyman Bryson, Time for Reason About Radio (New York: George W. Stewart, Inc., 1948), pp. 115, 118.

[46]Jack Gould, New York Times, October 19, 1952.

[47]Seldes, The Great Audience, p. 132.

[48]Williams, *op. cit.*, p. 48.

[49]Seldes, The Great Audience, pp. 223-27.

[50]*Ibid.*, p. 225.

[51]*Ibid.*, p. 228.

[52]Jack Gould, *New York Times*, September 7, 1947.

[53]Seldes, *The Great Audience*, p. 111.

[54]Marya Mannes, *Reporter*, May 2, 1957, p. 21.

[55]*Ibid.*, p. 19.

[56]Gilbert Seldes, *The Public Arts* (New York: Simon and Schuster, 1956), p. 177.

[57]Ace, *op. cit.*, p. 7.

[58]Jack Gould, *New York Times*, November 18, 1951.

[59]Saul Carson, *New Republic*, September 25, 1950, p. 31.

[60]John Crosby, *Herald Tribune* (New York), January 4, 1953.

[61]John Crosby, *ibid.*, January 9, 1953.

[62]Jack Gould, "Television: Boon or Bane?" *Public Opinion Quarterly*, X (Fall, 1946), 318.

[63]Goodman Ace, *Saturday Review*, October 1, 1955, p. 35.

[64]Jack Gould, *New York Times*, March 6, 1955.

[65]Seldes, *The Great Audience*, pp. 137-38.

[66]Seldes, *The Public Arts*, p. 178.

[67]Ace, *The Book of Little Knowledge*, p. 50.

[68]*Ibid.*

[69]Jack Gould, *New York Times*, February 17, 1946.

[70]*Ibid.*

[71]Jack Gould, *New York Times*, December 18, 1955.

[72]Saul Carson, *New Republic*, October 6, 1947, pp. 35-36.

[73]Ace, *The Book of Little Knowledge*, p. 41.

[74]Philip Hamburger, *New Yorker*, October 13, 1951, p. 123.

[75]Jack Gould, *New York Times*, June 20, 1954.

[76]Seldes, The Public Arts, p. 199.

[77]Harriet Van Horne, "It Is Later Than Radio Thinks," Saturday Review of Literature, February 19, 1944, p. 29.

[78]Leslie Allen, Christian Science Monitor, March 29, 1930.

[79]Cyrus Fisher [Darwin Teilhet], Forum, LXXXIX (January, 1933), 64.

[80]John Crosby, Wisconsin State Journal (Madison), December 11, 1955.

[81]Robert Lewis Shayon, Saturday Review, November 18, 1950, p. 34.

[82]Gilbert Seldes, Saturday Review, September 20, 1952, p. 35.

[83]Marya Mannes, Reporter, March 2, 1954, p. 40.

[84]Marya Mannes, ibid., October 7, 1954, pp. 42-43.

[85]Marya Mannes, ibid., March 2, 1954, p. 42.

[86]John Crosby, Wisconsin State Journal (Madison), December 20, 1955.

[87]John K. Hutchens, New York Times, January 25, 1942.

[88]Jack Gould, New York Times, August 27, 1944.

[89]Jack Gould, ibid., December 5, 1954.

[90]Seldes, The Great Audience, p. 5.

[91]Gould, loc. cit.

[92]Williams, op. cit., p. 74.

[93]Marya Mannes, Reporter, March 17, 1953, p. 41.

[94]Jack Gould, New York Times, March 7, 1955.

[95]Mannes, loc. cit.

[96]Jack Gould, New York Times, December 11, 1955.

[97]Gilbert Seldes, "Radio, TV, and the Common Man," Saturday Review, August 29, 1953, p. 40.

CHAPTER X

CRITICS' OPINIONS ABOUT OPERATIONAL STRUCTURES FOR BROADCASTING

Obviously, the financial base of broadcasting in the United States has never been unconditionally accepted by professional critics. Eternally anticipating cultural rather than monetary ends for these media, the critics have kept a wary eye on our system of privately owned networks and stations supported by advertising revenues. They realize that in an imperfect world art and entertainment, information and education must make economic compromises. But they also realize that the machinery for compromise can vary in its ability to nurture cultural excellence and to serve the diverse needs of a complex audience.

From the earliest days of radio when the dominant question was, "Who foots the bill?" to the present when the persistant question is, "How much should the person who picks up the tab control the program?" critics have examined, condemned, and promoted differing systems and combinations of systems for the prosecution of audience broadcasting. Their musings about operational structures are sometimes at variance, although commonly inspired by concern for quality programing rather than by any slavish regard for either conservative or radical economic and political systems of control.

Lacking any other compelling pattern of organization, this chapter shall discuss the critics' ideas somewhat chronologically, somewhat topically, touching in turn upon such matters as special tax plans, reactions to federal control, toll broadcasting, and complementary systems of operation. An important segment of the chapter will discuss the critics' common belief in the necessity for any operational system to provide for maximum devotion to genuine public interest on the part of broadcasting's leaders and for audience participation in policy making.

Early in 1925, Miss Jennie Mix explained to the readers of her critical column in Radio Broadcast magazine that the only alternative for station owners who insisted they had to engage in direct advertising was to leave the air. "No one asked these broadcasters to erect and operate their stations . . . good broadcasters can be found."[1] But, of course, the solution to quality programing was not that simple. Artists were no longer intrigued enough by the new gadget to offer their talents for a pittance. A steady source of revenue was imperative as the editors of Miss Mix's magazine themselves had realized several months before when they sponsored a contest for the best financing suggestion. The winning proposal was advocated by Zey Bouck, radio critic for the New York Sun, who had been one of the judges. Purchasers of radio sets and parts would pay a special tax on each tube and crystal with the resultant program fund to be administered by the government.[2]

A similar idea was set forth in desperation by Darwin Teilhet ten years later when he wrote "Clear the Air," his last piece for Forum magazine. After stating that the popular theater has always rested on public support, Mr. Teilhet urged the imposition of a yearly two dollar tax on each receiving set, plus a two to five percent manufacturer's tax on each new set. The revenue derived from these taxes would be distributed by the government to privately owned and operated stations selected by listeners in each area of the country as having the most enjoyable programs. Thus, stations would be rewarded not by any government or self-appointed body of critics but by the listeners themselves. Approximately twenty-five percent of this income would have to be used for the production of specifically cultural programs. Although sponsors would still be welcomed, advertising time would be strictly regulated. Any station receiving too little public appreciation year after year would have its wave length assigned to another broadcaster. It was Mr. Teilhet's conviction that these government collected but privately received operating funds would permit audience control, while simultaneously subsidizing many less popular but culturally superior programs. He carefully pointed out that he had polled two hundred sixty-five radio editors of whom two hundred two approved the general objectives of his plan, if not its specific details.[3]

However sincere and reasonable the suggestions of one or two professional critics may have been, there was never a concerted drive toward any implementation. Despite prophetic warnings of audience revolutions in the early twenties, broadcasters who had somewhat cautiously received minor assistance from the advertising industry found themselves by the middle thirties utterly and not unhappily dependent on that industry. Nor was advertising alienating listeners to any frightening degree.

Although direct taxation of the public was never again proposed by a professional critic, Albert Williams and Jack Cluett did indicate, after the passage of more than another decade, that advertisers might assume more civic responsibility and actually assess themselves in order to provide an outlet for programs of a public service nature. In 1947, Mr. Williams commended the Rocky Mountain Radio Council of Denver, which, under the aegis and financial backing of local broadcasters, organized a pool of the cultural, informational and educational resources of the community for the use of advertisers, stations, and member organizations of the council. "In many respects," said Mr. Williams, "the idea of the advertisers indirectly footing the bill for an adequate public service comes closest to the ideal of a strong and free commercial radio system."[4] And at the time reserved channels for educational television were being discussed, Mr. Cluett declared his support for the Brockway plan (see p. 384) which would have required donations of time from advertisers for educational programing over commercial channels.[5]

Of more interest than the fact that none of these critical proposals for a modification of our commercial broadcasting system ever came to fruition, is the fact that the professional critics, almost to a man, have never seriously suggested a policy of all-out federal control. To be sure, Leslie Allen, in 1931, toward the end of his tenure with the Christian Science Monitor, reported rather wistfully on the British plan of government operated broadcasting,[6] and Darwin Teilhet (as we have seen) was actively opposed to any further growth of commercialism; but in general, critics have been less than enthusiastic about a government system.

Their chief fear concerns program censorship. In the early fifties, when the Congress was investigating the relationship between crime, delinquency and television programing, Senator William Benton of Connecticut proposed a national advisory board which would make suggestions for the improvement of broadcasting. The fact that the board would not be empowered to act made little difference to Gilbert Seldes. He sensed that its very prestige "would only add to the confusion over Federal influence on program content" and that the measure was "in the direction of Federal pressure."[7] The House of Representatives' companion measure drew even more scorn from Jack Gould who urged broadcasters to fight back at "the spectre of a group of politicians arrogating unto themselves the authority to decide what should or should not be put on the air. . . . For the government to explore the business and legal aspects of radio and TV is one thing; for it to judge moral conduct is censorship pure and simple."[8]

With characteristic verve, John Crosby condemned both industry and government censorship. In one of his earliest Herald Tribune columns, he recognized the praiseworthy motives of the network's private censor but scored the impracticality of the operation:

> There is nothing wrong with this desire to please [all segments of an audience] except that in many cases it is pursued to such lengths that radio programs are robbed of much of their vitality. The intentions are good, but the administration is ridiculous.[9]

Mr. Crosby's comment on Senator Joseph McCarthy's displeasure with the Voice of America stands as an incisive warning to those who would treat the matter of government censorship lightly, whether it be concerned with a service of its own state department or with private broadcasting operations:

> The one basic flaw in the Voice is a sort of occupational timidity which prevents it from speaking with or even formulating a clear, coherent, positive philosophy of democracy. And the reason for that timidity is the constant threat of investigation.[10]

Secondary to the curse of potential censorship in a government operated broadcasting system is the suspicion of some critics that monopoly ownership might result in aesthetic rigidity and creative mediocrity. In this regard, Mr. Crosby, Mr. Gould, and Miss Mannes have observed government owned British broadcasting and have returned with mixed feelings. It was in 1946 that John Crosby praised B.B.C. radio's lofty concept of leadership and compared it to our networks' humiliating anxiety about giving the public only what it wants. But his final judgment was that the "B.B.C.'s performance is not as high as its intentions," and he predicted that if Americans heard a full day of British programs "the outcry would be louder than anything that ever went up over our soap operas."[11] After Jack Gould had viewed B.B.C. television in 1953, he was understandably pleased with its lack of advertisements, its uninterrupted programs, and the fact that its cultural fare was "spread throughout the main fabric of the evening schedule and accordingly . . . seen by maximum audiences." On the other hand, Mr. Gould felt that our multiple network system actually offered more public service and cultural programs and provided more outlets for artistic experimentation. In fact, Mr. Gould even stated that an American in Britain would "yearn for some trivia professionally turned out."[12] Similar conclusions were reached by Marya Mannes, although she predicted in 1955 after the advent of commercial television in Britain that the government network would now have to become "funny and gay and impudent." Of perhaps even greater interest was her feeling that the B.B.C.'s healthy relaxation of discipline would soon be matched by the tightening of cultural discipline in our own studios, resulting finally in fresh, improved standards for both countries.[13]

Even though many of America's professional critics might not be as optimistic as Miss Mannes about the future of our cultural and intellectual attainments in broadcasting, they are not yet ready to endorse any program of federal control. Their position is accurately stated by Robert Lewis Shayon:

> This nation . . . can have a better pattern of broadcasting without sacrificing its traditional method of commercial operation within the framework of public interest.[14]

Periodically, as a matter of fact, an entirely voluntary plan intended to improve the pattern of broadcasting has been suggested. As early as 1933 Darwin Teilhet wondered why "family listening tickets" could not be sold. They would be good for one year, and the income would be used to produce programs of higher quality than general commercial fare, although it too would continue to be broadcast.[15] Apparently Mr. Teilhet's idea would have depended merely upon the appreciative generosity of individual listeners, since it did not involve any private wave lengths.

A refinement of his suggestion was made in 1944 by a broadcaster who petitioned the Federal Communications Commission for a frequency modulation channel which no one but subscribers could receive and over which quality, minority-taste programs would be transmitted. Jack Gould's reaction to the proposal is particularly interesting because it represents a stand which this leading critic completely reversed later when initial plans for toll television were being considered. Mr. Gould's argument in this instance rested on his objection to a subversion of the democratic principle of public broadcasting. If anyone wanted to raise radio's standards, let him be willing to express his faith in quality programing by encouraging its free competition with the offerings of existing stations. "Opening the door to a whole series of exclusive squeals, each representing a different fee to the listener, seems an undemocratic means to a generally desirable end."[16]

Mr. Gould's new position in 1951 may have resulted simply from seven more years of observing American radio and television. He now voiced the common critical complaint that broadcasting often functions at the mercy of sponsor whim, a situation scarcely exemplifying pure democracy at work. At any rate, the New York Times critic was willing to support experimentation with subscription television:

> [It alters] the fundamental concept of programing in broadcasting and at long last puts it into proper and constructive focus.
>
> . . . .
>
> Subscription television puts the emphasis where it is in all other entertainment media: on the person who is looking, on the audience. . . . Where subscription television would appear to offer an exciting new area of conjecture is in the field of minority cultural tastes.[17]

The tactics of commercial broadcasters continued to block government approval of toll experimentation as late as 1955, but critics like Robert Lewis Shayon, John Crosby, and Gilbert Seldes, nevertheless, waited with patience and interest for the new pattern to take shape. If there were any shared misgivings, they were similar to those voiced by Mr. Gould in May, 1955, when he urged proponents of the plan to describe their program service more clearly. "We don't want present fare just to leave free TV and go over to toll TV."[18]

This last objection stems, of course, from one of the most highly regarded concepts in the critics' credo: the belief that any structure within which the broadcasting arts are to operate must permit constant change in the hope of achieving more frequent pinnacles of excellence. To approve toll television only to see last month's feature movie from Hollywood instead of the last decade's, or to watch this week's situation comedy only without commercials, is certainly not the way to inject variety into broadcasting's present offerings. No, if changes are to be made in our present operating structure, many critics believe they might better be made by establishing dual or even triple systems in such a way that they could not simply imitate each other.

This is the belief which motivated the vigorous critical advocacy of reserved channels for education (see pp. 382-86). This is the belief which prompted Saul Carson time and again to point with pride to WNYC, the municipally owned and operated radio outlet of the city of New York: "If there were a dozen others like it across the country, radio and television would be light years above their present intellectual levels."[19] This is the belief which prompted Jack Gould to write:

> The best guarantee of democratic broadcasting is participation in the medium by both commercial and non-commercial interests truly representative of a free-enterprise society. American broadcasting must move ahead on all fronts.[20]

If the public interest is to be more completely met by the addition of locally subsidized (even tax supported) educational channels and by the adoption of subscription broadcasting, then these are new patterns which the critics would generally encourage. Of more immediate importance, on the other hand, is the constant, goading encouragement they reserve for commercial broadcasters in an effort to elicit the best our present system can produce. Rather than condemning sponsored broadcasting to eternal damnation, the critics prefer exhorting it to repent and mend its ways by becoming aware of its responsibilities, by obeying its own codes, by accepting reasonable help from the F.C.C., and by encouraging more listener control.

A major flaw, say the critics, lies not in the structure of our broadcasting system but in the leadership, not in the fact that a manufacturer wants to advertise, but in the fact that the broadcaster hedges on setting responsible conditions (particularly with respect to type and duplication of programs) under which he can advertise. Like electron guns which bombard a piece of steel in order to reveal its inner weakness, the critics produce a steady barrage of caustic comments about the management of these media. At a time when industry officials were complaining about a government investigation into programing, Jack Gould gave them short shrift. He felt the networks had only themselves to blame for the major criticism concerning excessive crime shows, and he wrote with exasperation, "Broadcasters cannot get through their heads a realistic concept of their own freedom and responsibilities."[21]

Perhaps the most important of the industry's responsibilities, at least as far as critics are concerned, is the duty to develop audience desires for new forms of entertainment and for pleasurable experiences which may tax the intellect and the spirit as well as drug them. After quoting Sir William Haley, director general of the British Broadcasting Corporation, who outlined his organization's task as that of drawing "more and more listeners to all that is worthwhile," John Crosby reproved American broadcasters for eternally replying to the charge of low standards by quoting the latest audience statistics as evidence that the public was getting what it wanted. "It is the responsibility of the artisan to elevate public tastes, not vice versa. The public has created a demand for entertainment, education and news on the radio but the quality of that product should be determined by the broadcasters."[22] Or to paraphrase Gilbert Seldes, broadcasters must be made aware of the central question: Are we supplying the best service we can? And they must not be permitted to substitute a tangential question: Is this service what the public wants?[23]

Another responsibility which broadcasters must assume is that of not airing programs deemed downright harmful rather than merely uninspiring and mediocre. Such exercise of judgment is necessary not only with respect to violence viewed by youngsters (see pp. 217-18), but even with respect to some adult fare. Jack Gould, for example, questioned the wisdom of televising certain medical programs which, devoid of a question-answer period, could stimulate fear and actually lead some viewers to draw entirely erroneous conclusions. He is unconvinced that the satisfactory answer to the entire problem of questionable shows is simply to have the viewer turn off his set. "TV viewers are seldom apprised of what is going to happen until it has happened. . . . To shift the responsibility to the amorphous public mass is to evade the practical issue."[24]

To be sure, most stations subscribe to voluntary broadcasting codes, representing a step in the direction of commendable self-regulation. But any critic is quick to remind broadcasters that these codes, proffering general advice on advertising quantity and content as well as program content, are frequently disregarded. They feel that in a system of comparatively free broadcasting such as ours no code making high aesthetic and ethical demands will be observed with alacrity unless broadcasting personnel are motivated by a strong spirit of public service.

The term "comparatively free" was used advisedly, since the Federal Communications Commission does operate to see that the transmitting frequencies, the property of all the people, are legally and technically supervised. However, the Commission has traditionally refrained from any strong pronouncements on programing which could be construed as government censorship. In Albert Williams' words, the F.C.C. "indicated that its proprietorship over broadcasting is that of an uneasy well-wisher rather than that of a tribunal aware of the crime and capable of the punishment."[25] Despite the industry's need for support and guidance in the exercising of leadership, it is understandably content with the Commission's historical reluctance to supervise programing. Conversely, though no professional critic would relish the prospect of the Commission in the role of all powerful tribunal, he would and has urged this guardian of the public air waves to exert itself more frequently and more forcefully in matters of programing.

Although Mr. Gould was speaking only for himself, he expressed a logical, moderate view in this regard which would very likely be acceptable to many of the other critics. The F.C.C. had announced a spring meeting to consider the role of television in serving the needs and interests of the public, and Mr. Gould took the occasion to remind his readers of the single, unfavorable Commission report on radio programing (1946 Blue Book) and of the value a similar report might have for the new medium:

> [At that time, the F.C.C.] took the constructive and positive view that the problem was not so much what was on as what was not. Significantly, that is the crux of the problem facing television.
>
> . . . .
>
> A Blue Book policy in TV, with each station aware that it would be asked for a public explanation if there were complaints that it had not lived up to its promises, would provide the incentive, not only for maintenance of standards but their improvement. If one network were prepared to go on record as promising a given diversity of programing, another of like stature could hardly drag its feet for long.
>
> But such constructive competition will never be possible either culturally or economically if there is no agency to see that everybody follows the rules of the game. That is where the F.C.C. properly must exercise its authority to the end that the broadcasters may continue to control their own affairs and not allow selfishness under the guise of competition to invite greater government control.[26]

In the last analysis, of course, selfishness, overt as well as covert, weakens the will of the managers of commercial broadcasting. And it is against this vice that critics have inveighed over the years. Sometimes their technique has been to use sarcasm as the following lines from Mr. Teilhet's pen indicate. He had just been pitying the unenlightened Canadians who had decided not to adopt the commercial system of the

United States:

> The Canadians were unable to understand the simple truth repeatedly presented to the American public by conscientious public relations counsels, that privately owned stations really operate for the public good.[27]

At other times, the critics have been too disgusted to utilize the humor implicit in sarcasm. Then, like Marya Mannes in the following passage, they have turned to a more powerful assault upon the conscience of the industry:

> It is of cosmic indifference to the producers of TV whether children's homework suffers, or whether the baby in the pen hasn't a quiet moment. It is of equal indifference to them that they may be upsetting an order of living for adults as well as children to the real detriment of human welfare. . . . Never will they ask themselves whether it is right that people should be entertained four-fifths of the day and night and informed one-fifth or whether the complete reverse might be the only justifiable path to follow.
>
> They never will ask themselves so long as programs depend on selling goods.[28]

Self probing is undeniably painful, and it may be too much to expect the leadership of the industry to delve deeply. Perhaps we should be grateful for some respectable codes of operation, some occasional bursts of genuine public concern, and periodic magnificent programs. But the question still remains: Where can our present system turn for the correctives most critics believe it needs? The stimulus of new, competing systems (educational and toll) may be a partial answer. The stern interest of the F.C.C. may be another. Still, a third may lie in the establishment of an academy of broadcasting which would serve to inspire and guide present station managers. Saul Carson elaborated on a plan by Norman Corwin and spoke out vigorously for what he called a "yardstick station" against which private broadcasting could be measured. Robert Lewis Shayon did the same. (see pp. 386-87.) Another critic, Albert Williams, proposed "a meeting place for thinking men and women whose interest in radio is speculative rather than practical." This institute would provide a place where the businessman, the philosopher, the scientist, and the artist, including industry personnel, could exchange ideas with "the object of perpetuating that which is good and thinning out obsolete attitudes."[29]

Apparently the critics feel that broadcasting is an endeavor which should challenge the courage and creativity of those to whom it is a livelihood, while at the same time arousing cooperative suggestions from many other sources. Gilbert Seldes may have accurately analyzed the situation in commercial broadcasting when he said, "I think the managers have been caught in a complicated piece of machinery and haven't seen the faintest necessity for getting out of it. As soon as enough people see that the machinery is working against the public interest, the managers will be adroit enough to make changes which even they realize are needed."[30] The people referred to by Mr. Seldes may be the professionals attending Mr. Williams' academy, but the people are also the non-professionals who qualify simply because they are perceptive members of radio and television audiences. Here is a vast, unorganized listener-viewer group who, according to the critics, have an important role to play in our system of broadcasting.

Audience apathy, tinged with the kind of courtesy that makes us reluctant to criticize a gift, is an understandable concomitant of "toll-free" radio and television. To arouse the consumers of programs has been no less a task for the critics than to shame the producers of programs. From a time when Leslie Allen explained to his readers that "the leaven of intelligent [listener] criticism can eventually leaven the whole radiocasting lump,"[31] to a time, sixteen years later, when Jack Gould wrote that television needed what radio never got: "an alert, critical, articulate audience,"[32] the professional critics have been anxious to enlist support. In general, the critics would agree with Saul Carson's rebuke that "we get the kind of broadcasts--and the kind of F.C.C.--that our indifference deserves."[33]

To a public willing to cast off indifference, critics, over the years, have suggested a variety of techniques which will assist audiences in actually shaping broadcasting's operational structure. The first and easiest way to register a protest is to turn off the receiver. This can be effective, but it is a vague device at best and should be followed by specific appraisals sent to the appropriate program officials. Mr. Allen reminded his readers that "the listener can prove his power by writing constructive letters of criticism;"[34] and Saul Carson, for one, offered this bit of evidence garnered at an educational conference:

> A minor network executive said, "Once in a while I can get peak time for a real public service show by telling the boss that it's worth it to keep the 'long hairs' quiet. If these educators and their buddies ever stop sounding off, we're sunk."[35]

Of course, the critics are interested in having their readers realize that compliments as well as barbs will help indicate future programing patterns to producers. Jack Gould described a simple post-card form devised and printed by a concerned family. They kept a stack of these cards on the television set and sent them off to sponsors, networks, and entertainers immediately after a program. Mr. Gould urged others to follow suit, cautioning them to be as quick to praise as to blame, and to be specific in their remarks.[36]

Although the critics recognize advantages in personal, pointed audience mail, many of them have also encouraged the formation of listener-viewer councils which can bring intelligent, organized pressure to bear upon program procedures. An early example of critical sympathy for this kind of activity can be seen in the following comment by Darwin Teilhet with respect to the National Advisory Council on Radio in Education, and the National Committee on Education by Radio:

> [They are] the only non-partisan forces we have on the listeners' side of the fence. . . . They should do much to co-ordinate, direct, and express the inchoate but growing displeasure of the radio audience with the present sacrosanct "American System."[37]

Not all listener groups, of course, functioned as councils of war and revolution. In the late forties, Albert Williams described organizations in some twenty American cities (see pp. 34-35) which solicited program evaluations from the community, edited them into constructive critiques and forwarded them to networks and local stations who received them with appreciative interest. Said Mr. Williams, "Such groups provide broadcasters with a set of checks and balances that will guarantee full freedom of the air because of the guarantee to the listener against inroads on his patience and privacy."[38]

With the arrival of television and the repetition (only in a new dimension) of radio's lapses of taste in programing and excesses in advertising, it would seem as if the council idea would have been invigorated. To some extent, perhaps, its energies were focused upon reserving separate channels for education. At any rate, despite occasional columns of support given them by a critic like Saul Carson, who even suggested that the Ford Foundation subsidize two of the more vigorous societies for better radio and television,[39] the movement has declined rather than increased in power. Audience lethargy, it would seem is more than enough to counteract the guiding influence of diffuse arrivals of studio mail, and scattered reports from organized councils. And yet, at least one professional critic's interest in a citizens' department to assist the commercial broadcasters has not yet waned.

In 1952, Gilbert Seldes proposed (as a counter measure to Senator Benton's idea for a government advisory board) an organization of regional citizens' groups working with a small national body to prepare an annual report on the state of television. The unique feature of the plan lay in the fact that the report and a thorough discussion of its implications would be broadcast by the television networks. He felt that public indifference with respect to evaluating broadcasting operations might change, "that people would observe, comment, question, and when necessary, protest, if a channel for these activities were available."[40] Three years later, when Frank Stanton, the president of CBS, announced that his network wanted to solicit public opinion about the role of television in our society, Mr. Seldes saw a way to implement his original idea. He congratulated Mr. Stanton for understanding "that to fulfill his legal obligation to operate 'in the public interest' he must consult the public as to its basic wants--which means as to his basic policies." Now, said Mr. Seldes, the way for the public to communicate with Mr. Stanton is to go on the air to try to answer "the real $64,000,000 question--which is what the broadcasters ought to be doing."[41] Neither Mr. Seldes nor Mr. Crosby (who raised specific objections to the Stanton proposal in his column[42]) is interested in watching a public committee try to dictate on matters of program art to professional artists. But Mr. Seldes still feels that, even though frank, "on the air" consultations with the public may mean the deletion of a few poor programs, it will also mean a restoration of confidence in commercial broadcasting and perhaps even a release for the broadcaster from some of the more irritating restrictions imposed on him by his sponsors.[43]

Whether lay critics who organize themselves for listening and watching will ever be permitted to speak and to be seen on the air is still a matter for conjecture. But this latest in a long line of ideas from professional critics with respect to improved audience controls represents an important advance. Beyond its immediate functions in any one period, a council which actually broadcast its deliberations would, in time, become a teacher, instructing the entire nation in the principles, practices and evaluation of radio and television programing. Such an activity would be an extension of the kind of emphasis many critics, Mr. Gould in particular, feel should be supplied by our schools:

> It is an irony of contemporary education that it will devote infinite care . . . to stimulating interest and better taste in books, but will allow no specific or regular time for the study of a medium which may fill more of a child's time than reading. . . . Now is the time for the schools to start teaching tomorrow's adult audiences what is worthwhile in television.[44]

In summary, the professional critics, who, perhaps more than the rest of us, have agonized over the weaknesses of the American system of broadcasting, are apt also to see more of its strengths. An operation which divides responsibility between the broadcasting industry, the government, and the audience, can, through its very flexibility and its broad access to a variety of ideas, produce a remarkable range of programs. The persistent challenge of the critics has been that if each segment of the operation would take its responsibilities seriously (and many of these, the critics have carefully delineated), the system would further produce a remarkable range of <u>superior</u> programs. It requires a steady exercise of the will to assume responsibility, and the managers, the F.C.C., and the audiences must have the will to see that the public interest is truly served.

Albert Williams was thinking only of radio at the time he wrote the following passage, but it stands as a common critical summons to the television industry as well:

> Radio can rearrange its position, even at this late date, if the broadcasters care to make the effort.
>
> . . . .
>
> They can decide in the light of their broader experience, demagnetized of allegiance to a particular brand of soap, what the public interest and necessity really is, and they can become experts in radio instead of advertising specialists, relegating the sale of products to the same importance that it has in journalism--the back of the book.
>
> And then, when the people of the United States rather than the board of directors of a patent medicine company are recognized as the true audience, radio can, perhaps, take it's rightful place as a private enterprise, with whom the regulatory commissions have protective and constructive, rather than merely punitive, relationships.[45]

As for the regulatory body and its function in our broadcasting scheme, it would probably be most severely criticized by the professional critics for sins of omission (a pleasant irony in view of its official title). Certainly, early critics like Leslie Allen and Darwin Teilhet would have expected more from the Federal Communications Commission in matters of program guidance and advertising control. Most of the later critics approved the strong tone of the Blue Book and have taken the Commission to task for its dilatory technical decisions about color telecasting, the use of ultra-high frequency channels, and toll television. Although current critics are more cautious about suggesting any direct intervention by the F.C.C. into programing problems, they do not hesitate to periodically remind the industry of its "regulated" status. They may feel that the indirect threat is powerful enough.

On the other hand, the critics would feel that indirection on the part of audiences has too long been the case. They continually urge upon the public a clearer understanding of its function as a partner in our broadcasting enterprise. Saul Carson concluded a column entitled "Broadcasters Have Big Ears" with a four-point program of action. His remarks summarize the thinking of most critics with respect to audience participation in broadcasting control:

What Can the Listener Do?

> 1. Accept certain conditions as they are, because they will not change unless the United States changes not only its economic system, but also its cultural makeup. . . . Advertising mores are pretty well fixed, and as a matter of fact, some good programing comes from advertising agencies. . . . As for government control, well, if most Americans liked . . . B.B.C. [programing], American advertisers probably would produce that kind of programs.
>
> 2. Watch the networks . . . Criticize them often and sharply. Write direct to the network heads as well as to the affiliate . . . Pat them on the back whenever you hear a good show. . . . Ask the network to inform you in advance when it is going to broadcast sustainers.
>
> 3. Urge local stations to carry the network sustainers and public service programs. If the local affiliate won't carry a show, ask its competitor.
>
> 4. Follow regularly one or more of the better radio critics and occasionally take a look at one of the trade papers.[46]

Despite occasional outbursts of disillusionment, the critics generally have advocated accommodation to the commercial structure for broadcasting. But this is to be an active accommodation consonant with that requirement in our communications law which licenses broadcasters to operate in the "public interest, convenience and necessity." As the desires and needs of the public change, commercial broadcasters and the Federal Communications Commission may have to accommodate themselves to additional broadcasters who plan other program patterns and other systems of finance. And the public whose "interest" is to be served must accommodate itself to an active role in continually defining what that interest is. Mediating between these groups are the critics whose interpretations, and warnings and encouragements are intended to help any structures for broadcasting function at their best.

Notes

[1]Jennie Mix, Radio Broadcast, VI (February, 1925), 691.

[2]Zey Bouck, "Can We Solve the Broadcast Riddle?" Radio Broadcast, VI (April, 1924), 1040-44.

[3]Cyrus Fisher [Darwin Teilhet], "Clear the Air," Forum, XCI (June, 1934), 323-37.

[4]Albert Williams, Listening (Denver: University of Denver Press, 1948), p. 132.

[5]Jack Cluett, Woman's Day, XV (December, 1951), 140.

[6]Leslie Allen, Christian Science Monitor, June 6, 1931.

[7]Gilbert Seldes, Saturday Review, March 15, 1952, p. 31.

[8]Jack Gould, New York Times, May 18, 1952.

[9]John Crosby, Out of the Blue (New York: Simon and Schuster, 1952), p. 272.

[10]John Crosby, Herald Tribune (New York), March 13, 1953.

[11]Crosby, Out of the Blue, p. 271.

[12]Jack Gould, New York Times, July 12, 1953.

[13]Marya Mannes, Reporter, October 6, 1955, pp. 43-44.

[14]Robert Lewis Shayon, Television and Our Children (New York: Longmans, Green and Co., 1951), p. 82.

[15]Cyrus Fisher [Darwin Teilhet], Forum, LXXXIX (May, 1933), 318.

[16]Jack Gould, New York Times, November 12, 1944.

[17]Jack Gould, ibid., June 10, 1951.

[18]Jack Gould, ibid., May 8, 1955.

[19]Saul Carson, New Republic, March 5, 1951, p. 22.

[20]Jack Gould, New York Times, August 19, 1951.

[21]Jack Gould, ibid., May 18, 1952.

[22]Crosby, Out of the Blue, pp. 269-70.

[23]Gilbert Seldes, The Public Arts (New York: Simon and Schuster, 1956), p. 265.

[24]Jack Gould, New York Times, December 12, 1954.

[25]Williams, op. cit., p. 69.

[26]Jack Gould, New York Times, February 4, 1951.

[27]Cyrus Fisher [Darwin Teilhet], Forum, LXXXVIII (August, 1932), 125.

[28]Marya Mannes, Reporter, June 30, 1955, p. 43.

[29]Williams, op. cit., pp. 135, 138.

[30]Gilbert Seldes, The Great Audience (New York: Viking Press, 1950), p. 6.

[31]Leslie Allen, Christian Science Monitor, May 31, 1930.

[32]Jack Gould, "Television: Boon or Bane?", Public Opinion Quarterly, X (Fall, 1946), 320.

[33]Saul Carson, New Republic, September 5, 1949, p. 23.

[34]Allen, loc. cit.

[35]Saul Carson, New Republic, May 17, 1948, pp. 33-34.

[36]Jack Gould, New York Times, April 5, 1953.

[37]Cyrus Fisher [Darwin Teilhet], Forum, XC (November, 1933), 318.

[38]Williams, op. cit., p. 127.

[39]Saul Carson, New Republic, September 3, 1951, p. 23.

[40]Gilbert Seldes, Saturday Review, March 15, 1952, p. 31.

[41]Gilbert Seldes, ibid., June 25, 1955, pp. 25-26.

[42]John Crosby, Wisconsin State Journal (Madison), June 4, 1955.

[43]Seldes, The Public Arts, pp. 281-82.

[44]Jack Gould, New York Times, February 26, 1950.

[45]Williams, op. cit., p. 76.

[46]Saul Carson, New Republic, September 15, 1947, pp. 22-24.

CHAPTER XI

RESPONSE TO THE CRITICS AND SUGGESTIONS FOR STRENGTHENING CRITICISM

After examining an activity as young and faltering as the professional criticism of radio and television broadcasts, it is interesting to chart reactions to the behavior of this neophyte in the critical fraternity. Lest the word "chart" imply computations based on a broad sample let it be stated at the outset that there has been no specific survey of the critics' readers. Section one primarily concerns responses (and in a few cases, rebuttal by the critics) which studio spokesmen including executives, production personnel and performers have made. Section two deals with estimates the critics, themselves, have offered about their effect on the industry and on the public. From this mixture of thoughtful opinion and defensive indignation interspersed with statistical evidence and objective fact comes the conclusion that a sizeable portion of broadcasting's vast audience is at least sporadically conscious of critical ferment. The third and concluding section of this chapter considers some ideas the critics have had for strengthening their impact on society.

The Broadcasters' Response

John Crosby once wrote, "Critics should be belted once in awhile. It restores their sense of humor, their sense of proportion, and just possibly, their sense of humility."[1] Starting with a few legal brickbats, pausing for a brief respite of compliments, and resuming with stinging verbal retorts, these next pa es will attempt to describe the restoratives concocted by the industry for the critics. Unfortunately, there is no evidence to indicate whether the critics ever experienced Mr. Crosby's list of beneficial effects. At least they had no doubt that someone read their columns, and that in itself is beneficial.

Performers, in particular, have been known to strike back at the critics in no uncertain terms. Ring Lardner once informed his readers that Jerry Wald, a radio reviewer for the New York Graphic, lost his job because he mentioned Graham McNamee was through as a sporting events announcer. "In future reviews," Ring quavered with mock solemnity, "I [will] stick to a eulogy of important artists and sponsors--a eulogy of everybody who is in a position to blast me out of mine."[2] On a few other occasions artists instituted law suits involving critics. Bob Hope, for example, brought a two million dollar suit (which he subsequently dropped) against Life magazine for printing a quip by John Crosby to the effect that Hope paid writers two thousand dollars a week for scouting Fred Allen's program to add to his supply of jokes.[3] A case of more significance for the entire critical profession has been just recently ajudicated. In November, 1957, Marie Torre, a television columnist for the Herald Tribune (New York), was sentenced to ten days in prison for refusing to divulge the name of a CBS executive who had given her material for a piece about Judy Garland. The singer was suing the broadcasting system, and the court felt Miss Torre's assistance was needed. Pleading that the protection of information sources is essential to a free press, the Herald Tribune carried Miss Torre's case to the U. S. Supreme Court which refused, in December, 1958, to review the verdict against the columnist. Although this decision could conceivably hamper the effectiveness of the professional critic, it is possible that the New York State legislature will pass a law granting members of the fourth estate immunity in such instances.[4] Since the major critics are employed by New York City publications, they would thus be protected in the future.

Even though the loss of a job or the prospect of a law suit are convincing evidence that readers in the industry pay attention to a critic's comments, there are pleasanter ways to be reassured of one's influence. Whereas Miss Torre faced a jail sentence for arousing the ire of an entertainer, a predecessor, Stuart Hawkins, critic on the Herald Tribune three decades earlier, elicited the following praise from announcer Ted Husing:

> I took from him the most public razzing I have ever received. . . . It did me good though, I admit, for while sore at his diatribes, I unconsciously took them to heart and amended my microphone ways.[5]

How much other prominent industry representatives have taken the critics' words to heart is largely a matter for conjecture. But at least the scattered occasions when they have testified to the value of critical commentary are in the record. At a convention of the National Association of Broadcasters in 1946, William Paley, CBS board chairman, heralded the increasing importance of the new profession:

> As for professional by-lined criticism in newspapers and magazines, I believe all broadcasters should welcome it. It is desirable that radio should receive the same sort of intelligent reviewing which books, plays, movies, concerts and so on receive. Formal published criticism of individual radio programs promotes better artistic standards all around. I have noted with genuine satisfaction the recent introduction of departments of radio program criticism in a number of periodicals.[6]

A year later Norman Corwin, after delivery of the professional broadcasters' usual but severe castigation of literary specialists who infrequently dabble in radio criticism, commended the generally sensible and constructive criticism of radio editors and qualified critics in corollary fields. He even urged the industry to pay attention to the reliable critics: "The chronic abuses of broadcasting have been persistently exposed and attacked by these writers, who, as a rule, are far from snobs."[7]

Benefits, which accrued to a performer like Ted Husing, could, in the opinion of director-writer Eric Barnouw, also accrue to the radio writer who familiarized himself with the critics' work. Mr. Barnouw told a conference of educators in 1948:

> The writer in radio has always had a puzzling feeling of isolation from his audience--the balance wheels of the theater (audience reaction, professional critic reaction) were lacking, so that the writer was thrown to the amateur critic, the pressure group critic, the crackpot critic. Radio writers welcome the advent, in the past two years, of the professional radio critic engaging in a public discussion of what in radio is desirable, and what is bad. They are certain to influence radio standards. . . . Informed criticism is important if radio is to achieve a real maturity.[8]

Although radio, unfortunately, advanced to a kind of second childhood with the arrival of television, officials were apparently grateful for the assistance critics gave the new medium. Not infrequently, notes pass from the studios to the critics or their publications. The Reporter magazine, for example, printed the following compliment from Irving Gitlin, CBS Director of Public Affairs;

> Many thanks for Marya Mannes' comments on "Out of Darkness." We have come to look upon her as a really intelligent voice of support for the kind of programing that we do--programing which is so important for the future well-being of television and its public. We are very proud to have met with her approval.[9]

NBC executives, too, have indicated their interest in what the critics have to say. Sidney Eiges, Vice President in Charge of Press, wrote:

> In general, the reviews of the leading critics receive wide circulation within the industry and are carefully read by management and particularly by those in charge of programing. On this basis I guess it would be safe to say that their views are taken into consideration in appropriate situations, but I am somewhat at a loss in supplying you with specific information.
>
> . . . .
>
> About the most definite thing that can be said about TV critics is that TV as a whole welcomes responsible, intelligent and knowledgeable criticism and gives every consideration to such criticism.[10]

Mr. Eiges' statement would seem to be borne out by Robert Sarnoff, NBC president, who told a group of television editors that the broadcasting company's scrapbooks are carefully kept up to date and that everyone's word was sifted and respected.[11]

Whether anyone's word is subsequently acted upon is more difficult to ascertain. The critics will indicate, shortly, specific events which they think can be attributed to their comments. For the moment suffice it to say that the industry has written and revised, and often closely observed, codes of operation; it has checked and even deplored advertising excesses; and it has produced culturally stringent programs. That these happen to be policies urged time and again by professional critics is surely no mere coincidence, although additional credit, of course, is due many other pressure groups and due the industry itself.

To some extent the critics can discount private feuds with individual performers which may erupt in the courts; this is a common journalistic hazard. To some extent they can also discount the general public statements of gratitude from the industry; this is diplomacy even though it is appreciatively received. What they must weigh carefully before discounting them are the major charges of ineptitude flung at them by the industry. These unfavorable responses from broadcasters may be irrelevant, worthy of thoughtful rebuttal, or even valid guides toward the strengthening of future critical commentary.

The one charge which has recurred throughout thirty years of critical endeavor and will undoubtedly never be resolved to everyone's satisfaction is the opinion on the part of broadcasters that most critics indicate in their writings that they simply do not understand these mass media. Broadcasters feel that critics do not understand the masses and that this lack of understanding betrays their lack of faith in the people, in majority tastes, and ultimately (as some broadcasters would have it) in the democratic way of life.

The charge was strongly phrased by Merlin Aylesworth, president of NBC, in 1935. Although he was not specifically addressing the mere handful of professional critics writing at that time, variations of his theme were directed at the critics in later years:

> There is a small minority to whom radio offers little, . . . the recluse, the intellectually superior person who voluntarily separates himself from the living, breathing, moving America in which he lives. . . . But these folk really do not belong to the great, vibrant mass and soul of America. . . . The American people are to be judges of radio's performance. Uppermost in the minds of those who guide this industry, therefore, there is but one major consideration. . . . It is the public interest.[12]

Mr. Paley of CBS repeated the accusation six years later, shifting the argument from the legal, FCC ground of "public interest" to the broader area of democratic fundamentals:

> [Many critics] hold, even though they may not say so explicitly, that it is the duty of radio to turn one kind of public into another kind of public, one of which they approve more highly. It is the feeling of broadcasters that in the first place this is rather an appalling responsibility . . . and . . . such deliberate planning is pretty hard to square with the principles of a democracy.
>
> The most I think we may do is to experiment with the public acceptance.[13]

With television well on its way in 1951, NBC executive Sylvester

Weaver, Jr. indicated that the critics were still uncomprehending:

> My hatred is aimed . . . at the intellectuals of our country who write for the publications which should influence the various leadership groups of our nation. . . . The critics simply do not understand mass media and what makes mass media work. . . . Television is a communications instrument, and that means far more than just another art form like theater or movies. . . . [The intellectuals] distrust the basic American public. For my money, I will take the public any time, and you can have the intellectuals.[14]

What had become by now a standard reaction from the broadcasting industry was intensified in 1955 when Max Wylie, television writer, producer, and (at least in the critics' eyes) notorious guide for the sobbing charity show, "Strike It Rich," pummeled his tormentors in a book entitled Clear Channels. His thesis is that too many critics are intellectual snobs, who, in their ignorance of these media of the common people, threaten to smash broadcasting's structure by their false but highly articulate expressions of disdain. Singling out Mr. Seldes as the super symbol of snobbery, Mr. Wylie declares:

> For the Harvards to urge on the non-Harvards what they think is good for the non-Harvards, is Gilbert Seldes' special dilemma and Harvard's. Not television's dilemma, and not radio's. . . . We talk to anybody.[15]

"Why is it not possible," he continues later, "for the critics of radio and television to realize just as a basic and practical platform from which to draw judgment and make comparison, that these media are for all the people?"[16] And then in the final section of his book Mr. Wylie concludes:

> Perhaps TV isn't for critics. . . . Audiences don't need a critic to tell them what they are looking at, and they don't need a sociologist to tell them what it is doing to them.[17]
>
> . . . .
>
> The average critic of television is not an average American, and he does not like being around average Americans. And to the degree by which he separates himself from this average -- through sensitivity, superior education, keener native discriminations or whatever it is that makes him think he is more

civilized than the average man--to that degree he will find (in hours of television per week) less that he prefers.[18]

It should be noted that Mr. Wylie at least recognizes degrees of critical isolation, and he ranks Gilbert Seldes, Robert Lewis Shayon, Jack Gould and John Crosby in descending order as they move into closer communion with the "jerks" (his sympathetic title for the rank and file of broadcasting's audience).

To refer to Mr. Crosby's comment at the beginning of this section, if reactions like these are intended to humble the critics, it is possible they have had some effect, for one factor of which the critics are increasingly aware is the need to construct a relevant frame of reference for their criticism, to reach a working agreement with the concept "mass media."

On the other hand, even if the critics are realistic enough about their readership not to claim to be spokesmen for the masses, Jack Gould, for one, would vigorously deny that his profession does not attempt to represent a large segment of the viewers. He feels that the critic is first and foremost a proxy or stand-in for his readers (see p. 117). Certainly this representative function is part and parcel of democratic structure, and one small piece of evidence is offered to indicate that critics may not be as divergent from the general audience as industry executives might wish. In the November 6, 1957 issue of Variety the following item appeared:

> In the showdown argument of whether the critic reflects audience tastes in his evaluations, the first Nielsen's of the new season appear to support the critics.
> . . . .
> In virtually every case where a show was unanimously panned, its showing on the Nielsen list is a poor one.

An additional comment by Mr. Crosby might be relevant here. Speaking with reference to an actress who complained of their stuffiness, he said, "Critics are a lot closer to the public than she is, surrounded as she is by press agents, talent agents and all manner of back-slappers."[19] Not only performers, but the entire industry, because of its close dependence upon sponsors, is given to back-slapping. It, too, needs the kind of objectivity it claims critics lose when they observe the mass media.

Even when Mr. Weaver, in the same article quoted earlier, stated that broadcasters have statistical data to prove their performance, unlike the critics who merely exist on opinion, Robert Lewis Shayon was ready with a reply: "The record of radio and television is a highly debatable one, as Mr. Weaver knows, otherwise, he would not be defending it in such heat."[20] This eternal debate was carried on much more coolly by Marya Mannes who, for example, commented on Mr. Wylie's book, first by complimenting him for his belief in the good things of television (He was particularly eloquent about the medium's educational uses.); and then by underscoring a basic inconsistency: "He likes slobs [or jerks]. And yet . . . he has disarming enthusiasm for television's potentialities for diminishing slobhood in general."[21]

Such remarks are, of course, only samples of continual attacks and counter attacks. If the professional critics constantly ride the horns of a dilemma with respect to standards for evaluating programs for the mass audience, so do the producers and managers in the industry. On the one hand industry personnel want the commendation and happy conscience that comes from high quality programing, and on the other hand they want the cash that comes from the satisfied sponsor with a large audience. Perhaps the only solution is for critic and broadcaster to accept the jabs as they bounce from horn to horn, as prods toward constant improvement in their respective fields. Radio and television might thus benefit all the way around.

As if it were not bad enough for critics to be accused of generally not understanding the mass media, they have also been accused of not fulfilling specific duties successfully. This information comes second-hand from Jack Gould, who summarized and then refuted items he had gleaned from conversations with dozens of industry personnel. Briefly, the plaintiffs charge that: (1) Critics are arrogant even to attempt to comment on television's wide variety of program types. (2) They are sour and frustrated because their reviews are ineffectual, since they appear after a program has had its first and last presentation. (3) They ignore regular programs and are unfair to criticize fresh, original, even off-beat material without seeming to take into account the realistic compromises dictated by executives and sponsors.[22]

After stating his basic belief that television cannot be criticized simply with respect to standards applicable only to that medium but must be evaluated in conjunction with its place in the rest of contemporary life, Mr. Gould proceeded to answer these three charges.

> 1. If criticism is to be comprehensive and meaningful somebody must be responsible for looking at the whole.
>
> 2. A favorable review does have a beneficial influence on those who prepared and presented a program. . . . [Also] it is of no long range service to TV to let utter trash and rubbish go unnoticed. (see pp. 100-101)
>
> 3. Critics could do more in checking established routine fare and pointing up its dominant force. [As for the compromises necessary in new programs], a critic must understand why they are made but he cannot be sanguine about them. . . . Are the creative people thus affected truly asking for compassion and understanding, or are they asking a critic's surrender to the gospel of commercial opportunism? To each and every program must be applied the same acid tests: What is it trying to do and how well is it done?[23]

Even though Mr. Gould cannot speak for all the critics, it is safe to say that complaints of this sort are received by most of them and that their answers would be similar to those of the New York Times critic.

A final but allied reason for unpleasant responses from the industry rests in the fact that broadcasters feel only partial truths about radio and television are emphasized. Obviously, even though critics thoroughly understood mass media operations and even though they corrected the three specific complaints mentioned above, they could still distort the total view by concentrating their fire solely on broadcasting's weak points. To Harold Fellows, president of the National Association of Radio-Television Broadcasters, this is, indeed, the situation, and it calls for immediate adjustment.

> We in broadcasting have been living in a hail of words --flung at us by the Carrie Nations of the kilocycles, by magazine critics, by newspaper critics, by a substantial and thinking segment of the public and by public office holders. Much of this battering . . . takes into account only our weaknesses. . . . Those who weigh our deficiencies against our great contributions of fine showmanship and superb informational service, and emerge with a tempered and reasoned appraisal of our industry, are men and women whose voices should be heard.[24]

In Mr. Seldes' opinion the lack of balance is not as serious as Mr. Fellows implies, and whatever negativism does exist is motivated only by the sincere desire of the critics to aid these media. He had just concluded an informal comparison of Mr. Ace's, Mr. Shayon's and his own columns in the Saturday Review and was impressed by "the general harmony of our principles and the diversity of our enthusiasm within the circumference of these principles." "We each communicate, on the average, one satisfaction to one or two dislikes. . . . I would say we love broadcasting and consequently hate its lower manifestations."[25]

Most critics would agree that the hypersensitive attitude of Mr.

Fellows and his colleagues could perhaps elicit a kind of malicious carping, but they would also say that the truly professional critics try to be aware of balance in their evaluations. Jack Gould stated the point this way:

> Radio's traditional irritability toward any form of complaint, no matter how well reasoned or temperate, long has been a basic industry weakness [which has cost] public esteem, [and has been] responsible for criticism which to some extent has been unfair and unwarranted.[26]

Like critics of any media, the critics of broadcasting have enjoyed as well as endured the responses of the industry. From law suits, to compliments, to harsh (though often helpful) comments, critics have the satisfaction of having aroused attention and perhaps of having stimulated the industry's interest in some of their goals for radio and television. To add to this record of response, it is now necessary to turn to the accounts of critics and their friends.

The Critics Weigh Their Influence

Any person likes to be assured of the value of his contribution to society, and this is probably particularly true of critics whose admittedly parasitic profession requires, in addition, that they occupy the constantly uncomfortable position of judge. Leslie Allen expressed his feelings on the matter with disarming frankness: "Often the columnist feels he's writing in the dark . . . give him a hand now and then; he needs guidance; he'd like to know when what he says is warm or cold."[27]

As we have seen, the critic frequently receives the back of the industry's hand, at least, in print, but he is also the frequent recipient of letters and phone calls some of which disagree with his comments but more of which re-enforce his opinions. The following sampling of statements by the leading critics indicates, to some extent, the influence they have on their readers.

> In memory, my feeling is the reader response and cooperation [in getting background information] from below-executive level at the broadcasting stations was enthusiastic.[28]
> (Darwin Teilhet)

> Organized pressure groups sometimes deluge me with mail. For example, I received three-thousand letters in connection with a column I wrote castigating the Oral Roberts' faith-healing television program.[29] (Jack Gould)

> For three years I received more mail than any other column in the back-of-the-book [literary, theater, film reviews]. This mail generally agreed with my point of view since people who disagree do not bother to write.[30] (Saul Carson)

> Producers of shows frequently call me up to tell me why they disagree with my negative opinion about a particular show. I usually receive 25-30 letters a week, although I recall one time when I opposed the cancellation of an opera festival on a local station and received one thousand letters from sympathetic readers.[31] (Jay Nelson Tuck)

Critics for publications outside the main center of broadcasting would report an equally appreciative response to their columns, if the following comments by Donald Kirkley of the Baltimore Sun, and Paul Cotton of the Register and Tribune (Des Moines) are a valid indication:

> Response to my column has been excellent--intimate, intelligent letters from the readers, flattering responses from actors and agencies. I go to New York once a month and am surprised by the deference paid this one newspaper.[32]

> There has been a heavy and continuing response from the readers of the columns. . . . Des Moines is a long way from New York but apparently everything I write is screened by the advertising agencies or agents and passed around. The industry and the artists seem to be past masters at public relations. They write and thank me for favorable mentions and don't argue about unfavorable mentions. . . . [For example], when [Ed Sullivan] has had a flop, he has written agreeing that it was a flop and telling why things went wrong.[33]

One additional example would indicate that beyond receiving a satisfying amount of mail, a critic will occasionally reach an even higher pinnacle of popularity. Concerning John Crosby's rapid rise to fame, Time magazine wrote: "Crosby's brash columns have brought baskets of fan mail, offers from book publishers, and four salary boosts in three months."[34] In fact, the columnist even ventured into CBS video for several weeks in the winter of 1957 as master of ceremonies for an interesting but uneven series of programs entitled "The Seven Lively Arts."

Tallying popularity at mail call is one thing; detecting an actual critic-motivated change in broadcasting practice is another, less accurate matter. Certainly, one of the most important questions concerns the role critics play in insuring the continuance, the dropping, or the effecting of changes within a series of programs. Ever since Leslie Allen claimed his crusade was responsible for bringing back to the air a 1930 NBC music program called "The Slumber Hour,"[35] critics or their friends have been pointing with cautious pride to successes in this area. There would be little reason to doubt _Variety's_ authoritative voice to the effect that the prestige of the _New York Times_ makes Jack Gould "tremendously influential." "A peep out of him will bring a dozen memos flying from top executives. The 'evil' complained about may not be straightened out immediately--or at all, but the problem is certainly weighed."[36] And Dickson Hartwell contributes an example of John Crosby's influence: "When he described a character in 'My Friend Irma' as too weak to be real, Hubbell Robinson, vice president in charge of CBS programs, telegraphed the producer to have the character strengthened."[37] Mr. Gould, himself, feels that his reviews and those of other critics have kept some programs on the air longer than they would have been otherwise.[38] His opinion is re-enforced even more specifically in this comment by Gilbert Seldes:

> Perhaps the praise of critics has kept shows alive, at least at the very beginning of a series. It is probable that "Omnibus" was kept alive through critical acclaim, just as it is probable that the critics helped kill "Junior Omnibus."

> The vulgarity of the Easter parade on television was denounced by the critics in 1954 and 1955, and this year it was changed. As a matter of specific influence, Jack Gould criticized the scheduling of a horror show between two children's programs and the objectionable show was removed. [see p. 217][39]

Walter Winchell adds another bit of testimony to critical influence by reminding his readers that two television series, "Mr. Peepers" and "I Remember Mama," were saved for a few more seasons by listener protest stirred up by the critics. In addition single dramas like "Patterns" and "A Night to Remember" were repeated as a direct result of critical acclaim.[40]

When all is said and done, critics admit that their influence on programing is a real, though somewhat indeterminate one. Mr. Peter Whitelam, in a Master's study, asked seven professional critics two questions relevant to this point. (Mr. Seldes and Mr. Hamburger were the only critics of those presently under discussion who were interviewed by Mr. Whitelam.) To the question, "How influential is the present day critic in forming public opinion?" two of the seven felt he was "highly influential," and five "moderately influential." When asked, "Can the critic make or break a work of art?" two felt it depended on the critic; two said he could if other critics were to agree with him; and two thought this could happen only in the theater, not in broadcasting.[41]

Such carefully qualified appraisals of their own impact on broadcasting and its audience is an indication of the critics' knowledge that they exert only a small amount of control over programs tightly supervised by advertisers and received by millions of people who are scarcely aware of the leading critics' existence. Even the comfort of readership ratings is a small one to journalists so familiar with the staggering computations of Neilsen or Trendex. However, the following statistics are not discouraging. In radio's heydey one authoritative study indicated that about a third of the subscribers whose newspaper carried a column of radio news, gossip and criticism, read it.[42] And recent studies of newspaper readers, according to Ben Gross, indicate that the television column has three to five times more readers than either the drama or movie columns.[43] John Crosby, through syndication, was even reported at one time as having 15,000,000 avid readers![44] In addition, the writers for periodicals whose subscribers can be numbered only in the thousands, can still fall back on the sociologists' promise that they reach "the solid citizens, the well-educated men and women able to express themselves clearly and likely to influence others."[45]

In the last analysis, the hope that keeps the critic writing may be just this: the fact that one intelligent reader will talk to another and both of them may eventually be persuaded to write to a station. The technique of becoming a vocally perceptive viewer or listener is not too difficult to learn with the stimulating examples of professional critics close at hand and a constant source of new criticism at the flick of a switch. Mr. Gould, in speaking of the average television viewer who has already seen some of the best entertainers in the world, said, "The woods west of the Hudson are filled with astute critics."[46] Here, indeed, is encouragement for professional critics who would like to increase their reading audience, add new critics to the profession, and generally broaden their small but sturdy influence. If Mr. Shayon, with more cynicism than his colleagues, is correct when he says, "My persuasive powers and those of other critics have no real impact on the industry. We are read by people in the trade as entertainers. The public are the masters of the trade, not the critics who write for minority groups of readers,"[47] then this is all the more reason for the critics to strengthen their profession so that the public becomes a careful appraiser instead of remaining a passive master.

Some attention has already been given (at least by inference) to the matter of strengthening the critical profession. As the third chapter of this study indicates, critics realize that if their work is to have any significance, their observations and judgments must be relevant to the area under scrutiny. Consequently, their knowledge of broadcasting's economic structure, of the conditions under which programs are prepared, and of the vast, heterogeneous home audiences is slowly forcing them to adopt new and as yet uncertain definitions of standards and goals for these mass media. Their final aim is not to arouse violent antagonistic responses from the industry and strong partisan support from a handful of readers; it is to involve broadcasters and the public in a cooperative critical endeavor. In addition, however, to wrestling with fundamental concepts about broadcasting and with other normal critical duties, the professional critics have also offered specific suggestions for the strengthening of their work, and it is these suggestions with which the final section will deal.

Strengthening the Critics' Role

The broadcast media, whose avenues of transmission are held in trust for the people and whose programs are able to be received by most of the people, have become true public services. The public, then, is derelict in its duty if it remains unconcerned with the improvement of these services. As a group, professional critics function to inform and stimulate public concern. Their activities, therefore, need to be demanded by more people and made available to more people.

The public has taken broadcasting for granted for so many years that the very concept of careful, regular, conscious appraisal is strange to them. No one has roused their interest in criticism; why then should they demand critics? For this reason current professional critics, as well as other persons interested in better radio and television service, urge the schools to focus some attention on this area.

Robert Lewis Shayon, for example, is convinced that the most important place to strengthen criticism is in the school rooms at the elementary level.

> Children must be taught to criticize. The schools are monasteries as far as true culture is concerned. The kids are going to discuss shows with friends--why not with the teacher? There is a hopeful trend toward aligning the school with outside culture. Schools must orient their procedures in terms of outside environment.[48]

And Marya Mannes speaks in similar vein:

> Schools and colleges must not only use the media, but they must get used to criticizing it. Children in the school should have practice in writing reviews of programs. On the upper levels, professors have been at fault in weakening criticism. They must know what 60,000,000 other people are watching. Scorning television and ignoring it is not enough.[49]

Although isolated courses in mass media criticism are offered in some of our universities[50] and many more units in better listening and viewing are included in public school curricula, students, having lived so intimately with radio and television, still comprise the single most fertile source from which to elicit a lively concern with critical activity. It is of interest to note that within recent years teachers' journals and at least one student magazine have initiated critical departments.[51]

Critics also feel that their profession would be strengthened, if critical comment were available in more newspapers. Although syndicated columns, such as those contributed by Jack Gould and John Crosby, are a partial answer, obviously, only the top network programs can be discussed. Vigorous evaluations by local critics of local and network shows would probably generate more reader interest. The major difficulty, of course, lies in discovering a writer who can be profound as well as popular, wise as well as witty, erudite as well as entertaining. Current critics only compound the difficulty by listing other factors which would enable a new colleague to uphold their profession's wobbly standards. He must have "a serious background in arts and letters."[52] He "must be more than a gossip-columnist and item-lister without knowledge or viewpoint."[53] "He must not be simply some nice, young fellow who has no qualifications for the job."[54]

These last comments imply that an important responsibility rests on the editor or publisher who hires the critic. If his attitude toward criticism is a healthy one, he will support his columnist in inevitable rows with advertisers, and he will not spread the talents of his broadcasting critic over such diverse areas as movie reviewing, book reviewing and society notes.[55]

Finally, all noble criteria aside, Harriet Van Horne states with incontrovertible logic her panacea for the dearth of professional newspaper critics:

> If newspapers paid higher salaries they could draw better people into the profession. And there you have it in one sentence--what's wrong with TV criticism . . . and what's wrong with the newspaper business. You've got to love it with all your heart to stay in it. For in the immortal words of Phil Silvers, "You'll never get rich!"[56]

Nor will the newspaper critic ever achieve his share of readers, say the critics, if his column remains buried in some inappropriate section. To emphasize this point, Gilbert Seldes, a few years ago, reminded Mr.

Sulzberger, editor of the New York Times, that Jack Gould's Sunday column was lost in the middle of the drama section when it should at least be on the front page of that section, since it concerned a medium which was having a far greater effect on people than either the drama or the movies.[57] The suggestion has not yet been acted upon.

In addition to developing critical attitudes in young people and increasing the staff of professional critics, the suggestion has been advanced at various times that a national magazine of criticism be launched. Presumably, the well-established critics would be the contributors. When some of them were asked for an opinion on the matter, the concensus was that the idea, though worthwhile, would be impractical. For one thing, the inescapable time-lag between programs and commentary would place a serious handicap on public acceptance of such a journal. For another, "a magazine which would try to sift hours of programing per week down to ten hours per week simply could not take into account various audience tastes."[58] Mr. Seldes once suggested to the networks that they collaborate on a national magazine but nothing came of it.[59] It was Mr. Carson's opinion that a magazine which attempted criticism of all the arts, including broadcasting, might have a better chance for survival.[60]

A somewhat more practical suggestion would be to arrange regular broadcast time on either of the media for the leading critics. Once again, since the airwaves are public property, perhaps the government and the broadcasters could be convinced that it is not entirely unreasonable for the people or their representatives to utilize station facilities for discussing programing and other common broadcasting problems.

As a matter of fact, during this last decade some critics have occasionally been invited to appear on the air. Gilbert Seldes broadcast a weekly, fifteen minute program of commentary for three whole years during the late forties over WNEW, an independent New York City station. His discussion of radio and television, however, was only incidental to a broader treatment of all the arts. Both he and Marya Mannes have appeared several times on New York's municipal station WNYC,[61] and some of the network owned stations in the city have even played host on occasion to critics Harriet Van Horne, John Crosby, and Jay Nelson Tuck.[62]

During this same period, two interesting projects in "on-the-air" criticism were proposed, but for financial reasons never came to fruition. WNYC had at one time considered Saul Carson for a radio program to be called "Critic's Choice" on which he would have played outstanding tapes and discs and then discussed them.[63] The lack of a sponsor prevented ABC from carrying a program devised by an advertising agency, no less, which would have employed a regular professional critic and a panel of laymen to discuss broadcasting.[64]

Two projects that failed and a handful of appearances spotted over the years do not add up to a very strong precedent for critic broadcasting. And of course, it is too much to expect that the industry would be enthusiastic over the delicate task of ushering sponsors out one door and critics in another. Yet, the possibility remains that a powerful network like CBS, which has publicized the Stanton plan (see p. 451) and in days past has discussed on the radio its philosophy of operation with John Crosby as one-time guest,[65] that such a network could successfully schedule a critical program that would bring it honor as well as be of inestimable service to the public. To use a mass medium for criticism of a mass medium would seem to be an immensely sensible course.

One final idea for strengthening criticism was announced for a tryout during the 1958-59 television season. For years, critics have urged either the repetition of programs or some type of preview system which would permit them to exercise the important critical function of evaluating a program in time for audiences to act upon the advice in the review. They feel that their work would immediately gain greater relevancy and prestige. When the Dupont Company announced that its ninety minute dramas would be performed for critics a day before the broadcast, industry reaction was mixed, although critical reaction was highly favorable.[66] As yet the plan is too small in scope and has been too recently implemented for any accurate appraisal of its success.

Practical or impractical, in summary, all these ideas seem based on the reasonable assumption that if more people become active critics in their own right, they will strengthen the hand of the professional critics, thus assuring radio and television of a generally more alert, demanding, and appreciative audience. An industry response which is more negative than positive to critical writings serves notice to professional critics that broadcasters are not too anxious to have an alert audience. It is thus even more imperative for critics to concern themselves with increasing their own ratings, not with tactics of the hard-sell, but with the continued demonstration of their indispensibility as guide and conscience for the managers of radio and television, and as teacher to listeners and viewers.

Notes

[1]John Crosby, Wisconsin State Journal (Madison), July 19, 1955.

[2]Ring Lardner, New Yorker, July 16, 1932, p. 22.

[3]"Hope Drops Life Suit," New York Times, May 26, 1951, p. 10.

[4]"Law to Permit Newsmen to Guard Sources Sought," Courier Express (Buffalo), December 26, 1958, p. 2.

[5]Ted Husing, Ten Years Before the Mike (New York: Farrar and Rinehart, Inc., 1935), p. 265.

[6]William Paley, quoted in Ned Midgley, The Advertising and Business Side of Radio (New York: Prentice-Hall, Inc., 1948), pp. 318-19.

[7]Norman Corwin, Preface to Joseph Liss (ed.), Radio's Best Plays (New York: Greenberg, 1947), p. iv.

[8]Erik Barnouw, panel member discussing radio criticism, Education on the Air, 18th Yrbk., O. Joe Olson (Columbus: Ohio State University Press, 1948), p. 112.

[9]Irving Gitlin, "Correspondence," Reporter, May 3, 1956, p. 5.

[10]Letter from Mr. Sydney H. Eiges, Vice President in Charge of Press, National Broadcasting Company, May 21, 1956.

[11]Variety, November 13, 1957, p. 29.

[12]Merlin Aylesworth, "Broadcasting in the Public Interest," Annals of the American Academy of Political and Social Science, CLXXVII (January, 1935), 118.

[13]William Paley, "Broadcasting and American Society," the Annals, CCXIII (January, 1941), 66.

[14]Sylvester Weaver, Jr., "The Public Makes the Hits," Variety, January 3, 1951, p. 101.

[15]Max Wylie, Clear Channels (New York: Funk and Wagnalls Co., 1955), p. 69.

[16]Ibid., p. 15.

[17]Ibid., pp. 235-36.

[18]Ibid., p. 277.

[19]John Crosby, Wisconsin State Journal (Madison), November 23, 1955.

[20]Robert Lewis Shayon, Saturday Review, January 27, 1951, p. 30.

[21]Marya Mannes, Reporter, March 24, 1955, p. 37.

[22]Jack Gould, New York Times, May 19, 1957.

[23]Jack Gould, ibid., May 26, 1957.

[24]Harold Fellows, "Address, NARTB Convention," Broadcasting-Telecasting, April 23, 1956, p. 35.

[25]Gilbert Seldes, Saturday Review, June 27, 1953, p. 32.

[26]Jack Gould, New York Times, August 10, 1947.

[27]Leslie Allen, Christian Science Monitor, July 12, 1930.

[28]Letter from Mr. Darwin Teilhet, former critic, Forum, May 18, 1956.

[29]Interview with Mr. Jack Gould, critic, New York Times, April 2, 1956.

[30]Interview with Mr. Saul Carson, former critic, New Republic, April 4, 1956.

[31]Interview with Mr. Jay Nelson Tuck, critic, New York Post, April 6, 1956.

[32]Letter from Mr. Donald Kirkley, critic, Baltimore Sun, April 16, 1956.

[33]Letter from Mr. Paul Cotton, critic, Register Tribune (Des Moines), September 6, 1956.

[34]Time, August 5, 1946, p. 61.

[35]Leslie Allen, Christian Science Monitor, July 5, 1930.

[36]George Rosen, "Appraising the Radio Editors," Variety, January 23, 1946, p. 30.

[37]Dickson Hartwell, "John Crosby: Gadfly of Radio," Coronet, XXVIII (July, 1950), 112.

[38]Interview with Mr. Jack Gould, loc. cit.

[39]Interview with Mr. Gilbert Seldes, critic, Saturday Review, April 5, 1956.

[40]Walter Winchell, "Are Critics People," TV Guide, February 1, 1958, p. 7.

[41]Peter Temple Whitelam, "The Critic in the Mass Media" (unpublished Master's thesis, Boston University, 1955) pp. 75-76. This study concerns the degree to which readers and listeners are influenced by, primarily, literary, film and drama critics. Some attention is given to broadcasting

critics.

[42]Paul F. Lazarsfeld and Patricia Kendall, Radio Listening in America, (New York: Prentice-Hall, Inc., 1948), p. 146.

[43]Interview with Mr. Ben Gross, radio-TV editor, Daily News (New York), April 5, 1956.

[44]"Out of the Blue," Time, August 20, 1956, p. 71.

[45]Lazarsfeld and Kendall, op. cit., p. 84.

[46]Jack Gould, New York Times, December 11, 1955.

[47]Interview with Mr. Robert Lewis Shayon, critic, Saturday Review, April 4, 1956.

[48]Ibid.

[49]Interview with Miss Marya Mannes, critic, Reporter, April 3, 1956.

[50]The University of Southern California, for example, offers a course in the area of "Telecommunications--Criticism" in which writers like Jack Gould, John Crosby, Gilbert Seldes, and Robert Lewis Shayon are studied.

[51]In October, 1955, Senior Scholastic, a magazine for high school students, started a department called "Teleguides" conducted by Patrick D. Hazard in which comments about future programs and questions for class discussion were included.

An article by Robert J. Landry in Variety, August 8, 1956, listed new departments of monthly comment on the popular arts in the following teacher publications: Elementary English, English Journal, and College English.

[52]Interview with Mr. Robert Lewis Shayon, loc. cit.

[53]Interview with Miss Marya Mannes, loc. cit.

[54]Interview with Mr. Ben Gross, loc. cit.

[55]Interview with Mr. Robert J. Landry, managing editor, Variety, April 3, 1956.

[56]Letter from Miss Harriet Van Horne, critic, New York World Telegram, May 7, 1956.

[57]Interview with Mr. Gilbert Seldes, loc. cit.

[58]Interview with Mr. Jack Cluett, critic, Woman's Day, April 4, 1956.

[59]Interview with Mr. Gilbert Seldes, loc. cit.

[60]Interview with Mr. Saul Carson, loc. cit.

[61]Obviously, non-commercial stations find themselves much more at liberty to schedule programs of criticism; and many of them do, particularly university outlets. An outstanding example is a program by Phillip Gelb, staff member of KUOM, the University of Minnesota radio station, called "Critic at Large," on which radio and television fare, as well as other art forms, are pungently and perceptively discussed. (See Variety, October 26, 1955, p. 32, for a review of one program.)

[62]For brief comments about a few of the critics' appearances, see Jack Gould, New York Times, May 4, 1947 and July 30, 1952, and John Crosby, Herald Tribune (New York), June 22, 1953.

[63]Interview with Mr. Saul Carson, loc. cit.

[64]Interview with Mr. Jay Nelson Tuck, loc. cit.

[65]Lyman Bryson, Time For Reason About Radio (New York: George W. Stewart, Inc., 1948).

[66]Jack Gould, New York Times, June 29, 1958.

CONCLUSION

The professional critics' appraisal of American broadcasting's first thirty-five years is an account of some fine achievements and of many frustrating disappointments. The high incidence of unfavorable reactions is the result of the critics' talent for double vision. Behind the immediate stimulus, they see always the image of what could be. Only on occasion do these two phenomena coincide so that some phase of broadcasting is momentarily revealed in a thoroughly satisfying dimension. In the final analysis, the function of the critic is to suggest ultimate values which, if they were demanded by audiences and purused by the industry, would act as forces to insure a more frequent coinciding of reality with hope.

Likewise, the final function of this study in criticism is to resolve the substance of the professional critics' observations into a set of values which are significant for the improvement of radio and television operations. These values are abstracted from all that the critics have said they liked or disliked in programs, in our system of broadcasting, and in the public's response to these media.

First, the critics like honesty. They like the sight and sound of truth within a program and within a commercial message. They also appreciate evidence that a broadcast licensee's performance measures up to his public declarations of intent.

The criterion of honesty applied to drama explains the critics' praise for an adaptation which remains faithful to the theme and mood of the original, and it explains their severe castigation of the industry when it bows to the pressure of time or timidity and distorts a previously valid work of art.

The criterion of honesty applied to drama accounts for the pleasure critics take in an original play which treats life realistically and follows plausible premises to their logical conclusions even when such conclusions are at variance with the mores of the sponsor or the public. It is an awareness of this same criterion which impels the critic to ask that the mildest domestic comedies or the wildest farces still have their roots in believable characters. They deplore the dishonesty of the daytime serials' mawkish sentimentality and have urged the form to deal straight-forwardly with major ethical problems. The critics dislike seeing crime or medical thrillers (no matter how realistically performed) masquerade as serious, informational programs.

And so it goes throughout the gamut of broadcast types. Sincerity is preferred to condescension, not only in children's shows but in programs which attempt to bring "culture" to the mass audience. Insincerity in any communicative form is suspect, whether it be reflected in the frantic sensationalizing of a commentator or in the "planned" spontaneity of the quiz game which must insure the presence of bon mots and innuendoes.

Although the dubbing of laughter onto the tape of a comedy show and the rigging of a contest to manipulate a program's emotional tension are minor sins in an operation which must try to deliver to a sponsor a large and appreciative public, control of audience response to certain types of programs may be more seriously dishonest. Critics believe that some kinds of truth cannot be made to conform to show business techniques, that the honest exploration of a problem in a documentary or in a discussion program may be a quiet, deep process generating an excitement and a drama quite unrelated to popular entertainment. If this be the case, say the critics, the informational program must proceed on its own merits. To let it do otherwise would be to tamper with the public's right to an accurate and thoughtful consideration of serious issues.

Obviously, the criterion of honesty when applied to advertising has called forth expressions of disgust from the critics. But they still insist (and have pointed to some commercials for proof) that merchants can sell their products without resorting to falsehoods.

And finally, many critics have called industry leaders to account, just as they have suggested the government do, in cases where published statements of production standards, of advertising regulations, of plans for community service are disregarded in day to day operations. Honesty, whether in a line of dialogue, in a memo to a producer, or in the slogan of a product is a supreme value for the broadcaster who wishes to earn the confidence of the public and the approval of the critics.

A second value the professional critic would stress is the value of program variety. This is particularly important for media dedicated to serving the public interest, which is, after all, a collective term for many separate interests. The broad categories into which this study is divided already stand as evidence of some variety, but within these categories there is room for improvement. Two areas largely undeveloped by radio and television are those dealing with serious themes and cultural experiences. Consequently, the excursions of dramatic or musical forms or of informational programs into these areas command the close attention of the critics.

This is not to say that the critics equate the serious in drama with melancholy or violence. The prestige television theater programs threaten to exhaust the vein of melancholia; and the formula shows, which drained dry the wells of violence in the early days of radio, continue only by the rearrangement of minor trappings in an endless succession of standard plots, genuinely exciting only to the youngsters for whom such stimulation is, unfortunately, of dubious value. If anything, the critics would like to see and hear more controversial themes in serious broadcast drama. And they would appreciate, even in children's shows, more cerebral action as a substitute for the unimaginative, meaningless physical action of violence and adventure.

The lack of variety in serious drama is matched by the dullness of repetition in comedy shows. Since comedy, however, seems to be the necessary foundation upon which broadcast entertainment rests, the critics suggest a brilliant solution to the problem of maintaining fresh comic material without forsaking important serious issues. Radio and television have almost totally ignored the value of satire, which is, of course, a form employing comic variations on serious themes. Here, they feel, is an untapped resource for topical and cultural humor that would lend significant variety to the total broadcast schedule.

In addition to injecting fresh twists of controversy, of intelligence, and of satire into drama and comedy routines, the professional critics believe broadcasting would benefit by shifting some of its broad emphasis on the anti-cultural. The berating of the school marm and the artist, in particular, has become a tired business carried, perhaps, to its most appalling exhibition in the vulgar gag trading of serious artists with clowns.

The anti-cultural monotony of steady, popular music programs on radio has made that medium almost sterile in the critics' opinions.

Variety is also welcome in the informational area, with the critics encouraging experimentation in news in depth as well as breadth, and in the thoughtful interpretation as well as plain dissemination of facts.

Finally, it is the critics' recognition of the need for program variety which elicited their support for distinct educational stations and which aroused initial favorable interest in toll broadcasting proposals. Broadcasting has generally been content to exploit the large public interest in light amusement. It must now exert its leadership to create substantial public interest in more stimulating forms of amusement and, particularly, in more challenging forms of a serious-cultural nature.

To mention exploitation is to call to mind the maintenance of human dignity as a third value by which the critics have measured broadcasting's performance. They find it difficult, for example, to laugh at the bumbling idiot domestic comedy makes of father, or difficult to listen to great artists deliver cheap commercials. These are experiences in the destruction of human dignity.

Even more painfully embarrassing to critics have been the bewildered antics of often willing contestants caught in the clever surprises of an audience participation show. While the emotions of the participants range from uncontrolled laughter to hysterical sobbing, the empathic responses of a vast home audience represent, as far as the critics are concerned, a useless, often shameful waste of a basically fine desire. To share in the joys and sufferings of our fellows is a noble urge. But to capitalize on it by making private emotions public is to momentarily destroy human dignity in observer as well as victim. Despite the undeniable virtue of honesty in these all too realistic displays, the critics still damn the commercial motive underlying such programs and they still insist that splendid gifts are too small a reward for recipients who debase themselves.

It may be at this point that the materialistic milieu in which radio and television operate becomes most apparent and is seen by the critics as a basic threat to dignity. To make the movement of goods and the desire for goods the prime force in broadcasting is to thwart the operation in these media of non-materialistic, spiritual forces which are uniquely human. These are the forces which critics believe should infuse more programs and the forces which inspire them to praise a few.

Regardless of whether radio and television are to be thought of as arts or crafts, their critics, like the critics of any media, stress the value of excellence in writing and production. They feel that broadcasting must not be an area where attitudes of indifference and concepts of second-rate hold sway. From authors, performers, and technicians (although the last mentioned have been less guilty in this respect) have come expressions of contempt for these media. Though such reactions may well be the result of the studios' frightening ability to drain-off creativity, the solution is not for personnel to acquiesce so that production becomes even more mechanical. The critics would urge the extension of activities they have already heralded: the beneficial intermingling of artists and production staffs from theater, cinema and concert hall which television has promoted, and the presentation of outstanding special events which jolt broadcasting from its penchant for the routine. In addition, the critics have repeatedly emphasized the value of utilizing the slack summer season for careful experimentation and for the polishing period which new programs so often need.

Concepts of excellence, they hasten to point out, are also necessary for non-commercial stations whose personnel may be apt to excuse laziness or incompetence in the name of academic purity and who may need the guidance of more talented communicators. Only through the skill, the diligence, and the dedication of those who labor in this new area will the art of broadcasting ever bear relevance to art in general.

As a corollary (almost opposing) value to excellence in writing and production, the critics have come to recognize a fifth criterion applicable to many programs in broadcasting: the element of relaxation and informality which actually enhance intimate media like radio and television. The absence of force and a prevailing mood of quietness contribute to an ease of spectator perception which is an important positive virtue. Casualness can also be an art, whether it is evident in the rambling humor of a pleasant master of ceremonies or a comfortable ad-lib session with a candidate running for office. In the tense atmosphere of push and hard sell, which is too often apparent in broadcasting, the quiet moments and the unplanned segments have often become the periods when these media project the vital element of personality with gratifying results.

Taken as a whole, the values of honesty, variety, dignity, excellence, and informality reflected in the output of any broadcasting system would be conclusive evidence of the operation of the last value professional critics wish for radio and television: the existence of a strong sense of responsibility.

These new media, these recent guests in the home have now become close relatives and are undoubtedly here to stay. Their fundamental characteristics are shaped by the industry for whom they are the means to substantial profits. And yet, the positive contribution the media make to the relaxation, the information, and the cultural maturity of the whole family depends to a large extent on the fine sense of social responsibility which the industry must exhibit even as it is impelled by the money motive.

Further, the public, which so eagerly opened its doors to accommodate the guests and which has so willingly shifted its social routines and perhaps some of its former values as a result, must now exert its responsibilities toward controlling the media's behavior. Uncritical acceptance, total indifference, or fastidious fault-finding are all attitudes inimical to a constructive sense of responsibility on the part of the public.

In addition, the critics believe that the responsibility of the federal government toward the active encouragement of improved programing has not yet been satisfactorily defined.

Although radio is still in middle-age and television merely in early adolescence, both media have created countless segments of respectable quality and many occasions of magnificence. But only keen awareness on the part of the audience, broadcaster, and government will divert the media from an innate tendency to forget minority tastes and to perpetuate adolescent interests. Professional critics are an abrasive upon which the evaluative faculties of these three groups can be sharpened. Their influence, as far as is known, (And here, it would seem, is a most fruitful area for further research.) is small, but their profession is young and full of promise.

BIBLIOGRAPHY

Books

Ace, Goodman. The Book of Little Knowledge. New York: Simon and Schuster, 1955.

Allen, Fred. Treadmill to Oblivion. Boston: Little, Brown and Co., 1954.

Broadcasting--To All Homes. Broadcasting--Music, Literature, Drama, Art. Broadcasting--Religion, Education, Agriculture. Broadcasting--Public Affairs. New York: National Broadcasting Company, Inc., 1935.

Brown, John Mason. Upstage. New York: W. W. Norton and Co., 1930.

Bryson, Lyman. Time For Reason About Radio. New York: George W. Stewart, Inc., 1948.

Candee, Marjorie Dent. Current Biography. Vols. XIV, XV. New York: H. W. Wilson, 1953, 1954.

Chase, Francis, Jr. Sound and Fury. New York: Harper and Brothers, 1942.

Chester, Giraud, and Garrison, Garnett. Radio and Television. 1st ed. New York: Appleton-Century-Crofts, Inc., 1950.

Cooke, Alistair. "The Critic in Film History." Footnotes to the Films. ed., Charles Davy. London: Lovat Dickson, Ltd., 1937.

"A Critical Look at Radio Criticism." Education on the Air. 18th yrbk. ed., Joe Olson. Columbus: Ohio State University Press, 1948.

Crosby, John. Out of the Blue. New York: Simon and Schuster, 1952.

Denison, Merrill. "The Preparation of Dramatic Continuity for Radio." Education on the Air. 3d yrbk. ed., Josephine H. MacLatchey. Columbus: Ohio State University Press, 1932.

Directory: Newspapers and Periodicals. Vols. 1927, 1930, 1933, 1936. Philadelphia: N. W. Ayer and Sons.

Edman, Irwin. Arts and the Man. New York: W. W. Norton and Co., Inc., 1939.

Elder, Donald. Ring Lardner. Garden City, N. Y.: Doubleday and Co., Inc., 1956.

Farrel, Tom (ed.). The Working Press of the Nation. New York: Public Relations Press, 1950.

Gross, Ben. I Looked and I Listened. New York: Random House, 1954.

Grunwald, Edgar A. (ed.). Radio Directory 1937-1938. New York: Variety, Inc., 1937.

Head, Sydney. Broadcasting in America. New York: Houghton Mifflin Co., 1956.

Husing, Ted. Ten Years Before the Mike. New York: Farrar and Rinehart, Inc., 1935.

Krutch, Joseph Wood. Experience and Art. New York: Harrison Smith and Robert Haas, 1932.

Kunitz, Stanley J., and Haycroft, Howard. Twentieth Century Authors. New York: H. W. Wilson Co., 1942.

Landry, Robert J. This Fascinating Radio Business. Indianapolis: Bobbs-Merrill Co., 1946.

_______. Who, What, Why Is Radio?. New York: George W. Stewart, Inc., 1942.

Lardner, Ring. The Portable Ring Lardner. ed., Gilbert Seldes. New York: Viking, 1946.

Lazarsfeld, Paul F., and Field, Harry. The People Look at Radio. Chapel Hill: University of North Carolina Press, 1947.

Lazarsfeld, Paul F., and Kendall, Patricia L. Radio Listening in America. New York: Prentice-Hall, Inc., 1948.

Liss, Joseph (ed.). Radio's Best Plays. New York: Greenberg, 1947.

McLuhan, Marshall. The Mechanical Bride. New York: Vanguard Press, 1951.

Midgley, Ned. The Advertising and Business Side of Radio. New York: Prentice-Hall, Inc., 1948.

Parker, DeWitt H. The Principles of Aesthetics. 2d ed. New York: J.S. Crofts and Co., 1947.

"Radio Critics Talk to Program Directors!". Education on the Air. 16th yrbk. ed., I. Keith Tyler and Nancy Mason Dasher. Columbus: Ohio State University Press, 1946.

Rothe, Anna, and Ellis, Constance. Current Biography. Vol. IX. New York: H. W. Wilson, 1948.

Seldes, Gilbert. The Great Audience. New York: Viking Press, 1950.

_______. The Public Arts. New York: Simon and Schuster, 1956.

_______. The Seven Lively Arts. New York: Harper and Brothers, 1924.

Shayon, Robert Lewis. Television and Our Children. New York: Longmans, Green and Co., Inc., 1951.

Shurick, E. P. J. The First Quarter-Century of American Broadcasting. Kansas City: Midland Publishing Co., 1946.

Siepmann, Charles A. Radio's Second Chance. Boston: Little, Brown and Co., 1946.

Smith, S. Stephanson. The Craft of the Critic. New York: Thomas V. Crowell Co., 1931.

Stallman, Robert W. The Critic's Notebook. Minneapolis: University of Minnesota Press, 1950.

Stephan, Robert. "Informing the Listener". Education on the Air. 9th yrbk. ed., Josephine H. MacLatchey. Columbus: Ohio State University Press, 1938.

Thonssen, Lester, and Baird, A. Craig. Speech Criticism. New York: Ronald Press Co., 1948.

Waller, Judith C. Radio, the Fifth Estate. 2d ed. Boston: Houghton Mifflin Co., 1950.

White, Llewellyn. The American Radio. Chicago: University of Chicago Press, 1947.

Who's Who in America. Vol. XXIX. Chicago: Marquis, 1956.

Williams, Albert. Listening. Denver: University of Denver Press, 1948.

Wylie, Max (ed.). Best Broadcasts of 1939-40. New York: McGraw-Hill Book Co., Inc., 1940.

_______. Clear Channels. New York: Funk and Wagnalls Co., 1955.

Newspapers and Periodicals

Ackerman, William C. "U. S. Radio: Record of a Decade," Public Opinion Quarterly, XII (Fall, 1948), 440-54.

Adams, Jack. "Proposed FCC Policy," Capital Times, (Madison, Wisconsin), June 27, 1956.

Adorno, T. W. "How to Look at Television," Quarterly of Film, Radio and Television, VIII (Spring, 1954), 213-35.

"Air Uplift," Newsweek, October 27, 1934, p. 36.

Allen, Leslie. "The Week's Program Trend" later called "Speaking From New York," weekly columns in Christian Science Monitor, January 25, 1930--October 17, 1931.

Ames, Richard Sheridan. "The Art of Pleasing Everybody," Atlantic Monthly, CLVIII (October, 1936), 444-52.

Arnold, Frank A. "Radio and the Newspaper," Editor and Publisher, February 20, 1937, p. 22.

Atkinson, Brooks. "Credo of a Critic," Saturday Review, August 6, 1949, p. 136.

Aylesworth, Merlin. "Broadcasting in the Public Interest," Annals of the American Academy of Political and Social Science, CLXXVII (January, 1935), 114-18.

_______. "Men, Mikes, and Money," as told to Ben Gross, Collier's, April 17, 1948, pp. 13-15, 65-67.

_______. Ibid., April 24, 1948, pp. 26-27, 96-97.

_______. Ibid., May 1, 1948, pp. 68-72.

_______. Ibid., May 8, 1948, pp. 30,32, 34, 36-39.

Bartlett, Kenneth G. "Trends in Radio Programs," Annals of the American Academy of Political and Social Science, CCXIII (January, 1941), 15-25.

Best, Katherine. "'Literature' of the Air, Radio's Perpetual Emotion," Saturday Review of Literature, April 20, 1940, pp. 11-13.

Bliven, Bruce. "How Radio is Re-Making Our World," Century Magazine, CVIII (June, 1924), 147-54.

Bouck, Zey. "Can We Solve the Broadcast Riddle?," Radio Broadcast, VI (April, 1924), 1040-44.

_______. "What the Air Waves Are Saying," New York Sun, January 30, 1924.

_______. Ibid., January 10, 1925.

_______. Ibid., January 8, 1927.

Bretz, Rudy. "TV As An Art Form," Hollywood Quarterly, V (Winter, 1950-51), 153-163.

Broadcasting-Telecasting, November 22, 1954, p. 54.

Broun, Heywood. "Radio," Nation, May 27, 1936, p. 686.

Bryson, Lyman. "Broadcasting and the Cultivated Minority," American Scholar, XX (Autumn, 1951), 221-24.

Canby, Henry Seidel. "Good and Bad Reviewing," Saturday Review of Literature, I (August 2, 1924), 1.

Carpenter, Ford A. "First Experiences of a Radio Broadcaster," Atlantic Monthly, CXXXII (September, 1923), 386-88.

Carson, Saul. "Notes Toward an Examination of the Radio Documentary," Hollywood Quarterly, IV (Autumn, 1949), 69-74.

_______. "On the Air," weekly columns in New Republic, Vols. CXVI-CXXVI (March 31, 1947-March 24, 1952).

Cluett, Jack. monthly columns in Woman's Day, Vols. VII-XVIII (March, 1944-December, 1955).

Collison, Perce. "Shall We Have Music or Noise?," Radio Broadcast, I (September, 1922), 434-38.

Crosby, John. "Radio and Who Makes It," Atlantic Monthly, CLXXXI (January, 1948), 26-29.

_______. "Radio and Television," columns appearing four times weekly including Sunday in Herald Tribune (New York), January 1, 1952-March 31, 1952; 1st-10th of each month thereafter from April, 1952-February, 1953; 11th-20th of each month from February, 1953-February, 1954; all columns in Wisconsin State Journal (Madison), March 15, 1954-December 31, 1955.

_______. "TV and the 1952 Elections," American Magazine, CLIII (April, 1952), 21, 108-12.

"Crosby's First Birthday," Newsweek, May 19, 1947, p. 66.

Denison, Merrill. "The Actor and Radio," Theater Arts, XVII (November, 1933), 849-55.

DeVoto, Bernard. "The Easy Chair," Harper's Magazine, CXCI (July, 1945), 33-36.

_______. Ibid., (October, 1945), 325-28.

"Editorial," Saturday Evening Post, August 23, 1924, p. 24.

Fellows, Harold. "Address, NARTB Convention," Broadcasting-Telecasting, April 23, 1956, p. 35.

Fisher, Cyrus [Darwin Teilhet]. "Radio Reviews," monthly columns in Forum, Vols. LXXXVIII-XCI, (July, 1932-March, 1934).

"For Listeners Only," Time, August 5, 1946, p. 61.

Frankel, Lou. "In One Ear," Nation, November 9, 1946, p. 528.

_______. Ibid., January 18, 1947, p. 73.

_______. Ibid., February 15, 1947, p. 187.

_______. Ibid., March 15, 1947, p. 304.

Gitlin, Irving. "Correspondence," Reporter, May 3, 1956, p. 5.

Gould, Jack. "How Comic Is Radio Comedy," New York Times Magazine, November 21, 1948, pp. 22, 64-68.

_______. "The Paradoxical State of TV," New York Times Magazine, March 30, 1947, pp. 14, 34-35.

_______. "A Primer of TV Comics," New York Times Magazine, May 3, 1953, pp. 12, 37, 39, 42, 44.

_______. "Radio" later called "Radio and Television," Sunday columns in New York Times, August 13, 1944-December 25, 1949; one hundred and forty-seven Sunday columns, sixty-six week-day columns, January 2, 1949-December 25, 1955.

_______. "Television: Boon or Bane?," Public Opinion Quarterly, X (Fall, 1946), 314-20.

_______. "Television Today--a Critic's Appraisal," New York Times Magazine, April 8, 1956, pp. 12-13, 36, 38.

_______. "They Say the Right Things at the Wrong Time," New York Times Magazine, March 24, 1946, pp. 22-23.

_______. "TV at the Crossroads: A Critic's Survey," New York Times Magazine, March 9, 1952, pp. 12-13, 49-50.

_______. "What TV Is--And What It Might Be," New York Times Magazine, June 10, 1951, pp. 18, 22-24.

_______. "Why Millions Love Lucy," New York Times Magazine, March 1, 1953, p. 16.

Hamburger, Philip. "The Crier," New Yorker, January 20, 1945, pp. 23-33.

_______. "Television," columns appearing bi-monthly for three years; three times a month for two years in New Yorker, Vols. XXV-XXX (October 29, 1949-January 15, 1955).

Hart, Joseph K. "Radiating Culture," Survey, March 18, 1922, pp. 948-49.

Hartwell, Dickson. "John Crosby: Gadfly of Radio," Coronet, XXVIII (July, 1950), pp. 110-12.

Hawkins, Stuart. "On the Radio," Herald Tribune (New York), July 12, 1926.

Hazard, Patrick D. "Teleguides," Senior Scholastic, LXVII (October, 1955), 35T.

Herzog, Herta. "Radio--The First Post-War Years," Public Opinion Quarterly, X (Fall, 1946), 297-313.

Hettinger, Herman S. "Broadcasting in the United States," Annals of The American Academy of Political and Social Science, CLXXVII (January, 1935), 1-13.

_______. "Organizing Radio's Discoveries for Use," Ibid., CCXIII (January, 1941), 170-89.

Hobson, Rixey. "Radio With the Romance Tuned Out," Journal of the American Bankers Association, XVI (February, 1924), 479-82.

"Hope Drops Life Suit," New York Times, May 26, 1951, p. 10.

Hudson, Robert D., and Weibe, Gerhart D. "A Case for Listener Participation," Public Opinion Quarterly, XII (Summer, 1948), 201-208.

Hutchens, John K. "Crime Pays--On the Radio," New York Times Magazine, March 19, 1944, pp. 16-17, 31.

Hutchens, John K. "Radio," eighty-five Sunday columns appearing in New York Times between July 27, 1941-July 16, 1944.

_______. "Same Time, Same Station," Saturday Review, May 4, 1946, pp. 16-17.

_______. "The Secret of a Good Radio Voice," New York Times Magazine, December 6, 1942, pp. 26-27, 39.

Kaltenborn, H. V. "On the Air," Century, CXII (October, 1926), 666-76.

Knight, Raymond. monthly columns in Woman's Day, Vols. III-VII (March 1940-February, 1944).

Krutch, Joseph Wood. "Theater...Cultural Common Denominator," Theater Arts, XL (February, 1956), 24-25, 82-83.

Landry, Robert J. "Every Schoolmarm a Critic," Variety, August 8, 1956, p. 1.

_______. "The Improbability of Radio Criticism," Hollywood Quarterly, II (1946-47), 66-70

_______. "Memo to Young Scholars, Critics," Variety, February 1, 1956, pp. 30, 34.

_______. "Wanted: Radio Critics," Public Opinion Quarterly, IV (December, 1940), 620-29.

Lardner, Ring. "Over the Waves," columns appearing approximately every three weeks in New Yorker, Vols. VIII-IX (June 18, 1932-August 26, 1933).

"Law to Permit Newsmen to Guard Sources Sought," Courier Express (Buffalo, New York), December 26, 1958, p. 2.

Lazarsfeld, Paul F. "The Role of Criticism in the Management of Mass Media," Journalism Quarterly, XXV (June, 1948), 115-126.

Levin, Harvey J. "Competition Among the Mass Media and Public Interest," Public Opinion Quarterly, XVIII (Spring, 1954), 62-79.

"The Listener," Atlantic Monthly, CLXXIV (September, 1944), 115.

Loveman, Amy. "New Dimensions in Information," Saturday Review of Literature, May 17, 1941, p. 10.

Mackaye, Percy. "The University of the Ether," Popular Radio, V (January, 1924), pp. 37-40.

Mannes, Marya. "Channels," approximately monthly columns in Reporter, Vols. VIII-XIII (January 6, 1953-December 1, 1955).

________. Ibid., May 2, 1957, pp. 19-22.

Matthews, William. "Radio Plays As Literature," Hollywood Quarterly, I (October, 1945), pp. 40-50.

Mix, Jennie Irene. "The Listener's Point of View," Radio Broadcast, VI (January, 1925), 454-62.

________. Ibid., (March, 1925), 880-86.

________. Ibid., (February, 1925), 684-91.

"Non-New York Critics Demand Attention," Variety, November 13, 1957, p. 29.

"Out of the Blue," Time, August 20, 1956, p. 71.

Paley, William. "Broadcasting and American Society," Annals of the American Academy of Political and Social Science, CCXIII (January, 1941), 62-68.

Peter, Paul F. "The American Listener in 1940," Annals of the American Academy of Political and Social Science, CCXIII (January, 1941), 1-8.

Radio Age, IV (April, 1925).

"Radio Critics: Seven Programs Attacked by WNRC," Business Week, August 10, 1935, p. 23.

"Radio Department," Literary Digest, April 1, 1922, pp. 28-29.

________. Ibid., April 15, 1922, pp. 28-29.

________. Ibid., May 13, 1922, pp. 28-29.

________. Ibid., June 24, 1922, pp. 24-25.

________. Ibid., December 30, 1922, pp. 22-23.

"Radio Departments are Now Fixed Feature in Many Newspapers," Editor and Publisher Yearbook, January 31, 1926, p. 202.

Radio Digest, XXX (February, 1933).

"Radio Editor's Annual Poll," Newsweek, February 17, 1934, p. 34.

"Radio Favorites," Fortune, XVII (January, 1938), 88-89.

"Radio Reviews," Variety, October 26, 1955, p. 32.

"Radio Test," Literary Digest, December 23, 1933, pp. 8-9.

"Ratings Make Heroes of Critics," Variety, November 6, 1957, p. 30.

"Results of Recent Survey," Printer's Ink, January 21, 1944, p. 38.

Rosen, George. "Appraising Radio Editors," Variety, January 23, 1946.

"Second Annual Awards of WNRC," Literary Digest, May 2, 1936, p. 34.

Seldes, Gilbert. "Life on the Tinsel Standard," Saturday Review, October 28, 1950, pp. 9-10, 55-56.

_______. "The Nature of Television Programs," Annals of the American Academy of Political and Social Science, CCXIII (January, 1941), 138-44.

_______. "Radio, TV and the Common Man," Saturday Review, August 29, 1953, pp. 11-12, 39-41.

_______. "Screen and Radio," Scribner's, CII (July, 1937), 56-58.

_______. "Television," Nation, May 26, 1956, pp. 457-58.

_______. "TV and Radio," columns appearing approximately every three weeks in Saturday Review, Vols. XXXV-XXXVIII (March 15, 1952-December 31, 1955).

_______. "TV and the Voter," Saturday Review, December 6, 1952, pp. 17-19, 57-59.

"Shall We Advertise by Radio?," Literary Digest, May 26, 1923, p. 27.

Shayon, Robert Lewis. "Radio--TV," weekly column in Christian Science Monitor, June 10, 1950-February 13, 1951.

_______. "Toynbee, TV, and Chicago," Christian Science Monitor, June 3, 1950.

_______. "TV and Radio," columns appearing approximately every other week in Saturday Review, Vols. XXXIII-XXXIX (October 28, 1950-March 3, 1956).

Siepmann, Charles. "Further Thoughts on Radio Criticism," Public Opinion Quarterly, V (June, 1941), 308-12.

_______. "Radio Starts to Grow Up," Nation, December 27, 1947, pp. 697-98.

"Stupid and Irresponsible," Time, November 12, 1956, p. 106.

Teilhet, Darwin L. "On the Summer Air," Forum, LXXXVIII (June, 1932), 383-84.

_______. "What America Listens To," Forum, LXXXVIII (May, 1932), 275-79.

Theater Arts, XXV (February, 1941), 54.

Thurber, James. "Onward and Upward with the Arts," New Yorker, May 15, 1948, pp. 34-38.

_______. Ibid., May 29, 1948, pp. 30-38.

_______. Ibid., June 12, 1948, pp. 48-58.

_______. Ibid., July 3, 1948, pp. 40-48.

_______. Ibid., July 24, 1948, pp. 63-68.

Time, April 16, 1956, p. 72.

Trumbo, Dalton. "Frankenstein in Hollywood," Forum, LXXXVII (March, 1932), 142-46.

"Two Exciting Decades," Broadcasting--Telecasting, October 16, 1950, pp. 67-168.

Van Horne, Harriet, "It Is Later Than Radio Thinks," Saturday Review of Literature, February 19, 1944, pp. 26-30.

_______. Monthly column in Theater Arts, Vols. XXXV-XXXVI, (June, 1951-December, 1952).

Variety, January 4, 1956, p. 152.

"Variety Tells All," Printer's Ink, August 24, 1933, pp. 90-91.

Volkening, Henry. "Abuses of Radio Broadcasting," Current History, XXXIII (December, 1930), 396-400.

Wallace, John. "The Listener's Point of View," monthly columns in Radio Broadcast, Vols. VIII-XIII (January, 1926-August, 1928).

Weaver, Sylvester, Jr. "The Public Makes the Hits," Variety, January 3, 1951, p. 101.

Welles, Kingsley. "The Listener's Point of View," Radio Broadcast, VII (August, 1925), 472-76.

Williams, Albert. "Radio and the Writer," Saturday Review, October 24, 1942, p. 44.

Winchell, Walter. "Are Critics People?," TV Guide, February 1, 1958, pp. 6-7.

Yates, Raymond. "The Broadcast Listener," monthly columns in Popular Radio, Vols. VIII-X (July, 1925-November, 1926).

_______. "Last Night On the Radio," New York Tribune, February 25, 1924.

_______. Ibid., Herald Tribune (New York), June 3, 1924.

_______. Ibid., September 1, 1924.

_______. Ibid., June 1, 1925.

_______. Ibid., February 6, 1926.

Young, James C. "New Fashions in Radio Programs," Radio Broadcast, VII (May, 1925), 83-89.

Other Sources

Carson, Saul, former critic, New Republic, personal interview. April 4, 1956.

Cluett, Jack, critic, Woman's Day, personal interview. April 4, 1956.

Cotton, Paul, critic, Register-Tribune (Des Moines) letter to the author. September 6, 1956.

Eiges, Sydney H., Vice-President in Charge of Press, National Broadcasting Company, letter to the author. May 21, 1956.

Gerling, George Fernand. "Trends in the Early Relationships between Newspapers and Radio Broadcasting." Unpublished Master's thesis, Department of Journalism, University of Wisconsin, 1946.

Gibbs, Richard Leslie. "Motion Picture Reviewing in the Daily Newspaper." Unpublished Master's thesis, Department of Journalism, University of Illinois, 1950.

Gould, Jack, critic, New York Times, personal interview. April 2, 1956.

Gross, Ben, radio-tv editor, Daily News (New York), personal interview. April 5, 1956.

Hurd, Volney D., former radio editor now Chief of the Paris Bureau, Christian Science Monitor, letter to the author. May 29, 1956.

Kirkley, Donald, critic, Baltimore Sun, letter to the author. April 16, 1956.

Landry, Robert J., managing editor, Variety, personal interview, April 3, 1956.

McNeely, Jerry Clark. "The Criticism and Reviewing of Brooks Atkinson." Unpublished Ph. D. dissertation, Department of Speech, University of Wisconsin, 1956.

Mannes, Marya, critic, Reporter, personal interview. April 3, 1956.

Rosen, George, radio-tv editor, Variety, personal interview. April 5, 1956.

Seldes, Gilbert, critic, Saturday Review, personal interview. April 5, 1956.

Shayon, Robert Lewis, critic, Saturday Review, personal interview. April 4, 1956.

Teilhet, Darwin, former critic, Forum, letter to the author. May 18, 1956.

Tuck, Jay Nelson, critic, New York Post, personal interview. April 6, 1956.

________. Ibid., letter to the author. May 14, 1956.

Van Horne, Harriet, critic, World Telegram (New York) letter to the author. May 7, 1956.

West, Edna. "The Broadway Critics." Unpublished Ph.D. dissertation, Department of Speech, University of Wisconsin, 1952.

Whitelam, Peter Temple. "The Critic in the Mass Media." Unpublished Master's thesis, School of Public Relations and Communications, Boston University, 1955.

Woods, David Lyndon. "The Criteria of the Radio and Television Criticism of Gilbert Seldes." Unpublished Master's thesis, Stanford University, 1955.

DISSERTATIONS IN BROADCASTING

An Arno Press Collection

Bailey Robert Lee. **An Examination of Prime Time Network Television Special Programs, 1948 to 1966.** *(Doctoral Thesis, University of Wisconsin, 1967)* 1979

Burke, John Edward. **An Historical-Analytical Study of the Legislative and Political Origins of the Public Broadcasting Act of 1967.** *(Doctoral Dissertation, The Ohio State University, 1971)* 1979

Foley, K. Sue. **The Political Blacklist in the Broadcast Industry:** The Decade of the 1950s. *(Doctoral Dissertation, The Ohio State University, 1972)* 1979

Hess, Gary Newton. **An Historical Study of the Du Mont Television Network.** *(Doctoral Dissertation, Northwestern University, 1960)* 1979

Howard, Herbert H. **Multiple Ownership in Television Broadcasting:** Historical Development and Selected Case Studies. *(Doctoral Dissertation, Ohio University, 1973)* 1979

Jameson, Kay Charles. **The Influence of the United States Court of Appeals for the District of Columbia on Federal Policy in Broadcast Regulation, 1929-1971.** *(Doctoral Dissertation, University of Southern California,1972)* 1979

Kirkley, Donald Howe, Jr. **A Descriptive Study of the Network Television Western During the Seasons 1955-56 to 1962-63.** *(Doctoral Dissertation, Ohio University, 1967)* 1979

Kittross, John Michael. **Television Frequency Allocation Policy in the United States.** *(Doctoral Dissertation, University of Illinois, 1960)* 1979

Larka, Robert. **Television's Private Eye:** An Examination of Twenty Years Programming of a Particular Genre, 1949 to 1969. *(Doctoral Dissertation, Ohio University, 1973)* 1979

Long, Stewart Louis. **The Development of the Television Network Oligopoly.** *(Doctoral Thesis, University of Illinois at Urbana-Champaign, 1974)* 1979

MacFarland, David T. **The Development of the Top 40 Radio Format.** *(Doctoral Thesis, University of Wisconsin, 1972)* 1979

McMahon, Robert Sears. **Federal Regulation of the Radio and Television Broadcast Industry in the United States, 1927-1959:** With Special Reference to the Establishment and Operation of Workable Administrative Standards. *(Doctoral Dissertation, The Ohio State University, 1959)* 1979

Muth, Thomas A. **State Interest in Cable Communications.** *(Doctoral Dissertation, The Ohio State University, 1973)* 1979

Pearce, Alan. **NBC News Division:** A Study of the Costs, the Revenues, and the Benefits of Broadcast News and **The Economics of Prime Time Access.** *(Doctoral Dissertation, Indiana University, 1972)* 1979

Pepper, Robert M. **The Formation of the Public Broadcasting Service.** *(Doctoral Dissertation, University of Wisconsin, 1975)* 1979

Pirsein, Robert William. **The Voice of America:** A History of the International Broadcasting Activities of the United States Government, 1940-1962. *(Doctoral Dissertation, Northwestern University, 1970)* 1979

Ripley, Joseph Marion, Jr. **The Practices and Policies Regarding Broadcasts of Opinions about Controversial Issues by Radio and Television Stations in the United States.** *(Doctoral Dissertation, The Ohio State University, 1961)* 1979

Robinson, Thomas Porter. **Radio Networks and the Federal Government.** 1943

Sadowski, Robert Paul. **An Analysis of Statutory Laws Governing Commercial and Educational Broadcasting in the Fifty States.** *(Doctoral Thesis, The University of Iowa, 1973)* 1979

Schwarzlose, Richard Allen. **The American Wire Services:** A Study of Their Development as a Social Institution. *(Doctoral Thesis, University of Illinois at Urbana-Champaign, 1965)* 1979

Smith, Ralph Lewis. **A Study of the Professional Criticism of Broadcasting in the United States. 1920-1955.** *(Doctoral Thesis, University of Wisconsin, 1959)* 1979

Stamps, Charles Henry. **The Concept of the Mass Audience in American Broadcasting:** An Historical-Descriptive Study. *(Doctoral Dissertation, Northwestern University, 1956)* 1979

Steiner, Peter O. **Workable Competition in the Radio Broadcasting Industry.** *(Doctoral Thesis, Harvard University, 1949)* 1979

Stern, Robert H. **The Federal Communications Commission and Television:** The Regulatory Process in an Environment of Rapid Technical Innovation. *(Doctoral Thesis, Harvard University, 1950)* 1979

Tomlinson, John D. **International Control of Radiocommunications.** 1945

Ulloth, Dana Royal. **The Supreme Court:** A Judicial Review of the Federal Communications Commission. *(Doctoral Dissertation, University of Missouri-Columbia, 1971)* 1979